Strategic Science Communication

T0146194

Strategic Science *Communication*

A GUIDE to
Setting the Right Objectives
for More Effective
Public Engagement

JOHN C. BESLEY *and* ANTHONY DUDO

JOHNS HOPKINS UNIVERSITY PRESS | *Baltimore*

© 2022 Johns Hopkins University Press
All rights reserved. Published 2022
Printed in the United States of America on acid-free paper
2   4   6   8   9   7   5   3   1

Johns Hopkins University Press
2715 North Charles Street
Baltimore, Maryland 21218-4363
www.press.jhu.edu

Library of Congress Cataloging-in-Publication Data

Names: Besley, John C., 1976– author. | Dudo, Anthony, author.
Title: Strategic science communication : a guide to setting the right objectives
for more effective public engagement / John C. Besley and Anthony Dudo.
Description: Baltimore : Johns Hopkins University Press, 2022. |
Includes bibliographical references and index.
Identifiers: LCCN 2021045394 | ISBN 9781421444208 (paperback) |
ISBN 9781421444215 (ebook)
Subjects: LCSH: Communication in science. | Public relations.
Classification: LCC Q223 .B47 2022 | DDC 501/.4—dc23/eng/20211130
LC record available at https://lccn.loc.gov/2021045394

A catalog record for this book is available from the British Library.

*Special discounts are available for bulk purchases of this book. For more information,
please contact Special Sales at specialsales@jh.edu.*

CONTENTS

CONTENTS

ACKNOWLEDGMENTS

Writing a book is an odd, challenging, and extended undertaking. We greatly appreciate everyone who has made it possible, including our collaborators on the research underlying the work and the people who read various chapters or provided forums for us to share ideas, including Nichole Bennett, Sharon Dunwoody, Sarah Garlick, Samantha Hautea, Maria Lapinski, Bruce Lewenstein, Laura Lindenfeld, Reyhaneh Maktoufi, Todd Newman, Dennis Martell, Nalini Nadkarni, Brooke Smith, Amanda Stanley, Leigh Anne Tiffany, Sara Yeo, and Shupei Yuan. We also thank the team at Johns Hopkins University Press for shepherding us through our first book project.

We are also appreciative of the organizations that have financially supported various elements of the research that led to this this project, including the National Science Foundation (grants #1049476, #1138296, #1421214, #1421723, #1713197), the United States Department of Agriculture (NIFA: 1011210), the Burroughs Wellcome Fund, the Chan Zuckerberg Initiative, the David and Lucille Packard Foundation, the Gordon and Betty Moore Foundation, the John Templeton Foundation, the Kavli Foundation, the John S. and James L. Knight Foundation, and the Rita Allen Foundation. A portion of this writing also occurred during a sabbatical that was supported by both the Wee Kim Wee School of Communication and Information at the Nanyang Technological University in Singapore and the Ellis N. Brandt Endowment at Michigan State University. Indeed, we are both grateful for the support that colleagues at our home universities continue to provide us for this work.

Of course, none of the errors or omissions in this book is the fault of either our colleagues or our funders. They are ours. Indeed, any opinions, findings, conclusions, or recommendations expressed in this material are those of the authors and do not necessarily reflect the views of any of these people or groups.

Finally, we are both deeply grateful to our spouses and children (Andrea, Alex, and Marshall for John; Megan, Rose, Reid, and Marin for Anthony) for all the ways they help make being a researcher, partner, and parent possible.

Strategic Science Communication

Introduction

THIS BOOK IS ABOUT SCIENCE communication strategy. We wrote it for our colleagues in the scientific community who want to take an evidence-based, long-term approach to communication. This community includes natural scientists, social scientists, engineers, and mathematicians, as well as the broad range of professional communicators, informal educators, and "boundary spanners." These are the people we have spent almost two decades learning from and trying to help as social scientists focused on science communication.

By communication strategy we mean the process of establishing long-term behavioral goals for communication and then working backward to figure out what intermediate communication objectives a communicator might seek to achieve, over time, that could contribute to achieving their goals. Only then should strategic communicators choose communication tactics—behaviors, messages, styles, sources, channels—that offer the possibility of achieving the prioritized objectives. We have not always been interested in the strategic side of communication, but our many opportunities to work with science communicators wrestling with decisions about how to prioritize and evaluate their communication efforts have helped us see the potential value of writing this book. Our hope is that the book enables people like you to think more deeply about how to have a sustained impact through intentional communication choices. For those who don't know us yet, please let us share a little bit about ourselves to explain why we wrote this book.

To start, John (Besley) is the only one in his family without a biology degree; instead he trained to be a journalist and science policy analyst. He ended up in government, writing briefing notes for senior environmental officials in Ottawa, Canada. He found that his friends thought the reason politicians enact weak environmental policy is because they lack guts. John's sense was that his bosses would be happy to make stronger policies if citizens demanded them. Consequently, he left government to get a communication PhD at Cornell University.

At Cornell, John collaborated with pioneers in the social scientific study of science, environmental, and risk communication. He completed his PhD with a focus on understanding the relationship between how people think about decision-makers and their willingness to accept risk-related decisions. He also studied cumulative media effects. His first faculty position was in University of South Carolina's School of Journalism and Mass Communications where the number of journalism students was dropping and the number of strategic communication students was rising. He therefore began teaching basic social science research methods, persuasion theory, and crisis communication to advertising and public relations students. Later, he also started helping to bring these students to visit strategic communication agencies and firms around Atlanta. He did this both out of curiosity and because he thought it might allow him to do a better job teaching his students.

Partially as a result of this shift, the Department of Advertising and Public Relations at Michigan State University recruited John to join one of the country's top communication colleges. (It also meant he was able to move closer to his Ontario-based family so that his kids would be able to see more of their grandparents.)

John had not intended to change his research focus away from public opinion about science. However, at about the same time that he switched universities, he also had the chance to use a data set that focused on scientists' views about the public rather than the public's views about science. This switch in focus brought him into contact with new people who were curious about how to use communication research to convince *more* scientists to communicate *more* often and *more* effectively. John did not want to do this research by himself, so he approached a colleague who had similar interests and a good reputation for collaborating.

This other guy (Anthony Dudo) had done his PhD at the University of Wisconsin, which, along with Cornell, is one of the centers of science communication scholarship. Anthony's first gig out of college—where he also studied to become a journalist—was in the communications department of a prestigious but dusty natural history museum. In working to publicize the museum's research, he realized how communication practices he took for granted were not widely shared. Anthony's sense was that the frequent misalignments among the museum's experts, educators, staff, and external audiences were undercutting the museum's ability to fulfill its mission. He wondered what types of communication tweaks would allow these well-meaning professionals to achieve more gratifying engagement experiences with their many stakeholders. He internalized this issue as a research question and it eventually led him to graduate school with hopes that he could develop the skills needed to help tackle it.

Upon completing his doctorate, Anthony also found himself appointed as faculty in a top advertising and public relations program at a large communication college. While settling into life in Austin, Texas, he regularly did two things: he continued to research scientists' communication activities and he taught strategic communication courses. These efforts led him to think more about how the fundamentals of strategic communication (e.g., audience analysis, goal setting, message testing) could be applied to science communication contexts.

Our initial project together was funded by the National Science Foundation and gave us the chance to do one of the most extensive surveys of scientists, that we know of, to date. Additional research interviews and face-to-face encounters at conferences and smaller symposia also gave us a chance to get to know the passionate community of people who were training and supporting scientists in their efforts to communicate more effectively. Among them, the Kavli Foundation, the Rita Allen Foundation, the Packard Foundation, the Moore Foundation, the Lasker Foundation, and the John Templeton Foundation have all contributed ideas and funding to this work, which in turn has allowed us to interview many people in the science communication community while also giving us informal opportunities to build relationships. These many relationships have helped us both develop and test the ideas we present in this book.

One key challenge we learned through the back-and-forth discussions with our new network is that the science communication research community has operated in near isolation from the practitioner community. From the researcher side, a chief reason for this seems to be a demand from communication journals and researchers' home departments for scholarship that advances theory coupled with relatively low demand for applied research that might answer the practitioners' day-to-day questions about how to do better public engagement. Communication scholars also publish in journals that practitioners rarely read and spend their travel dollars going to conferences that few practitioners attend. We know that most of our academic colleagues want to see improved communication but face the challenge that academic success often requires focusing on relatively small pieces of the communication puzzle. Many practitioners' background in the natural sciences and journalism—rather than the social sciences or strategic communication—also likely makes the challenge of connecting theory and practice more difficult. While such backgrounds are useful, they might also mean that the communities start further apart without a shared language or evidence base.

As we got to know the people involved in the practitioner community, we realized that our position as social scientists in advertising and public relations departments was helping us think about communication somewhat differently than many of our colleagues, and we found an appetite for our ideas. We also heard tough critiques of the available research from communication practitioners alongside many,

many ideas for things that these practitioners would like to know. More importantly, we realized that we enjoyed doing increasingly applied research in collaboration with this growing, and increasingly sophisticated, community of practitioners. And, fortunately for us, the fact that we were in strategic communication departments meant that our home units valued this work.

We hope to continue down this path, and this book takes stock of how we currently think about science communication. Our goal in sharing this work is to help the scientific community make smart, strategic decisions and thus improve the long-term impact of science communication efforts. In other words, we want the scientific community to turn to social science when faced with communication challenges and opportunities. We do this by sharing what we have come to learn about 12 types of communication objectives that any communicator could choose to prioritize as part of a long-term communication strategy. And in the end, helping the scientific community communicate more effectively could mean that our society will be more likely to turn to the sciences for guidance when faced with challenges and opportunities.

That being said, we are also quite sure that we do not fully understand how science communication works. So our second goal for this book is to invite debate and testing of our ideas.

But why did we start by telling you all of this?

It is part of our communication strategy. Look at what we told you and think about what we want you to believe and feel as you decide whether to continue reading this book. You might also consider *how* we want you to think and what we want you to *do*. To start, we told you our primary behavioral goal: We want scientists to devote effort to communicating more effectively (so that citizens are more likely to turn to science when faced with difficult decisions). We have only started to share what we mean by effective, but we promise we will share more on that topic soon. Right now, what is important is that we thought it might be useful for you to believe and feel some specific things to help get you to consider reading this book. We also wanted to frame the discussion in a certain way.

First, we suspect it is important for you to believe that we have some level of competence or expertise (chapter 7). We are not pretending we are the best scholars in the world, but we do want you to believe that our experiences and training make us capable of the current task. We therefore told you about our professional and academic histories, and our research successes. *Competence beliefs* are a core element of how social scientists understand trustworthiness [1] and should make it more likely that you will pay attention to what we write. We think sharing information about *why* we think you should believe we are competent (despite self-doubt) is probably ethical because everything we said is true. In other words, we understand beliefs as a person's estimate of whether something is true or false, and we would like you to evaluate us and decide we are competent enough to provide you with insight about strategic science communication. We are especially interested throughout this book in *evaluative beliefs*, which include some sort of affective judgement. Believing someone is honest or that a technology creates benefits, for example, are evaluations that generally carry positive affective meaning [2]. In contrast, *descriptive beliefs*, such as "ice is usually cold," do not have inherent positive or negative connotations.

Second, we want you to believe that we care about science communication quality and chose our research to make the world a better place. We might also call these *warmth* or *benevolence beliefs* (chapter 3). We really do care about improving society, and we think it is important you believe we care because perceived caring is another aspect of how social scientists think people make trust judgements [1,3]. We also provided information about our commitment to listening and our sense that we have become part of the science communication practitioner community. Being perceived as *honest* (chapter 4), and *willing to listen* (i.e., open) (chapter 5) are both additional potential communication objectives. Trying to communicate a *shared identity* as members of the scientific community and people embedded within families and communities like everyone else is a fifth communication objective (chapter 6). Again, we want you to believe these things because they are true and because evidence suggests that fostering these beliefs will increase the odds that you will consider the advice we share. We recognize that, as two heterosexual, white, 40-something male professors, we have different life experiences than many other people we want to reach, but we also believe it is important to recognize that we share many similarities with the diverse range of people that we work with and who we hope will read this book.

And it does not stop there. We think this book is more likely to succeed in improving the quality of science communication practice if we achieve several other objectives.

At the most basic level, we hope to share social scientific research knowledge that makes a case for the types of content that you could include in your communication efforts. The *sharing knowledge* objective is always going to be an objective of science communication projects. That being said, one of the most interesting aspects of knowledge (as an objective) is how minimally factual knowledge about the natural world seems to impact many behaviors that scientists care about (chapter 2) [4]. We eschew definitions of science communication that suggest it is only about communicating scientific facts, processes, and the results of research. In contrast, we understand science communication in the broadest possible terms as simply communication done in the context of scientific issues. And the specific type of communication we focus on in this book is intentional communication done to affect the long-term behaviors (very broadly understood, see chapter 1) of both scientists and the people with whom they communicate. Ultimately, the idea of knowledge sharing as an objective is important because it should raise the question of what "knowledge" needs to be shared to affect behavior. What true beliefs do we hope you hold when you finish the book? The knowledge we are sharing is knowledge about what social science tells us about the range of beliefs, feelings, and frames that science communicators could seek to achieve. Your knowing about our trustworthiness could be understood as type of knowledge (chapter 3-7) but let us also suggest some additional potential beliefs that we touch on and that any science communicator could choose to prioritize in their own communication.

Beyond sharing knowledge, given our desire to change behavior, we also want readers to believe that being more strategic when communicating will result in *more benefits than risks* to themselves and the scientific community (chapter 8). We will therefore spend time talking about the expected benefits and potential risks of choosing to prioritize the communication objectives we detail in most chapters. A focus on evaluative beliefs about risks and benefits can also be understood as an attempt to shape your general attitudes toward strategic communication. We understand attitudes, in this regard, as a sum of evaluative beliefs [2].

We will also describe what our research shows about how the scientific community thinks about different communication objectives and the community's own behavior. In other words, based on our data, we want our scientist readers to believe that other people in the scientific community would be okay if you pursued most communication objectives and that many of your colleagues would be willing to pursue many of these objectives themselves. Similarly, we want communication professionals who read this book to know that scientists are open to a range of communication objectives. We have substantial data on this from our scientist surveys and interview work. We also have examples from practice. In social science, beliefs about what others think and do are often called *normative beliefs* (i.e., what is normal) and strategic communicators may sometimes want to shape or reshape such beliefs if they are inaccurate or when norms are not clear (chapter 9) [5].

Another type of belief we seek to foster through this book—and that we suggest you consider in your own communication—are beliefs about the degree to which communicators believe that they are personally capable of communicating more strategically. Social scientists call these *self-efficacy beliefs* (chapter 10) [6].

Beliefs are not the only things that communication can change, however. Thinking about the emotions that different communication choices can engender, including both overall positive or negative affect as well as discrete emotions that have the potential to draw people in or cause people to shift away, is also very important (chapter 11).

The ethics of communicating feelings seem more challenging, but they represent an important potential objective that needs to be considered.

Finally, you might note that our whole discussion so far frames the challenge of communicating strategically as a question of adapting and using social science. This framing can also be seen in terms such as the "science of science communication" [7] or the idea of "evidence-based science communication" [8]. Unlike communicating to change beliefs or to evoke feelings, the final communication objective this book offers is framing issues in ways that help achieve goals or avoiding framing that gets in the way of achieving those goals (also chapter 11).

Our Book

In the end, given all the potential objectives that communicators can choose, we wanted to write a book that would bring together a range of literature in a way that can help people in the science community make evidence-based choices. We thought we could do this by sharing what we know about communication objectives and inviting potential communicators to think about (1) what objectives they should consider prioritizing given their ultimate communication goals and (2) what tactics they might want to use to meet those objectives.

Our surveys and interviews tell us that many science communicators start with a limited perspective on the strategic choices they have available when it comes to tactics, objectives, and goals. To us, this is like a musician playing only two chords or a chef cooking with only two ingredients. In the long run, successful communicators need to choose from the full range of available options, and we see our task as writing about those options that exist. We also share when one should expect specific beliefs, feelings, or frames to lead to behavior change, as well as what tactics might be the most useful in changing those underlying beliefs, feelings, and frames themselves. Our "tactics-objectives-goals" framework (chapter 1) explains how we see objectives, in particular, as central to improving the quality of science communication.

We do not pretend to be experts in every area we discuss—each area has its own extensive body of literatures and subliteratures—but we hope we are able to provide a useful overview that could help readers better think about the choices they could make when communicating. In some cases, we talk about specific theories by name and describe specific studies that deserve attention. We do this because we expect that most of our readers are highly educated (or on their way to being highly educated) and that such people would want us to use the terms that social scientists really use. We do not seek to invent new terms that make it hard to dig deeper if you choose. You should feel free to skip these theory bits if you are so inclined, but we also hope that some of you will use our work as a guide into this fascinating and still-emerging field of research and practice.

REFERENCES

1. Fiske, Susan T., Amy J. C. Cuddy, and Peter Glick. "Universal Dimensions of Social Cognition: Warmth and Competence." *Trends in Cognitive Sciences* 11, no. 2 (2007): 77–83. https://doi.org/10.1016/j.tics.2006.11.005.

2. Oskamp, Stuart, and P. Wesley Schultz. *Attitudes and Opinions.* 3rd ed. Mahwah, NJ: Lawrence Erlbaum Associates, 2005.

3. Schoorman, F. David, Roger C. Mayer, and James H. Davis. "An Integrative Model of Organizational Trust: Past, Present, and Future." *Academy of Management Review* 32, no. 2 (2007): 344–54. https://doi.org/10.2307/20159304.

4. Allum, Nick C., Patrick Sturgis, D. Tabourazi, and I. Brunton-Smith. "Science Knowledge and Attitudes across Cultures: A Meta-Analysis." *Public Understanding of Science* 17, no. 1 (Jan 2008): 35–54. https://doi.org/10.1077/0963662506070159.

5. Rimal, Rajiv N., Maria K. Lapinski, R. J. Cook, and K. Real. "Moving toward a Theory of Normative Influences: How Perceived Benefits and Similarity Moderate the Impact of Descriptive Norms on Behaviors." *Journal of Health Communication* 10, no. 5 (Jul–Aug 2005): 433–50. https://doi.org/10.1080/10810730591009880.

6. Bandura, Albert. "Social Cognitive Theory of Mass Communication." In *Media Effects: Advances in Theory and Research*, edited by Jennings Bryant and Dolf Zillman, 121–53. Mahwah, NJ: Lawrence Erlbaum Associates, 2002.

7. Fischhoff, Baruch. "The Sciences of Science Communication." *Proceedings of the National Academy of Sciences* 110, Supplement 3 (2013): 14033–39. https://doi.org/10.1073/pnas.1213273110.

8. Jensen, Eric A., and Alexander Gerber. "Evidence-Based Science Communication." *Frontiers in Communication* 4, January 23, 2020. https://doi.org/10.3389/fcomm.2019.00078.

1

What It Means to Be a Strategic Science Communicator

THE FRAMEWORKS INSTITUTE is a good place for us to start our exploration into strategic science communication. Their approach to helping scientists communicate effectively makes it an important voice in our field. FrameWorks began its efforts in 1999 and continues to thrive as one of a growing number of entities trying to help scientists communicate more effectively. These organizations are full of creative and clever communication experts, but we suspect Frame-Works has excelled because of its evidence-based efforts to help its partners think strategically.

The FrameWorks Institute starts by helping to identify the behavioral goals their clients want to achieve. Setting goals is essential to the idea of effective communication, but FrameWorks's real expertise is in the way they think about one specific (but broad) type of communication objective: how people frame an issue in their mind (chapter 11). Behavior change is typically their clients' ultimate goal, but (re)framing is the primary communication objective for which Frame-Works has unique expertise.

Once FrameWorks helps organizations set goals for the behaviors they want to shift, the organization's researchers begin to systematically scour news stories, websites, and other types of content to understand how an issue is being talked about. They also talk to experts and nonexperts both to better understand the dominant "frame" for an issue and to begin to work toward identifying alternative framing that might shift behavior. Once they identify promising alternative frames, they test these frames using social science tools such as interviews, experiments, and surveys. They then share their recommendations with those who might use their insights. As part of their recommendations, they often include ideas and templates aimed at helping their clients use specific tactics, such as storylines and metaphors, that their evidence suggests may be particularly effective.

Let's look at an example. A group of foundations sponsored Frame-Works to build strategy to ensure strong support for better integrating in-school and out-of-school science, technology, engineering, and math (STEM) education [1]. Building on their previous work, Frame-Works recommended that proponents of integrating STEM education frame their discussions in terms of "collective prosperity" and "future preparation" of fellow citizens. They also suggested emphasizing that STEM education is a process of "weaving" together a range of skills that young people need and ensuring "fairness across places" so that all children have access to these skills. Additional suggested frames addressed related issues but the important point is that FrameWorks's strategy involves trying to change behavior through a focus on a specific type of communication objective: how an issue is framed. And once FrameWorks identifies a framing objective, they suggest a range of tactics that have the potential to help achieve that objective. For FrameWorks, the tactics used to achieve the stated objectives often involve the careful selection of words and metaphors, but it could also involve choices about things such as *who* communicates and with what tone, timing, and channel.

Tactics to achieve selected objectives. Objectives to achieve priority goals.

The Central Role of Communication Objectives

This book focuses on communication objectives because of their central role (figure 1.1) in strategic science communication. In that spirit, we argue there are at least 12 specific communication objectives that represent a core pantry from which to choose. Some of these objectives are well known, while others—including the research on why the objective matters—may be less familiar to many readers. The potential outcome of wise choices about communication objectives, however, could include stronger financial and political support for scientific research as well as broader acceptance of scientific evidence as a central source of insight for societal decisions. This in turn could

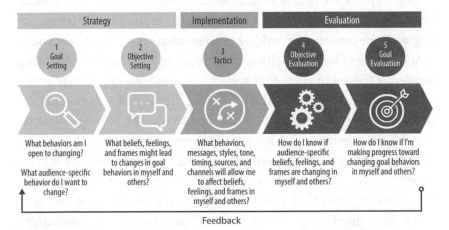

Figure 1.1. Goals-Objectives-Tactics-Objectives-Goals Model of Strategic Communication. The strategy phase involves identifying goals—typically behaviors or pseudo-behaviors like "support" or "acceptance"—that a communicator wants a specific group to consider and then setting communication objectives that might help achieve those goals. The objectives are often various evaluative beliefs, feelings, or frames (see figure 1.2). The implementation phase involves choosing communication tactics that might help achieve those beliefs, feelings, or frames in a specific group. And the evaluation phase entails assessing whether the chosen tactics affected priority objectives and whether, over time, these objectives are associated with changes in desired behaviors. One important element to recognize is that strategic communicators can set goals and objectives that involve changing their *own* behaviors (e.g., they might consult to see if they are pursuing the best possible research path) and then choose tactics that make changes to their own behavior more likely.

help friends, neighbors, and fellow humans make evidence-based personal and societal decisions about health, the environment, and other sources of well-being.

We know that science is not infallible and we don't believe that scientists should make decisions for others in society. There are, however, issues where we hope there is broad agreement; for instance, that the world would be a better place if we could ensure that scientists have a meaningful voice in decision-making. Scholars and practitioners focused on science communication are, in fact, becoming aware of how achieving specific communication objectives might affect science-relevant behaviors (i.e., goals) as well as the tactics communicators can use to achieve their objectives.

Our experience is that most science communication texts seek to help communicators focus on tactical skills related to clarity, working with the media, and making presentations [2–5]. Another type of work—some of which we have contributed to—focuses on building academic theory in ways that are often not as clearly tied to practice as communicators might like [6–8]. One element of this theoretical discussion addresses important questions about the economic and societal forces behind the apparent increasing demand for science communication and the changing nature of the community [9]. We deeply appreciate our colleagues' work on tactics and theory but believe we can provide additional insight into how academic research can inform the strategic use of communication to achieve community goals and objectives through a range of tactics. For example, research tells us that avoiding jargon is a tactic that might affect how a message or messenger is perceived (not just understood), and so we would like to focus on what specific types of content science communicators could build into their communication. Similarly, while we agree that storytelling is an important communication tactic, our focus is on the potential content for such stories and how scientists could best use stories to achieve specific communication objectives. We also assume that readers already agree that the scientific community needs to communicate. We do not make an argument for why scientists should communicate but instead focus on helping science communicators make strategic choices that are likely to be both effective and ethical.

Strategy is needed to ensure effectiveness because science communicators can make so many different choices about tactics, objectives, and goals. Tactically, they need to choose what to say or write. Indeed, choosing whether to say anything at all is in itself a tactical communication choice. They need to choose the tone of what they share and how to frame their content. They can also often choose where to communicate and who should do the communication. The challenge is how to make these choices. A strategic communicator needs to avoid making these tactical decisions too early in the communication planning process. We thus argue that the most important choices—the choices that should drive the tactics—are what a communicator wants to achieve by communicating. This includes both their ultimate goals and their immediate communication objectives.

Choosing Goals

Choosing ultimate goals may seem easy but many science communicators seem to struggle with identifying what they *really* want to achieve through communication. When asked, many scientists say their goal is to raise awareness or interest in an issue or new research. Sometimes they say they just want people to enjoy themselves in the context of science. And that's . . . fine. Those are meaningful communication objectives. However, when pushed, most will agree that they would not be happy if they *only* raised awareness, helped someone understand new (or old) science, or provided an enjoyable experience.

Pushing potential communicators to identify their true goals is central to any strategic process. When pressed, science communicators will often agree that they want to see their efforts result in behavior change, broadly defined. Ideally, a science communicator will identify these behavioral goals based on where they sit within the scientific community, whether as the member or leader of an organization such as a lab, scientific society, business, or group. For example, in a company, we would expect the communication team to support the company's business goals, and we think it makes equal sense that science communicators should also consider looking to their organizations and colleagues for guidance on potential goals (more on this in chapter 12). These behaviors might be individual in nature and involve increasing how often some groups of people do something, such as buy environmentally friendlier products, wear sunscreen, or choose a science career.

The behavior might also involve *not* doing something. Examples might include wanting people to consider eating less beef or other foods that are bad for the planet and health, refusing unprotected sex, or not dropping out of school. Some of the desired behaviors may be more civic in nature, including goals such as increasing policymakers' use of science or ensuring government funding for scientific research. This support could be explicit in the form of wanting to see votes or donations, but it could also be more tacit or implicit in cases where the goal is simply "support" in an abstract sense. Indeed, we would argue that one of the most important long-term goals of science communication is to ensure that people see science as a legitimate source of insight when making decisions in society [9]. In other words, the goal may not be support for every decision but, rather, acceptance of the fairness of science decision-making processes [10].

Some science communicators have a goal to advance their own careers and, while we are fine with that, this book is not really about that inasmuch as the literature we focus on is about the factors that seem to affect behavior. We suppose the behavior that some communicators want is to be read and cited by others (a key metric of academic success) [11], and the ideas discussed here could be used to try to foster such behavior. Nevertheless, we focus primarily on prosocial goals because, as we will discuss, our sense is that these are the goals that drive most of the scientists we interact with, and we have little desire to help science communicators who are only focused on themselves. That being said, we are perfectly comfortable with the idea that scientists or scientific organizations that believe they are doing useful work could use the ideas in this book to help get their work recognized by others as part of a strategy to have a broader positive impact on the world.

Whatever the case, our view is that effective communication can only be sustained when you are clear about your long-term goals. You are an effective communicator when your communication efforts help you achieve your goals. Indeed, the idea of effectiveness only makes sense if you have goals. There may be some science communicators who genuinely do not care if people consider scientific advice, but we also think that communication simply for the sake of communication seems wasteful in a world where many scientists are busy and starved for resources. We also worry that communicators who communicate without purpose may strike audiences as either disrespectful or unprofessional. For example, few people like being asked to participate in a meeting where there is no clear purpose.

For evidence to support the idea that most scientists have substantive goals for communication, we included a battery of questions on a survey of scientists we conducted in late 2015 and early 2016. The survey was done with a range of different US-based scientific societies. We focused on societies because the journals, groups, and conferences that scientific societies manage are a primary place where scientists go to hear from one another and keep up with trends in research, teaching, and (increasingly) how their field is interacting with the world beyond academia. Using data from seven scientific societies from different fields, we found that scientists are almost unanimous in their belief that getting policymakers and our culture to value science are important goals for public engagement activities (table 1.1). On a scale from 1 to 7, the average scores for these two goals were near or above 6 for all seven societies.

The survey was also divided up so that some respondents were asked about goals in the context of face-to-face engagement, engagement through the news media, or online engagement. And again, no matter the context, scientists indicated that they wanted to see something happen because of public engagement. What is more, even the lower-ranked goals were rated well above the middle of the scale, suggesting that scientists see a range of goals as potentially useful. Also

Table 1.1.

Scientists' ratings (on a scale of 1 to 7) of the importance of various public engagement goals in the context of different communication channels

Type of society and mode of engagement	Ensure policymakers use science	Ensure culture values science	Increase own research impact	Fulfill own duty to society	Help others make better decisions	Ensure science funding	Ensure youth choose science careers	Obtain own funding	Diversify STEM	Sample size range
General										
Face-to-face	6.32	6.15	5.83	5.72	5.58	5.50	5.25	5.09	5.02	381–384
Media	6.45	6.10	5.84	5.80	5.50	5.68	5.19	4.67	5.07	328–332
Online	6.36	6.15	5.73	5.55	5.41	5.55	5.25	4.73	4.96	382–389
Biological										
Face-to-face	6.32	6.29	5.84	5.68	5.82	5.73	5.50	5.00	5.19	354–356
Online	6.27	6.08	5.77	5.59	5.68	5.82	5.43	5.06	5.25	336–339
Geophysical										
Face-to-face	6.38	6.08	5.84	5.67	5.51	5.00	5.02	4.98	5.05	313–316
Media	6.50	6.10	5.90	5.77	5.48	5.22	5.13	4.76	5.12	317–322
Online	6.23	6.07	5.75	5.53	5.37	4.99	5.07	4.88	4.99	275–276
Geological										
Face-to-face	6.36	6.10	5.56	5.60	5.71	5.18	5.43	5.06	5.00	257–259
Media	6.48	6.07	5.57	5.60	5.77	5.20	5.39	4.91	5.03	242–248
Online	6.41	6.15	5.53	5.40	5.69	5.03	5.64	5.01	5.00	234–241
Ecological										
Face-to-face	6.43	6.13	5.89	5.79	5.65	4.91	5.07	4.97	5.13	345–350
Chemical										
Face-to-face	6.16	6.23	5.35	5.52	5.60	5.48	5.41	5.11	5.02	181–184
Media	6.11	5.97	5.46	5.54	5.37	5.57	5.25	4.76	4.84	157–160
Online	6.01	5.93	5.52	5.31	5.44	5.39	5.13	5.15	4.91	156–157
Biochemical										
Face-to-face	6.29	6.19	5.90	5.53	5.58	5.95	5.18	4.87	5.19	371–375
Social										
Media	6.12	5.47	5.12	5.88	5.12	4.68	4.08	3.80	4.45	921–930

Notes: Respondents were all faculty with PhDs at US-based universities. They were asked to rate each goal on how important they thought it was for scientists such as themselves, from "very low importance" (1) to "very high importance" (7). In addition, the survey was designed so that respondents from larger societies were chosen at random to answer in the context of either face-to-face public engagement with adults, engagement of adults through the news media, or online public engagement with adults. Data was collected between October 2015 and April 2016. See appendix A for additional details about survey methods.

noteworthy is that the goals that tended to score highest were those focused on improving society rather than helping the individual scientist.

One key goal missing from this project is that respectful, ethical, and smart communicators communicate to see if their own behaviors need to change. This goal is central to ethical and effective communication but frequently forgotten. It could involve scientists realizing that there is an unmet need that research could address or that a current research approach might not be the best approach. In some cases, the science communicator might decide that they are on the right track, whereas in others they might realize they could better use their time and resources in another way. Ironically, we realized we had missed this goal in our research by actively talking with communication practitioners.

Goals and the Centrality of Objectives

A practical problem with talking about behavior as a communication goal is that communication does not lead directly to behavior change. Instead, communicators who want to affect behavior must find ways to affect a range of evaluative beliefs, feelings, and frames,* including their own. These beliefs, feelings, and frames are the essential objectives of science communication practice and research as well as the primary subject of this book. Ultimately, we think that science communicators who know something about the range of different objectives they could pursue are more likely to make better communication choices when it comes to tactics and thus will be more likely to achieve their ultimate goals.

We could call objectives something else (e.g., short-term goals) but we prefer the term "communication objectives" to better differentiate them from goals, building on foundational scholarship in strategic

---

* We are aware that "beliefs, feelings, and frames" could be made into the acronym BFF and that BFF is also understood to stand for "best friends forever." We agree that beliefs, feelings, and frames are communicators' best friends (forever), but we are choosing not to make a big point of this fun fact.

communication [12,13] and broader discussions on strategy [14]. Communication tactics are not the only thing that shapes beliefs and feelings, but they are the primary ingredients that communicators have available to work with. For example, personal characteristics such as age, sex, education, ideology, and values are important concepts in any discussion of communication because they can shape how communication efforts are perceived, but they are not typically amenable to change through communication. We therefore reserve the term "communication objectives" for things that can change directly as a result of communication.

The expectation is that communicators who can foster the necessary evaluative beliefs, feelings, and frames in the people they are interested in reaching will get closer to achieving their behavioral goals. Our view is that a strategic communicator is therefore someone who first identifies realistic, audience-specific goals they want to achieve and then uses logic or evidence-based theories to decide what beliefs, feelings, and frames might help achieve those goals. Only then do they make choices about communication tactics such as their own behavior, word choice, tone, channel, and communicator. Tactics should be chosen for their ability to achieve their chosen objectives given one's resources and opportunities. In our view, the choice to avoid things like jargon and telling personal stories are thus tactics that science communicators can choose to use and that have an impact on a range potential communication objectives. They are not the essence of science communication. Some communicators are so charismatic, creative, or lucky that they can have positive effects by winging it, but we cannot trust society's long-term relationship with science to serendipity.

Another thing that's important to note is that we recognize our strategic communication approach to differentiating goals, objectives, and tactics is somewhat different than two important reports by groups working through the process of the prestigious US National Academies of Sciences, Engineering, and Medicine [15,16]. We feel somewhat self-conscious suggesting that our approach is preferable, but our sense is that both these reports lump things together that we have separated out and ordered in the way that we learned from strategic communication scholarship [12].

Knowledge Is Not the Only Communication Objective

One potential problem with some science communication discussion is that too much time is focused on too few objectives. We know from our own research that the outcome that science communicators typically prioritize as their objective is increasing scientific knowledge [17,18], including beliefs related to both the facts and processes of science. The hope seems to be that people will rationally choose to do the right behavior if they are provided with the correct way to understand an issue. For example, many people seem to think that, if people only knew the basic science of climate change, they would use fewer fossil fuels. Or, if people only knew how genetic engineering works, they would be happy to eat foods with genetically engineered ingredients. However, research suggests that it is naive to expect that people will change their behavior just because a scientist clearly shares the best scientific evidence [19].

The relationship between knowledge and behavior is an empirical question that researchers have asked many times and in many contexts. Unfortunately, as further discussed in chapter 2, the evidence is clear that filling deficits in science knowledge has only limited impact on behavior [15,19]. More broadly, research trajectories of both science [20] and risk communication [21] have highlighted how communication efforts will rarely succeed if they simply focus on increasing knowledge.

That being said, as (social) scientists and citizens, we agree that scientists need to meaningfully share what research shows when they communicate. Having scientists share what they are learning is probably a big reason that people are willing to provide scientists with so many communication opportunities. And while individual-level science knowledge is not likely to drive most behaviors, the National Academies report on science literacy still emphasized the importance of ensuring that communities can collectively access and use scientific information. For example, not everyone affected by HIV needed to become medical experts in the area, but it is important that at least some members of this community had the ability to communicate with scientists [22]. Further, scientists who do not appear willing or able to share meaningful insight when given the opportunity to communicate will likely generate a host of negative beliefs and feelings. The point in highlighting the limits of transferring scientific facts as the primary objective of science communication is simply to make clear that sharing our hard-won scientific knowledge is not enough.

Similarly, it is not enough for science communication researchers to tell practitioners that they should not focus so much effort on filling knowledge deficits. We need to find ways to share what we know about nonknowledge objectives that communicators might wish to pursue. This book is part of our attempt to do so. Building on our shared research will provide science communicators with novel ways to think about effectiveness.

In addition to research on public opinion about science, our work includes both surveys of scientists and how they see public engagement efforts as well as more than 1,000 hours of interviews with trainers, leaders of scientific societies, fellowship directors, science funders, and scientists themselves. It also draws on evidence from across the social sciences and the experiences of some of the world's most experienced trainers and others who are working directly with scientists to communicate more effectively. As noted, most science communication books have focused on tactical-level skills such as jargon-free writing, compelling storytelling, and gaining access to audiences through various media. Our sense is that too little attention has focused on understanding *what* content needs to be shared in a clear, compelling, and accessible way.

We have chosen to specifically focus on a set of 12 objectives—including knowledge (chapter 2)—that the research literature suggests are at the heart of effective communication (figure 1.2). These objectives are all outcomes that strategic communicators could choose to prioritize through their tactical choices when they communicate. We arrived at this list of 12 objectives from our own experience as researchers in the field and in the process of ongoing and active discus-

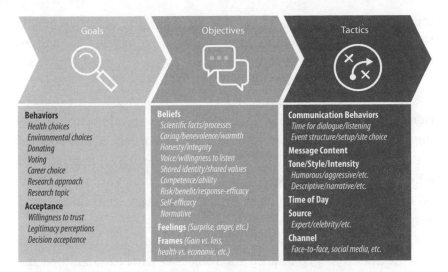

Goals	Objectives	Tactics
Behaviors	**Beliefs**	**Communication Behaviors**
Health choices	*Scientific facts/processes*	*Time for dialogue/listening*
Environmental choices	*Caring/benevolence/warmth*	*Event structure/setup/site choice*
Donating	*Honesty/integrity*	**Message Content**
Voting	*Voice/willingness to listen*	**Tone/Style/Intensity**
Career choice	*Shared identity/shared values*	*Humorous/aggressive/etc.*
Research approach	*Competence/ability*	*Descriptive/narrative/etc.*
Research topic	*Risk/benefit/response-efficacy*	**Time of Day**
Acceptance	*Self-efficacy*	**Source**
Willingness to trust	*Normative*	*Expert/celebrity/etc.*
Legitimacy perceptions	**Feelings** *(Surprise, anger, etc.)*	**Channel**
Decision acceptance	**Frames** *(Gain vs. loss,*	*Face-to-face, social media, etc.*
	health vs. economic, etc.)	

Figure 1.2. Goals-Objectives-Tactics. Communication objectives sit at the center of strategic communication thinking because they are both the evaluative beliefs, feelings, and frames that most behavior change theories typically associate with behavior change as well as the immediate expected outcome of communication tactics. Communication tactics from this perspective affect behavior only indirectly and as a result of successful shifts in beliefs, feelings, and frames. Recall also that strategic communicators should almost always set goals and objectives that involve changing their own behaviors, beliefs, feelings, and frames and then choose tactics that make such changes more likely.

sion with practitioners over about a decade. Five of these objectives are related to trustworthiness. These include the communication objectives of shaping evaluative beliefs associated with perceptions that the scientific community:

is warm, caring, or motivated by helping society (chapter 3);
is honest and honorable (chapter 4);
is open and willing to listen (chapter 5);
shares values with their audiences (chapter 6); and
is competent or able (chapter 7).

These trustworthiness-related objectives seem particularly important for behavioral goals associated with policy support or acceptance and also as a means of increasing the odds that someone will pay attention to what scientists have to share. They also represent beliefs that members of the scientific community need to develop about those with whom they want to communicate.

Four additional concepts central to the behavior-change literature are the objectives of shaping beliefs: both risk and benefit perceptions as the foundation of attitudes (chapter 8); social norms, including perceptions about what important people do, expect, and endorse (i.e., descriptive, subjective, and injunctive norms) (chapter 9); and efficacy, including the degree to which people believe that a particular behavior will be both possible and useful (i.e., self-efficacy and response efficacy) (chapter 10).

One thing this initial set of eight chapters will have in common is that the underlying communication objective can be understood as a belief that someone might hold. For example, ecologists who prioritize being perceived as caring might choose to spend time talking or writing about how they chose their topic to make their community safer or healthier (assuming this is true). The hope would be that those with whom they are speaking will come to believe in the scientists' goodwill. Similarly, a communicator who prioritizes getting someone to recognize their own ability to stop smoking might choose to share content aimed at instilling beliefs about success rates in people similar to their audience and the benefits of success (i.e., efficacy beliefs).*

The final objectives chapter will focus on both emotions and framing (chapter 11). These two types of objectives are somewhat different because they are less directly tied to evaluative beliefs. That chapter starts with a discussion of the traditional communication objective of providing people with positive affective experiences with science and scientists and addresses the importance of having communication that is perceived as relevant or interesting [23–25]. It then transi-

---

* We think that it is important to recognize these types of objectives as beliefs because knowledge and interest can also be understood as beliefs about how the world works and what is important to a respondent. In this regard, it would makes sense for people to say things like they believe the Earth goes around the sun or that they believe energy research is important to understand in order to make smart political and personal decisions.

tions to the role of negative affect [26] and the potential value of communication aimed at evoking discrete emotions, such as excitement, fear, or disgust, that communicators might seek through communication activities.

Similarly, the section on framing will address what we know about why science communicators might want to prioritize encouraging their audience to think about an issue in one way rather than another [27,28]. This could involve, for example, talking about an issue in terms of gains versus losses, or perhaps immediate versus long-term impacts, or local versus global impacts. Similarly, a communicator might want to encourage others to think about the same issue in terms of economic, environmental, health, or other societal impacts.

Focusing on these 12 objectives provide a useful framework within which to understand the value of strategic science communication. Key elements of this approach include differentiating communication goals from objectives and tactics, as well as the need to make choices. This need to make choices comes both from the fact that not all objectives are equally likely to affect every behavior and the fact that different tactics are likely better at achieving certain objectives in any given context. The chapters will therefore describe both what we know about how various tactics might help achieve specific objectives and the degree to which we might expect that achieving an objective is likely to help a communicator achieve the goals they have identified.

The need for choices also stems from the fact that communicators are typically faced with constraints in terms of time, space, and other resources. One way we think about this is to ask a science communicator how they would use 60 minutes of a group's time if asked to give a talk. Any communicator faced with this decision, for example, needs to decide how much time to spend sharing scientific facts or processes and how much time to devote to other topics. Should they devote some time to hearing from the audience? How much? Should they spend time trying to make the topic relevant or interesting to their audience? How much extra time will that take? Should they talk about why they do their work to assure their audience that they have the best interests of the community at heart or what they have done to avoid a conflict of interest? Again, these things take time from a talk or space in writing. Furthermore, beyond how to fill the 60 minutes, a science communicator needs to make choices about how to dress, how to set up the room, how early to get there, how late to stay, and many other things that will affect their own experience and the experience of those with whom they interact.

The solution is probably not trying to just do a little of everything. Those who design communication campaigns emphasize the value of theory and formative research to identify objectives that are both associated with the desired behavior and that are amenable to change [29]. For example, it might be a waste of effort to focus on a science decision-maker's credentials if the target audience already believes that the decision-maker is competent or if there is no evidence of a relationship between perceived competence and the desired behavior. There may not be *exact* answers to many of the types of questions we have raised, but our hope is that communicators will still make their choices with intention.

What about Two-Way Dialogue and Public Engagement?

Much of the recent discussion around effective communication highlights the importance of two-way communication in the context of "public engagement." We have been part of this research stream, discuss some of this research throughout the book, and think dialogue is a powerful tool. However, we also think our views are somewhat different than many other scholars.

It appears that many researchers talk about public engagement in a way that suggests that it *requires* two-way dialogue and represents an alternative to one-way communication focused on the objective of filling knowledge deficits. For example, it is common to talk about the history of science communication as moving from deficit to dialogue in the context of a need to stop talking about the public *understanding of* science and technology and instead talk about public *engagement with* science and technology [30]. We share the sentiment behind these calls—and will highlight dialogue-focused tactics in various places in the book—but worry that the deficit to dialogue discussion often seems to conflate tactics (i.e., fostering high quality dialogue) with objectives (i.e., filling a knowledge deficit). We therefore suggest that, from a social science perspective, it makes sense to think of engagement in a more limited way.

Building on the idea of cognitive engagement and opinion quality, we focus on the idea of public engagement *activities* and understand these as tactics designed to increase the odds that participants will actively think about a topic in a way that allows for the development of new or changed beliefs. In other words, they *engage* deeper, more effortful cognitive processes. From an academic perspective, this way of thinking about public engagement is consistent with much scholarship on cognitive processing that calls attention to the fact that people often conserve mental resources by reacting automatically to stimuli. Whether you call it system 1, heuristic, or peripheral processing [31–34], it seems useful to recognize that people are frequently cognitive misers [34,35]. On the other hand, while recognizing debates among social psychologists about the precise nature of the types of processing systems [34], there also appear to be circumstances that can get people to think more deeply and develop more stable beliefs. So, we think of public engagement activities as attempts to foster such effortful and deliberative system 2, systematic, or central processing. It is this type of processing that seems to largely shape the types of beliefs we emphasize in this book.

Taking a broad dual-process (i.e., fast vs. slow) approach to understanding engagement could also help practitioners and applied researchers make sense of how tactics relate to specific objectives. For example, we suspect one reason that dialogue is so important to discussions about public engagement is because having a meaningful conversation with a respectful partner likely promotes higher levels of cognitive engagement (i.e., deeper thinking) by participants [36]. This deeper cognitive engagement likely increases the odds that a science communicator could successfully share information that actually affects beliefs about scientific facts and processes, as well as beliefs related to other objectives (e.g., beliefs about scientists or the efficacy of specific alternatives). In later chapters we further highlight how fostering engagement through dialogue can often contribute to a range of other desirable objectives, including trustworthiness-related beliefs (chapter 3–7) and self-efficacy-related beliefs (chapter 10).

For now, understanding public engagement activities as tactics that increase the likelihood of deeper-than-usual cognitive processes also means that engagement does not always require dialogue. For example, one barrier to higher-level cognitive processing is comprehension [37]. If someone cannot make sense of something because a communicator uses jargon, then it seems reasonable to hypothesize that they are also less likely to sustain their attention. Similarly, audiences seem unlikely to devote scarce cognitive resources to a poorly targeted talk or personally irrelevant, poorly designed, or uninteresting-looking exhibit. We also would not expect people to pay as much attention to messages communicated by someone who does not seem to know much about the topic or care about their audience [33,38].

What about Audience Goals?

Another challenge with writing about being an ethical strategic communicator is how to take others' goals into account. For us, we start with the belief that the people with whom scientists communicate generally want to hold accurate beliefs about the world and are more likely to thrive when they hold such beliefs. We will argue in chapter 2 that holding correct beliefs is part of being knowledgeable. The information environment and our cognitive biases (as discussed in more detail in chapter 6) sometimes makes developing correct beliefs difficult [39], but we have little reason to believe that people want to hold incorrect beliefs. Similarly, we would expect that most people want to find ways to frame the world so that it makes sense to them, and that they generally want their emotions to reflect their experiences. In other words, they want to feel joyful when they have reason to feel joyful and sad when they have reason to feel sad. Together, this suggests that science communicators could be understood as *helping people meet* their goals if they communicate information that helps people form correct evaluative beliefs and feelings about the natural world (i.e., factual knowledge and risk/benefit reliefs), other people (i.e., trustworthiness-related beliefs and normative beliefs), and themselves (i.e., self-efficacy beliefs).

Second, we think that it is ethical for people within the science community to have communication goals that emerge from their own priorities and are not necessarily tied to other peoples' goals. For example, a climate scientist might want a congressperson to consider climate evidence when deciding whether to devote resources to alternative energy regardless of the congressperson's goals. Indeed, our understanding is that it is acceptable to pursue one's own goals through communication, even in situations where achieving these goals might conflict with other peoples' wants or desires, if the pursuit is done in an ethical way. So, we argue that communicators can openly, honestly, and respectfully try to change behavior by changing what other people believe and feel, as well as how they frame issues, so long as scientists recognize that they also need to remain open to changing their own beliefs, feelings, framing, and behavior. We would further argue that people in a pluralistic society sometimes *need* to be challenged as part of a competition of ideas, even if they do not recognize this need explicitly.

We also recognize a point made by historian of strategy Sir Lawrence Freedman that "strategies that depend on others to act out of character, beyond their competence, or against their declared interests and preferences, are gambles" [40]. Science communicators may thus often benefit from providing information that help other people achieve goals. For example, a science communicator who wants support for science funding might be wise to share information about the economic benefits of such funding (assuming it exists) to a decision-maker who seems to be interested in that type of information. Similarly, a guerilla science communicator who thinks they can advance science by giving unexpecting patrons of a bar a positive science experience on a Friday night may want to ensure that they also respect their audiences' desire for a relaxing and enjoyable time out with friends. More pointedly, to state the obvious, science communicators should not expect to succeed if they try to foist solutions on individuals or communities. The history of economic development is full of efforts by outsiders thinking that they know what some other group needs, and nothing in our current book should be understood to encourage such ill-considered activity.

Our emphasis is on asking science communicators to reflect pragmatically on why they might want to help stakeholders achieve their long-term goals (and short-term objectives). Scientists may sometimes want to help others out of a sense of ethical obligation, but they might also want to help others in ways that support science. And we think that is okay too. For us, understanding what audiences think they want can help communicators decide what information to emphasize when planning communication in order to have the most effect. Although we know of no specific research on the subject, a congressperson who *thinks* they want benefit information may in fact be convinced by additional benefit information, and a community member trying to figure out if they can trust a local scientist may really want to know what motivates that scientist or where that scientist gets their funding. On the other hand, it is important to recognize that people do not necessarily know what information is going to affect their behavior; they will give you an answer if you ask them, but "introspective illusion" research suggests that people often do not have direct knowledge about why they act and think in certain ways [41]. Therefore, a more immediate reason to provide someone with the information they expect to receive is that failing to do so could violate that person's expectations, an outcome that interpersonal communication research suggests could have a host of negative consequences [42]. Although we know of no research specifically focused on this question in the context of scientists' communication choices, we would expect, for example, that an audience would have negative reactions to a scientist who fails to share a meaningful amount of scientific evidence or explain why that evidence is important to their audience.

On the other hand, while providing people with the type of experience they expect (or better, that seems important), we would also expect strategic communicators to do more than "give people what they want." Strategic communicators should also consider whether they can use an interaction opportunity to provide other types of information that they think might be relevant to their audience. For example, a community group might invite a group of scientists to speak with them to learn about the potential risks and benefits of a new technology. In such a case, the scientists should share their findings, but they should also consider whether they could use the opportunity to try to foster a deeper relationship with the community group by focusing on outcomes such as building trustworthiness-related beliefs (chapter 3-6). It might similarly be useful and appropriate for a scientist who accepts a speaking invitation to try to learn more about the community and ask about potential research questions that might benefit themselves and the community. In this situation, scientists should be open about their rationale for participating but not feel bad about having their own long-term goals and immediate communication objectives.

One thing we would argue against is any suggestion that the scientific community should simply help others achieve their goals out of a sense of duty. While we might agree that scientists—especially scientists who receive public support—have an obligation to do and share work that ultimately contributes to the public good, we do not think this means that they should speak to whoever makes a request. This reaction-based approach seems inherently problematic and dangerous for any group, including scientists. Although it is beyond the scope of this book, we encourage everyone in the science community to figure out their obligations for themselves while also thinking carefully about how to best allocate precious time and other resources.

What about Uncertainty and Misinformation?

Uncertainty and misinformation are also topics we weave throughout the book but do not emphasize on their own. Communicating uncertainty and correcting misinformation are two topics that have been raised when we have asked whether there are any goals or objectives that our approach (figure 1.1) has missed. We do not include uncertainty or misinformation as stand-alone objectives because we see both as relevant to any of the belief-based objectives we discuss in chapters 2 through 10. For example, someone could be uncertain about the state of scientific knowledge on a topic (chapter 2) or whether a group of scientists is caring (chapter 3), honest (chapter 4), willing to listen (chapter 5), or competent (7). They could also be uncertain about a scientist's values (chapter 6), whether a specific technology or behavior presents risks or benefits (chapter 8), and whether they have the capacity (i.e., self-efficacy beliefs) to achieve those benefits (10). Uncertainty about others' beliefs (i.e., normative beliefs) is also common (chapter 9). There are many reasons why someone might be uncertain, but it is also clear that ill-informed or bad actors sometimes propagate misinformation (or disinformation) about any of these belief types. Such bad actors may even use such information in efforts to frame an issue as being about uncertainty in order to delay societal action, such as by claiming that we do not yet know enough about smoking or climate change to take action [43,44] (chapter 11).

A second reason we do not emphasize communicating uncertainty and misinformation is because we see that decision as ethical and tactical rather than strategic. The question of whether to communicate uncertainty about what is known or unknown seems like an ethical question because our sense is that science communicators should provide such uncertainty information if they think it is relevant not because they think it might have a negative or positive effect. Put differently, we would not suggest hiding uncertainty information because of a fear about an audience's response. Similarly, we would never advocate communicating misinformation. Rather, this book focuses on providing insight into the range of evaluative beliefs, feelings, and frames that science communicators could choose to try to affect through their own communication choices and does not dwell on lamenting others' poor or unethical choices to share misinformation. The one exception to this is our admonition that strategic communicators can usually benefit from formative research aimed at understanding what those with whom they are communicating are hearing, believing, and feeling when deciding what to prioritize through their communication choices.

On the tactical side, researchers continue to study how to best communicate uncertainty when presenting [45,46]—a skill set we do not seek to teach here (or possess)—but the evidence to date does not suggest that science communicators should worry excessively that communicating uncertainty will have substantive negative effects on how people feel about science or the scientific community. In contrast, a recent review of research in this area noted that introducing uncertainty about whether there is a scientific consensus on an issue (chapter 10) can have negative effects but that sharing uncertainty about something like the likelihood of risks or benefits (chapter 9) can either slightly improve perceptions of the communicator or have little overall effect, in most known cases [47].

And communicating uncertainty doesn't just have the potential to improve trustworthiness beliefs. We also highlight uncertainty as a reason science communicators need to care about how people perceive the scientific community because of the role uncertainty plays in how people use their trustworthiness beliefs. Specifically, as we will discuss, it appears that people use evaluative beliefs about trustworthiness to decide whether decisions are legitimate when we are uncertain about whether a decision is right or wrong. In contrast, as we hope people have learned in recent years, it's hard to ask someone to accept a decision about which you have incomplete information if you don't think a decision-maker is trustworthy (chapters 3-6).

And What about Ethics?

Understanding public engagement activities largely as efforts to foster belief formation through meaningful cognitive engagement also speaks to the importance of ethics in any discussion of strategic science communication. Therefore, we highlight throughout the book the importance of making ethical strategic communication choices. To start, we hope readers agree that it is more ethical to communicate in ways that encourage deeper processing rather than relying on the biased or heuristic reasoning that can arise when people lack the motivation or ability to process (or are encouraged to process in way that protects a cherished identity group) [39]. This is why we focus on the idea of helping people form meaningful beliefs and make choices about their behaviors. We also argue that it is not inherently problematic to devote communication resources to the types of objectives addressed in the core chapters if the beliefs being communicated are true and communicators are open to changing their own beliefs.

On the question of truthfulness, it would be clearly unethical to argue that a science communicator should, for example, try to build trust by saying that they care about their community if they do not, in fact, care about their community. But this seems banal. A more subtle aspect of truthfulness might be the willingness to be open and transparent about why you are sharing certain information. This might mean having a communicator say they know that some people worry about scientists' motives and then talking about their own motives or talking about why a specific frame was chosen, for example. This might not always be practical or necessary, but it is possible and might make sense in cases where a substantial effort is being put into achieving a specific objective.

Beyond transparency, it might also be unethical and unwise to ignore certain communication objectives. For example, some audience members may want science communicators to spend some of their time explaining why scientists chose a specific research topic or highlighting what a research group is doing to avoid conflicts of interest. This is important information in helping us make decisions in cases where we cannot know everything. Similarly, they might want to know why a topic is relevant for them or different ways an issue might be understood (i.e., framed). As already noted, to not share such information would be to disrespect the needs or desires of those with whom one is communicating.

On the issue of openness to changing one's own mind, a science communicator who is not eager to truly hear from others would also be both unethical and unwise. It seems clear that ethical communicators need to be willing to change their own beliefs, feelings, or ways of thinking. This is why two-way dialogue is so important. While this book largely focuses on helping science communicators figure out how to better think about affecting others through communication, we also offer suggestions about how scientists themselves might seek to create communication opportunities in which they change their own beliefs, feelings, and frames.

Another reason that prioritizing a range of communication objectives might be ethical is that a failure to prioritize an objective does not mean that one's communication does not affect that potential outcome. In other words, science communicators may inadvertently impart various beliefs, feelings, and frames through a failure to make careful, strategic decisions. For example, scientists who fail to ensure that those with whom they are communicating understand their motives or expertise risk being ignored or dismissed. In civic contexts, science communicators who do not think through what they hope to achieve through communication may naively use terms such as "denier" that increase the risk of alienating potential allies [48]. Similarly, science communicators who say things that create fear or anxiety without prioritizing helping people understand potential solutions (i.e., efficacy beliefs) may make beneficial behavior change more difficult [49].

The issue of ethics is also relevant to goals, not just objectives or tactics. Science communicators should obviously not encourage behavior they suspect might not be in the best interests of their audience, and they should also be open to discussing their own goals. The more interesting issue, however, is the degree to which science communicators might need to be more reflective with themselves about their own goals. As noted, there may be cases where communicators would truly be happy if people just learned something or just became more interested in the topic. In fact, this is exactly what we hope journalists will do as nonstrategic communicators whose purpose is to shine attention on issues of potential importance. However, while scientists and journalists may share values associated with seeking out truth and being as fair as possible to the evidence, most science communicators are not journalists precisely because they often want things such as public funding for their fields' researchers and input to decision-making processes where they have expertise. They should be honest about the behaviors they want to achieve through communication and find ways to achieve those goals in transparent ways.

Finally, we emphasize that being strategic should increase the odds that the resources we put into communication will be well spent. This is especially important because much of the money researchers spend comes from government or philanthropic funding. A built-in benefit of being explicit about communication objectives and behavioral goals is that well-articulated goals and objectives are meant to be measurable. If you say your goal is to get people in a community to choose more fuel-efficient vehicles and your strategy involves objectives such as getting people to recognize a broad community of support for such vehicles (i.e., subjective norms, chapter 9) and to see the environmental benefit of these vehicle (i.e., attitudes or response efficacy, chapter 8), then you are on the path of being able to gauge communication effectiveness.

Some Caveats

We are proud to be part of the science communication researcher community and feel fortunate to have so many superb colleagues across the United States and around the world. However, working with trainers, practitioners, and scientists has also convinced us that too little science communication research provides actionable insight. The lack of research means this book is therefore necessarily incomplete and, in some cases, speculative. We do our best to highlight social science research that we think suggests how specific beliefs, feelings, and frames may shape strategy-relevant behavior and how specific tactical choices might shape beliefs, feelings, and frames. We also, however, try to be clear about the limits of this research in the hope that we might encourage our colleagues to pursue more research that has the potential to improve science communication quality, not just describe current practices or advance narrow segments of theory.

A second caveat is that we recognize that our book does not put a direct focus on issues of diversity, equity, and inclusion (DEI) in science communication. Ensuring opportunities for a diverse range of science communicators is crucial both for ethical and strategic reasons [50–52], but these are not topics where we feel we have substantial insight or expertise at present. We do, however, think the arguments we make here about the potential value of putting more focus on audience-specific communication objectives (as well as tactics and goals) is fully relevant to discussions about proactively advancing DEI in science. One way in which we are committed to supporting efforts to advance DEI in science is by helping to apply the ideas in this book to those efforts. One tenet of public relations theory is that organizations cannot generally be excellent unless they build diversity into all aspects of communication decision-making and implementation [53]. This points to the fact that the scientific community seems unlikely to succeed in broadly building the types of beliefs, feelings, and frames that we address in these chapters unless we can find authentic ways to ensure that science communicators, as well as the people making strategic decisions about communication, reflect and respect society in all its wonderful diversity. Worse, there is a real danger that science communicators could cause harm to others by communication decisions that fail to respect others' contexts. Historian of science Naomi Oreskes makes a similar point in her arguments about the importance of consensus in her book *Why Trust Science?* She highlights the fact that we should trust science when there is a consensus within the scientific community. Further, she argues the power of a consensus is strengthened when that consensus includes the widest possible breadth of potential voices [54]. A consensus of mostly white, middle-age men is not a true consensus.

We are not in a position to write a book directly about how to make sure that the scientific community doesn't exacerbate or perpetuate inequality or how to advance equity and inclusion, but we are fully convinced that a failure to advance DEI by the scientific community will make it impossible to achieve the goals that scientists have told us they want to achieve (table 1.1). Further, one big advantage of becoming more strategic when making communication choices is that it gives us the opportunity to explicitly prioritize goals related to diversity, equity, and inclusion (e.g., recruiting and retaining a diverse workforce, ensuring inclusive workplaces, etc.), as well as associated objectives (e.g., fostering trust beliefs within specific groups). In later chapters, we highlight examples of research that speak to efforts to achieve goals or objectives in the context of efforts to consider or enhance DEI. Ultimately, we think that scientists want to be recognized as legitimate sources of insight for personal and civic behavior and believe that such legitimacy needs to be earned through behavior, not just communication.

One additional aspect of being strategic that we worry about is that it is easier to be strategic when you have power and privilege. This might mean that the powerful and privileged could use the ideas presented here to maintain their position. This is a perennial risk of strategic communication, but we reiterate our hope that the scientific community will use the science of science communication to help make positive changes in the world. We also support efforts to ensure marginalized communities have equitable access to the types of resources needed to ensure an inclusive science communication environment [50]. We will return to this issue in chapter 12.

A third caveat is that no one should expect that the potential communication effects we are discussing are immediate or especially powerful in the short term. The science community needs to see strategic science communication as a long-term process where smart communication choices increase the odds that their fellow citizens will develop their science beliefs gradually, over time [55]. Even minor behavior change is hard. We therefore need to create a communication environment in which people are regularly exposed to opportunities to engage cognitively with scientific ideas and people. Most of these experiences will be small. Others will be larger. Not all will be positive. But, if the science community does its job well, the expectation is that we can minimize the negative experiences and increase the positive ones such that, over time, people will be more likely to frame an issue in a constructive way and be more likely to draw on positive beliefs and feelings than on negative ones when making a science-relevant decision. One of our trusted practitioner friends encouraged us to use declarative language more freely in this book, and while we took much of this person's advice, we do not want to oversell the research or the challenge of effective communication.

A further corollary of this caveat is that not every problem can be solved by communication, at least as it is narrowly understood. In many cases, real historical and structural problems limit our ability to solve problems. For example, in the United States, an organization called 3.14 Action is trying to get more scientists to run for elected political office based on the hypothesis that a lack of scientific thinking in the halls of government creates a barrier that prevents the advancement of science [56]. We are not sure if 3.14 is right, but we would argue that they seem to be behaving strategically in the face of a perceived structural barrier. We also note that 3.14 Action uses communication to enact their strategy. They have identified a very specific set of upstream audience-specific behavioral goals that they want to achieve and are using communication strategies to try and make it happen. First, they want to get scientists to run for office, and then they want to help those candidates reach voters with compelling messages. We would similarly hope that any discussion of goals and strategy would delve into the range of barriers (and opportunities) associated with a goal and work through them systematically. This will often require finding barriers deep in systems and then finding ways (often through targeted communication) to weaken these barriers. We are focused here on what can be done through strategic choices about communication, but writing this book also highlighted to us a need for broader strategy discussions by the scientific community focused on figuring out how to identify and clarify community-wide goals and the resources needed to achieve those goals (more on this in the conclusion, chapter 12).

The Good News

The good news is that scientists want to share what they are learning with people outside their fields. Some of our initial survey research on scientists' communication behaviors focused on what might drive scientists to be willing to communicate and we found that some of the best statistical predictors are if the scientist expects to have a positive experience and make an impact [57,58]. Indeed, this book and much of our recent research has focused on improving the quality of communication (rather than quantity) because our survey work makes us confident that the science community contains many people who are eager to communicate with their fellow citizens.

For example, we asked the scientists we surveyed about their overall willingness to participate in four different types of public engagement activities in the same 2015–16 survey where we as asked about engagement goals. Using a seven-point scale where 1 meant "not at all willing" and 7 meant "very willing," the responding scientists indicated they were especially willing to participate in face-to-face public engagement activities, engagement through the news media, and direct engagement with policymakers (table 1.2). For these types of engagement activities, almost all the scores are typically between 5 and 6, well above the scale midpoint. The responding scientists indicated they were somewhat less willing to attempt online engagement, with typical scores between about 4 and 4.5 out of 7, but even these are above the scale midpoint. These scores also occurred despite the fact that the average age within all of the societies surveyed was above 50 (see appendix A) and the reality that older scientists are a bit less willing to engage online than younger ones [57].

It is not that scientists just say they are willing, either. Our data also showed that many scientists are already participating in public engagement activities (table 1.3). The numbers varied by society, but at least half of the scientists surveyed from every society said they had done some sort of face-to-face activity in the previous year. In most cases, almost 1 in 10 scientists said they were doing face-to-face and online activities at least monthly. Interviews with the news media and

Table 1.2.

Scientists' ratings (on a scale of 1 to 7) of their willingness to participate in various types of public engagement

	Face-to-face	Sample size	News media	Sample size	Online	Sample size	Direct with policymakers	Sample size
General	5.63	1,105	5.13	1,102	3.97	1,103	5.25	1,103
Biological	5.79	688	5.00	685	4.48	685	5.28	686
Geophysical	5.96	917	5.43	916	4.61	913	5.42	916
Geological	5.93	738	5.15	735	4.24	735	5.13	735
Ecological	6.09	349	5.55	349	4.45	349	5.62	349
Chemical	5.37	495	4.61	494	4.12	494	4.71	495
Biochemical	5.46	372	4.82	370	4.07	369	5.06	371
Social	5.98	932	5.79	930	4.83	930	5.79	930

Notes: Respondents were all faculty with PhDs at US-based universities. They were asked to "loo[k] forward" and indicate "how willing [they] would be to take part in" four different types of adult-focused public engagement activities "in the next 12 months." Respondents were asked to answer using a 7-point scale, from "not at all willing" (1) to "very willing" (7) with "neutral" as the middle option (4). Each type of public engagement was briefly defined with examples. Face-to-face engagement was described as "where you discuss science with ADULTS who are not scientists (e.g., giving a public talk or doing a demonstration)." New media engagement was described as "interviews with a journalist or other media professional (e.g., from a newspaper, television, online news site, documentary film)." Online engagement was described as communication "through websites, blogs and/or social networks (e.g., Facebook, Twitter) aimed at communicating science with ADULTS who are not scientists." Direct policymaker engagement was described as "direct interaction with government policymakers (e.g., elected officials, government officials, lobbyists, etc.)." Data was collected between October 2015 and April 2016. See appendix A for additional details about survey methods.

direct interaction with policymakers was somewhat rarer but still relatively common. Further, those types of activities depend more on the decisions of other people and may not make sense for many scientists.

While we would love to see more scientists communicating, we also do not think every scientist needs to be the headliner who appears in front of an audience, on camera, in the byline, or in the halls of government. What matters more to us is finding ways to help the scientific community communicate more effectively. In many cases this likely involves scientists playing a central role, but there are many supporting roles that scientists can play. We wrote this book for members of the whole scientific community, and this includes people who help run organizations that include communicators. Our sense is that one way to improve the quality of communication is to help foster demand for communicators who start planning for public engagement activities with a discussion of goals and objectives before making decisions about tactics. Alyssa Mastromonaco titled her book about working for President Barack Obama *Who Thought This Was a Good Idea? And Other*

Table 1.3.
Scientists' self-reported public engagement in previous 12 months

	Frequency	Face-to-face (%)	News media (%)	Online (%)	Direct with policymakers (%)
General	Never	34	46	59	59
(Sample size ~1,109)	Once	13	18	5	14
	2 to 5	29	25	15	19
	6 to 11	9	7	6	4
	Monthly+	15	5	16	5
Biological	Never	41	55	52	70
(Sample size ~696)	Once	13	18	9	11
	2 to 5	27	20	18	13
	6 to 11	7	4	5	3
	Monthly+	12	2	16	2
Geophysical	Never	26	38	47	59
(Sample size ~918)	Once	16	20	7	13
	2 to 5	33	30	18	18
	6 to 11	9	6	7	5
	Monthly+	15	6	22	5
Geological	Never	21	42	52	62
(Sample size ~754)	Once	13	23	6	15
	2 to 5	35	26	14	14
	6 to 11	12	6	5	4
	Monthly+	18	3	23	5
Ecological	Never	18	37	45	45
(Sample size ~350)	Once	16	21	9	18
	2 to 5	38	27	18	25
	6 to 11	12	10	8	6
	Monthly+	15	5	21	7
Chemical	Never	41	63	62	79
(Sample size ~501)	Once	13	20	9	9
	2 to 5	31	13	13	9
	6 to 11	6	3	4	2
	Monthly+	9	1	13	1
Biochemical	Never	47	62	64	71
(Sample size ~375)	Once	11	18	5	14
	2 to 5	26	17	15	13
	6 to 11	8	3	5	2
	Monthly+	7	0	11	1
Social	Never	30	21	35	44
(Sample size ~375)	Once	14	16	7	15
	2 to 5	32	30	20	25
	6 to 11	10	12	8	8
	Monthly+	14	21	30	15

Notes: Respondents were all faculty with PhDs at US-based universities. They were asked to indicate how often in the previous year they had participated in four different types of public engagement activities. Each type of public engagement was briefly defined with examples. Face-to-face engagement was described as "where you discuss science with ADULTS who are not scientists (e.g., giving a public talk or doing a demonstration)." New media engagement was described as "interviews with a journalist or other media professional (e.g., from a newspaper, television, online news site, documentary film)." Online engagement was described as communication "through websites, blogs and/or social networks (e.g., Facebook, Twitter) aimed at communicating science with ADULTS who are not scientists." Direct policymaker engagement was described as "direct interaction with government policymakers (e.g., elected officials, government officials, lobbyists)." Data was collected between October 2015 and April 2016. Sums herein may not equal 100% due to rounding of frequencies. See appendix A for additional details about survey methods.

Preparing to Identify Your Communication Goals

Later chapters will conclude with summaries encouraging science communicators to think about the short- or medium-term communication objective described in that chapter. The start to any communication discussion, however, should be identifying audience-specific goals to prioritize. Science communicators should consider the following six questions when deciding their goals for public engagement-focused communication.

THE BIG GOAL QUESTION

1. What specific change in a specific group do you want to see as a result of the time and other resources that you put into communication?
   a. Do you want to advocate for specific new rules/laws by decision-makers?
   b. Do you want decision-makers to consider scientific evidence when making new rules/laws?
   c. Do you want to affect a group's personal behaviors (e.g., smoke less, conserve more energy, communicate differently, choose a STEM career)?
   d. Do you want to help ensure the overall legitimacy of science as a source of evidence in societal decision-making?
   e. Do you want to consider changes to your own research choices (e.g., the questions you ask, how you ask those questions)?

THE COLLABORATION QUESTIONS

2. Have groups or organizations you support or belong to identified goals that you could try to help advance?
3. Could you work with groups or organizations you belong to or support to prioritize a goal that you have identified as a personal priority?

THE RESEARCH QUESTION

4. What does the group you want to change think about the change you want?

THE EVALUATION QUESTION

5. How would you know if you were making progress toward your goal?

THE ETHICS QUESTION

6. Are you being open about your goals?

Questions You Should Have Answers to When You Work in the White House, but the same idea applies to any communication activity. Strategic science communicators should be able to say exactly why their communication choices are good ideas, and the people providing the resources to communicators should demand to know.

REFERENCES

1. Moyer, Jessica, Moira O'Neil, Kevin Levay, and Andrew Volmert. *Wiring across Sites So STEM Learning Can Flow: Strategies for Communicating More Effectively About Connecting STEM Learning Environments (A FrameWorks Strategic Brief)*. Washington, DC: FrameWorks Insitute, May 2019. https://www.frameworksinstitute.org/wp-content/uploads/2020/05/FamLAB-Strategic-Brief.pdf.

2. Baron, Nancy. *Escape from the Ivory Tower: A Guide to Making Your Science Matter*. Washington, DC: Island Press, 2010.

3. Olson, Randy. *Don't Be Such a Scientist: Talking Substance in an Age of Style*. Washington, DC: Island Press, 2009.

4. Hayes, Richard, and Daniel Grossman. *A Scientist's Guide to Talking with the Media: Practical Advice from the Union of Concerned Scientists*. New Brunswick, NJ: Rutgers University Press, 2006.

5. Dean, Cornelia. *Am I Making Myself Clear? A Scientist's Guide to Talking to the Public*. Cambridge, MA: Harvard University Press, 2009.

6. Jamieson, Kathleen Hall, Dan Kahan, and Dietram A. Scheufele, eds. *The Oxford Handbook on the Science of Science Communication*. Oxford Library of Psychology. New York: Oxford University Press, 2017.

7. Kahlor, LeeAnn, and Patricia A. Stout, eds. *Communicating Science: New Agendas in Communication*. New York: Routledge, 2010.

8. Bucchi, Massimiano, and Brian Trench, eds. *Routledge Handbook of Public Communication of Science and Technology*. 2nd ed. London: Routledge, 2014.

9. Davies, Sarah R., and Maja Horst. *Science Communication: Culture, Identity, and Citizenship*. London: Palgrave MacMillan, 2016.

10. Besley, John C., and Katherine A. McComas. "Fairness, Public Engagement and Risk Communication." In *Effective Risk Communication*, edited by Joseph L. Arvai and Louie Rivers, 108–23. New York: Routledge/Earthscan, 2013.

11. Shema, Hadas, Judit Bar-Ilan, and Mike Thelwall. "Do Blog Citations Correlate with a Higher Number of Future Citations? Research Blogs as a Potential Source for Alternative Metrics." *Journal of the Association for Information Science and Technology* 65, no. 5 (2014): 1018–27. https://doi.org/10.1002/asi.23037.

12. Hon, Linda Childers. "Demonstrating Effectiveness in Public Relations: Goals, Objectives, and Evaluation." *Journal of Public Relations Research* 10, no. 2 (1998): 103–35. https://doi.org/10.1207/s1532754xjprr1002_02.

13. Hallahan, Kirk. "Organizational Goals and Communication Objectives in Strategic Communication." In *The Routledge Handbook of Strategic Communication*,

edited by Derina Holtzhausen and Ansgar Zerfass, 244–66. London: Routledge, 2015.

14. Rumelt, Richard P. *Good Strategy, Bad Strategy: The Difference and Why It Matters.* 1st ed. New York: Crown Business, 2011.

15. National Academies of Sciences, Engineering, and Medicine. *Communicating Science Effectively: A Research Agenda.* Washington, DC: National Academies Press, 2016.

16. National Research Council. *Learning Science in Informal Environments: People, Places, and Pursuits.* Edited by Philip Bell, Bruce Lewenstein, Andrew W. Shouse, and Michael A. Feder. Washington, DC: National Academies Press, 2009.

17. Besley, John C., Anthony Dudo, and Shupei Yuan. "Scientists' Views About Communication Objectives." *Public Understanding of Science* 27, no. 6 (2018): 708–30. https://doi.org/10.1177/0963662517728478.

18. Besley, John C., Anthony Dudo, Shupei Yuan, and Niveen AbiGhannam. "Qualitative Interviews with Science Communication Trainers About Communication Objectives and Goals." *Science Communication* 38, no. 3 (2016): 356–81. https://doi.org/10.1177/1075547016645640.

19. National Academies of Sciences, Engineering, and Medicine. *Science Literacy: Concepts, Contexts, and Consequences.* Washington, DC: National Academies Press, 2016. https://doi.org/10.17226/23595.

20. Bauer, Martin W., Nick Allum, and Steve Miller. "What Can We Learn from 25 Years of PUS Survey Research? Liberating and Expanding the Agenda." *Public Understanding of Science* 16, no. 1 (January 2007): 79–95. https://doi.org/10.1177/0963662506071287.

21. Fischhoff, Baruch. "Risk Perception and Communication Unplugged: Twenty Years of Process." *Risk Analysis* 2 (1995): 137–44. https://doi.org/10.1111/j.1539-6924.1995.tb00308.x.

22. Epstein, Steven. *Impure Science: Aids, Activism, and the Politics of Knowledge.* Berkeley: University of California Press, 1996.

23. Baram-Tsabari, Ayelet, and Elad Segev. "Exploring New Web-Based Tools to Identify Public Interest in Science." *Public Understanding of Science* 20, no. 1 (2011): 130–43. https://doi.org/10.1177/0963662509346496.

24. Bybee, Rodger, and Barry McCrae. "Scientific Literacy and Student Attitudes: Perspectives from PISA 2006 Science." *International Journal of Science Education* 33, no. 1 (2011): 7–26. https://doi.org/10.1080/09500693.2010.518644.

25. Dahlstrom, Michael F. "Using Narratives and Storytelling to Communicate Science with Nonexpert Audiences." *Proceedings of the National Academy of Sciences* 111, Supplement 4 (2014): 13614–20. https://doi.org/10.1073/pnas.1320645111.

26. Finucane, Melissa L., Ali Alhakami, Paul Slovic, and Stephen M. Johnson. "The Affect Heuristic in Judgments of Risks and Benefits." *Journal of Behavioral Decision Making* 13, no. 1 (2000): 1–17.

27. Nisbet, Matthew C. "Framing Science: A New Paradigm in Public Engagement." In *Communicating Science: New Agendas in Communication*, edited by LeeAnn Kahlor and Patricia A. Stout, 40–67. New York: Routledge, 2010.

28. Bolsen, Toby, James N. Druckman, and Fay Lomax Cook. "How Frames Can Undermine Support for Scientific Adaptations: Politicization and the Status-Quo Bias." *Public Opinion Quarterly* 78, no. 1 (2014): 1–26.

29. Hornik, Robert, and Kimberly Duyck Woolf. "Using Cross-Sectional Surveys to Plan Message Strategies." *Social Marketing Quarterly* 5, no. 2 (1999): 34–41. https://doi.org/10.1080/15245004.1999.9961044.

30. Stilgoe, Jack, Simon J. Lock, and James Wilsdon. "Why Should We Promote Public Engagement with Science?" *Public Understanding of Science* 23, no. 1 (2014): 4–15. https://doi.org/doi:10.1177/0963662513518154.

31. Kahneman, Daniel. *Thinking, Fast and Slow.* 1st ed. New York: Farrar, Straus and Giroux, 2011.

32. Chaiken, Shelly. "Heuristic Versus Systematic Information Processing and the Use of Source Versus Message Cues in Persuasion." *Journal of Personality and Social Psychology* 39, no. 5 (1980): 752–66. https://doi.org/10.1037/0022-3514.39.5.752.

33. Petty, Richard E., John T. Cacioppo, and D. Schumann. "Central and Peripheral Routes to Advertising Effecitiveness: The Moderating Role of Involvement." *Journal of Consumer Research* 10, no. 2 (1983): 135–46.

34. Evans, Jonathan St. B. T., and Keith E. Stanovich. "Dual-Process Theories of Higher Cognition: Advancing the Debate." *Perspectives on Psychological Science* 8, no. 3 (2013): 223–41. https://doi.org/10.1177/1745691612460685.

35. Fiske, Susan T., and Shelley E. Taylor. *Social Cognition: From Brains to Culture.* 1st ed. Boston, MA: McGraw-Hill Higher Education, 2008.

36. Eveland, W. P. "The Effect of Political Discussion in Producing Informed Citizens: The Roles of Information, Motivation, and Elaboration." *Political Communication* 21, no. 2 (April–June 2004): 177–93.

37. Hafer, Carolyn L., Kelly L. Reynolds, and Monika A. Obertynski. "Message Comprehensibility and Persuasion: Effects of Complex Language in Counterattitudinal Appeals to Laypeople." *Social Cognition* 14, no. 4 (1996): 317–37. https://doi.org/10.1521/soco.1996.14.4.317.

38. Petty, Richard E., and John T. Cacioppo. *Communication and Persuasion: Central and Peripheral Routes to Attitude Change.* Springer Series in Social Psychology. New York: Springer-Verlag, 1986.

39. Kahan, Dan M. "The Politically Motivated Reasoning Paradigm, Part 1: What Politically Motivated Reasoning Is and How to Measure It." In *Emerging Trends in the Social and Behavioral Sciences,* edited by Robert A. Scott, Marlis C. Buchmann, and Stephen M. Kosslyn, Wiley Online Library. Hoboken, NJ: John Wiley & Sons, 2015-. https://onlinelibrary.wiley.com/doi/10.1002/9781118900772.etrds0417.

40. Freedman, Lawrence. *Strategy: A History.* New York: Oxford University Press, 2013.

41. Pronin, Emily. "The Introspection Illusion." In *Advances in Experimental Social Psychology,* vol. 41, edited by Mark P. Zanna, 1–67. Cambridge, MA: Academic Press, 2009.

42. Burgoon, Judee K. "Interpersonal Expectations, Expectancy Violations, and Emotional Communication." *Journal of Language and Social Psychology* 12, no. 1–2 (1993): 30–48. https://doi.org/10.1177/0261927X93121003.

43. Oreskes, Naomi, and Erik M. Conway. *Merchants of Doubt: How a Handful of Scientists Obscured the Truth on Issues from Tobacco Smoke to Global Warming.* New York: Bloomsbury, 2011.

44. Oreskes, Naomi. "The Fact of Uncertainty, the Uncertainty of Facts and the Cultural Resonance of Doubt." *Philosophical Transactions of the Royal Society A: Mathematical, Physical and Engineering Sciences* 373, no. 2055 (2015): 20140455. https://doi.org/10.1098/rsta.2014.0455.

45. van der Bles, Anne Marthe, Sander van der Linden, Alexandra L. J. Freeman, James Mitchell, Ana B. Galvao, Lisa Zaval, and David J. Spiegelhalter. "Communicating Uncertainty About Facts, Numbers, and Science." *Royal Society Open Science* 6, no. 5 (2019): 181870. https://doi.org/doi:10.1098/rsos.181870.

46. Politi, Mary C., Paul K. J. Han, and Nananda F. Col. "Communicating the Uncertainty of Harms and Benefits of Medical Interventions." *Medical Decision Making* 27, no. 5 (2007): 681–95. https://doi.org/10.1177/0272989X07307270.

47. Gustafson, Abel, and Ronald E. Rice. "A Review of the Effects of Uncertainty in Public Science Communication." *Public Understanding of Science* 29, no. 6 (2020): 614–33. https://doi.org/10.1177/0963662520942122.

48. Yuan, Shupei, John C. Besley, and Wenjuan Ma. "Be Mean or Be Nice? Understanding the Effects of Aggressive and Polite Communication Styles in Child Vaccination Debate." *Health Communication* 34, no. 10 (2019): 1212–21. https://doi.org/10.1080/10410236.2018.1471337.

49. Maloney, Erin K., Maria K. Lapinski, and Kim Witte. "Fear Appeals and Persuasion: A Review and Update of the Extended Parallel Process Model." *Social and Personality Psychology Compass* 5, no. 4 (2011): 206–19. https://doi.org/10.1111/j.1751-9004.2011.00341.x.

50. Canfield, Katherine N., Sunshine Menezes, Shayle B. Matsuda, Amelia Moore, Alycia N. Mosley Austin, Bryan M. Dewsbury, Mónica I. Feliú-Mójer, et al. "Science Communication Demands a Critical Approach That Centers Inclusion, Equity, and Intersectionality." *Frontiers in Communication* 5, January 30, 2020. https://doi.org/10.3389/fcomm.2020.00002.

51. Dawson, Emily. *Equity, Exclusion, and Everyday Science Learning: The Experiences of Minoritised Groups.* New York: Routledge, 2019.

52. Polk, Emily, and Sibyl Diver. "Situating the Scientist: Creating Inclusive Science Communication through Equity Framing and Environmental Justice." *Frontiers in Communication* 5, February 21, 2020. https://doi.org/10.3389/fcomm.2020.00006.

53. Grunig, James E. (ed.), and IABC Research Foundation. *Excellence in Public Relations and Communication Management.* Communication Textbook Series: Public Relations. Hillsdale, NJ: Lawrence Erlbaum Associates, 1992.

54. Oreskes, Naomi. *Why Trust Science?* Princeton, NJ: Princeton University Press, 2019.

55. Brossard, Dominique, and Anthony D. Dudo. "Cultivation of Attitudes toward Science." In *Living with Television Now: Advances in Cultivation Theory & Research*, edited by Michael Morgan, James Shanahan, and Nancy Signorielli, 120–46. New York: Peter Lang, 2012.

56. 3.14 Action. "About Us: Our Mission." Accessed January 7, 2021. https://314action.org/about-us.

57. Besley, John C., Anthony Dudo, Shupei Yuan, and Frank Lawrence. "Understanding Scientists' Willingness to Engage." *Science Communication* 40, no. 5 (2018): 559–90. https://doi.org/10.1177/1075547018786561.

58. Besley, John C., and Anthony Dudo. "Scientists' Views About Public Engagement and Science Communication in the Context of Climate Change." *Oxford Encyclopedia of Climate Science*, April 26, 2017. https://doi.org/10.1093/acrefore/9780190228620.013.380.

2

Science Knowledge as a Communication Objective

WE LOVE THE ALAN ALDA Center for Communicating Science at Stony Brook University for all the work they have done to get people in the scientific community thinking about improving the quality of science communication. Alan Alda himself is a hero to us both because of his role in some of our favorite television programs (*M*A*S*H* and *The West Wing*, especially) and for his intelligence and warmth in sharing science through programs such as *NOVA*. We also sometimes work with the Alda Center team on research projects and know how dedicated and smart they are when it comes to training. While we'll write more about them later, we want to start by talking about communication objectives by asking a potentially provocative question about one of their most prominent former programs: the Flame Challenge [1].

On the face of it, the Flame Challenge sounds like a great idea. Between 2012 and 2018, the Alda Center held a competition in which they asked scientists to describe a scientific concept in a way that 11-year-olds from the around the world would find understandable and interesting. The first year (2012) saw scientists answering the question "What is a flame?," but the question changed every year of the competition and included topics such as "What is sleep?" (2015), "What is energy?" (2017), and "What is climate?" (2018). The questions asked resulted in a series of wonderful videos of scientists doing a fantastic job sharing scientific information. Alda doubled down on this comprehension and captivation focus when he named his podcast *Clear + Vivid*.

So, what potential problem do we see here? Our fear is that the framing of the Flame Challenge and the title of Alda's podcast (which is run separately from the Alda Center) seem to suggest that effective communication is largely about being understandable and interesting. Research suggests that science communication training has also taken this approach and prioritizes similar objectives [2]. What is wrong with that? Sharing knowledge will always be an important science communication objective, and we understand the desire to want to tell others about scientific findings. Indeed, we started studying scientists' opinions about communication because we wanted to find ways to share evidence-based methods with practitioners and hear their perspectives. However, a central argument of this book is that sharing scientific knowledge and getting people to feel things like excitement or interest (chapter 11) are only two of many potentially important communication objectives that communicators need to focus on if they have goals that involve affecting actual, real-world behavior. Being clear and being vivid should also be understood as tactics that might help achieve objectives but are also only two of many potential tactics. Our hope in respectfully critiquing ideas like the Flame Challenge is that foregrounding these types of examples can allow us to suggest alternative ways to think about science communication and encourage additional strategic thinking.

Communication Is Not Translation, Distillation, or Decoding

There are several reasons we think too many people in science communication focus so heavily on knowledge transfer, and the first is the language often used in communication training efforts. Specifically, a great number of the North American science communication trainers we have interviewed state that they want to teach scientists how to "translate," "distill," or "decode" their research so that their audiences can understand their results [3]. Researchers sometimes also use such metaphors [4] or evaluate science communicators by their clarity and ability to hold interest [2]. As with the Flame Challenge, the difficulty we see with this type of language dominating science communication discussions is that it frames the problem of science communication largely in terms of comprehension. As we discuss at length in a chapter 11, framing is all about how communicators signal—often unintentionally—how someone should make sense of some ambiguous topic or event [5]. At a psychological level, that might mean framing the same outcome as an equivalent potential loss or gain [6] while more sociologically focused scholars might think about whether, for example, we think about climate change in terms of environmental, health, or national security [7]. Metaphors, in this context, are a primary tool that people can use to frame reality (i.e., think of "life is like a box of chocolates"). Trainers' and others' use of the "translation" and "decoding" analogies suggests that science communication is mostly about being understood. Similarly, "distilling" suggests a need to extract an existing message from a messy slurry of information. It would be nice if this were the case. First, as discussed in chapter 1, we do not think most scientists would be happy just to be understood. At minimum, they want people to consider their advice. However, the more direct problem with putting a primary focus on knowledge transfer is that it is like going on a date and expecting that the other person would agree to a second date (a potential behavioral goal) if you successfully teach that person the right biological facts about you. There would be no demand for communication researchers or practitioners if scientists could just give people scientific facts and expect everything to turn out okay. We would just have education research and teachers. Fortunately for us, that's not the case.

It's not just communication trainers who seem to put a lot of emphasis on knowledge transfer either. In our surveys of scientists, we have consistently found that sharing knowledge is the communication objective that scientists prioritize most highly. We saw this in our 2015–16 survey data (table 2.1) as well as other surveys, such as a survey of Canadian scientists in 2018 and a 2019 survey of Association of American Universities (AAU) scientists. In our 2015–16 survey, we asked scientists to rate the importance of the knowledge objective, and almost all gave average scores of about 6 or higher on a 7-point scale. In the 2018 Canadian survey we asked a similar question using a 100-point slider, and the knowledge objective scored an average of 79. The average on the AAU survey was 81 out 100 using the same basic question.

Our 2015–16 survey also had additional questions about how scientists see various objectives. What we found is that scientists do not just prioritize the knowledge objective, they also rate it as the most ethical objective, the objective their colleagues would most respect, the objective their colleagues would be most likely to prioritize, the objective that's most feasible, and the objective for which they themselves are most skillful. Not surprisingly, it's also the one that they report having thought about the most.

Can Focusing on Science Knowledge Help Scientists Achieve Their Goals?

While we think sharing scientific knowledge is inherent to science communication, social scientists have found only small relationships between what people know and what they do on many of the issues that science communicators care about. One of us (Besley) had the opportunity in 2016 to be part of a US National Academies panel focused on the question of science literacy's relationship with attitudes and behavior. The panel ultimately concluded that the "available research does not support the claim that increasing science literacy will lead to appreciably greater support for science" [8]. While recognizing that more research might be helpful, the panel's finding was partly built on previous research by panelist Nick Allum from the University of Essex and his colleagues. This group gathered data from

Table 2.1.

Scientists' average assessments of the perceived importance of "helping to inform people about scientific issues" and associated beliefs about this objective in the context of different communication channels and different scientific societies (on a scale of 1 to 7)

	Priority[1]	Ethicality[2]	Peer norms[3]	Peer priority[4]	Achievability[5]	My skills[6]	Prior thought[7]	Sample size range
General								
Face-to-face	6.21	6.07	5.70	5.31	6.11	5.34	5.02	373–376
Media	6.26	6.16	5.79	5.29	6.06	5.12	4.89	321–324
Online	6.08	5.96	5.57	5.11	5.89	4.97	4.80	373–378
Biological								
Face-to-face	6.21	5.92	5.59	5.19	6.12	5.33	4.86	348–353
Online	6.26	5.88	5.54	5.01	5.96	5.05	4.67	326–327
Geophysical								
Face-to-face	6.22	6.04	5.69	5.35	6.09	5.51	5.26	314–315
Media	6.34	6.05	5.81	5.40	6.19	5.40	5.34	313–314
Online	6.19	5.86	5.54	5.04	5.98	5.23	4.92	270–274
Geological								
Face-to-face	6.21	5.94	5.58	5.16	5.99	5.45	5.11	249–251
Media	6.34	6.08	5.76	5.39	6.07	5.25	5.14	234–243
Online	6.29	5.92	5.62	5.24	5.93	5.33	5.07	232–35
Ecological								
Face-to-face	6.18	6.10	5.78	5.50	6.20	5.48	5.57	343–346
Chemical								
Face-to-face	6.15	5.83	5.51	5.08	5.90	5.23	4.77	178–179
Media	5.99	5.81	5.66	5.18	5.82	4.88	4.67	156–157
Online	5.85	5.86	5.51	4.93	5.82	4.87	4.43	154–155
Biochemical								
Face-to-face	6.07	5.96	5.55	5.05	5.99	5.09	4.80	368–371
Social								
Media	6.06	5.99	5.55	5.12	5.86	5.41	5.01	880–882

Notes: For the "priority" statement, respondents were given a list of objectives (including the objective noted in the table title) and asked to rate each objective between "very low importance" (1) and "very high importance" (7). For all other statements, respondents selected between "strongly disagree" (1) and "strongly agree" (7). Respondents were all faculty with PhDs at US-based universities. Standard deviations in appendix B tables.

[1] "In general, what are the most important or unimportant communication objectives that scientists such as yourself should have when taking part in [mode*]? Please remember that not every objective can be the most important objective." *Respondents were assigned to see all questions in the context of only one of three potential modes: face-to-face engagement, media engagement, or online engagement.

[2] "This objective is ethical."

[3] "Scientists who pursue this objective would be well regarded by their peers."

[4] "My colleagues would put a high priority on this objective."

[5] "Achieving this objective is possible for a good communicator."

[6] "I have the skills needed to achieve this objective."

[7] "Prior to this survey, I had thought a lot about this potential objective."

almost 200 science-focused surveys from around the world on a range of topics and found only a small relationship between knowledge and attitudes, no matter how they did the analysis [9]. Our own work in this area has similarly found that science knowledge is a relatively weak predictor of views about scientists [10].

We would go so far as to say that getting science communicators to think beyond knowledge objectives is the core challenge facing science communication researchers today. It's what we spend a lot of our time rehashing at the start of many collaborations with natural and physical scientists who are convinced that their problem is people just do not understand their work. If communication researchers cannot get communicators to think beyond knowledge transfer, then all the research they're doing—some of which we describe in this book—is not going to have any impact. In communication circles, as some readers will know, the belief that knowledge will be associated with attitudes or behavior is sometimes called the "knowledge deficit hypothesis." This is based on the idea that the underlying empirical question is about whether removing a "deficit" in what people know will have some sort of additional impact on other beliefs, feelings, frames, or behavior. Dan Kahan, who has done some of the most important recent work in this area, similarly calls the expectation that knowledge will shape attitudes and behavior as the "science comprehension thesis" [11]. Those who have been in science communication for any period of time will likely come across the "deficit model" idea, and some people seem to use the term as a catchall critique of communication efforts where there is a suggestion that communicators might have an objective of increasing knowledge.

We often think these critiques go too far and instead prefer to see the problem of deficit thinking as an overreliance on a single objective. At the same time, we also think it would be odd if knowledge was not an important objective for science communicators. We suspect—although have not yet examined in a study—that most audiences would be justifiably annoyed if they showed up at an event to hear a scientist talk and did not hear anything about scientific findings. In the language of persuasion research, we suspect scientists would violate peoples' expectations in a negative way [12] if they showed up to see a scientist talk about science and the scientist talked about something else. Similarly, we suspect it would be odd if scientists regularly appeared in the media and did not contribute any evidence-based insight into the public dialogue. A science center or museum would seem even odder if it did not feature science.

We sometimes say that researchers' unique access to hard-won knowledge is the ticket that gets us invited to play a central role in public (and private discussions) about issues in which we have expertise. This means researchers—including us—are going to share our own findings and our disciplines' findings when appropriate. The important point here is that once you are in the door, we think there is often an opportunity to do more than just share what you have found, and people, quite often, want more than just those facts. In our experience, people want us to share information about ourselves as well as provide insight into the views of others (i.e., the type of trustworthiness-related information, normative information, and efficacy information discussed in later chapters).

Our even bigger concern is that critics of the idea of "deficits" sometimes go so far as to say that the alternative to focusing on public deficits in knowledge is to focus on fostering public dialogue or engagement. There is generally nothing wrong with finding ways to generate good dialogue between scientists and the public, but this formulation replaces an objective—knowledge as holding true, justified beliefs about the types of facts and processes described in textbooks—with the activity of public dialogue. As discussed in chapter 1, we think of dialogue-focused events as one great way to deeply engage people with scientific ideas by overriding our cognitive-miser tendencies. However, it is challenging to talk about the effectiveness of engagement without thinking about what changes might occur in what participants (including scientists) believe and feel about science, as well as changes to how people frame relevant issues. In other words, while we think science communicators often focus too much on trying to share their knowledge given its likely minimal impact, it's impossible to talk about science communication without recognizing that one potential desirable outcome of things like dialogue might be changes in what participants know. And we're fine with that. We do not see any problem with making sure that the efforts put into sharing knowledge are maximized.

What Tactics Can Help Science Communicators Share Knowledge?

First, it's probably not a great idea to rely on communication researchers—at least ones like us—to provide advice on how to best educate audiences through science communication activities. Formal and informal education researchers are more directly focused on this objective. Informal science education researchers who study learning from things like after-school programs, museums, zoos, aquariums, and educational media are especially well placed to provide such advice, although much of this work focuses on younger audiences. The informal science education community has provided several attempts to summarize what the community has learned about passing along knowledge in recent decades, including a range of prominent reports from National Academies committees, such as a 2009 report specifically on informal environments and a 2016 report on informal chemistry education [13,14].

Our reading of these reports is that efforts to increase science knowledge and skills should start with a clear identification of what you want a specific group of people to learn and then figuring out what these people already think they know about that topic. From there the challenge is to build interesting and interactive activities that motivate people in the target group to learn the content you want them to learn, with each lesson building on previous lessons. In other words, the basic tactic is to create a series of contexts in which people teach themselves rather than trying to give people information and hoping they retain that information. An inherent challenge with this approach is that it may sometimes take more time than simply having people memorize facts, but the hope is people will retain more knowledge over the long term while also fostering their ability to learn and their own belief in their ability to learn. In academic language, you are increasing people's actual knowledge and self-efficacy as well as their perception of self-efficacy (see chapter 10 on self-efficacy beliefs as a communication objective).

Portal to the Public is a training organization that straddles the informal science education and science communication space. The Portal team has built a successful train-the-trainers program whose primary purpose is to prepare local scientist volunteers to talk with visitors at science centers and museums. The program started at the Pacific Science Center next to the Space Needle in downtown Seattle and has been implemented at more than 50 sites across the United States. Their recent efforts have sought to find ways to expand beyond the science centers and museums into places such as zoos, aquariums, and any other venue where people might enjoy talking with a working scientist.

The logistical core of Portal to the Public's approach—as explained in an "implementation manual" they share on their website [15]—is that scientists sign up to take a series of workshops with a cohort of colleagues in which they learn about the type of educational theories that the National Academies have shared [16]. While Portal to the Public puts a lot of emphasis on building relationships between scientists and their communities, their training typically starts with activities and discussion about "how people learn." The training then builds on these discussions—consistent with an emphasis on a "learning by doing" approach for interesting and enjoyable things— by helping the scientists develop some sort of hands-on activity or demonstration that is both interesting to the potential audience and related to the scientist's work.

And the training is not just an academic exercise. The participating scientists agree at the outset that they're going to bring whatever they develop into the real world for the organization that provided the training. For some, this means setting up a table on the floor of the museum with things for visitors to touch and manipulate. For others, it could mean putting on a portable microphone to try to attract a crowd like a street busker. The range of activities (i.e., tactics) that participants have developed has expanded as the training has moved beyond science centers and museums, but there is always face-to-face interaction and an emphasis on helping people learn, rather than trying to teach. A central point is that scientists who participate commit to meeting directly with people in their community, sharing their work in evidence-based ways, and reflecting on their experiences to improve future interactions for all involved.

One thing that strikes us when learning about programs coming from the informal science education world is how often they are consistent with ideas found in persuasion research. We know persuasion sometimes evokes negative reactions for some people because it suggests manipulation, but a central question of persuasion research [17]—like education research—is how people come to believe what they believe. Inasmuch as we understand knowledge as "correct and justifiable beliefs," this overlap should not seem surprising. The idea of avoiding scientific jargon exemplifies this overlap.

The Thing about Jargon

The Portal to the Public training focuses on how people learn, which puts a lot of emphasis on helping experts recognize that people are unlikely to learn if they cannot understand the discussion. This might seem obvious, but almost every training program and book on applied science communication spends a lot of time on jargon or the broader idea of using clear language. Our sense is that this emphasis is not because trainers think scientists do not intellectually know that technical language can cause problems. Instead, we think it probably reflects the "curse of knowledge" idea that it is hard to know what terms or concepts people are going to find confusing or incomprehensible [18]. And it's even harder to keep oneself from using jargon-y language if we have not consciously chosen to do the hard work that it takes to come up with—and use—alternative language.

The persuasion literature poses other considerations for how to think about jargon within the context of communicating science. One of the dominant models used in the communication literature to help understand how people process information is the elaboration likelihood model [17]. As noted in chapter 1, this is one of several dual-process cognitive engagement models that focuses attention on the idea that people sometimes think about messages carefully but often do not have the time or inclination to engage with what they are hearing or seeing. The elaboration likelihood model calls effortful engagement "central route processing" (a.k.a., systematic or type-2 processing) while the more limited processing is termed "peripheral processing" (a.k.a., heuristic or type-1 processing). As also noted in chapter 1, we think that science communicators are attracted to the idea of public engagement because it seems to emphasize finding ways to get people to slow down and think about issues. It is this slower thinking, in turn, that seems to lead to the development of long-term beliefs.

The elaboration likelihood model (similar to related models) highlights that two initial elements of getting people to process messages more deeply is ensuring that they are (1) motivated to process and (2) able to process. The motivation might come from interest or need (i.e., perceived risk or opportunity) and is consistent with the informal science education emphasis on creating opportunities where people want to engage. Alan Alda addresses interest through the idea of being "vivid." The focus on ability to cognitively process highlights the fact that people will not be able to engage deeply if the language used is inaccessible, there are too many distractions, the person is too tired, or many other potential barriers. Alda similarly talks about "clear" communication. In formal school settings, the motivation to pay attention may come from things like demand from parents or college admissions officers, but these sorts of extrinsic pressures are less meaningful when there are no grades to earn or bosses to impress. Similarly, compared to informal settings, formal settings typically allow for more time to build up to key ideas and bring audience members to at least roughly the same level. This means that the people in classrooms and similar settings have more opportunity to build up to the use of more formal language.

And the Thing about Dialogue

Thinking about knowledge change in the context of persuasion can also help us understand why so many trainers—including Portal to the Public—put so much emphasis on two-way dialogue. In this regard, it seems reasonable to expect that people involved in real-life conversations related to science—especially nonscientists—might be motivated to slow down their thinking processes. The reason might be a desire not to look dumb, but it could also be a desire to try to make sense of something new, whether that something is related to a potential risk or a potential benefit [19]. In some cases, the desire to think through an issue might be built into the situation inasmuch as someone might come to an event where they hear from a scientist with the hope and expectation of learning something new.

The "deliberative polling" and "deliberative democracy" processes that became popular in the 1990s and 2000s are good examples of the hope that creating dialogue-focused situations can help people think through science and technology issues [20]. Edna Einsiedel, a former editor of the journal *Public Understanding of Science*, provided small-scale examples of these types of processes in a series of four articles between 2000 and 2002. In the first, she describes working with the Canadian government to organize and study a Citizen Conference on Food Biotechnology [21] to bring together small, diverse groups of nonscientists to talk about an important issue. The meeting was specifically built on previous efforts pioneered in Europe [22,23] and elsewhere [24]. An advisory committee with a range of viewpoints led the process and used newspaper ads and public service announcements on television and radio to solicit interest and then selected 15 people (balanced by demographics and geography) that did not have a connection to the topic. "The youngest panelist was a seventeen-year-old twelfth grader, while the oldest was a fifty-nine-year-old retiree. Occupations represented included a letter carrier, two teachers, a geological engineer, a ranch hand, a heavy equipment mechanic, a management consultant, an administrative secretary, a restaurant manager, a grocery store manager, and two students" [21, p. 330].

These 15 citizen panelists were provided with a carefully selected set of readings along with plane tickets and hotel reservations needed to meet twice as a group to begin learning about food biotechnology (i.e., genetically modified or engineered organisms). The advisory group selected an initial set of experts to meet with the citizen panel but also asked the panel to come up with additional types of people whom they wanted to hear from. Time was devoted to hearing from experts as well as talking within the citizens' group with the help of a moderator. The discussions initially focused on a set of questions drafted by the advisory group and branched out from there. The citizen participants were also put in touch through email between meetings.

The two initial meetings were designed to work toward a three-day public conference. At this final conference, the 15 selected citizens asked questions of the experts that they had helped choose to provide a range of viewpoints. Other attendees to the final conference—which included anyone who wanted to come as well as invited journalists and policymakers—could also ask questions on the second day. The public part of the meeting ended midafternoon, but the citizen panel members stayed up until 6:00 the following morning to write a report that summarized what they had come to believe about the use of biotechnology in food, including perceived benefits and risks, as well as any remaining questions.

In the context of this chapter, we found it interesting that Einsiedel's descriptions of the meetings focused heavily on what the citizen participants learned through the process [21]. Much of the learning involved increased understanding about the science underlying biotechnology. She describes the citizens' own sense that they had learned, participating experts' positive perceptions of citizen learning, and a sense that the transcripts suggest increasing sophistication. Einsiedel also noted that the citizens learned about regulatory and policy processes and expressed a desire for broader interactions between scientists and citizens going forward. Her later articles reiterated some of these themes looking at different issues and contexts [24-26], but the key point is that these types of studies strongly suggest that dialogue, as a tactic, can contribute to learning as a function of cognitive processing. What is also key to recognize (in the context of later chapters of this book) is that learning about science was not the only type of "learning" that occurred; participants also developed a range of other types of beliefs about the technology, key actors, and their own selves.

An obvious critique of deliberative events—whether called "citizen conferences" [21], "consensus conferences" [27], "citizen juries," [28], or something else [29]—is that they often involve only a small number of participants and the amount of interaction is so high that learning is inevitable. In contrast, less ambitious attempts to foster citizen discussion are unlikely to foster equally substantive learning in more traditional representative samples of citizens. In light of this critique, researchers such as James Fishkin have pioneered efforts to show that it's possible to bring hundreds of citizens together to hear from experts, foster small-group discussion, and change both knowledge and related attitudes [30]. While expensive and complicated, these types of processes can potentially help decision-makers learn where discussions around an emerging issue might go over time as people learn about the topic. In essence, part of the idea is to create an artificial, sped-up process of discussion and learning to see what kinds of new or altered beliefs emerge while trying to avoid allowing interest groups (whether for or against a technology) to hijack the dialogue. And again, the evidence seems to be that people can and do learn as a result of dialogic processes [31–33], although it is also hard to know what they might have learned through other similarly resourced efforts. In addition, others have called into question the idea that science engagement efforts foster more sophisticated thinking [34]. In our own earlier research, we argued that people who organize existing or traditional ways of bringing together community members, especially the various forms of public meetings that are common in the United States and Canada, should put more emphasis on providing high quality opportunities for dialogue [35,36].

Even more broadly, researchers have found that exposure and attention to a range of ideas through media and interpersonal discussion is associated with relatively higher levels of knowledge, among other potential outcomes. The idea here is that news can be partly thought of as mediated dialogue or deliberation [37] and should be expected to have cumulative effects over time, similar to what might occur from direct participation in dialogue [38]. Much of this research developed from political communication scholarship conducted by Jack McLeod [39] and his former graduate students (e.g., William Eveland, Patricia Moy, and Dietram Scheufele) at the University of Wisconsin. McLeod's students have often focused on civic engagement, but most have also occasionally looked at science and health communication questions. Scheufele, in particular, has largely transitioned to study science communication as political communication and has become one of the main proponents of making science communication more evidence-based through his research and work with the US National Academies [40–42]. Overall, the body of scholarship that these researchers have produced highlights the fact that people who read, talk, watch, and listen to content about civic and science issues tend to have relatively higher knowledge levels (as well as other outcomes) [43]. Reading and talking are especially important, likely because they tend to require higher levels of cognitive effort. Further, it seems that the best way to measure the relationship between media use and belief development is to consider the combination of both exposure and attention [44,45]. Overall, the evidence showing a positive association between the amount of attention paid and the amount of knowledge gained suggests to us that dialogue—whether experienced directly or through mediated communication—is a tactic that can affect knowledge, as well as other beliefs.

It is also important to recognize that the objective behind fostering dialogue in the deliberative democracy literature is not only about transferring knowledge. Knowledge is one potential outcome of deliberation, but the suggested objectives for sponsoring deliberative opportunities include a range of beliefs about policy, policy process, policymakers, and fellow citizens. Further, the ultimate hope is that changes in such beliefs will increase overall satisfaction with decision-making systems [46–48], in science and nonscience contexts.

In our way of thinking, deliberation or dialogue is often about the goal of perceived legitimacy [20]. Legitimacy as a goal is a bit difficult to discuss—we decided not to directly ask about it in our surveys of scientists, focusing instead on fostering a culture that values science (table 1.1)—in that the point is not really to get people to do a behavior, it's more about getting people to accept decisions with which they may disagree. A classic book on participation in decision-making, called *Exit, Voice, and Loyalty,* talked about how people in organizations faced with a decision they do not like must choose to either voice their objection and seek an acceptable solution . . . or quit [49]. The core argument is that those who believe they can voice their views and be heard are likely to remain loyal, whereas those who cannot voice their views will feel the need to exit. In the context of deliberation, this suggests that an end goal of providing voice is to foster legitimacy, not just knowledge [20,50,51]. We return to this idea in later chapters when talking about the importance of dialogue in fostering trustworthiness-related communication objectives more directly related to legitimacy.

Two Concerns about Knowledge as an Objective

There are two other things anyone considering prioritizing knowledge as a communication objective should consider. The first deals with the reality that motivating someone to think more deeply about an issue sometimes seems to lead people to learn incorrect science. The second addresses the danger that focusing too much on knowledge may lead scientists to act like jerks.

Scholars such as Dan Kahan have provided compelling evidence over a series of studies that getting people to think more about science topics can sometimes lead people to believe things that are inconsistent with the scientific community's best understanding of reality. One type of evidence that Kahan and others have used to support this argument is that, for example, higher knowledge is only associated with belief in human-caused climate change for liberals [52,53]. Worse, relatively strong conservatives with relatively high science knowledge are sometimes less likely than otherwise-similar conservatives with less knowledge to support climate change mitigation [52,53]. Sol Hart and Erik Nisbet have shown similar patterns using social science experiments [54,55].

Another piece of evidence that Kahan notes is that there is little reason for (incorrect) beliefs related to climate change, concealed-carry benefits, and nuclear energy to be correlated in the ways they are unless group membership is driving belief formation. Underlying these findings is the hypothesis that it makes psychological sense that people would be more likely to devote effort to processing information in a way that will help them fit into their group or feel good about their group, rather than learning information that makes group membership more difficult [56,57]. While we discuss this research more in chapter 6, it is important here to further highlight the danger of focusing too much on just sharing knowledge. Whereas the typical research highlighted in the deficit model literature shows that knowledge only has a small relationship with attitudes and behavior [8], researchers focused on motivated reasoning show that only focusing on knowledge can make things worse. The following chapters on trustworthiness expand on both the dangers and opportunities of developing a broader perspective about what objectives can be prioritized and achieved through science communication.

Our second concern about focusing on knowledge as an objective is that it may increase the odds you will communicate like a jerk. We have no published studies to back up this concern, but our hypothesis would be that focusing on people's science knowledge deficiencies could lead science communicators to share information in unproductive, aggressive ways [12]. We come back to our concern about aggressive science communication in the coming chapters on trustworthiness as well. At the minimum, however, we are wary of putting too much emphasis on any objective that frames interactions between scientist and nonscientists as a situation where scientists are teachers and other people are students who need to be taught. Instead, we encourage any science communicator to think carefully about what knowledge they may want to share or that their audience may want

Preparing to Prioritize Sharing Knowledge as a Communication Objective

The following are eight questions that science communicators should consider when deciding whether to prioritize sharing knowledge as a communication objective. As this chapter emphasizes, communicators should note that increasing knowledge is unlikely to directly change behavior, but this does not mean that they shouldn't share what they are learning in an accessible way.

THE GOAL QUESTION

1. Given the behavior you want from your chosen audience (i.e., your goal), what scientific concepts do you think they need to understand more about?

THE PREPARATION QUESTIONS

2. What does your chosen audience know about your topic?
3. What do you know about what your audience may want to better understand?

THE TACTICS QUESTIONS

4. What could you do to potentially increase the likelihood that your desired audience will understand your topic, including choices about messages, behaviors, tone/style, communication channel, and communication source?
5. What could you do to learn about your chosen audience's current knowledge, including potential insights you may not have considered?

THE EVALUATION QUESTIONS

6. Did your desired audience better understand some aspect of your topic after communicating with you?
7. What did you learn about your audience's knowledge?

THE ETHICS QUESTION

8. Were you clear about what you know and do not know?

to learn about, but they should not mistake being clear as effective communication, or expect people to change their mind just because they learn something new. Learning about the other potential objectives discussed in this book will help communicators see sharing knowledge as an important ingredient of communication but not the *only* ingredient.

REFERENCES

1. Alda, Alan. "The Flame Challenge." *Science* 335, no. 6072 (2012): 1019. https://doi.org/10.1126/science.1220619.

2. Rubega, Margaret A., Kevin R. Burgio, A. Andrew M. MacDonald, Anne Oeldorf-Hirsch, Robert S. Capers, and Robert Wyss. "Assessment by Audiences Shows Little Effect of Science Communication Training." *Science Communication* 43, no. 2 (2021): 139–69. https://doi.org/10.1177/1075547020971639.

3. Besley, John C., and Anthony Dudo. *Landscaping Overview of the North American Science Communication Training Community: Topline Takeaways from Trainer Interviews.* N.p.: Kavli Foundation, Rita Allen Foundation, David and Lucille Packard Foundation, and Gordon and Betty Moore Foundation, 2017. http://www.informalscience.org/sites/default/files/Communication Training Landscape Overview Final.pdf.

4. Altman, Katya, Brooks Yelton, Zac Hart, Margaret Carson, Louisa Schandera, R. Heath Kelsey, Dwayne E. Porter, and Daniela B. Friedman. "'You Gotta Choose Your Words Carefully': Findings from Interviews with Environmental Health Scientists About Their Research Translation Perceptions and Training Needs." *Journal of Health Communication* 25, no. 5 (2020): 454–62. https://doi.org/10.1080/10810730.2020.1785060.

5. Nisbet, Matthew C. "Framing, the Media, and Risk Communication in Policy Debates." In *The Sage Handbook of Risk Communication*, edited by Hyunyi Cho, Torsten Reimer, and Katherine A. McComas, 216–27. Thousand Oaks, CA: Sage, 2015.

6. O'Keefe, Daniel J., and Jakob D. Jensen. "The Relative Persuasiveness of Gain-Framed Loss-Framed Messages for Encouraging Disease Prevention Behaviors: A Meta-Analytic Review." *Journal of Health Communication* 12, no. 7 (2007): 623–44. https://doi.org/10.1080/10810730701615198.

7. Myers, Teresa A., Matthew C. Nisbet, Edward W. Maibach, and Anthony A. Leiserowitz. "A Public Health Frame Arouses Hopeful Emotions About Climate Change." *Climatic Change* 113, no. 3–4 (2012): 1105–12. https://doi.org/10.1007/s10584-012-0513-6.

8. National Academies of Sciences, Engineering, and Medicine. *Science Literacy: Concepts, Contexts, and Consequences.* Washington, DC: National Academies Press, 2016. https://doi.org/10.17226/23595.

9. Bauer, Martin W., Nick Allum, and Steve Miller. "What Can We Learn from 25 Years of PUS Survey Research? Liberating and Expanding the Agenda." *Public*

Understanding of Science 16, no. 1 (January 2007): 79–95. https://doi.org/10.1177
/0963662506071287.

10. Besley, John C. "The National Science Foundation's Science and Technology Survey and Support for Science Funding, 2006–2014." *Public Understanding of Science* 27, no. 1 (2018): 94–109. https://doi.org/10.1177/0963662516649803.

11. Kahan, Dan M., Ellen M. Peters, Maggie Wittlin, Paul Slovic, Lisa Larrimore Ouellette, Donald Braman, and Gregory Mandel. "The Polarizing Impact of Science Literacy and Numeracy on Perceived Climate Change Risks." *Nature Climate Change* 2, no. 10 (2012): 732–35. https://doi.org/10.1038/nclimate1547.

12. Yuan, Shupei, John C. Besley, and Chen Lou. "Does Being a Jerk Work? Examining the Effect of Aggressive Risk Communication in the Context of Science Blogs." *Journal of Risk Research* 21, no. 4 (2018): 502–20. https://doi.org/10
.1080/13669877.2016.1223159.

13. National Academies of Sciences, Engineering, and Medicine. *Effective Chemistry Communication in Informal Environments.* Washington, DC: National Academies Press, 2016.

14. National Research Council. *Learning Science in Informal Environments: People, Places, and Pursuits.* Edited by Philip Bell, Bruce Lewenstein, Andrew W. Shouse, and Michael A. Feder. Washington, DC: National Academies Press, 2009.

15. Portal to the Public Network. *Implementation Manual and Catalog of Professional Development Elements.* Seattle, WA: Pacific Science Center and Institute for Learning Innovation, 2018. https://popnet.instituteforlearning innovation.org/implementation-manual.

16. National Research Council. *Learning Science in Informal Environments: People, Places, and Pursuits.* Edited by Philip Bell, Bruce Lewenstein, Andrew W. Shouse, and Michael A. Feder. Washington, DC: National Academies Press, 2009.

17. Petty, Richard E., and John T. Cacioppo. *The Elaboration Likelihood Model of Persuasion.* New York: Springer-Verlang, 1986.

18. Heath, Chip, and Dan Heath. "The Curse of Knowledge." *Harvard Business Review* 84, no. 12 (2006): 20–23.

19. Griffin, Robert J., Sharon Dunwoody, and Kurt Neuwirth. "Proposed Model of the Relationship of Risk Information Seeking and Processing to the Development of Preventive Behaviors." *Environmental Research* 80, no. 2 (1999): S230–S45. https://doi.org/10.1006/enrs.1998.3940.

20. Gastil, John. "Designing Public Deliberation at the Intersection of Science and Policy." In *The Oxford Handbook of the Science of Science Communication*, edited by Kathleen Hall Jamieson, Dan M. Kahan, and Dietram A. Scheufele, 233–42. New York: Oxford University Press, 2017.

21. Einsiedel, Edna F., and Deborah L. Eastlick. "Consensus Conferences as Deliberative Democracy: A Communications Perspective." *Science Communication* 21, no. 4 (2000): 323–43.

22. Grundahl, Johs. "The Danish Consensus Conference Model." In *Public Participation in Science: The Role of Consensus Conferences in Europe*, edited by

Simon Joss and John Durant, 31–40. London: British Science Museum & European Commission Directorate General XII, 1995.

23. Joss, Simon, and John Durant. "The UK National Consensus Conference on Plant Biotechnology." *Public Understanding of Science* 4 (1995): 195–204.

24. Einsiedel, Edna F., Erling Jelsoe, and Thomas Breck. "Publics at the Technology Table: The Consensus Conference in Denmark, Canada, and Australia." *Public Understanding of Science* 10, no. 1 (January 2001): 83–98.

25. Einsiedel, Edna F. "GM Food Labeling: The Interplay of Information, Social Values, and Institutional Trust." *Science Communication* 24, no. 2 (2002): 209–21.

26. Einsiedel, Edna F. "Assessing a Controversial Medical Technology: Canadian Public Consultations on Xenotransplantation." *Public Understanding of Science* 11, no. 4 (October 2002): 315–31. https://doi.org/10.1088/0963-6625/11/4/301.

27. Joss, Simon, and John Durant, eds. *Public Participation in Science: The Role of Consensus Conferences in Europe.* London: British Science Museum & European Commission Directorate General XII, 1995.

28. Finney, Colin. "Implementing a Citizen-Based Deliberative Process on the Internet: The Buckinghamshire Health Authority Electronic Citizens' Jury in the UK." *Science and Public Policy* 27, no. 1 (2000): 45–64. https://doi.org/10.3152/147154300781782165.

29. Gastil, John, and Peter Levine, eds. *The Deliberative Democracy Handbook: Strategies for Effective Civic Engagement in the Twenty-First Century.* San Francisco: Jossey-Bass, 2005.

30. Fishkin, James S. *The Voice of the People: Public Opinion and Democracy.* 2nd ed. New Haven, CN: Yale University Press, 1997.

31. Fishkin, James S., and Peter Laslett, eds. *Debating Deliberative Democracy.* Philosophy, Politics, and Society, vol. 7. Malden, MA: Blackwell, 2003.

32. Delli Carpini, Michael X., Fay Lomax Cook, and Lawrence R. Jacobs. "Public Deliberation, Discursive Participation, and Citizen Engagement: A Review of the Empirical Literature." *Annual Review of Political Science* 7 (2004): 315–44. https://doi.org/10.1146/annurev.polisci.7.121003.091630.

33. Ryfe, D. M. "The Practice of Deliberative Democracy: A Study of 16 Deliberative Organizations." *Political Communication* 19, no. 3 (July–September 2002): 359–77. https://doi.org/10.1080/01957470290055547.

34. Sturgis, Patrick, Caroline Roberts, and Nick C. Allum. "A Different Take on the Deliberative Poll: Information, Deliberation, and Attitude Constraint." *Public Opinion Quarterly* 69, no. 1 (Spring 2005): 30–65.

35. McComas, Katherine A., Craig W. Trumbo, and John C. Besley. "Public Meetings About Suspected Cancer Clusters: The Impact of Voice, Interactional Justice, and Risk Perception on Attendees' Attitudes in Six Communities." *Journal of Health Communication* 12, no. 6 (2007): 527–49.

36. Besley, John C., Katherine A. McComas, and Craig W. Trumbo. "Local Newspaper Coverage of Health Authority Fairness during Cancer Cluster Investigations." *Science Communication* 29, no. 4 (2007): 498–521.

37. Page, Benjamin I. *Who Deliberates? Mass Media in Modern Democracy.* American Politics and Political Economy. Chicago: University of Chicago Press, 1996.

38. McLeod, Jack M., Dietram A. Scheufele, and Patricia Moy. "Community, Communication, and Participation: The Role of Mass Media and Interpersonal Discussion in Local Political Participation." *Political Communication* 16, no. 3 (July–September 1999): 315–36.

39. Dunwoody, Sharon, Lee B. Becker, Douglas M. McLeod, and Gerald M. Kosicki, eds. *The Evolution of Key Mass Communication Concepts: Honoring Jack McLeod.* Cresskill, NJ: Hampton Press, 2005.

40. Scheufele, Dietram A., and Anthony D. Dudo. "Emerging Agendas at the Intersection of Political and Science Communication: The Case of Nanotechnology." In *Communication Yearbook*, edited by Charles T. Salmon, 143–66. Newbury Park, CA: Sage, 2010.

41. Scheufele, Dietram A. "Science Communication as Political Communication." *Proceedings of the National Academy of Sciences* 111, Supplement 4 (2014): 13585–92. https://doi.org/10.1073/pnas.1317516111.

42. Jamieson, Kathleen Hall, Dan Kahan, and Dietram A. Scheufele, eds. *The Oxford Handbook on the Science of Science Communication.* Oxford Library of Psychology. New York: Oxford University Press, 2017.

43. Eveland, William P., Jr., and Josephine B. Schmitt. "Communication Content and Knowledge Content Matters: Integrating Manipulation and Observation in Studying News and Discussion Learning Effects." *Journal of Communication* 65, no. 1 (2014): 170–91. https://doi.org/10.1111/jcom.12138.

44. Slater, Michael D., and Kenneth A. Rasinski. "Media Exposure and Attention as Mediating Variables Influencing Social Risk Judgments." *Journal of Communication* 55, no. 4 (December 2005): 810–27. https://doi.org/10.1111/j.1460-2466.2005.tb03024.x.

45. Chaffee, Steven H., and Joan Schleuder. "Measurement and Effects of Attention to Media News." *Human Communication Research* 13, no. 1 (Fall 1986): 76–107. https://doi.org/10.1111/j.1468-2958.1986.tb00096.x.

46. Burkhalter, Stephanie, John Gastil, and Todd Kelshaw. "A Conceptual Definition and Theoretical Model of Public Deliberation in Small Face-to-Face Groups." *Communication Theory* 12, no. 4 (November 2002): 398–422.

47. Rowe, Gene, and Lynn J. Frewer. "Evaluating Public-Participation Exercises: A Research Agenda." *Science Technology & Human Values* 29, no. 4 (Fall 2004): 512–57.

48. Rowe, Gene, Roy Marsh, and Lynn J. Frewer. "Evaluation of a Deliberative Conference." *Science Technology & Human Values* 29, no. 1 (Winter 2004): 88–121.

49. Hirschman, Albert O. *Exit, Voice, and Loyalty: Responses to Decline in Firms, Organizations, and States.* Cambridge, MA: Harvard University Press, 1970.

50. Cohen, Joshua. "Deliberation and Democratic Legitimacy." In *The Good Polity: Normative Analysis of the State*, edited by Alan Hamlin and Philip Pettit, 17–34. New York: Basil Blackwell, 1989.

51. Hibbing, John R., and Elizabeth Theiss-Morse. *Stealth Democracy: Americans' Beliefs About How Government Should Work.* Cambridge Studies in Political Psychology and Public Opinion. New York: Cambridge University Press, 2002.

52. Kahan, Dan M. "'Ordinary Science Intelligence': A Science-Comprehension Measure for Study of Risk and Science Communication, with Notes on Evolution and Climate Change." *Journal of Risk Research* 20, no. 8 (2017): 995–1016. https://doi.org/10.1080/13669877.2016.1148067.

53. Hart, P. Sol, Erik C. Nisbet, and Teresa A. Myers. "Public Attention to Science and Political News and Support for Climate Change Mitigation." *Nature Climate Change* 5 (2015), 541–45. https://doi.org/10.1038/nclimate2577.

54. Hart, P. Sol, and Erik C. Nisbet. "Boomerang Effects in Science Communication: How Motivated Reasoning and Identity Cues Amplify Opinion Polarization About Climate Mitigation Policies." *Communication Research* 39, no. 6 (2012): 701–23. https://doi.org/10.1177/0093650211416646.

55. Nisbet, Erik C., P. Sol Hart, Teresa A. Myers, and Morgan Ellithorpe. "Attitude Change in Competitive Framing Environments? Open-/Closed-Mindedness, Framing Effects, and Climate Change." *Journal of Communication* 63, no. 4 (2013): 766–85. https://doi.org/10.1111/jcom.12040.

56. Byrne, Sahara, and Philip Solomon Hart. "The Boomerang Effect a Synthesis of Findings and a Preliminary Theoretical Framework." *Annals of the International Communication Association* 33, no. 1 (2009): 3–37. https://doi.org/10.1080/23808985.2009.11679083.

57. Kahan, Dan M. "The Politically Motivated Reasoning Paradigm, Part 1: What Politically Motivated Reasoning Is and How to Measure It." In *Emerging Trends in the Social and Behavioral Sciences,* edited by Robert A. Scott, Stephen M. Kosslyn, and Marlis Buchmann, Wiley Online Library. Hoboken, NJ: John Wiley & Sons, 2015–. https://onlinelibrary.wiley.com/doi/10.1002/9781118900772.etrds0417.

3

Show Warmth

THE NEXT FIVE CHAPTERS ARE ABOUT trustworthiness-related science communication objectives: one chapter each on perceptions of
warmth as caring, integrity, willingness to listen, shared identity, and
competence. We focus a lot on trust because fostering trustworthiness-
related beliefs is central to any long-term communication strategy. It is
so important that a multibillion-dollar public relations (PR) industry
has developed to serve all kinds of organizations' needs to actively
build positive relationships with a range of different stakeholders (i.e.,
"publics"), including customers, regulators, fellow community members, employees, and others [1]. People in the PR field have done a lot of
unethical, unprofessional, and outright dumb things over the years,
but this does not take away from the need organizations have to build
and maintain trusting relationships nor the excellent work that many
PR professionals have done. Science communication researcher and
PR practitioner Rick Borchelt and his colleague Kristian Nelson have
called this "managing the trust portfolio" of science [2].

We always encourage science communicators to consider devoting
effort to fostering trustworthiness-related beliefs when they are
thinking about their communication strategy. This might often mean

taking a few minutes or words to share why someone should trust you as a scientist, but it could also mean ensuring that you, as a communicator, have an opportunity to learn (i.e., generate new beliefs) about some aspect of someone else's trustworthiness. It will also often require doing research to find out what others think about you or evaluating how you were perceived during a communication activity.

It frustrates us when people talk about building trustworthiness beliefs as though it is one thing. Strategic communicators should probably avoid saying things such as "we need to build trust" because that is too vague. A core argument we make over these five chapters is that thinking about trustworthiness at a granular level helps when it comes to thinking about communication strategy. For example, the tactics (i.e., communication choices about messages, behaviors, style, channel, and source) you might use to show you are competent (i.e., using technical language, casually mentioning your PhD from an Ivy League university) may not be the same as what you might do to look caring (i.e., sharing your motivations). On the other hand, it is also likely that some tactics, such as creating communication activities that provide people with opportunities for real, respectful dialogue, could affect a range of trustworthiness-related outcomes, including beliefs about others' warmth and openness.

Trustworthiness-related beliefs are also different from trusting behavior. Trust researchers typically conceptualize trusting behavior as "a willingness to be vulnerable" to someone else [3]. Science-related examples of making oneself vulnerable through behavior might include going ahead and eating the genetically engineered salmon, accepting a plan to build a new nuclear plant near your community, getting on the plane and flying across an ocean, getting a vaccine, or even accepting that some of your tax dollars will go toward long-term scientific research, even if the ultimate benefit is uncertain. Trusting behaviors are often the type of semi- or pseudobehaviors mentioned as potential behavioral goals in chapter 1 because they do not require specific action. Instead, they involve accepting the legitimacy of scientific decision-making or scientific consensus. We see evaluative beliefs about trustworthiness, in contrast, as key communication objectives.

To preview, in this initial chapter we focus on a broad category we're calling "warmth beliefs," to be consistent with the work of Princeton University professor Susan Fiske [4] and social science pioneer Solomon Asch [5], though we sometimes prefer to call them "benevolence beliefs" from work in organizational psychology [3] because this term puts a focus on scientists' motivations. Other terms we could use include "communion judgments" from European work on social psychology [6], or something like "caring beliefs" from work on risk perception [7]. It also seems reasonable to consider the literature on likeability [8] and interpersonal or interactional fairness [9] from the social psychology of justice in any discussion of communicating trustworthiness beliefs as these two bodies of work also address how people are perceived in the context of decision-making. This means trying to integrate insights from researchers looking at a range of substantive topics, including science communication, but also areas such as social psychology, organizational psychology, various pieces of strategic communication, persuasion, health communication, and promotion, among others. The literature on empathy [10] is also potentially relevant, but we largely save that research for the chapter on perceived willingness to listen (chapter 5) because much of the focus on communicating empathy is about demonstrating that you are listening and ensuring that people feel heard.

For some, our attempts to meld these literatures will seem clumsy, but our sense is that the evidence base that communicators might want to have to help build trustworthiness-related beliefs in the science community remains scattered.* And, while we do our best to

---

* We feel comfortable integrating research from different traditions because we focus on the underlying words scholars have used to measure constructs such as warmth and benevolence rather than the umbrella terms they use to describe what they are studying. Looking at question wording suggests substantial overlap in the literature despite the fact that many scholars, such as Susan Fiske and Amy Cuddy, focus their attention on overall perceptions of groups of people (e.g., scientists, specific races, or whole organizations such as a company) whereas others, in areas such as organizational psychology, focus on people who actually know each other (e.g., workplace peers or employees and their managers). For example, some warmth researchers ask people to rate groups on such attributes as warmth, tolerance, and good-naturedness (e.g., Fiske's work [14]) whereas researchers who look at the idea of benevolence ask people to rate specific people in their lives on their level of concern for others and the degree to which they try to be helpful. Similarly, the

summarize current knowledge, we ultimately conclude that there is an ongoing need to test ideas in science-specific contexts, something colleagues and ourselves have begun to explore [11,12].

Do You Care About People Like Me?

In reviewing trust research, author and Harvard University lecturer Amy Cuddy argues that people have an evolutionary need to prioritize quick judgments about whether or not the stranger who just came around the corner *intends* us harm [13]. Of secondary—but still important—concern is whether or not they have the *ability* to do us harm. The first question is about warmth. The second is about competence. Some of Cuddy's work focuses on the stereotypes around things like race and gender [14] that can drive quick perceptions, and she notes that it seems even young children tend to make quick judgments about warmth first and then competence.

Most important to us is Cuddy notes that warmth perceptions are both important and not entirely dependent on first impressions (which can be hard to control). The evidence that they are important comes from the fact that warmth is a key statistical predictor of overall evaluations of other groups [15].* Evidence that warmth-like beliefs are somewhat open to change is based on findings that

---

idea of interpersonal or interactional fairness focuses on perceived politeness and respectful treatment by direct decision-makers (whether managers, or police and judges, although groups of people have also been looked at), while the idea of likability has been measured by asking respondents to rate the degree to which they perceive someone as friendly, warm, and approachable. While efforts continue to be done to try to statistically and theoretically integrate different perspectives, we argue that, from a communication perspective, there appears to be value in highlighting the potential impact of getting scientists to show that they care about others' well-being and that "warmth" seemed to be a term that captures what we want scientists to consider communicating.

* Other research simply shows that perceived benevolence shares similar levels of importance when it comes to predicting trusting behavior in organizations. One complicating factor in this regard is that the type of warmth measure used by Cuddy includes typically integrity-focused questions whereas typical measures of benevolence do not. We fully recognize the strong relationship between integrity perceptions and warmth perceptions, but we prefer to treat them separately as communicators because our expectation is that the things scientists need to do to communicate that they care are different than what they need to do to communicate integrity. We therefore deal with integrity on its own in chapter 4.

suggest that people tend to look for evidence that their initial, quick warmth judgments may have been faulty. Research in organizations highlights how "continued demonstrations of benevolence can deepen . . . a mutual sense of fondness and respect" [16]. While this research often focuses on workplaces, our expectation would be that the same holds true for how people see categories of people such as scientists. We would thus expect that regular, ongoing exposure to direct and mediated communication that shows scientists behaving in a caring way will tend to lead to increasingly positive beliefs about scientists.

A potential downside of people's tendency to monitor for warmth-related information is a possible urge to look mostly for clues of fake warmth rather than looking for hidden signs of benevolence. It's hard to pretend to be competent for very long in most roles (at some point, people will expect you to cook that eggplant or surf that wave), whereas faking warmth, at least for a time, seems more feasible. It makes evolutionary sense that people might therefore devote cognitive resources to monitoring others' warmth. Further, exhibiting coldness—perhaps an angry outburst or sneering comment—seems to damage perceptions in a way that may be hard to repair [17,18].

This concern about the danger of cold behavior by scientists is one thing that prompted our colleague to study the effect of aggressive communication around such hot-button topics as genetically modified food, vaccines, and climate change. Shupei Yuan built her studies on prior work in the area of political incivility [19] and how people perceive mean teachers [20], and she has shown fairly clearly that "being a jerk" does not "work" when it comes to making a science writer more likable [21]. A typical study of Yuan's involves exposing someone to an opinion column from a scientist that has been altered to be either relatively neutral or really antagonistic toward people who disagree with a scientific consensus. What typically happens is that people see scientists who are mean as less likeable (which is measured with questions about warmth, friendliness, and approachability) and scientists who are polite as more likeable [22,23].

Sadly, the effect of aggressiveness (and politeness) seems to work largely through whether someone's expectations have been violated. In other words, aggressive communication by a scientist does not seem to negatively (or positively) affect people who expect scientists to be aggressive. Similarly, those who expect politeness and see politeness tend not to be affected. However, this also suggests that people who expected the scientist to be a jerk and experienced unexpected politeness are especially likely to have a positive outcome. Our view is that science communicators should therefore strategically focus on reaching the people who were surprised that a scientist could be warm (or not aggressive) and try to garner additional supporters over time [23]. There may be times (e.g., fundraising calls) when it makes sense to "preach to the choir" or rally supporters by harshly criticizing opponents, but both need to be done carefully and in recognition that private conversations are rarely private.

Yuan's studies communicated warmth through the choice available to scientists to be nice by *not* overtly calling people morons when they disagree with a scientific consensus. However, one thing that surprises us is the degree to which researchers focus on nonverbal cues, such as smiling and posture, as well as preexisting stereotypes when they write about communicating warmth. In contrast, there seems to be less attention on "overt behaviors" [13, p. 88] that someone could enact in order to try to foster warmth perceptions. Of course we agree that science communicators could benefit from attention to choices about things like personal style (clothing, hair, makeup, etc.) and that scientists should avoid nonverbal bad habits (such as arm crossing, insufficient eye contact, and similar communicative body language). Social scientists have shown the importance of nonverbal communication with studies on how employee smiles can be somewhat contagious and that smiling employees contribute to experience quality [24,25]. However, while we appreciate the value of managing nonverbal cues, we suspect science communicators should think more about how to purposefully communicate reasons about why people should see scientists as well-meaning and focused on improving the public good [26,27].*

Communicating Warmth

As noted, we try to think broadly about research on warmth beliefs and include related constructs such as benevolence, caring, interactional fairness, and others because we have not found much direct evidence focused on purposefully shaping warmth-related beliefs about scientists. There appears to be some evidence about how certain communication choices might hurt warmth-related perceptions (e.g., Yuan's work described earlier), but this literature is also somewhat limited. This means that, for now, we must extrapolate from studies that are not quite as clear as we would like. This includes relying on studies that use single surveys to see if there is a statistical relationship between warmth-like beliefs and other variables [28] or experiments where the researcher does pretests to find a source that is already perceived as warm and caring (e.g., a parental figure) [29] to compare the impact of a message from that source against one that's seen as less warm (often based on a measure of the communicator's likability). For example, David Roskos-Ewoldsen has done a series of experiments showing that being reminded that one likes a source (Neil Armstrong, in one study) can increase the effort that individual will put into thinking about a message (i.e., engaging with the content). This is good if the message is strong, but weak arguments by a likable source can end up less persuasive because people appeared to be more likely to actually think about the message and then find it wanting [30,31]. On the survey side, results have shown that perceived interpersonal fairness of local university scientists (measured as such warmth-like beliefs as expected respectfulness

---

* A 2009 survey by the Pew Research Center for the People and the Press found that 81% of members of the American Association for the Advancement of Science—the world's largest multidisciplinary scientific society with more than 100,000 members—said that "a desire to work for the public good" was either a "very important" (41%) or "somewhat important" reason behind their decision to become a scientist [26].

and politeness) is somewhat associated with perceived satisfaction with local research efforts, but not associated with actual concern about specific technologies, such as genetically modified foods, underlying the research [32].

More compelling are results such as Jason Colquitt's efforts to combine more than 100 studies looking at a range of trustworthiness-related variables in workplaces. This meta-analysis showed that "perceived benevolence" of managers (along with perceived competence and integrity) is meaningfully associated with a range of positive workplace outcomes [28]. A challenge in extrapolating from these types of studies is that such research focuses on warmth perceptions about specific people (e.g., a manager or caregiver) rather than the development of warmth perceptions for entire groups (e.g., scientists).

We noted in chapter 1 that our focus on evaluative beliefs means we tend to think in terms of a cumulative-effects model of communication that suggests people develop beliefs about the world through their direct and mediated experiences over time [33]. Our expectation is that evidence about how experiences with managers or restaurant servers affect warmth beliefs can tell us something about how experiences with scientists likely shape beliefs about scientists [34]. On the other hand, Fiske and her colleagues treat beliefs about scientists' warmth (and competence) as stereotypes [4], highlighting the fact that views about groups emerge through complex social processes and are therefore hard to reshape [35]. And yet, the thing that most science communicators can partly control is how they communicate about themselves as individuals and as groups (through organizations like their labs, universities, and scientific societies). It is for this reason that we think people in the scientific community should make the effort to share as many examples as possible about their specific desire to help make the world a better place through their research.

Recognizing that evaluative beliefs build up over time does not mean that any single event cannot affect how people think about members of the scientific community. Among the best evidence we know of for why scientists need to prioritize warmth-related beliefs comes from research on how doctors break bad news. These studies contain heartbreaking accounts of how doctors have treated patients or their families coldly. For example, a quotation from one such study describes the mother of a child recently diagnosed with autism and severe learning disabilities describing how her child's doctor provided the diagnosis. She says that he was "so horrible in handling us we tried not to pay his bill! He was terribly abrupt, businesslike, no compassion. . . . I feel they must have been taught in 'med' school to detach—stay distant and controlling" [36, p. 544].

Another study quoted a set of parents describing how a medical team doing hospital rounds dropped news about their child's "cerebral palsy and spastic quadriplegia" in an "appalling" and "blunt" way: "The facts were laid out as black and white and plain as they could be. They called us in and said, 'Right, we've had the results and she has severe brain damage which means [she'll] . . . never be able to do anything for herself' and that was it . . . and then they were off doing the ward round" [37, p. 80]. These types of results call to our minds survey results from the National Science Board showing that the percentage of Americans who express a "great deal" of confidence in medicine has declined slowly since the 1970s, even as views about scientists have stayed relatively stable [38]. There's no direct connection showing that people's views of doctors has declined because of bad experiences with the medical community—perhaps including long waiting times and excessive charges—but we would hypothesize that such experiences might drive some of the emphasis now being placed on improving doctors' bedside manner [39,40].

Another body of research suggests that groups can communicate warmth by looking at how people perceive companies, especially companies that do an active job in promoting their social responsibility. Fiske again, this time with marketing research consultant Chris Malone, conducted studies [41] and wrote a book for business leaders [42] to explain why it makes sense to think about businesses in terms of their warmth and competence. They highlight how a range of North American companies, such as Sprint (a mobile serve provider), Lululemon (a clothing company), Zappos (an online shoe company), and Chobani (a Greek yogurt company), have communicated their "worthy intentions" toward communities and customers to achieve success. On the flip side, they also describe companies they feel have underperformed because they failed to treat others with respect. Their ultimate argument is that tracking warmth perceptions—in addition to competence perceptions—is a good way to understand an organization's reputation. It is also noteworthy, in this regard, that literature on "reputation" measurement similarly involves some focus on the degree to which stakeholders think a company cares about others [43].

Beyond Fiske and Malone, public relations scholars have also tried to show that companies can affect perceptions by communicating about their corporate social responsibility efforts. One well-cited study suggested that about a sixth of Fortune 500 companies put a substantial focus in their Facebook profiles, for example, on things their companies do to be socially responsible [44]. Earlier research also highlighted a substantial amount of social responsibility content on websites, especially the websites of companies nearer the top of the Fortune 500 list [45]. More importantly, a thorough analysis of comments on Facebook posts showed that people were more likely to make comments indicating they believed a company was a "decent entity in society" when a company posted about their social responsibility activities then when they focused on their other abilities [44].

Even more interesting are the attempts to use experiments to see if a focus on social responsibility content can—at least temporarily—affect people's assessment of companies. For example, an early experiment by corporate social responsibility and public relations researcher Sora Kim involved giving about 300 American consumers information about the activities of either Motorola (the technology company) or Kellogg's (the food company). About a third of these people were given information about one of the company's efforts to make good products, another third were given information about their efforts to be socially responsible, and the final third were given information with a bit of both types of content. The results were consistent with the idea that messages focused on product quality (i.e., competence beliefs, chapter 7) had little impact but that simple messages focused on corporate responsibility topics seemed to increase people's beliefs that the company was doing pro-social activities. Specifically, people who read only about Motorola's product quality efforts gave the company only about 3.99 out of 7 on a measure of pro-social behavior compared to 4.64 by people told a bit about both ability and social efforts, and 5.01 by those who received a social responsibility-focused message. For Kellogg's, the score climbed from 4.38 to 4.64 for the hybrid strategy to 5.05 for the social responsibility messaging. In terms of impact, additional associations seemed to suggest that, beyond product quality, people's beliefs about the companies' activities translated into positive evaluations of the underlying company and, in turn, affected views about the quality of the products [46].

Together, these results suggest that there are at least two good bets for science communicators who want to be perceived as warm and who do not want to rely on nonverbal cues. The first one should be obvious: Try to treat others well and avoid being a jerk. Scientists should avoid being jerks in any direct interaction with others, when talking to journalists, and when sharing material online. Beyond being nice, however, it also seems possible that science communicators should actively seek to share information about the degree to which a desire to help others motivates their research. We have not found any direct evidence about what such "pro-social motivation" communication would accomplish for scientists, but our expectation is that it would lead to warmth perceptions and boost warmth beliefs in the short term, and possibly over time.

It is important to note that we have not found literature exploring whether common tactics emphasized by science communication trainers [47] affect warmth. Specifically, we looked for evidence that activities designed to engage audiences in dialogue, allow stories from scientists, or encourage scientists to speak clearly might have impacts on warmth, but we came up blank. This is a big gap in the literature given how important warmth beliefs are in trust research. We suspect all three tactics are beneficial. We would expect, for example, that the interpersonal interaction inherent in dialogue-based events could provide an opportunity for the type of sharing that the literature suggests could contribute to warmth, although it would partly depend on how scientists behaved during the interactions. Similarly, we would expect that having scientists focus more on telling stories could give them the opportunity to highlight the deep concerns and hopes that drive much research. But again, the nature of the story matters. Finally, we would also expect that scientists who take the time and effort to speak using language and style that are appropriate and clear for their specific audiences would be seen as warmer and more caring then a scientist who does not make this effort.

What Do Warmth Beliefs Affect?

Susan Fiske's model of "people perceptions" includes an argument that people tend to want to actively help those whom they perceive as warm. We may admire individuals and groups seen as both warm and competent, but being perceived as "competent but cold"—a danger for scientists [4]—seems to lead to envy. People may even tend to actively impede those we see as cold [13,48]. These types of patterns are hard to study (you generally cannot easily or ethically run experiments where you present someone as cold to see if participants attack them), so initial data supporting this view comes from research finding fairly strong relationships between survey participants' ratings (whether student or nonstudent samples) of how they think a group is perceived by their fellow citizens. Consistent with the model, the people that participants believe are cold and incompetent tend to be the same people that respondents say evoke negative emotions and that people want to impede or even harm [48]. It is noteworthy in these studies, however, that respondents are not describing how *they* feel about people from specific groups or what they would personally do to those groups. They are asked to describe what they think other people would feel and do.

Fiske's work with market researcher Chris Malone also brought this perspective into a discussion about consumers' attitudes toward companies and brands. At the core of this discussion is the idea that consumers tend to prefer to buy from companies that care about the communities where they operate, their employees, and the issues that matter to their customers. Researchers have been collecting survey and experimental evidence of the relationship between beliefs about an organization's caring-related behavior and willingness to buy or support that organization for a long time [49]. While people often have doubts about why any given organization behaves well—is it just because they're afraid to look bad?—people still tend to prefer companies that seem well-meaning. More directly related to the model put forward by Fiske—and in a nonconsumer context—are a series of studies by German social psychologists Julia Becker and Frank Asbrock. In one of their studies, they found that students said they would be more likely to do things to impede a group of hypothetical yuppies (e.g., sign a petition or hand out oppositional leaflets) whose new presence was gentrifying a neighborhood against the wishes of existing residents when these yuppies were described as lacking warmth (versus being described as busy or not being described at all) [50].

As a practical matter, it almost seems too obvious to make the argument that it is helpful for groups to be perceived as warm rather than cold. However, what may be worth remembering is that "obvious" things are sometimes wrong, and it can be nice to have direct evidence for our arguments in a case where we think it is worth encouraging science communicators to put more priority on communicating scientists' desire to improve the lives of others. Nagwan Zahry has started to provide such evidence in exploratory studies showing that using posters that portray smiling young scientists working in groups are particularly compelling to potential science students [51], and the perceived warmth of scientists in various science areas was among the better statistical predictors of student interest in that area [52]. However, the evidence remains limited. We just do not know enough about how scientists can affect warmth beliefs.

Demand for Warmth-Related Information

It is one thing to argue that nurturing warmth beliefs might affect how people see science, but it also seems people want warmth-related information. A subcomponent of the "breaking bad news" literature from the health field are findings that suggest people often say they want warmth from people whose jobs require them to share scientific information, such as doctors. One set of researchers, for example, directly asked parents of children with developmental disabilities what they wanted from doctors who were sharing bad news. As part of the study they contacted about 200 parents and asked about their experiences hearing bad medical news as well as what they would want when hearing future bad news. The experiences described included both good examples and heartbreaking ones, wherein the doctors were described as being brusque and unfeeling: "The doctor simply stated the diagnosis, handed us some papers with general information, . . . told us to institutionalize him, and walked out the door. We would like to have been treated like human beings" [36, p. 544].

Ultimately, about two thirds said that the doctor controlled the conversation and only about half said that the doctor allowed the parents to talk or show feelings. Only about 4 in 10 said the doctor tried to make the parent feel better and provided substantial amounts of information. In contrast, essentially all of the respondents said they wanted the doctor to let them talk and express their feelings [36,37,53]. Outside of the medical context, corporate social responsibility researcher Sora Kim has shown that American respondents also say they want companies to provide more specific information about the motives behind their efforts to be socially responsible [54].

Scientists' Willingness to Prioritize Warmth Objectives and Associated Tactics

We need to learn much more about the potential impact of sharing warmth-related information, but our past surveys make us confident that many scientists are willing to prioritize this objective. On average, the members of the scientific societies we surveyed in 2015–16 gave communicating warmth an importance score of about 5.5 out of 7 (table 3.1). This is higher than most other objectives with the

Table 3.1.

Scientists' average assessments of the perceived importance of "showing that the scientific community cares about society's well-being" and associated beliefs about this objective in the context of different communication channels and different scientific societies (on a scale of 1 to 7)

	Priority[1]	Ethicality[2]	Peer norms[3]	Peer priority[4]	Achievability[5]	My skills[6]	Prior thought[7]	Sample size range
General								
Face-to-face	5.71	5.79	5.25	4.81	5.76	4.82	4.11	370–374
Media	5.74	5.79	5.20	4.70	5.68	4.54	4.01	326–328
Online	5.43	5.65	4.98	4.52	5.62	4.38	3.82	370–376
Biological								
Face-to-face	5.80	5.62	5.19	4.73	5.79	4.89	4.18	346–349
Online	5.79	5.74	5.29	4.69	5.66	4.58	3.98	326–329
Geophysical								
Face-to-face	5.44	5.60	5.10	4.67	5.71	4.99	4.21	313–316
Media	5.49	5.60	5.17	4.73	5.67	4.72	4.23	310–313
Online	5.44	5.55	4.99	4.43	5.63	4.57	3.94	265–268
Geological								
Face-to-face	5.60	5.60	4.92	4.51	5.68	4.94	4.22	246–248
Media	5.68	5.70	5.13	4.75	5.58	4.69	4.09	235–240
Online	5.58	5.66	5.07	4.59	5.63	4.77	4.10	230–233
Ecological								
Face-to-face	5.46	5.73	5.04	4.64	5.76	4.81	4.32	339–342
Chemical								
Face-to-face	5.62	5.54	5.12	4.66	5.67	4.72	4.11	180–181
Media	5.56	5.55	5.22	4.74	5.56	4.42	3.96	157–158
Online	5.38	5.50	5.03	4.45	5.61	4.43	3.77	151–152
Biochemical								
Face-to-face	5.71	5.68	5.17	4.66	5.72	4.66	4.13	363–370
Social								
Media	5.05	5.50	4.87	4.40	5.36	4.87	3.97	876–880

Notes: For the "priority" statement, respondents were given a list of objectives (including the objective noted in the table title) and asked to rate each objective between "very low importance" (1) and "very high importance" (7). For all other statements, respondents selected between "strongly disagree" (1) and "strongly agree" (7). Respondents were all faculty with PhDs at US-based universities. Standard deviations in appendix B tables.

[1] "In general, what are the most important or unimportant communication objectives that scientists such as yourself should have when taking part in [mode*]? Please remember that not every objective can be the most important objective." *Respondents were assigned to see all questions in the context of only one of three potential modes: face-to-face engagement, media engagement, or online engagement.

[2] "This objective is ethical."

[3] "Scientists who pursue this objective would be well regarded by their peers."

[4] "My colleagues would put a high priority on this objective."

[5] "Achieving this objective is possible for a good communicator."

[6] "I have the skills needed to achieve this objective."

[7] "Prior to this survey, I had thought a lot about this potential objective."

exception of our questions about informing people (table 2.1) and getting people excited about science (table 11.1). This makes it similar to responses to a question about prioritizing communicating to affect beliefs about the scientific community's openness (chapter 5, see also appendix B tables). Our study looking at what variables might be most highly associated with giving certain objectives higher importance scores found that seeing the "warmth" objective as ethical was the only consistent predictor. Most scientists indicated that they thought the objective was fairly ethical, with the average agreement score being well above five out of seven (and often closer to six) on ethicality. Table 3.1 also highlights that many scientists thought that their peers would be accepting of a scientist who pursued this objective while being somewhat skeptical about whether their peers themselves prioritize warmth. Similarly, most respondents seemed to think having people see scientists as caring was possible for a skilled communicator but were a little less likely to feel that they had such skills. The lowest score was for prior thought about this objective, where the mean score was around four of out seven. This suggests that many scientists surveyed had not previously thought deeply about warmth beliefs as a potential communication objective. Similar to prioritization, all these scores are at the high end when compared to scores for many of the other objectives discussed in this book (see appendix B tables).

Our past survey work also tells us that scientists are also quite willing to tell stories about their research processes and talk about their motivations [55]. Overall, we would expect people advising science communicators to receive a fairly positive reaction to suggesting such tactics. Specifically, our initial tactics study asked about two things:

1. "Willingness to tell first person stories in a way that helps to connect with an audience. This might mean spending less time talking about scientific findings to have more time for providing a clear, compelling narrative about why you study your topic, your research choices, the challenges you faced and how you overcame them."

2. "Willingness to talk about the role a desire to help their community or society plays in shaping their research. This might mean spending less time talking about scientific findings to have time to talk about why you chose a science career or what you hope to achieve through your science."

For both tactics, we used a 7-point "strongly disagree" to "strongly agree" scale, and the average willingness score was well above 5, while the average agreement score was 5.49 for the storytelling tactic and 5.16 for the talking-about-a-desire-to-help tactic. Similarly, respondents clearly agreed that both of these tactics are ethical (5.55 and 5.59 average agreement, respectively) and likely to have an impact (5.27 and 4.96 average agreement, respectively). They also tend to believe that their colleagues would see these tactics as acceptable (4.96 and 4.93 average agreement, respectively) and that they personally had the skills to implement these tactics (5.73 and 5.62 average agreement, respectively). Unfortunately, as with the warmth objective, the data does not suggest that scientists have spent much time thinking about these tactics (4.06 and 3.83). Whether or not a scientist said they had thought much about the tactics was also a relatively important predictor of willingness to choose the tactic [55].

Given the overall positive views about these tactics, our fear is that many science communicators may simply fail to prioritize communicating warmth because the objective and associated tactics simply are not choices they have spent much time thinking about. We'll come back to this in the concluding chapter, but these types of findings suggest at least two things: (1) that training needs to address a broader range of objectives, and (2) that we may not be putting enough resources into providing scientists with access to communication experts who understand the full pantry of potential objectives that scientists may want to consider using.

Next we tackle integrity and honesty beliefs. The lack of attention to communicating about the scientific community's integrity may be even more pressing than beliefs about warmth.

Preparing to Prioritize Warmth Beliefs
as a Communication Objective

The following are eight questions that science communicators should consider when deciding whether to prioritize the communication objective of being perceived as warm. In many cases, warmth-related communication might involve sharing information about the degree to which scientists are motivated by a desire to help others (i.e., they're caring or benevolent).

THE GOAL QUESTION

1. Given the behavior you want from your specific audience (i.e., your goal), why do you think it would be helpful if your chosen audience saw you as motivated by concern about the well-being of others?

THE PREPARATION QUESTIONS

2. What does your chosen audience believe about your motivations and is there meaningful room to improve?
3. What do you believe about your chosen audience's motivations?

THE TACTICS QUESTIONS

4. What could you do to potentially increase the likelihood that those with whom you are communicating will you see you as motivated by a concern about others' well-being, including choices about messages, behaviors, tone/style, communication channel, and communication source?
5. What could you do to learn about your chosen audiences' motivations?

THE EVALUATION QUESTIONS

6. Did your chosen audience perceive you as motivated by a desire to help?
7. What did you learn about your audience's motivations?

THE ETHICS QUESTION

8. Are you being honest about your motivations?

REFERENCES

1. Ledingham, John A., and Stephen D. Bruning. "Relationship Management in Public Relations: Dimensions of an Organization-Public Relationship." *Public Relations Review* 24, no. 1 (1998): 55–65. https://doi.org/10.1016/S0363-8111(98)80020-9.

2. Borchelt, Rick E., and Kristian H. Nielsen. "Public Relations in Science: Managing the Trust Portfolio." In *Routledge Handbook of Public Communication of Science and Technology*, 2nd ed., edited by Massimiano Bucchi and Brian Trench, 58–69. London: Routledge, 2014.

3. Schoorman, F. David, Roger C. Mayer, and James H. Davis. "An Integrative Model of Organizational Trust: Past, Present, and Future." *Academy of Management Review* 32, no. 2 (2007): 344–54. https://doi.org/10.2307/20159304.

4. Fiske, Susan T., and Cydney Dupree. "Gaining Trust as Well as Respect in Communicating to Motivated Audiences About Science Topics." *Proceedings of the National Academy of Sciences* 111, Supplement 4 (September 2014): 13593–97. https://doi.org/10.1073/pnas.1317505111.

5. Asch, Solomon E. "Forming Impressions of Personality." *Journal of Abnormal and Social Psychology* 41, no. 3 (1946): 258–90. https://doi.org/10.1037/h0055756.

6. Abele, Andrea E. "Agency and Communion from the Perspective of Self Versus Others." *Journal of Personality and Social Psychology* 93, no. 5 (2007): 751–63. https://doi.org/10.1037/0022-3514.93.5.751.

7. Kasperson, Roger E., Dominic Golding, and Seth Tuler. "Social Distrust as a Factor in Siting Hazardous Facilities and Communicating Risks." *Journal of Social Issues* 48, no. 4 (Winter 1992): 161–87.

8. Reysen, Stephen. "Construction of a New Scale: The Reysen Likability Scale." *Social Behavior and Personality: An International Journal* 33, no. 2 (2005): 201–08. https://doi.org/10.2224/sbp.2005.33.2.201.

9. Bies, Robert J., and John S. Moag. "Interactional Justice: Communication Criteria of Fairness." In *Research on Negotiations in Organizations*, vol. 1, edited by Roy J. Lewicki, Blair H. Sheppard, and Max H. Bazerman, 43–55. Greenwich, CT: JAI Press, 1986.

10. Kim, Sung Soo, Stan Kaplowitz, and Mark V. Johnston. "The Effects of Physician Empathy on Patient Satisfaction and Compliance." *Evaluation & the Health Professions* 27, no. 3 (2004): 237–51. https://doi.org/10.1177/0163278704267037.

11. Besley, John C., Nicole M. Lee, and Geah Pressgrove. "Reassessing the Variables Used to Measure Public Perceptions of Scientists." *Science Communication* 43, no. 1 (2021): 3–32. https://doi.org/10.1177/1075547020949547.

12. Hendriks, Friederike, Dorothe Kienhues, and Rainer Bromme. "Measuring Laypeople's Trust in Experts in a Digital Age: The Muenster Epistemic Trustworthiness Inventory (METI)." *PLOS ONE* 10, no. 10 (2015): e0139309. https://doi.org/10.1371/journal.pone.0139309.

13. Cuddy, Amy J. C., Peter Glick, and Anna Beninger. "The Dynamics of Warmth and Competence Judgments, and Their Outcomes in Organizations."

Research in Organizational Behavior 31 (2011): 73–98. https://doi.org/10.1016/j.riob
.2011.10.004.

14. Fiske, Susan T., Amy J. C. Cuddy, Peter Glick, and Jun Xu. "A Model of
(Often Mixed) Stereotype Content: Competence and Warmth Respectively Follow
from Perceived Status and Competition." *Journal of Personality and Social Psychology* 82, no. 6 (2002): 878–902. https://doi.org/10.1037/0022-3514.82.6.878.

15. Fiske, Susan T., Amy J. C. Cuddy, and Peter Glick. "Universal Dimensions of
Social Cognition: Warmth and Competence." *Trends in Cognitive Sciences* 11, no. 2
(2007): 77–83. https://doi.org/10.1016/j.tics.2006.11.005.

16. Colquitt, Jason A., and Sabrina Salam. "Foster Trust through Ability,
Benevolence, and Integrity." In *Handbook of Principles of Organizational Behavior*,
edited by Edwin A. Locke, 395. West Sussex, UK: Wiley, 2009.

17. Tausch, Nicole, Jared B. Kenworthy, and Miles Hewstone. "The Confirmability and Disconfirmability of Trait Concepts Revisited: Does Content Matter?"
Journal of Personality and Social Psychology 92, no. 3 (March 2007): 542–56. https://
doi.org/10.1037/0022-3514.92.3.542.

18. Rothbart, Myron, and Bernadette Park. "On the Confirmability and
Disconfirmability of Trait Concepts." *Journal of Personality and Social Psychology*
50, no. 1 (January 1986): 131–42. https://doi.org/10.1037/0022-3514.50.1.131.

19. Mutz, Diana C., and Reeves Byron. "The New Videomalaise: Effects of
Televised Incivility on Political Trust." *American Political Science Review* 99, no. 1
(2005): 1–15. https://doi.org/10.2307/30038915.

20. Myers, Scott A., and Kelly A. Rocca. "Students' State Motivation and
Instructors' Use of Verbally Aggressive Messages." *Psychological Reports* 87, no. 1
(August 2000): 291–94. https://doi.org/10.2466/pr0.2000.87.1.291.

21. Yuan, Shupei, John C. Besley, and Chen Lou. "Does Being a Jerk Work?
Examining the Effect of Aggressive Risk Communication in the Context of
Science Blogs." *Journal of Risk Research* 21, no. 4 (2018): 502–20. https://doi.org/10
.1080/13669877.2016.1223159.

22. Yuan, Shupei, John C. Besley, and Wenjuan Ma. "Be Mean or Be Nice?
Understanding the Effects of Aggressive and Polite Communication Styles in
Child Vaccination Debate." *Health Communication* 34, no. 10 (2019): 1212–21.
https://doi.org/10.1080/10410236.2018.1471337.

23. Yuan, Shupei, Wenjuan Ma, and John C. Besley. "Should Scientists Talk
About GMOs Nicely? Exploring the Effects of Communication Styles, Source
Expertise, and Preexisting Attitude." *Science Communication* 41, no. 3 (2019):
267–90. https://doi.org/10.1177/1075547019837623.

24. Söderlund, Magnus, and Sara Rosengren. "Revisiting the Smiling Service
Worker and Customer Satisfaction." *International Journal of Service Industry
Management* 19, no. 5 (2008): 552–74. https://doi.org/10.1108/09564230810903460.

25. Barger, Patricia B., and Alicia A. Grandey. "Service with a Smile and
Encounter Satisfaction: Emotional Contagion and Appraisal Mechanisms."
Academy of Management Journal 49, no. 6 (2006): 1229–38. https://doi.org/10.5465
/amj.2006.23478695.

26. Pew Research Center. *Public Praises Science; Scientists Fault Public, Media.* Washington, DC: Pew Research Center, 2009. https://www.pewresearch.org/politics/2009/07/09/public-praises-science-scientists-fault-public-media.

27. Besley, John C., Sang Hwa Oh, and Matthew C. Nisbet. "Predicting Scientists' Participation in Public Life." *Public Understanding of Science* 22, no. 8 (2013): 971–87. https://doi.org/10.1177/0963662512459315.

28. Colquitt, Jason A., Brent A. Scott, and Jeffery A. LePine. "Trust, Trustworthiness, and Trust Propensity: A Meta-Analytic Test of Their Unique Relationships with Risk Taking and Job Performance." *Journal of Applied Psychology* 92, no. 4 (2007): 909–27. https://doi.org/10.1037/0021-9010.92.4.909.

29. Zawisza, Magdalena, and Chelsea Pittard. "When Do Warmth and Competence Sell Best? The 'Golden Quadrant' Shifts as a Function of Congruity with the Product Type, Targets' Individual Differences, and Advertising Appeal Type." *Basic and Applied Social Psychology* 37, no. 2 (2015): 131–41. https://doi.org/10.1080/01973533.2015.1015130.

30. Roskos-Ewoldsen, David R., Jacqueline Bichsel, and Kathleen Hoffman. "The Influence of Accessibility of Source Likability on Persuasion." *Journal of Experimental Social Psychology* 38, no. 2 (March 2002): 137–43. https://doi.org/10.1006/jesp.2001.1492.

31. Roskos-Ewoldsen, David R., and Russell H. Fazio. "The Accessibility of Source Likability as a Determinant of Persuasion." *Personality and Social Psychology Bulletin* 18, no. 1 (1992): 19–25. https://doi.org/10.1177/0146167292181004.

32. McComas, Katherine A., John C. Besley, and Zheng Yang. "Risky Business: The Perceived Justice of Local Scientists and Community Support for Their Research." *Risk Analysis* 28, no. 6 (2008): 1539–52. https://doi.org/10.1111/j.1539-6924.2008.01129.x.

33. Morgan, Michael, James Shanahan, and Nancy Signorielli. "Growing up with Television: Cultivation Processes." In *Media Effects: Advances in Theory and Research*, edited by Jennings Bryant and Mary Beth Oliver, 34–49. Mahwah, NJ: Lawrence Erlbaum Associates, 2009.

34. Dudo, Anthony, Dominique Brossard, James Shanahan, Dietram A. Scheufele, Michael Morgan, and Nancy Signorielli. "Science on Television in the 21st Century: Recent Trends in Portrayals and Their Contributions to Public Attitudes toward Science." *Communication Research* 38, no. 6 (2011): 754–77. https://doi.org/10.1177/0093650210384988.

35. Fiske, Susan T. "Stereotyping, Prejudice, and Discrimination." In *The Handbook of Social Psychology*, 4th ed., edited by Daniel T. Gilbert, Susan T. Fiske, and Gardner Lindzey, 357–411, vol. 2. New York: McGraw-Hill, 1998.

36. Sharp, Michael C., Ronald P. Strauss, and Sharon Claire Lorch. "Communicating Medical Bad News: Parents' Experiences and Preferences." *Journal of Pediatrics* 121, no. 4 (1992): 539–46. https://doi.org/10.1016/S0022-3476(05)81141-2.

37. Davies, Ruth, Bryn Davis, and Jo Sibert. "Parents' Stories of Sensitive and Insensitive Care by Paediatricians in the Time Leading Up To and Including Diagnostic Disclosure of a Life-Limiting Condition in Their Child." *Child: Care,*

Health and Development 29, no. 1 (2003): 77–82. https://doi.org/10.1046/j.1365-2214 .2003.00316.x.

38. National Science Board. "Science and Technology: Public Attitudes and Public Understanding." In *Science & Engineering Indicators 2018*. Alexandria, VA: National Science Foundation, 2018. https://www.nsf.gov/statistics/2018/nsb20181 /report/sections/science-and-technology-public-attitudes-and-understanding /highlights.

39. Teding van Berkhout, Emily, and John M. Malouff. "The Efficacy of Empathy Training: A Meta-Analysis of Randomized Controlled Trials." *Journal of Counseling Psychology* 63, no. 1 (2016): 32–41. https://doi.org/10.1037/cou0000093.

40. Trzeciak, Stephen, and Anthony Mazzarelli. *Compassionomics: The Revolutionary Scientific Evidence That Caring Makes a Difference*. Pensacola, FL: Studer Group, 2019.

41. Kervyn, Nicolas, Susan T. Fiske, and Chris Malone. "Brands as Intentional Agents Framework: How Perceived Intentions and Ability Can Map Brand Perception." *Journal of Consumer Psychology* 22, no. 2 (2012): 166–76. https://doi.org/10 .1016/j.jcps.2011.09.006.

42. Malone, Chris, and Susan T. Fiske. *The Human Brand: How We Relate to People, Products, and Companies*. San Francisco: Jossey-Bass, 2013.

43. Fombrun, Charles J., Naomi A. Gardberg, and Joy M. Sever. "The Reputation Quotient[SM]: A Multi-Stakeholder Measure of Corporate Reputation." *Journal of Brand Management* 7, no. 4 (2000): 241–55. https://doi.org/10.1057/bm.2000.10.

44. Fraustino, Julia Daisy, and Colleen Connolly-Ahern. "Corporate Associations Written on the Wall: Publics' Responses to Fortune 500 Ability and Social Responsibility Facebook Posts." *Journal of Public Relations Research* 27, no. 5 (2015): 452–74. https://doi.org/10.1080/1062726x.2015.1098543.

45. Kim, Sora. "What They Can Do Versus How Much They Care." *Journal of Communication Management* 14, no. 1 (2010): 59–80. https://doi.org/10.1108 /13632541011017816.

46. Kim, Sora. "Transferring Effects of CSR Strategy on Consumer Responses: The Synergistic Model of Corporate Communication Strategy." *Journal of Public Relations Research* 23, no. 2 (2011): 218–41. https://doi.org/10.1080/1062726x.2011 .555647.

47. Besley, John C., Anthony Dudo, Shupei Yuan, and Niveen AbiGhannam. "Qualitative Interviews with Science Communication Trainers About Communication Objectives and Goals." *Science Communication* 38, no. 3 (2016): 356–81. https://doi.org/10.1177/1075547016645640.

48. Cuddy, Amy J. C., Susan T. Fiske, and Peter Glick. "The BIAS Map: Behaviors from Intergroup Affect and Stereotypes." *Journal of Personality and Social Psychology* 92, no. 4 (2007): 631–48. https://doi.org/10.1037/0022-3514.92.4.631.

49. Mohr, Lois A., Deborah J. Webb, and Katherine E. Harris. "Do Consumers Expect Companies to Be Socially Responsible? The Impact of Corporate Social Responsibility on Buying Behavior." *Journal of Consumer Affairs* 35, no. 1 (2001): 45–72. https://doi.org/10.1111/j.1745-6606.2001.tb00102.x.

50. Becker, Julia C., and Frank Asbrock. "What Triggers Helping Versus Harming of Ambivalent Groups? Effects of the Relative Salience of Warmth Versus Competence." *Journal of Experimental Social Psychology* 48, no. 1 (2012): 19–27. https://doi.org/10.1016/j.jesp.2011.06.015.

51. Zahry, Nagwan R, and John C Besley. "Warmth Portrayals to Recruit Students into Science Majors." *Visual Communication*, September 10, 2019. https://doi.org/10.1177/1470357219871696.

52. Zahry, Nagwan R., and John C. Besley. "Students' Perceptions of Agriculture and Natural Resources Majors: Understanding STEM Choice." *Natural Sciences Education* 46 (2017). https://doi.org/10.4195/nse2016.07.0019.

53. Wenrich, Marjorie D., J. Randall Curtis, Sarah E. Shannon, Jan D. Carline, Donna M. Ambrozy, and Paul G. Ramsey. "Communicating with Dying Patients within the Spectrum of Medical Care from Terminal Diagnosis to Death." *JAMA Internal Medicine* 161, no. 6 (2001): 868–74. https://doi.org/10.1001/archinte.161.6.868.

54. Kim, Sora, and Mary Ann T. Ferguson. "Dimensions of Effective CSR Communication Based on Public Expectations." *Journal of Marketing Communications* 24, no. 6 (2018): 549–67. https://doi.org/10.1080/13527266.2015.1118143.

55. Besley, John C., Kathryn O'Hara, and Anthony Dudo. "Strategic Science Communication as Planned Behavior: Understanding Scientists' Willingness to Choose Specific Tactics." *PLOS ONE* 14, no. 10 (2019): e0224039. https://doi.org/10.1371/journal.pone.0224039.

4

Show Integrity

IN THIS CHAPTER WE MAKE THE ARGUMENT that science communicators may sometimes need to prioritize ensuring that people believe in the scientific community's integrity. There will always be community members who do dishonest things for recognition, money, or because of some other weakness [1]. Integrity failures may be isolated or systematic, but we believe most people involved in science try to act ethically. Indeed, the social norms that underlie the scientific process [2] are designed to propel scientists toward ethical behavior. Unfortunately, as with many things in strategic communication, behaving ethically does not inherently lead to others' integrity beliefs. We could blame journalists or online commentators for putting too much emphasis on isolated cases, but these people are typically outside the science community's control and not the subject of this book. As already noted, what we can control are our own communication choices. And when it comes to integrity beliefs, the available public opinion evidence suggests that there is room for the scientific community to make substantial improvements.

In the previous chapter, we noted that trust researcher Susan Fiske alarmed the science communication and policy worlds when she showed that many people see scientists as similar to accountants and lawyers as a group of people who are "competent but cold" [3]. She partly based this argument on her own statistical analyses of a small (n=116), nonrepresentative sample of people recruited online through Amazon's Mechanical Turk, a crowd-sourcing website where researchers often recruit participants for experiments in exchange for a small amount of money. This made sense for her argument—which focused on the pattern of responses within the data rather than the absolute scores given by respondents—but we need to look elsewhere to get a more complete sense of how people perceive the scientific community.

For the United States, one source of such information is the biennial report *Science and Engineering Indicators* produced by the National Science Board that includes a section on public attitudes and knowledge about science [4]. The National Science Board is the high-level group of scientists from academia, government, and the private sector that oversees the National Science Foundation, the country's primary nonhealth, nondefense research funder. The biennial report is technically meant for the Executive Branch and Congress, but it has also served as a primary mechanism to consolidate research on such topics as how people perceive science [5]. The primary source of data for the report's section on public opinion since 2008 has been a set of questions that the National Science Foundation pays to have on the General Social Survey (GSS), a nationwide, biennial, face-to-face survey that is among the world's most important sources of social science data because of its high quality and longevity [6]. The GSS has long included questions about overall confidence in various institutions, including science, and the evidence is clear that scientists are among the country's most respected groups. Further, unlike most other groups, average views about scientists have stayed fairly stable over time [5].

A problem with this data—which we have often seen highlighted as evidence that Americans tend to trust science—is the same problem we raised in chapter 3 when we argued that it makes sense to focus on trustworthiness-related beliefs rather than overall trust. Knowing about overall confidence does not tell communicators much about the specific beliefs, such as warmth beliefs, that underlie people's views about scientists and could be prioritized as part of strategic science communication activities. The National Science Foundation survey has, unfortunately, only sporadically included information directly focused on Americans' specific trustworthiness-related beliefs. In contrast to Fiske's concern about perceived coldness, however, the available data seems to suggest that Americans have positive views about scientists' motives. In this regard, almost all respondents to surveys in 1985, 2001, 2012, 2016, and 2018 agreed that scientists "want to help solve problems," "want to work for the good of humanity," and "want to make life better for average person" (figure 4.1). Unfortunately, this data does not tell us much about perceived integrity.

Some of the most recent American integrity data comes from a 2019 survey by the Pew Research Center that found while 89% of Americans see scientists as intelligent (chapter 7), only 71% see scientists as honest, and this number falls to 64% among Republicans and to 59% for those with relatively less science knowledge. Many groups might see 71% as positive, but it still means 3 in 10 Americans worry about scientists' integrity [7]. Similarly, the 2006 GSS survey data featured in the 2008 version of *Indicators* asked respondents to assess the degree to which they thought three different groups would "support doing what is best for the country or what serves their own narrow interest" when "making policy decisions" about such issues as global warming, stem cell research, federal income taxes, and genetically modified foods (figure 4.2). The results showed that experts were generally seen as more likely to put the interests of the country first, and much more likely than either business leaders or elected officials. However, there was still substantial room for improvement.

More broadly, the United Kingdom's Wellcome Trust—undertaken with Gallup—surveyed 1,000 people from each of 140 countries around the world in 2019 about how they felt about science and health [8]. The data collected included a question about how much respondents "trust science" overall, as well as questions consistent with the three-dimensional approach to measuring trustworthiness [9] in the form of ability beliefs (i.e., competence), benevolence beliefs (i.e., warmth),

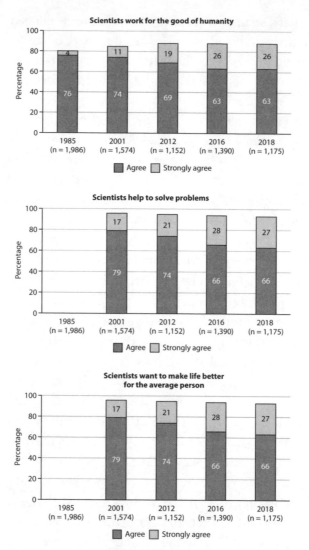

Figure 4.1. Public perception of scientists: Selected years, 1983–2018. Data represent respondents who "strongly agree" and "agree" with the following statements: *Scientific researchers are dedicated people who work for the good of humanity*; *Scientists are helping to solve challenging problems*; and *Most scientists want to work on things that will make life better for the average person*. Not all questions were fielded in all years.

SOURCE: J. C. Besley and D. Hill, "Science and Technology: Public Attitudes, Knowledge, and Interest," *Science & Engineering Indicators*, May 2020, Figure 7.6. https://ncses.nsf.gov/pubs/nsb20207/public-attitudes-about-s-t-in-general#perceptions-of-scientists.

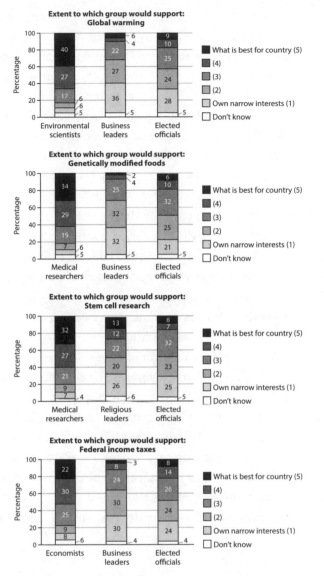

Figure 4.2. Extent to which certain groups would support specific public issues. Question wording was "When making policy decisions about [public issue], to what extent do you think [group] would support doing what is best for the country as a whole or what serves their own narrow interests?" Totals may equal between 99% and 101% of sample due to rounding of raw data.

SOURCE: *Science and Engineering Indicators 2008*, University of Chicago, National Opinion Research Center, General Social Survey (2006), appendix table 7–23, accessed October 13, 2021, https://wayback.archive-it.org/5902/20150818072959/http://www.nsf.gov/statistics/seind08/c7/c7s3.htm.

and integrity beliefs. The results show that in many countries—especially wealthier countries—most people say they generally believe that scientists have the ability to "find out accurate information" (i.e., they are competent; discussed in chapter 6). However, the pattern in countries such as the United States and the United Kingdom is that people become somewhat less positive when asked to report the degree to which they feel "college and university scientists do work that benefits the public," (i.e., warmth or benevolence as discussed in chapter 3) (see table 4.1). They are then even less positive when asked whether they say they trust "college and university scientists to be open and honest about who pays for their work" (i.e., honesty or integrity). The amount of positivity drops even further when asked about public benefits and integrity in the context of "corporate scientists." While the absolute level of trust beliefs seems to vary across countries and regions (with poorer regions expressing lower amounts of trust), the overall pattern is evident: many people do not believe in the integrity of the scientific community.

One basic idea of communication strategy is that it is helpful to know what people already think when setting communication priorities. For example, it might not make sense to spend a lot of effort communicating about how effective science is in solving difficult questions if people already strongly believe that scientists are competent when it comes to finding answers to complicated technical challenges. The Wellcome data could therefore be understood to suggest that there's room to make progress on the degree to which people see the scientific community—especially corporate scientists—as having integrity.

What Is Integrity and Why Treat Integrity as Separate from Warmth?

Many trust-focused researchers see integrity as an element of warmth [10], communion [11], character [12], or something else [13] when measuring how people perceive others. Practically, this involves asking survey respondents a series of questions about the degree to which

Table 4.1.

Mean scores (M) for trust-related beliefs in seven key countries based on the Wellcome Global Monitor 2018, conducted by the Gallup Corporation

	Australia			Brazil			China			Denmark			Germany			South Africa			UK			USA		
	M	SD	SE	M	SD	SE	M	SD	SE	M	SD	SE	M	SD	SE	M	SD	SE	M	SD	SE	M	SD	SE
Competence[1] (chapter 6)	3.48	0.65	.02	2.85	0.93	.03	3.19	0.66	.01	3.27	0.62	.02	3.33	0.75	.02	2.78	1.00	.03	3.47	0.68	.02	3.43	0.66	.02
Warmth/benevolence, Universities[2] (chapter 3)	3.38	0.69	.02	2.85	0.91	.03	3.17	0.57	.01	3.34	0.64	.02	3.31	0.79	.03	2.78	1.04	.04	3.39	0.69	.02	3.17	0.78	.03
Warmth/benevolence, Companies[3] (chapter 3)	2.96	0.74	.02	2.82	0.89	.03	3.04	0.71	.01	3.04	0.75	.02	2.68	0.92	.03	2.71	1.03	.04	2.99	0.76	.02	2.80	0.81	.03
Honesty/integrity, Universities[4] (chapter 4)	3.06	0.74	.02	2.53	0.89	.03	3.10	0.69	.01	3.03	0.70	.02	2.91	0.96	.03	2.54	1.05	.04	3.10	0.72	.02	2.88	0.84	.03
Honesty/integrity, Companies[5] (chapter 4)	2.75	0.77	.02	2.54	0.89	.03	2.97	0.72	.01	2.82	0.75	.02	2.67	0.97	.03	2.51	1.04	.04	2.77	0.86	.03	2.61	0.83	.03

Notes: Respondents scored their level of trust on a scale of 1 to 4 (1= Not at all, 2= Not much, 3= Somewhat, 4= A lot). Standard deviation (SD) and standard error (SE) are included here as well. Sample sizes were as follows: Australia, n=952–997; Brazil, n=952–997; China, n=885–944; Denmark, n=2,479–2,842; Germany, n=993–1,000; South Africa, n=870–917; United Kingdom, n=972–990; United States, n=834–961. Full data set available at https://wellcome.ac.uk/reports/wellcome-global-monitor/2018.

[1] "In general, how much do you trust scientists to find out accurate information about the world?"

[2] "How much do you trust scientists working in colleges/universities in this country to do their work with the intention of benefiting the public?"

[3] "How much do you trust scientists working for companies in this country to do their work with the intention of benefiting the public?"

[4] "How much do you trust scientists working in colleges/universities in this country to be open and honest about who is paying for their work?"

[5] "How much do you trust scientists working for companies in this country to be open and honest about who is paying for their work?"

they see a group as caring, benevolent, honest, and moral and then combining them into a single measure (i.e., using an average score of multiple questions connected to what we argue can be understood as two different constructs). One argument for this approach is that statistical analyses of trust-focused questions often show high levels of correlation between items meant to capture integrity and benevolence beliefs [14,15]. In contrast, measures aimed at capturing competence or ability are more clearly distinct from both integrity and benevolence measures. For example, researcher Jason Colquitt found in a study about trust in managers that integrity and benevolence correlated at $r = .78$ (i.e., about 60% of statistical overlap), whereas ability correlated with benevolence at $r = .67$ and with integrity at $r = .66$ (i.e., both about 45% of statistical overlap) at the start of the study. This high correlation between benevolence and integrity measures makes a great deal of sense when you consider that there are clear moral dimensions to being both honest and caring [10,16]. In other words, it makes some sense to expect a moral person to be both honest and focused on helping other people.

However, our perspective is that it is useful for science communicators to conceptualize integrity as distinct from benevolence or warmth. We often use the example of what we want out of a plumber. First, we want our plumbers to have the ability to fix our broken pipes. We also want our plumbers to not steal from us when we let them into our homes. It would also be nice if the plumber was polite and seemed to care about the welfare of our family, although that is probably not always a deal breaker. The key, however, is that these attributes seem distinct enough that plumbers might need to communicate in different ways to be seen as both honest (talking about what they do to avoid conflicts of interest, steps taken to ensure their work can be checked, etc.) and caring (talking about motivation, past efforts to help people, etc.).

One challenge to this distinction is that there are many cases where integrity issues might call people's motivations into question. For example, finding out that an environmental scientist conducting a study on fracking was getting money from an energy company involved in fracking might make you wonder about whether the scientist is both dishonest and more concerned about personal benefits than societal benefits [17]. It is also probably worth mentioning that when trust researchers Bill McEvily and Macro Tortoriello reviewed research on organizations (i.e., companies) they found that integrity was the most common aspect of trustworthiness that people included in their studies (when they included more than one dimension) [18]. Further, a team led by trust researcher Lisa PytlikZillig combined a number of data sets—including data related to perceptions of police, local government, natural resource governance, and state governance—and found that there was generally a reasonable statistical reason to separate warmth from integrity [19]. For us, the combination of theoretical research on the "dimensions of trustworthiness" and the survey evidence suggesting that many people worry about the integrity of the science community point toward the conclusion that science communicators should often consider prioritizing integrity beliefs as a distinct communication objective.

Communicating Integrity

As with warmth, we have been surprised with the challenge of finding literature that speaks directly to the question of how to communicate that you have integrity, especially in the context of science communication. Similarly, even though communication trainers often say they are trying to help scientists build trust for science, we have rarely heard trainers emphasize what they do to help the scientific community specifically communicate about their integrity [20]. The three closest sets of literature we are aware of come from work on perceived conflict of interest (COI), research on corporate communication strategy, and organizational research focused on workplaces. The conflict of interest literature does not paint an optimistic picture for communicating integrity, but the broader research related to corporate and organizational communication offers some hope.

The COI literature is of interest to John because of a set of studies he did with colleagues from various fields, including philosophy, sociology, and the natural sciences. Conflicts of interest are situations where there is the potential that someone could benefit financially or socially from decisions for which they are at least partly responsible. For science communicators, this might involve something like a scientist who advocates on behalf of the safety or effectiveness of a drug when doing so might personally benefit the scientist through a company with which they have a relationship. COIs are especially problematic when they are not adequately disclosed [21].

John's specific research was prompted because a project collaborator managed a food safety research center that occasionally accepted corporate funding, and there was a fear that accepting this type of funding might make it harder to have their findings accepted by stakeholders. Those involved in food science—especially at universities such as Michigan State where there is substantial expertise related to genetically modified food—are well aware of reputational challenges posed in the press and online as a result of being seen to accept money from agriculture companies (e.g., the former company Monsanto) who sometimes offer to provide resources to academics willing to make public arguments that might be seen as helping companies but that critics argue come at the expense of academic independence [22,23].

The first study in the project started with the idea that one way to communicate integrity is to pick research partners who might be expected to help keep the research team honest [24]. An experiment was developed in which participants were told about a research collaboration being assembled to study trans fats safety that involved some combination of a university (i.e., Purdue), a nongovernmental organization (i.e., the Union of Concerned Scientists), a government agency (i.e., the Centers for Disease Control and Prevention, commonly known as the CDC), and a company (i.e., the food company Kellogg's). These partners were selected using a pretest to ensure that participants were unlikely to start with negative predispositions to any of the organizations involved. The main experiment then involved randomly assigning a new set of participants to one of 16 different experimental conditions, such that one person would read about research involving just one of the partners, another might learn about all four of the partners, and the remaining were assigned to one of every other possible combination of partners. In the end, the evidence was clear that having Kellogg's in the partnership—even though people in pre-tests said they liked Kellogg's—meant that people thought the research would be biased (i.e., lack integrity) and did not think the evidence should be used in decision-making. What is more, qualitative responses provided a strong indication that people felt that any company involved would find a way to mess with the research.

Faced with these results, our same team conducted a second pair of studies on trans fats to see if there might be procedures research-ers could put in place that would mitigate the downside of accepting corporate funding beyond simply having additional partners. The ini-tial version of the study varied both the partners and whether they had one of three COI-mitigation procedures that seem relatively com-mon in the literature. These included (1) a commitment to make all data publicly available, (2) a commitment to have an independent ad-visory board oversee the project, or (3) a commitment to set up a sys-tem so that funders were kept at arm's length from researchers with no potential for oversight. Having a procedure in place seemed to make a very small positive difference on whether respondents saw the research as biased, but this was nothing compared to the negative impact of having a corporate partner. A follow-up experiment then involved assigning participants to read about a partnership that in-volved one, two, or three of the COI-mitigation processes (i.e., not just one process, as in the previous experiment). Once again, however, we found that having a process to try to mitigate COI might help a little when it comes to bias perceptions, but nothing compared to the downside of having a company involved. Also, having multiple COI-mitigation procedures was not any better than having a single procedure.

These were two relatively straightforward attempts to see if we could communicate simple procedures that might affect bias per-ceptions on a single issue, but the findings were consistent with earlier work showing how corporate involvement could make people question science [25–27]. The negative effect of corporate partners also echoes recent research on what happens when bloggers disclose that they have received money to post material [28]. This work finds that while disclosure may boost integrity beliefs for those who are not paying a lot of attention to the post, the same disclosure actually hurts integrity beliefs for people who are thinking about the post more deeply (i.e., processing systematically or engaging with the material). It might be that more detailed descriptions of the COI-mitigation procedures or justifications for the partnership might change the results. But we are not hopeful. Also, there may be issues or companies—perhaps ones that do not directly involve health and safety—where integrity is less of an issue.

Indeed, scattered examples from various parts of the corporate communication literature are more promising. For example, in one highly cited 2006 study, a group of marketing researchers created mock company websites and found that having a strong data security and privacy statement boosted the perceived integrity of the company by about a half point on a 5-point scale [29]. Another team of marketing scholars did an experiment using a made-up electronics company that was described as having gotten into trouble for a product that harmed either customers or the environment. Additional conditions varied whether the company apologized, provided compensation, or were open in providing information. The overall results suggested that apologizing and providing access to information (but not compensation) were associated with substantially higher integrity ratings. Apologizing also affected benevolence ratings, but not competence ratings (compensation and providing information did increase competence somewhat).

A bit more related to science communication—but still published within the management literature—is a study by leadership researcher William Gardner. This study is the type of project we would love to see adapted for science communication and involved using an actor to record fake interviews with a man ostensibly interviewing for a job as a business school dean. The research team made one version of the interview in which the prospective dean answers three questions in the middle of the interview to portray himself "as an honest and ethical individual who cannot tolerate deceit and prides himself on being fair and equitable." This was randomly shown to half of the participants in the experiment. A second version of the interview, shown to the other half, had the man describing himself as a "practical and adaptable person who strives to present information in the best possible light, even if it is necessary to stretch the truth to do so" [30, p. 510]. Other aspects of the experiment involved varying the quality of the delivery (i.e., dynamic with good eye contact and fluency vs. lower quality but still realistic delivery) and whether the prospective dean's references made any mention of potential ethical lapses that were consistent or inconsistent with how the man described himself in the interview.

As might be hoped, when the interviewee described himself in ethical terms, he was rated by study participants as almost seven-tenths of a point more ethical on a 5-point integrity measure. The reference checks were more damning, with negative reports dropping the scale by almost nine-tenths of a point. In contrast, delivery quality did not affect integrity ratings on its own but somewhat boosted the effect of having a positive reputation for integrity. These findings suggest that science communicators who want to be perceived as honest may want to directly communicate why they think they should be seen as honest. Also, it may be that the effectiveness of delivery quality on integrity ratings is partly a function of an existing reputation for integrity.

More recently, German science communication researchers Lars König and Regina Jucks created videos of a person described as scientist (and a lobbyist) talking about antidepressants in an aggressive or nonaggressive manner [31]. Their data also showed about a half-point negative impact on a 5-point integrity indicator (as well as somewhat bigger effects on expertise, benevolence, and overall likability) when the delivery was aggressive. Shupei Yuan's similar work on aggressive communication has not directly looked at how aggressiveness affects integrity, but her research has clearly shown that aggressiveness affects scientists' likability [32–34]. Given what we know about the tight connections between morality-related trustworthiness beliefs, Yuan's work adds additional weight to the argument that the choices science communicators make—whether they are explicit or implicit—will often affect others' perceptions of their integrity. On a positive note, recent research using written vignettes showed that communicating using personal narratives could increase perceptions of integrity [35].

Studies in organizational and crisis communication have also used manufactured videos to look at the value of apologies and denials, starting with a focus on job interviewees [36] and extended to a CEO [37] accused of making either integrity- or competency-based violations of trustworthiness. These provide a cautionary tale to those accused of integrity violations. A key finding of this research is that apologizing seems to work better when a lapse involves competence more so than when the error involves integrity. For integrity lapses, the advice this literature seems to suggest is denial. And while this advice may make sense if the denier truly did not do the problematic behavior, other situations may require an apology and corrective actions. In other words, there do not seem to be any easy answers to actual integrity violations beyond restarting the hard, long-term work of building back one's reputation [38–40].

The potential value of honesty—if you need convincing—is that there is some evidence that being open about negative information can have positive effects on others' assessments of your integrity. One corporate social responsibility (CRS) study, for example, randomly assigned people to read CSR-report cover letters from a made-up cosmetics company that had varying levels of negative disclosure about failures to reach environmental targets. The study found that these disclosures increased perceived integrity judgments and thus somewhat counteracted the negative effect of these disclosures on overall reputation for social responsibility [41].

What Do Integrity Beliefs Affect?

As with all trustworthiness-related beliefs, it matters if people believe that most members of the scientific community have integrity. A core element of trust-related theory is that trustworthiness-related beliefs contribute to people's willingness to make themselves vulnerable to someone else (i.e., to let the plumber into your home, to rehash our earlier metaphor) [42]. In our own initial work on COI, integrity-related beliefs were also associated with a willingness to accept underlying research findings as a legitimate source of information for personal and government decision-making [24]. This is consistent with past work on COI that found that perceived financial ties, for example, appeared to reduce people's faith in various aspects of the health care system [25,43].

The corporate communication literature argues that integrity beliefs are one key driver of overall reputation [44]. Reputation, in this regard, is not useful unto itself, but the expectation is that having a reputation as a good corporate citizen might lead to such outcomes as more favorable product evaluations [45], and thus increased sales. Furthermore, the hope might be, companies with such reputations—earned over time—might be better able to withstand ethical problems when and if they occur [46].

Demand for Integrity Information

Evidence suggests nonscientists seem to want integrity information from the scientific community. Political communication researcher Kathleen Hall Jamieson recently helped report that a solid majority of Americans say they want scientists to make their methods and data transparent, disclose funding, and state the peer review status of their work [47]. Sixty-eight percent of Americans said that they want to take scientists' methodological openness into account when judging research, and 63% said that they want to know who funded the research. While we are surprised these numbers are not higher, Jamieson and her coauthors go on to argue that scientists need to find ways to both signal integrity and talk about how new data can change their minds. Part of their argument is that the scientific community could help by making it easier for scientists to report conflicts and change or withdraw papers when inadvertent mistakes are found.

In addition to this direct work, research on CSR similarly suggests that people want companies to be, among other things, transparent and consistent in their reporting while also obtaining third-party endorsement [48]. The responses to the surveys reported at the beginning of this chapter also signal to us that people have concerns about scientists' integrity—especially when it comes to funding [8]—and thus might welcome an effort by science communicators to share all the hard work that goes into to trying to maintain the integrity of the scientific process.

Scientists' Willingness to Prioritize Integrity Objectives and Associated Tactics

As with most other objectives discussed in this book, the scientists we have surveyed seem quite open to prioritizing communication aimed at ensuring that people see them as having integrity. We are therefore not shy about encouraging science communicators to consider devoting time or space to making sure those with whom they are communicating perceive the scientific community as trustworthy. In our 2015–16 survey, we specifically asked about communicating aimed at "demonstrating the scientific community's openness and transparency" and found that assessments of the importance of such communication typically scored in the mid-5 range on 7-point scale (table 4.2). This is slightly lower than the importance score they gave to communicating about how much scientists care about societal well-being (which, as noted, averaged closer to 6 on our 7-point prioritization scale), but it is still quite high in an absolute sense (see appendix B tables).

Agreement about the ethicality of this objective was similarly high, and the scientists appeared to believe that a good communicator could achieve the objective. The average score was closer to 5 (getting closer to the scale midpoint) for the degree to which respondents felt that their peers would prioritize this objective or expect others to prioritize the objective. Respondents were even less likely—with average scores just above the scale midpoint—to say that they felt they had the skills to achieve this objective. The lowest agreement scores tended to be for when we asked respondents to indicate how much

Table 4.2.

Scientists' average assessment of the perceived importance of "demonstrating the scientific community's openness and transparency" and associated beliefs about this objective in the context of different communication channels and different scientific societies (on a scale of 1 to 7)

	Priority[1]	Ethicality[2]	Peer norms[3]	Peer priority[4]	Achievability[5]	My skills[6]	Prior thought[7]	Sample size range
General								
Face-to-face	5.49	5.79	5.15	4.65	5.57	4.77	3.96	369–377
Media	5.51	5.79	5.24	4.76	5.61	4.53	3.86	325–331
Online	5.44	5.65	4.99	4.52	5.49	4.43	3.74	375–384
Biological								
Face-to-face	5.47	5.62	5.13	4.68	5.66	4.81	4.06	345–352
Online	5.59	5.74	5.14	4.69	5.53	4.55	3.79	327–334
Geophysical								
Face-to-face	5.37	5.60	5.18	4.73	5.54	4.94	4.26	313–315
Media	5.44	5.60	5.36	4.78	5.60	4.74	4.09	315–322
Online	5.42	5.55	5.07	4.49	5.41	4.63	4.03	267–275
Geological								
Face-to-face	5.41	5.60	5.13	4.68	5.57	4.98	3.87	244–257
Media	5.53	5.70	5.32	4.81	5.56	4.73	4.03	234–247
Online	5.48	5.66	5.16	4.70	5.54	4.76	4.06	233–239
Ecological								
Face-to-face	5.23	5.73	5.06	4.61	5.60	4.78	4.15	342–347
Chemical								
Face-to-face	5.45	5.54	5.12	4.55	5.54	4.63	3.88	178–184
Media	5.16	5.55	4.93	4.53	5.39	4.37	3.64	157–158
Online	5.31	5.50	4.92	4.30	5.40	4.39	3.63	152–156
Biochemical								
Face-to-face	5.56	5.68	5.17	4.63	5.49	4.60	3.92	365–373
Social								
Media	4.95	5.50	5.05	3.97	5.30	4.92	3.92	874–918

Notes: For the "priority" statement, respondents were given a list of objectives (including the objective noted in the table title) and asked to rate each objective between "very low importance" (1) and "very high importance" (7). For all other statements, respondents selected between "strongly disagree" (1) and "strongly agree" (7). Respondents were all faculty with PhDs at US-based universities. Standard deviations in appendix B tables.

[1] "In general, what are the most important or unimportant communication objectives that scientists such as yourself should have when taking part in [mode*]? Please remember that not every objective can be the most important objective." *Respondents were assigned to see all questions in the context of only one of three potential modes: face-to-face engagement, media engagement, or online engagement.

[2] "This objective is ethical."

[3] "Scientists who pursue this objective would be well regarded by their peers."

[4] "My colleagues would put a high priority on this objective."

[5] "Achieving this objective is possible for a good communicator."

[6] "I have the skills needed to achieve this objective."

[7] "Prior to this survey, I had thought a lot about this potential objective."

they had thought about openness and transparency beliefs as a potential communication objective. In this case, scores were right at the scale midpoint, meaning that about as many of the scientists surveyed agreed that they had thought about the objective as the number who disagreed. What is more, these scores are pretty common across the range of scientific disciplines and channels included in the project (i.e., face-to-face, news media, online).

Unfortunately, we did not include any clear integrity-focused content in our initial study on how scientists think about tactics [49]. The closest thing we had was a section focused on attacking opponents which, as noted earlier, may make people see scientists as having lower levels of integrity [31]. Specifically, our initial tactics study asked respondents how willing they would be "to publicly question the credibility of those who disagree with a scientific consensus. This might mean describing such people as deniers, liars, anti-science, or otherwise criticizing their motives or knowledge." The findings made us a little sad, but they were not surprising given all the vitriol that ostensible science-lovers seem to share on social media in the form of insults directed toward people who (frustratingly, to be sure) question well-established scientific findings—such as the safety of most vaccines or genetically modified food.

We found the average willingness to use an attack as a communication tactic to be in the middle of the 7-point "strongly disagree" to "strongly agree" measure. The bulk of scientists said they had not given much prior thought to this tactic, but they indicated that attacking was ethical, somewhat acceptable to colleagues, and something that might be effective. We hope that future studies find fewer scientists giving these types of answers. And on that note, the next chapter dives into the idea of trying to communicate that scientists are open and willing to listen to others' views. This dimension of trustworthiness does not appear in the literature as often as benevolence (i.e., warmth) and integrity but is key to researching the fairness of decision-making procedures. Like integrity, we see openness-related beliefs as an objective all communicators should consider and one where there may be substantial room for improvement.

Preparing to Prioritize Integrity Beliefs as a Communication Objective

The following are eight questions that science communicators should consider when deciding whether to prioritize demonstrating integrity as a communication objective. In many cases, integrity-related communication might involve sharing information about actions taken to ensure that people can believe in the validity of results, including ensuring and communicating efforts to avoid conflicts of interest and otherwise protect the integrity of the scientific process.

THE GOAL QUESTION

1. Given the behavior you want from your specific audience (i.e., your goal), why do you think it would be helpful if your chosen audience saw you as honest or high in integrity?

THE PREPARATION QUESTIONS

2. What does your chosen audience believe about your integrity and is there meaningful room to improve?
3. What do you believe about your audience's integrity?

THE TACTICS QUESTIONS

4. What could you do to potentially increase the likelihood that those with whom you are communicating see you as high in integrity, including choices about messages, behaviors, tone/style, communication channel, and communication source?
5. What could you do to learn about your chosen audience's integrity?

THE EVALUATION QUESTIONS

6. Did your chosen audience perceive you as honest or otherwise high in integrity?
7. What did you learn about your audience's integrity?

THE ETHICS QUESTION

8. Are you being honest about your integrity? (And, yes, we see the irony in this question.)

REFERENCES

1. Vogel, Gretchen. "Picking up the Pieces after Hwang." *Science* 312, no. 5773 (2006): 516. https://doi.org/10.1126/science.312.5773.516.

2. Merton, Robert K. *The Sociology of Science: Theoretical and Empirical Investigations*. Chicago: University of Chicago Press, 1973.

3. Fiske, Susan T., and Cydney Dupree. "Gaining Trust as Well as Respect in Communicating to Motivated Audiences About Science Topics." *Proceedings of the National Academy of Sciences* 111, Supplement 4 (2014): 13593–97. https://doi.org/10.1073/pnas.1317505111.

4. National Science Board. *Science and Engineering Indicators*. Accessed October 4, 2021, https://ncses.nsf.gov/indicators.

5. Besley, John C., and Derek Hill. "Science and Technology: Public Attitudes, Knowledge, and Interest." In *Science and Engineering Indicators 2020*. Alexandria, VA: National Science Foundation, May 2020. https://ncses.nsf.gov/pubs/nsb20207. (John served as the primary author on this chapter of the *Science and Engineering Indicators* for the 2014, 2016, 2018, and 2020 editions.)

6. National Opinion Research Center. *The General Social Survey*. Accessed October 29, 2019. http://gss.norc.org.

7. Funk, Cary, and Meg Hefferon. "Most Americans Have Positive Image of Research Scientists, but Fewer See Them as Good Communicators." Pew Research Center, August 19, 2019. https://www.pewresearch.org/fact-tank/2019/08/19/most-americans-have-positive-image-of-research-scientists-but-fewer-see-them-as-good-communicators.

8. Gallup. *Wellcome Global Monitor: First Wave Findings*. London: Wellcome Trust, 2019. https://wellcome.ac.uk/sites/default/files/wellcome-global-monitor-2018.pdf.

9. Mayer, Roger C., James H. Davis, and F. David Schoorman. "An Integrative Model of Organizational Trust." *Academy of Management Review* 20, no. 3 (1995): 709–34. https://doi.org/10.5465/AMR.1995.9508080335.

10. Cuddy, Amy J. C., Susan T. Fiske, and Peter Glick. "Warmth and Competence as Universal Dimensions of Social Perception: The Stereotype Content Model and the BIAS Map." In *Advances in Experimental Social Psychology*, vol. 40, edited by Mark P. Zanna, 61–149. Cambridge, MA: Academic Press, 2008.

11. Wojciszke, Bogdan, and Andrea E. Abele. "The Primacy of Communion over Agency and Its Reversals in Evaluations." *European Journal of Social Psychology* 38, no. 7 (2008): 1139–47. https://doi.org/10.1002/ejsp.549.

12. McCroskey, James C., and Thomas J. Young. "Ethos and Credibility: The Construct and Its Measurement after Three Decades." *Central States Speech Journal* 32, no. 1 (1981): 24–34. https://doi.org/10.1080/10510978109368075.

13. Rosenberg, S. "A Multidimensional Approach to the Structure of Personality Impressions." *Journal of Personality and Social Psychology* 9, no. 4 (1968): 283–94. https://doi.org/10.1037/h0026086.

14. Besley, John C., Nicole M. Lee, and Geah Pressgrove. "Reassessing the Variables Used to Measure Public Perceptions of Scientists." *Science Communication* 43, no. 1 (2021): 3–32. https://doi.org/10.1177/1075547020949547.

15. Hendriks, Friederike, Dorothe Kienhues, and Rainer Bromme. "Measuring Laypeople's Trust in Experts in a Digital Age: The Muenster Epistemic Trustworthiness Inventory (METI)." *PLOS ONE* 10, no. 10 (2015): e0139309. https://doi.org /10.1371/journal.pone.0139309.

16. Wojciszke, Bogdan, Roza Bazinska, and Marcin Jaworski. "On the Dominance of Moral Categories in Impression Formation." *Personality and Social Psychology Bulletin* 24, no. 12 (1998): 1251–63. https://doi.org/10.1177/014616729 82412001.

17. Marshall, Eliot. "In the Wake of Scathing Review of Fracking Report, University of Texas Revises Conflict of Interest Policies." *Science*, December 7, 2012. https://www.science.org/content/article/wake-scathing-review-fracking -report-university-texas-revises-conflict-interest-rev2.

18. McEvily, Bill, and Marco Tortoriello. "Measuring Trust in Organisational Research: Review and Recommendations." *Journal of Trust Research* 1, no. 1 (2011), 23–63. https://doi.org/10.1080/21515581.2011.552424.

19. PytlikZillig, Lisa M., Joseph A. Hamm, Ellie Shockley, Mitchel N. Herian, Tess M. S. Neal, Christopher D. Kimbrough, Alan J. Tomkins, and Brian H. Bornstein. "The Dimensionality of Trust-Relevant Constructs in Four Institutional Domains: Results from Confirmatory Factor Analyses." *Journal of Trust Research* 6, no. 2 (2016): 111–50. https://doi.org/10.1080/21515581.2016.1151359.

20. Besley, John C., Anthony Dudo, Shupei Yuan, and Niveen AbiGhannam. "Qualitative Interviews with Science Communication Trainers About Communication Objectives and Goals." *Science Communication* 38, no. 3 (2016): 356–81. https://doi.org/10.1177/1075547016645640.

21. Field, Marilyn J., and Bernard Lo, eds. *Conflict of Interest in Medical Research, Education, and Practice*. Washington, DC: National Academies Press, 2009.

22. Lipton, Eric. "Food Industry Enlisted Academics in G.M.O. Lobbying War, Emails Show." *New York Times*, September 5, 2015. https://www.nytimes.com/2015 /09/06/us/food-industry-enlisted-academics-in-gmo-lobbying-war-emails-show .html.

23. Strom, Stephanie. "National Biotechnology Panel Faces New Conflict of Interest Questions." *New York Times*, December 27, 2016. https://www.nytimes .com/2016/12/27/business/national-academies-biotechnology-conflicts.html.

24. Besley, John C., Aaron M. McCright, Nagwan R. Zahry, Kevin C. Elliott, Norbert E. Kaminski, and Joseph D. Martin. "Perceived Conflict of Interest in Health Science Partnerships." *PLOS ONE* 12, no. 4 (2017): e0175643. https://doi.org /10.1371/journal.pone.0175643.

25. Licurse, Adam, Emma Barber, Steve Joffe, and Cary Gross. "The Impact of Disclosing Financial Ties in Research and Clinical Care: A Systematic Review." *Archives of Internal Medicine* 170, no. 8 (2010): 675–82. https://doi.org/10.1001 /archinternmed.2010.39.

26. Kesselheim, Aaron S., Christopher T. Robertson, Jessica A. Myers, Susannah L. Rose, Victoria Gillet, Kathryn M. Ross, Robert J. Glynn, Steven Joffe, and Jerry Avorn. "A Randomized Study of How Physicians Interpret Research

Funding Disclosures." *New England Journal of Medicine* 367, no. 12 (2012): 1119–27. https://doi.org/10.1056/NEJMsa1202397.

27. Hampson, Lindsay, Manish Agrawal, Steven Joffe, Cary P. Gross, Joel Verter, and Ezekiel J. Emanuel. "Patients' Views on Financial Conflicts of Interest in Cancer Research Trials." *New England Journal of Medicine* 355, no. 22 (2006): 2330–7.

28. Sah, Sunita, Prashant Malaviya, and Debora Thompson. "Conflict of Interest Disclosure as an Expertise Cue: Differential Effects Due to Automatic Versus Deliberative Processing." *Organizational Behavior and Human Decision Processes* 147 (July 2018): 127–46. https://doi.org/10.1016/j.obhdp.2018.05.008.

29. Schlosser, Ann E., Tiffany Barnett White, and Susan M. Lloyd. "Converting Web Site Visitors into Buyers: How Web Site Investment Increases Consumer Trusting Beliefs and Online Purchase Intentions." *Journal of Marketing* 70, no. 2 (2006): 133–48. https://doi.org/10.1509/jmkg.70.2.133.

30. Gardner, William L. "Perceptions of Leader Charisma, Effectiveness, and Integrity: Effects of Exemplification, Delivery, and Ethical Reputation." *Management Communication Quarterly* 16, no. 4 (2003): 502–27. https://doi.org/10.1177/0893318903251324.

31. König, Lars, and Regina Jucks. "Hot Topics in Science Communication: Aggressive Language Decreases Trustworthiness and Credibility in Scientific Debates." *Public Understanding of Science* 28, no. 4 (2019): 401–16. https://doi.org/10.1177/0963662519833903.

32. Yuan, Shupei, John C. Besley, and Wenjuan Ma. "Be Mean or Be Nice? Understanding the Effects of Aggressive and Polite Communication Styles in Child Vaccination Debate." *Health Communication* 34, no. 10 (2019): 1212–21. https://doi.org/10.1080/10410236.2018.1471337.

33. Yuan, Shupei, Wenjuan Ma, and John C. Besley. "Should Scientists Talk About GMOs Nicely? Exploring the Effects of Communication Styles, Source Expertise, and Preexisting Attitude." *Science Communication* 41, no. 3 (2019): 267–90. https://doi.org/10.1177/1075547019837623.

34. Yuan, Shupei, John C. Besley, and Chen Lou. "Does Being a Jerk Work? Examining the Effect of Aggressive Risk Communication in the Context of Science Blogs." *Journal of Risk Research* 21, no. 4 (2018): 502–20. https://doi.org/10.1080/13669877.2016.1223159.

35. Saffran, Lise, Sisi Hu, Amanda Hinnant, Laura D. Scherer, and Susan C. Nagel. "Constructing and Influencing Perceived Authenticity in Science Communication: Experimenting with Narrative." *PLOS ONE* 15, no. 1 (2020): e0226711. https://doi.org/10.1371/journal.pone.0226711.

36. Kim, Peter H., Donald L. Ferrin, Cecily D. Cooper, and Kurt T. Dirks. "Removing the Shadow of Suspicion: The Effects of Apology Versus Denial for Repairing Competence- Versus Integrity-Based Trust Violations." *Journal of Applied Psychology* 89, no. 1 (2004): 104–18. https://doi.org/10.1037/0021-9010.89.1.104.

37. Ferrin, Donald L. "Silence Speaks Volumes: The Effectiveness of Reticence in Comparison to Apology and Denial for Responding to Integrity- and

Competence-Based Trust Violations." *Journal of Applied Psychology* 92, no. 4 (2007): 893–908. https://doi.org/10.1037/0021-9010.92.4.893.

38. Sisco, Hilary Fussell. "Nonprofit in Crisis: An Examination of the Applicability of Situational Crisis Communication Theory." *Journal of Public Relations Research* 24, no. 1 (2012): 1–17. https://doi.org/10.1080/1062726x.2011.582207.

39. Coombs, W. Timothy. *Ongoing Crisis Communication: Planning, Managing, and Responding.* 3rd ed. Thousand Oaks, CA: Sage, 2012.

40. Gillespie, Nicole, and Sabina Siebert. "Organizational Trust Repair." In *The Routledge Companion to Trust,* edited by Rosalind H. Searle, Ann-Marie I. Nienaber, and Sim B. Sitkin, 284–301. New York: Routledge, 2018.

41. Jahn, Johannes, and Rolf Brühl. "Can Bad News Be Good? On the Positive and Negative Effects of Including Moderately Negative Information in CSR Disclosures." *Journal of Business Research* 97 (April 2019): 117–28. https://doi.org/10.1016/j.jbusres.2018.12.070.

42. Schoorman, F. David, Roger C. Mayer, and James H. Davis. "An Integrative Model of Organizational Trust: Past, Present, and Future." *Academy of Management Review* 32, no. 2 (2007): 344–54. https://doi.org/10.2307/20159304.

43. Chaudhry, Samena, Sara Schroter, Richard Smith, and Julie Morris. "Does Declaration of Competing Interests Affect Readers' Perceptions? A Randomised Trial." *BMJ* 325, no. 7377 (2002): 1391–92. https://doi.org/10.1136/bmj.325.7377.1391.

44. Park, Jongchul, Hanjoon Lee, and Chankon Kim. "Corporate Social Responsibilities, Consumer Trust, and Corporate Reputation: South Korean Consumers' Perspectives." *Journal of Business Research* 67, no. 3 (2014): 295–302. https://doi.org/10.1016/j.jbusres.2013.05.016.

45. Kim, Sora. "Transferring Effects of CSR Strategy on Consumer Responses: The Synergistic Model of Corporate Communication Strategy." *Journal of Public Relations Research* 23, no. 2 (2011): 218–41. https://doi.org/10.1080/1062726x.2011.555647.

46. Vanhamme, Joëlle, and Bas Grobben. "'Too Good to Be True!': The Effectiveness of CSR History in Countering Negative Publicity." *Journal of Business Ethics* 85, no. 2 (2008): 273. https://doi.org/10.1007/s10551-008-9731-2.

47. Jamieson, Kathleen Hall, Marcia McNutt, Veronique Kiermer, and Richard Sever. "Signaling the Trustworthiness of Science." *Proceedings of the National Academy of Sciences* 116, no. 39 (2019): 19231–36. https://doi.org/10.1073/pnas.1913039116.

48. Kim, Sora, and Mary Ann T. Ferguson. "Dimensions of Effective CSR Communication Based on Public Expectations." *Journal of Marketing Communications* 24, no. 6 (2018): 549–67. https://doi.org/10.1080/13527266.2015.1118143.

49. Besley, John C., Kathryn O'Hara, and Anthony Dudo. "Strategic Science Communication as Planned Behavior: Understanding Scientists' Willingness to Choose Specific Tactics." *PLOS ONE* 14, no. 10 (2019): e0224039. https://doi.org/10.1371/journal.pone.0224039.

5

Be Willing to Listen

WE GENTLY CRITIQUED THE ALAN ALDA Center for Communicating Science (which we quite like) in chapter 2 for sometimes suggesting that successful science communication is about being "clear and vivid" (which is also the name of Alda's podcast). One thing we appreciate about this strategy, though, is they put paying close attention to audiences at the core of their work. Their training draws heavily on improvisational theater games to get scientists to communicate in a way that makes sense to the specific people whom the scientist is trying to reach. However, while the Alda focus on audience attention is sometimes couched as a way to increase the likelihood of knowledge transfer, it is also clear the Alda team is committed to helping scientists truly empathize with others.

We initially considered including the concept of empathy as part our chapter on warmth, but in reading more about the concept—one we have not directly studied—we came to see empathy beliefs and empathetic behavior as being about truly listening rather than just showing warmth. It is not hard to imagine, for example, someone who appears to care deeply about others but who does not seem especially good at listening to what others need. A do-gooder showing up in a crisis with all the best intentions but who is, in fact, clueless as to what the people actually want or need. Ronald Reagan memorably said, "The nine most terrifying words in the English language are 'I'm from the government, and I'm here to help'" [1].

Similarly, it also seems possible to imagine perceiving someone as good at listening but not believing that the person is especially warm or caring. A stereotypical financial analyst or lawyer who is motivated to make informed decisions might fit this description. The behaviors underlying the differences between these two types are sometimes called cognitive versus affective (or emotional) empathy [2], but at the core of both types is the capacity to understand what others might be experiencing. Perceived empathy is the perception that one person understands what another person is thinking and feeling [3]. Training probably cannot make everyone truly empathetic—that would be difficult given that empathy seems to be partly genetic and partly developed through longer-term socialization [4]—but training does seem able to help many people, like scientists, demonstrate their existing capacity for empathy, including the degree to which they project that empathy to others. Indeed, Stanford University professor Jamil Zaki's book *The War for Kindness* makes a powerful argument that many of us can learn the skill of empathy [5]. This type of training objective is consistent with substantial discussions in medical training [6] and the Alda Center's effort to help medical students at Stony Brook University improve their communication with patients and caregivers.

While we appreciate the empathy literature, research on "procedural fairness as voice" is what truly drives us to believe that science communicators should focus attention on ensuring people see the science community as willing to listen to others' views. This body of research from the social psychology of fairness perceptions clearly shows that people feel more satisfied and accepting of many decisions—even decisions they disagree with—when they believe there was a meaningful opportunity to have their perspective heard during a decision-making process [7,8]. That is, it is possible to *accept* a decision as having been made in a legitimate way without necessarily supporting the decision itself.

Legal scholar Laurens Walker and social psychologist John Thibaut reported their classic studies on procedural justice in a 1975 book that included such methods as mock trials to understand what makes people see legal trials as fair [9]. Their conclusion was that participants and observers were more likely to see dispute resolutions (e.g., a trial or arbitration) as fair if both sides had the ability to exert a degree of control over the process. This could include, for example, the ability to put their own best argument and evidence forward. The view that people care about process challenges the idea that people only care about the fairness of outcomes (i.e., distributive justice), and a range of scholars have built on this initial argument that having a meaningful voice [10] in decision-making processes matters in a range of fields.

The work appears to have been especially useful in organizational [11] and policing [12] contexts because the work shows the value of paying attention to whether people feel like they can speak up for themselves and be heard. Fairness researcher Tom Tyler has done extensive work showing that the way police officers and judges treat suspects is central to policing being perceived as legitimate, even among those who end up going to jail [13]. Being heard, in this regard, requires a belief that the decision-maker is not unduly biased against them (as well as respectful). Paying attention often means ensuring the existence of quality procedures, including quality people to manage those procedures. The scientific community may not face the same depth of challenges as the justice system, but it still needs to find ways to continue to address its own deep history of racism, sexism, and other forms of oppression if we want people to make use of scientific evidence [14]. Finding a way for people—especially people from traditionally marginalized groups—to believe that they (or people like them) have a voice seems like a central element of ensuring society can benefit from science.

Why Treat Willingness to Listen as Separate from Integrity or Warmth?

We treat being perceived as willing to listen as a separate trust-worthiness-related objective from warmth and integrity beliefs with the full recognition that these concepts are likely to be linked both in people's minds (i.e., their evaluative beliefs) and in the real world [15]. As noted, it is hard—but not impossible—to imagine someone who seems to lack either warmth or integrity but could still be perceived as a good listener. We would argue that any good listening process must include at least some attention to all three elements—as well as other trustworthiness-related beliefs, such as competence—but we also think the tactics that communicators could use to enact and demonstrate listening are distinct enough that strategists should prioritize them separately. These tactics might include simple things, such as ensuring adequate time for questions and discussion, but they might also include more complex methods, such as creating a range of real (and visible) opportunities for hearing from a range of different voices or creating feedback mechanisms to show how input from stakeholders is regularly and continuously affecting decision-making.

John's dissertation research highlighted the challenge and importance of distinguishing between willingness-to-listen beliefs and other trustworthiness-related beliefs. This work—completed under the supervision of Katherine McComas, now the vice provost responsible for engagement at Cornell University—involved research into community meetings at which local people listened to the results of epidemiological research into whether public health authorities had found any evidence of elevated cancer rates in their community [16–18]. Cancer's ubiquity means that residents may believe that their community is seeing elevated rates and can point to potential local causes, but health authorities rarely find compelling evidence that allows them to say that a cluster is anything more than random chance. This does not mean that health authorities do not investigate potential clusters carefully, but the nature of the scientific process means they cannot substantially control the outcome of their investigation. One of the few things they can control is the degree to which they manage the investigation process in a way that tries to ensure local communities experience at least some satisfaction with the investigation process.

The research on community meetings about cancer clusters demonstrated the importance of fair process—including both perceived voice and perceived respectfulness of health authorities, both of which were highly correlated [16]. What struck John was that newspaper coverage of the cancer clusters often seemed to suggest that the reason public health officials were not doing more to respond to community concerns was that they did not care enough about the communities [18]. In other words, it is important to recognize that while perceptions about being willing to listen may represent conceptually unique objectives, we would also fully expect that people who do not feel listened to are likely to infer reasons for that lack of attention. Thus, putting a priority on listening seems integral to building trustworthiness-related beliefs. Ultimately, we recognize that current trust researchers typically do not treat perceived willingness to listen as distinct from benevolence, warmth, or integrity, but we still treat it here as a separate construct for discussing communication strategy. Our own research on trustworthiness perceptions in the context of communication suggests this makes at least some sense [15].

Communicating Willingness to Listen

A primary practical reason we suggest specifically prioritizing communicating willingness to listen is because such beliefs seem like a key initial outcome of so many of the tactics underlying effective science communication. Indeed, Martin Bauer's historical overview of the field emphasizes his belief that we are now in an era where it is important to look at the effect of dialogue on a range of outcomes (including behavior) rather than focus on how increasing knowledge impacts outcomes (such as attitudes and behavior) [19]. As noted earlier in the book, a mistake many people seem to make is to view dialogue as an objective when it is actually a tactic that can lead to a range of objectives [20], including perceptions about willingness to listen. In other words, one likely outcome of participating in high-quality dialogue—or even believing that one *could participate*, if desired [21]—is providing people a sense of their own voice. We often talk about this "sense of voice" as evaluative beliefs about the degree to which the scientific community seems willing to listen.

Cornell University wildlife researchers Bruce Lauber and Barbara Knuth conducted one early set of studies that suggests the ability of public participation activities to provide people with a belief in their own voice in the context of science . . . and moose [22,23]. They did their research in the early 1990s just after an extensive multiyear effort by New York's Department of Environmental Quality (DEQ) to get feedback on the possibility of accelerating the rate of moose return to the Adirondack Mountains. One part of the project involved a mail survey of people who had commented on the issue by either attending one of 15 public meetings, submitted written comments, or responded to a telephone survey. A total of 758 people took part, and Lauber and Knuth's data suggest that the people who were more satisfied with the process (and the final decision) were those who tended to believe the DEQ had been receptive to public comment and had done their best to provide a process in which citizens' views could be heard. These results were similar to what John has found studying public meetings about cancer clusters [16] and nuclear energy decision-making processes [24] but also similarly limited in that they all involved looking at the pattern of relationships within cross-sectional (i.e., one-time public) opinion surveys. To get at causality, it is not enough to say that participants are more likely to believe they were listened to. It is also important to do experiments where some people are given a voice and others are not. These types of studies do not seem to regularly occur within the context of scientific topics.

One exception might be the risk research done by Joe Arvai, now at the University of Southern California. For example, in 2010 he published a social science experiment focused on NASA's decision to use plutonium to power their Cassini satellite and the concern about potential consequences of an accident. The experiment involved randomly assigning participants into two groups, one of which learned about the Cassini mission through an information packet describing the planning process as involving both public and expert voice, whereas the second group received nearly identical information except that the planning process was described as being done exclusively by experts. The results were what we might expect; those who saw a packet that indicated the mission was designed with public input saw more benefits and were more in favor of the mission and satisfied with the decision-making process [25].

Later research by Arvai suggests that it is important to ensure that people experience good process before decisions get made. Even so, his work shows that the benefit of providing voice does not necessarily mean that people will not get upset if a decision goes against their preferences [26]. Such results echo research in social psychology that shows that the quality of procedures is unlikely to have much impact on how people see decisions where they have moral certainty about the correct outcome. For example, no amount of perceived listening is likely to make someone who strongly opposes abortion fully happy with a decision-making process that allows abortion [27]. However, not all science decisions seem quite so central to morality debates. It is important to remember you can try to give people direct or mediated experiences with a process before any final decision is made. The hope is that people might be more willing to develop beliefs about the quality of process before learning about the outcomes of the process.

Fairness researcher Kees van den Bos and his colleagues conducted a set of experiments in the mid-1990s on this type of question in the context of applying for a job [28]. In an initial study, participating Dutch students first read a scenario in which they were asked to imagine applying for a job and being selected to take part in a nine-part selection process, including a series of tests and an interview. The scenario described whether the hypothetical applicant was offered the job as well as whether the interview process went fairly. The results showed that fair process only really affected students who learned about the process before learning about whether they were offered a job.

A second study by van den Bos found the same thing using an actual task (estimating the number of squares in a series of images) in which students were told that they were assessed either fairly or unfairly and that they either succeeded or failed. Again, the fairness of the assessment only seemed to matter for students who were told about the quality of the process prior to the outcome. The results led van den Bos to propose that fair process works best in contexts where people are uncertain about the correct outcome and must therefore rely on process cues to begin making judgments [29]. This argument helps explain why process quality is unlikely to affect people who already feel morally certain about an issue. It also highlights that we can communicate fair process through both what we tell people (the first experiment) and how we treat people (the second experiment).

One formative thing about John's dissertation research was that it involved traveling to public meetings around the country to hear about the results of cancer cluster investigations. One such meeting occurred in Southampton, Massachusetts, in an old-style meeting room that looked straight out of a Norman Rockwell painting. The first half of the meeting involved a fairly typical report on the investigation; what struck John was the second half during which the two researchers from the state public health department sat on top of some tables and talked with the local residents. The way these two researchers interacted with local residents left no question in John's mind that they had already spent hours talking to people and being shown behind barns in search of potential sources of a pollutant (trichloroethylene) that the residents were worried was contaminating the local aquifer. Moreover, the two researchers seemed eager for any additional information that residents were willing to provide.

The second example of good listening John often describes is a series of meetings hosted by the federal Nuclear Regulatory Commission (NRC) in 2008 as part of an effort to build two new nuclear reactors just north of Columbia, South Carolina, in a relatively poor area with low levels of education and a relatively high proportion of African

Americans. The project was ultimately a disaster because of cost overruns and technical failures, but the NRC's hearing process impressed John in its focus on ensuring that local residents could comment on the proposed site. The process included the traditional opportunity to comment by standing up and talking at a public meeting, but attendees also were offered the option of providing written comments or either oral or video-taped conferences in a private room. Furthermore, the African American meeting facilitator from the NRC made a point of talking about how they would use and respond to the comments and made sure to work with local leaders, including pastors, to share information about the project.

This second story is especially important because it highlights the NRC's recognition that giving people a single opportunity to comment does not necessarily mean you have truly given people a meaningful voice [30]. Not everyone is going to stand up at a public meeting and share their perspective, so ethical and smart communicators work hard to provide multiple opportunities for people to share their views. A range of circumstances that includes current and past systematic racism, sexism, and classism more often means that not everyone has equal opportunity or ability to devote time and other resources to sharing their views. We know from decades of research on "intergroup contact" that interaction between different types of people can help develop positive impressions but only if the interactions are designed so they provide positive, meaningful experiences [31]. Those who face regular discrimination may conclude that it is not worth their effort to participate in dialogue exercises that enable such connections to get made. Science and technology studies professor Emily Dawson is perhaps the most well-known name in the informal science education and science communication research community highlighting the challenges faced by racialized and minoritized groups when they interact with the scientific community. Talking largely about informal science education (e.g., museums, public events), she writes, "We need to do more than tweak staff training or marketing materials if we want everyday science learning to be truly public. We need to radically overhaul the systems, practices and ways of thinking that shape everyday science learning" [32, p. 155]. We take this as a call to recognize the added onus on the scientific community—a community with high power and privilege in society—to take steps to actively ensure fair access to the opportunity to be truly heard. Only then can one hope that people will see scientists as willing to listen.

While this chapter is about trying to convince science communicators to consider prioritizing willingness-to-listen beliefs when they communicate, we also recognize there is a wide range of guidance aimed at helping leaders listen more effectively that is beyond our scope. For example, social work professor Brené Brown has published a range of books and other media on being courageous, vulnerable, and empathetic in giving and accepting feedback [33], while Jamil Zaki has highlighted concrete steps that organizations can take to make empathy more likely, including both training and organizational procedures [5]. Similarly, concepts such as active listening and patient-centered communication [34] have emerged to organize discussions around improving people's ability to listen to the views of others [35].

What Does Demonstrating a Willingness to Listen Affect?

A primary outcome of being seen as willing to listen to others' views is that people seem more willing to accept decisions they believe have been arrived at fairly (i.e., via procedural fairness). Ethically, getting an opportunity to learn others' views (and thus make better decisions) could be seen as a sufficient outcome (i.e., a goal described in chapter 1) to justify prioritizing listening, but our focus here is on the fact that being *perceived* as willing to listen has its own benefits for science communicators who want their advice considered. In John's early research in South Carolina, for example, one study compared the statistical predictors of favoring nuclear expansion in comparison to the statistical predictors of perceived decision legitimacy after a nuclear expansion decision-making process. What he found was that people's perceptions of whether they would get a fair share of the benefits and risks (chapter 8) of the new plant predicted support, but perceived voice was among the best statistical predictors of perceived decision legitimacy [24]. The central role of procedural perceptions in predicting an outcome similar to legitimacy or satisfaction is also described in Lauber and Knuth's study on moose [23] and Arvai's study on NASA's Cassini satellite [25].

Another useful study from outside the scientific space saw communication researcher John Gastil and his colleagues test the impact of jury deliberation on local election voting [36]. To do the study, the researchers used court records to find the names of 794 people who had participated in 110 criminal trials in one Washington State county over two years in the mid-1990s. They also went to the county's voter registration office and recorded whether those 794 people voted in the subsequent general election. What the team found was that people whose jury experience involved coming to a decision on the case were about 10% more likely to vote than people whose experience involved serving as an alternate, on a trial that ended early with a plea deal, or even on a hung jury. The number of charges, debate, and past voting history also mattered, but the length of the trial and length of jury deliberation did not. Gastil and his collaborators argued that this result is consistent with the idea that having a demonstrable voice in politics can lead people to become more attached to their political system. For us, this again speaks more broadly to the value of making sure people feel listened to when the goal is to enhance support for an existing system.

Demand for Listening

It may seem obvious that people want to feel listened to, so community-meeting organizers may therefore wonder why they see the same people over and over. Where is everyone if there is such a demand to be heard? A 2016 poll by the Pew Research Center indicated that only about 12% of Americans had been to a community meeting in the previous 12 months, while another 27% said that they had been to such a meeting at some point prior to the last 12 months [37]. And while people have many reasons for not attending meetings [38], political scientists John Hibbing and Elizabeth Theiss-Morse provided a now-classic argument that many—perhaps most—Americans are not especially interested in most policy debates and would often prefer experts (including politicians) to collaborate to come up with the best solution. At the same time, what Americans really want is to be "certain that if they ever did deign to get involved, if an issue at some point in the future happened to impinge so directly on their lives that they were moved to ask the system for something, elected officials would respond to their request with the utmost seriousness" [21, p. 131]. In practice, Hibbing and Theiss-Morse express concern that Americans' desire to shield themselves from having to participate in politics risks exposing them to undemocratic tendencies, but for our purpose, we simply want to highlight the point that it makes sense for science communicators to prioritize sharing information about their willingness to listen when it is also clear that people value being listened to by such people as their bosses [39] and doctors [40].

Scientists' Willingness to Prioritize Listening and Associated Tactics

Although the scientific community seems open to communication efforts aimed at ensuring people are heard (and thus communicate a willingness to listen), it is just not yet an objective many scientists have thought about and prioritized, especially when compared to other objectives. One might argue that our 2015–16 scientist surveys had two sets of questions focused on the idea of listening. In the previous chapter, we described how scientists felt about openness and transparency in the context of integrity. And we noted the difficulty of disentangling concepts such as integrity and a willingness to listen at the start of this chapter, but what needs highlighting here is the big difference between how the surveyed scientists rated the importance of "demonstrating the scientific community's openness and transparency" (table 4.1) versus how they rated the importance of "hearing what others think about scientific issues" (table 5.1) (see also appendix B tables).

Table 5.1.

Scientists' average assessment of the perceived importance of "hearing what others think about scientific issues" and associated beliefs about this objective in the context of different communication channels and different scientific societies (on a scale of 1 to 7)

	Priority[1]	Ethicality[2]	Peer norms[3]	Peer priority[4]	Achievability[5]	My skills[6]	Prior thought[7]	Sample size range
General								
Face-to-face	5.17	5.68	4.65	4.13	5.54	4.85	3.96	369–380
Media	4.84	5.64	4.67	4.10	5.42	5.4.4	3.76	318–331
Online	4.85	5.47	4.42	3.99	5.39	4.47	3.67	374–384
Biological								
Face-to-face	5.23	5.56	4.71	4.18	5.61	4.96	4.02	345–353
Online	5.15	5.57	4.70	4.18	5.39	4.71	3.83	324–333
Geophysical								
Face-to-face	4.89	5.58	4.45	3.98	5.57	5.03	4.06	312–316
Media	4.72	5.38	4.57	3.94	5.40	4.71	3.89	315–321
Online	4.76	5.35	4.36	3.76	5.29	4.56	3.58	268–275
Geological								
Face-to-face	4.93	5.52	4.55	4.03	5.55	5.02	4.04	243–255
Media	4.90	5.46	4.59	4.31	5.40	4.83	3.87	235–248
Online	4.89	5.31	4.54	4.19	5.41	4.71	3.98	229–239
Ecological								
Face-to-face	4.83	5.74	4.48	3.97	5.65	4.92	4.23	340–349
Chemical								
Face-to-face	4.93	5.49	4.61	4.12	5.44	4.78	3.91	181–189
Media	4.79	5.28	4.42	3.93	5.30	4.46	3.50	158–159
Online	4.98	5.30	4.53	3.94	5.38	4.58	3.46	152–156
Biochemical								
Face-to-face	5.10	5.47	4.55	4.05	5.48	4.69	3.83	366–374
Social								
Media	4.47	5.36	4.37	4.40	5.04	4.86	3.67	867–918

Notes: For the "priority" statement, respondents were given a list of objectives (including the objective noted in the table title) and asked to rate each objective between "very low importance" (1) and "very high importance" (7). For all other statements, respondents selected between "strongly disagree" (1) and "strongly agree" (7). Respondents were all faculty with PhDs at US-based universities. Standard deviations in appendix B tables.

[1] "In general, what are the most important or unimportant communication objectives that scientists such as yourself should have when taking part in [mode*]? Please remember that not every objective can be the most important objective." *Respondents were assigned to see all questions in the context of only one of three potential modes: face-to-face engagement, media engagement, or online engagement.

[2] "This objective is ethical."

[3] "Scientists who pursue this objective would be well regarded by their peers."

[4] "My colleagues would put a high priority on this objective."

[5] "Achieving this objective is possible for a good communicator."

[6] "I have the skills needed to achieve this objective."

[7] "Prior to this survey, I had thought a lot about this potential objective."

While scientists gave the objective of being seen as open and transparent a score just below 5.5 on our 7-point "very low importance" to "very high importance" measure, the importance score for "hearing what others think" was often about a half-point lower, almost always just below 5.0 on the 7-point scale. This means "hearing" was in the bottom tier of objectives, along with those related to demonstrating that scientists share the public's values (chapter 6) and demonstrating competence (chapter 7). On the other hand, the scientists surveyed generally thought that the objective of hearing from others was ethical and possible for a good communicator (average scores were in the mid-5s for each). They were less sure that their colleagues had thought about the objective or would themselves see hearing from others as important (average scores were in the mid-4s). They also were less sure about whether they had the skills to achieve this objective (average scores were between about 4.5 and 5.0).

When we modeled what might predict higher importance ratings for the hearing objective, we found that the best predictors were whether the scientist had previously thought about the objective (which many had not) and whether the scientist regarded hearing from others as being ethical (which most did) [41]. The degree to which scientists said they believed that their colleagues would prioritize hearing from others was also a substantive predictor in several samples. Practically, we might take this to mean that anyone who wants to get science communicators to place a higher priority on this objective might want to make sure scientists have thought about the objective and that they see it as ethical.

Keen observers may note that the question used to assess the "hearing what others think about scientific issues" objective looks slightly differently than most of the other objectives about which we asked. The hearing objective question, in this regard, asks about actually "hearing what others think" whereas the other questions focus on trying to ensure scientists are perceived in a certain way. So we worry about concluding from our 2015–16 surveys that scientists rate hearing from others as a relatively low-priority objective. We *are* comfortable saying that we had hoped this objective would have ranked higher among the list of objectives. It represents an objective that involves more than just perception and seems like a key outcome given the emphasis the science communication research community has placed on dialogue [42]. Specifically, we had hoped that scientists would put more priority on actually hearing from other people than on demonstrating openness and transparency or being seen as caring.

On a more positive note, our Canadian survey that focused on how scientists think about communication tactics [43] found that ensuring stakeholders "feel listened to" fared quite well, receiving an average score of 5.23 on the 7-point scale (a 7 meant that the scientists "strongly agreed" that they would "be willing to make this choice"). The Canadian scientists also saw this tactic as highly ethical, useful, and something that they had the ability to do (mean scores well above 5 out of 7). They were less sure if their colleagues would prioritize this tactic or expect the tactic to be prioritized (mean below 5 out of 7). The real surprise for us was how little scientists indicated they had thought much about such a tactic. The agreement score for the statement "prior to this survey I had thought a lot about this choice" was just 3.73, suggesting that ensuring that people feel heard was not something on scientists' minds.

Looking Forward

We would like more science communicators to actively prioritize both listening to people and ensuring that people feel listened to. Overall, the results in this chapter and the previous chapter on integrity beliefs are probably the ones where we are most excited about future work. The potential value of putting more attention on being perceived as open to scrutiny and others' perspective seems integral to ensuring a positive reputation for science, and ensuring that such a reputation is well deserved. Prioritizing hearing from others also represents a goal that might directly benefit the scientific community inasmuch as it allows the possibility of learning, which might help scientists achieve the potential goal of finding novel research ques-

Preparing to Prioritize Willingness-to-Listen Beliefs as a Communication Objective

The following are eight questions that science communicators should consider when deciding whether to prioritize the communication objective of showing a willingness to listen. In many cases, communicating this skill might involve sharing actions taken to ensure that people have the opportunity to share their views in a fair way as well as highlighting how past input has been used to shape decision-making.

THE GOAL QUESTION

1. Given the behavior you want from your specific audience (i.e., your goal), why do you think it would be helpful if your chosen audience saw you as willing to listen?

THE PREPARATION QUESTIONS

2. What does your chosen audience believe about your willingness to listen and is there meaningful room to improve?
3. What do you believe about your audience's willingness to listen?

THE TACTICS QUESTIONS

4. What could you do to potentially increase the likelihood that those with whom you are communicating see you as willing to listen, including choices about messages, behaviors, tone/style, communication channel, and communication source?
5. What could you do to learn about your chosen audience's willingness to listen?

THE EVALUATION QUESTIONS

6. Did your chosen audience perceive you as willing to listen?
7. What did you learn about your audience's willingness to listen?

THE ETHICS QUESTION

8. Are you being honest about your willingness to listen?

tions that are both scientifically interesting and have the ability to improve the lives of others. We will return to this theme in the final chapter.

REFERENCES

1. Ronald Reagan Presidential Foundation and Institute. "August 12, 1986: Reagan Quotes and Speeches." Accessed November 4, 2019. https://www.reaganfoundation.org/ronald-reagan/reagan-quotes-speeches/news-conference-1.

2. Smith, Adam. "Cognitive Empathy and Emotional Empathy in Human Behavior and Evolution." *Psychological Record* 56, no. 1 (2006): 3–21. https://doi.org/10.1007/bf03395534.

3. Kim, Sung Soo, Stan Kaplowitz, and Mark V. Johnston. "The Effects of Physician Empathy on Patient Satisfaction and Compliance." *Evaluation & the Health Professions* 27, no. 3 (2004): 237–51. https://doi.org/10.1177/0163278704267037.

4. Knafo, Ariel, Carolyn Zahn-Waxler, Carol Van Hulle, JoAnn L. Robinson, and Soo Hyun Rhee. "The Developmental Origins of a Disposition toward Empathy: Genetic and Environmental Contributions." *Emotion* 8, no. 6 (2008): 737–52. https://doi.org/10.1037/a0014179.

5. Zaki, Jamil. *The War for Kindness: Building Empathy in a Fractured World.* 1st ed. New York: Crown, 2019.

6. Spiro, Howard. "What Is Empathy and Can It Be Taught?" *Annals of Internal Medicine* 116, no. 10 (1992): 843–46. https://doi.org/10.7326/0003-4819-116-10-843.

7. Lind, E. Allan, Ruth Kanfer, and P. Christopher Earley. "Voice, Control, and Procedural Justice: Instrumental and Noninstrumental Concerns in Fairness Judgments." *Journal of Personality and Social Psychology* 59, no. 5 (1990): 952–59. https://doi.org/10.1037/0022-3514.59.5.952.

8. Colquitt, Jason A. "On the Dimensionality of Organizational Justice: A Construct Validation of a Measure." *Journal of Applied Psychology* 86, no. 3 (2001): 386–400. https://doi.org/10.1037/0021-9010.86.3.386.

9. Thibaut, John W., and Laurens Walker. *Procedural Justice: A Psychological Analysis.* Mahwah, NJ: Lawrence Erlbaum Associates, 1975.

10. Folger, Robert, David Rosenfield, Jacob Grove, and Louise Corkan. "Effects of 'Voice' and Peer Opinions on Responses to Inequity." *Journal of Personality and Social Psychology* 37, no. 12 (1979): 2253–61.

11. Colquitt, Jason A., Jerald Greenberg, and Cindy P. Zapata-Phelan. "What Is Organizational Justice? A Historical Overview." In *Handbook of Organizational Justice*, edited by Jerald Greenberg and Jason A. Colquitt, 3–58. Mahwah, NJ: Lawrence Erlbaum Associates, 2005.

12. Tyler, Tom R. *Why People Obey the Law.* Princeton, NJ: Princeton University Press, 2006.

13. Tyler, Tom R., and Yuen J. Huo. *Trust in the Law: Encouraging Public Cooperation with the Police and Courts.* New York: Sage, 2002.

14. Oreskes, Naomi. *Why Trust Science?* Princeton, NJ: Princeton University Press, 2019.

15. Besley, John C., Nicole M. Lee, and Geah Pressgrove. "Reassessing the Variables Used to Measure Public Perceptions of Scientists." *Science Communication* 43, no. 1 (2021): 3–32. https://doi.org/10.1177/1075547020949547.

16. McComas, Katherine A., Craig W. Trumbo, and John C. Besley. "Public Meetings About Suspected Cancer Clusters: The Impact of Voice, Interactional Justice, and Risk Perception on Attendees' Attitudes in Six Communities." *Journal of Health Communication* 12, no. 6 (2007): 527–49.

17. Trumbo, Craig W., Katherine A. McComas, and John C. Besley. "Individual- and Community-Level Effects on Risk Perception in Cancer Cluster Investigations." *Risk Analysis* 28, no. 1 (2008): 161–78.

18. Besley, John C., Katherine A. McComas, and Craig W. Trumbo. "Local Newspaper Coverage of Health Authority Fairness During Cancer Cluster Investigations." *Science Communication* 29, no. 4 (2007): 498–521.

19. Bauer, Martin W., Nick Allum, and Steve Miller. "What Can We Learn from 25 Years of PUS Survey Research? Liberating and Expanding the Agenda." *Public Understanding of Science* 16, no. 1 (January 2007): 79–95. https://doi.org/10.1177/0963662506071287.

20. Delli Carpini, Michael X., Fay Lomax Cook, and Lawrence R. Jacobs. "Public Deliberation, Discursive Participation, and Citizen Engagement: A Review of the Empirical Literature." *Annual Review of Political Science* 7 (2004): 315–44. https://doi.org/10.1146/annurev.polisci.7.121003.091630.

21. Hibbing, John R., and Elizabeth Theiss-Morse. *Stealth Democracy: Americans' Beliefs About How Government Should Work.* Cambridge Studies in Political Psychology and Public Opinion. New York: Cambridge University Press, 2002.

22. Lauber, T. B., and B. A. Knuth. "Fairness in Moose Management Decision-Making: The Citizens' Perspective." *Wildlife Society Bulletin* 25, no. 4 (Winter 1997): 776–87.

23. Lauber, T. B., and B. A. Knuth. "Measuring Fairness in Citizen Participation: A Case Study of Moose Management." *Society & Natural Resources* 12, no. 1 (1999): 19–37. https://doi.org/10.1080/089419299279867.

24. Besley, John C. "Public Engagement and the Impact of Fairness Perceptions on Decision Favorability and Acceptance." *Science Communication* 32, no. 2 (June 2010): 256–80. https://doi.org/10.1177/1075547009358624.

25. Arvai, Joseph L. "Using Risk Communication to Disclose the Outcome of a Participatory Decision-Making Process: Effects on the Perceived Acceptability of Risk-Policy Decision." *Risk Analysis* 23, no. 2 (April 2003): 281–89. https://doi.org/10.1111/1539-6924.00308.

26. Arvai, Joseph L., and Ann Froschauer. "Good Decisions, Bad Decisions: The Interaction of Process and Outcome in Evaluations of Decision Quality." *Journal of Risk Research* 13, no. 7 (2010): 845–59. https://doi.org/10.1080/13669871003660767.

27. Skitka, Linda J. "Do the Means Always Justify the Ends, or Do the Ends Sometimes Justify the Means? A Value Protection Model of Justice Reasoning."

Personality and Social Psychology Bulletin 28, no. 5 (May 2002): 588–97. https://doi .org/10.1177/0146167202288003.

28. van den Bos, Kees, Riël Vermunt, and Henk A. M. Wilke. "Procedural and Distributive Justice: What Is Fair Depends More on What Comes First Than on What Comes Next." *Journal of Personality and Social Psychology* 72, no. 1 (1997): 95–104.

29. van den Bos, Kees. "What Is Responsible for the Fair Process Effect?" In *Handbook of Organizational Justice*, edited by Jerald Greenberg and Jason A. Colquitt, 273–300. Mahwah, NJ: Lawrence Erlbaum Associates, 2005.

30. Sanders, Lynn M. "Against Deliberation." *Political Theory* 25, no. 3 (June 1997): 347–76.

31. Pettigrew, Thomas F., and Linda R. Tropp. "A Meta-Analytic Test of Intergroup Contact Theory." *Journal of Personality and Social Psychology* 90, no. 5 (2006): 751–83. https://doi.org/10.1037/0022-3514.90.5.751.

32. Dawson, Emily. *Equity, Exclusion, and Everyday Science Learning: The Experiences of Minoritised Groups.* New York: Routledge, 2019.

33. Brown, Brené. *Dare to Lead: Brave Work, Tough Conversations, Whole Hearts.* New York: Random House, 2018.

34. Swenson, Sara L., Stephanie Buell, Patti Zettler, Martha White, Delaney C. Ruston, and Bernard Lo. "Patient-Centered Communication." *Journal of General Internal Medicine* 19, no. 11 (2004): 1069–79. https://doi.org/10.1111/j.1525 -1497.2004.30384.x.

35. Jones, Susanne M., Graham D. Bodie, and Sam D. Hughes. "The Impact of Mindfulness on Empathy, Active Listening, and Perceived Provisions of Emotional Support." *Communication Research* 46, no. 6 (2016): 838–65. https://doi.org /10.1177/0093650215626983.

36. Gastil, John, E. Pierre Deess, and Phil Weiser. "Civic Awakening in the Jury Room: A Test of the Connection between Jury Deliberation and Political Participation." *Journal of Politics* 64 no. 2 (2002), 585–595. https://doi.org/10.1111 /1468-2508.00141.

37. Pew Research Center. *How "Drop-Off" Voters Differ from Consistent Voters and Nonvoters.* Washington, DC: Pew Research Center, September 2017. https:// www.people-press.org/2017/09/14/how-drop-off-voters-differ-from-consistent -voters-and-non-voters.

38. McComas, Katherine A., John C. Besley, and Craig W. Trumbo. "Why Citizens Do and Don't Attend Public Meetings About Possible Local Cancer Clusters." *Policy Studies Journal* 34, no. 4 (2006): 671–98.

39. Brownell, Judi. "Perceptions of Effective Listeners: A Management Study." *Journal of Business Communication (1973)* 27, no. 4 (1990): 401–15.

40. Epstein, Ronald M., Peter Franks, Kevin Fiscella, Cleveland G. Shields, Sean C. Meldrum, Richard L. Kravitz, and Paul R. Duberstein. "Measuring Patient-Centered Communication in Patient–Physician Consultations: Theoretical and Practical Issues." *Social Science & Medicine* 61, no. 7 (2005): 1516–28. https://doi.org/10.1016/j.socscimed.2005.02.001.

41. Besley, John C., Anthony Dudo, and Shupei Yuan. "Scientists' Views About Communication Objectives." *Public Understanding of Science* 27, no. 6 (2018): 708-30. https://doi.org/10.1177/0963662517728478.

42. Besley, John C., and Katherine A. McComas. "Fairness, Public Engagement, and Risk Communication." In *Effective Risk Communication*, edited by Joseph L. Arvai and Louie Rivers, 108-23. New York: Routledge/Earthscan, 2013.

43. Besley, John C., Kathryn O'Hara, and Anthony Dudo. "Strategic Science Communication as Planned Behavior: Understanding Scientists' Willingness to Choose Specific Tactics." *PLOS ONE* 14, no. 10 (2019): e0224039. https://doi.org/10.1371/journal.pone.0224039.

6

Show You Are Not That Different (and Respect Others' Differences)

THE STEM AMBASSADOR PROGRAM at the University of Utah is another of our favorite science communication training organizations [1]. Nalini Nadkarni, an accomplished forest canopy ecologist and science communication leader, developed the program to try to get scientists into places where they would not typically find themselves. The initial iteration of the program saw scientists developing activities for groups like cooking classes, religious congregations, homeschoolers, seniors living in assisted living facilities, people at a local family festival, and incarcerated adults and youth. This focus on trying to put scientists in rooms with people who might not otherwise interact with them reflects Nadkarni's belief that we need more communication focused on making sure more people know that scientists share many of the values and interests of their neighbors. This might mean helping young people see themselves as potential scientists, but for adults it might simply mean an opportunity to see scientists as fellow community members who are both eager to share their insights and learn from others. One of Nadkarni's most visible activities, for example, was working with her lab team to create "Tree Top Barbie" (with rope, crossbow, and safety helmet) to encourage Mattel into de-

138

veloping a series of scientist Barbies in cooperation with the National Geographic Society so that young people who like Barbies might see themselves as potential researchers [2].

This chapter focuses on the communication objective of trying to ensure people recognize and believe that people in the scientific community often share many of their values. At the same time, this might also mean trying to get people to recognize that they share key aspects of their self-identity with the scientific community. Self-identity and values both receive substantial attention in the social science literature; we cannot fully describe these bodies of research here. However, our core argument is simply that the communication choices science communicators could make can change the odds that people will feel similar to scientists and other science communicators. A key element of these similarity perceptions is beliefs about what values people think drive the scientific community. We want to highlight the importance that social scientists put on the degree to which people see someone as part of one of their own group (i.e., an in-group member) or as part of some other group (i.e., an out-group member). We start by talking about recent work on cultural values and then bring in social identity research. Together, this research is especially important in how it challenges us all to recognize that communication about some of the most important issues facing society may be intractable in the near term while also suggesting a long-term path forward.

Why Fostering Perception of Shared Values or Identity Is a Distinct Type of Objective

Dan Kahan, a psychologist with the Yale School of Law, was studying things that you might expect a psychologist at a law school to study in the 1990s and early 2000s. This included questions about perceptions of policing and punishment. In the early 2000s, Kahan had specifically turned to studying perceptions about gun control and began to argue that giving people more facts about the dangers of having—or not having—a gun were unlikely to sway public opinion around gun control (as discussed in chapter 2). Instead, he argued that people's views about gun control were likely swayed by the cultural values that he saw driving both proponents of gun rights and gun control. This includes values related to either "physical prowess and martial virtue to honor individual self-sufficiency" or "civilized nonaggression, racial and gender quality, and social solidarity" [3]. Kahan was highlighting classical work on risk perceptions and values by Mary Douglas and Aaron Wildavsky [4] and bringing them into contemporary discussions about what he sometimes calls areas of "decision-relevant science" [5].

Douglas and Wildavsky's work argued that available evidence suggests we can generally understand everyone's values by finding out the degree to which they prioritize what they called "individualism" in comparison to "communitarianism" and "hierarchy" in comparison to "egalitarianism." On average, individualists are those who want economic and personal freedom whereas communitarians are more concerned about ensuring the rights of the overall community rather than any individual. Individualists might therefore be attuned to risks associated with threats to freedom whereas communitarians worry more about collective threats, such as those posed by environmental pollution or public health concerns. Similarly, those who value hierarchy would prefer to see people respect and obey authorities whereas those who are more egalitarian see less value in having to attend to oppressive oversight.

Douglas and Wildavsky are not unique in pointing out these two basic dimensions of values. Scholars such as Shalom Schwartz [6,7], Milton Rokeach [8] and Ronald Inglehart [9,10] have proposed similar concepts. However, whereas Inglehart's work was influential on some past work in the area of environmental behavior [11], Kahan's work has driven much of the recent discussion on the role of values in science communication. Indeed, Kahan is one of the few researchers that science communication trainers have told us they see as valuable to training [12]. In all of this, cultural values should be understood as how individuals and groups think the world—including social relationships—should be structured. People use values to evaluate others and guide their own choices and thus can drive views about a range of issues [13]. As Schwartz argues, cultural values emphasize "shared conceptions of what is good and desirable in the culture" [14]. This means they are deeper and more strongly held than the evaluative beliefs that underlie attitudes.

Building on his foray into gun control, Kahan began working with a range of other scholars in the mid-2000s on a host of policy issues. Collaborating scholars included risk perception pioneer Paul Slovic [15], as well as legal scholar Donald Braman and political communication scholar John Gastil. Later research also included the University of Pennsylvania's Kathleen Hall Jamieson, a key player in contemporary debates in political communication who has recently focused some of her interest on science [16].

An early step in Kahan's collaboration was building out a set of measures to capture survey respondents' relative degree of individualism–collectivism and relative degree of hierarchicalism–egalitarianism. The goal was to create measures that were consistent with past theorizing [13,17] but suitable for broad, contemporary use [18]. In this regard, a short version of this measure categorizes respondents along the individualism–communitarianism dimension by asking them the degree to which they agree or disagree with statements like "the government interferes too much in our everyday lives" and "the government should do more to advance society's goals, even if it that means limiting the freedom and choices of individuals." The hierarchy–egalitarianism measure uses statements like "we have gone too far in pushing equal rights in this country" and "discrimination against minorities is still a very serious problem in our society" [19]. With an initial version of the survey developed, Kahan and his collaborators began to compare public opinion dynamics around issues such as gun control, the environment, the death penalty, and gay marriage [18]. They also soon turned to additional collaborations and issues, such as public perceptions of nanotechnology [20], synthetic biology [21], geoengineering [22], vaccines [23], and various aspects of climate change [22,24].

While the collaborations initially talked about a "Wildavsky Heuristic" [18], Kahan and his colleagues quickly refocused on the idea of "cultural cognition" [25]. The series of papers that since emerged has convincingly shown that, in a time where there are too many complicated issues for any of us to understand, we all use our values to make sense of the world. Specifically, as partly discussed in chapter 2, Kahan and his collaborators note that a "rational choice" argument (i.e., people judge science and technology based the accumulation of facts, including risk and benefit beliefs) does not account for the fact that you can often better predict someone's views about nuclear energy by knowing their views about gun control, health issues, or global warming. Similarly, the fact people do learn about new issues over time does not fit the argument that people are simply slaves to our many heuristics and biases, including our feelings. Instead, the cultural cognition argument is that people's values affect—and often bias—what they feel and learn about public issues, including science topics [25]. With Kahan's help, the idea that we all frequently engage in "motivated reasoning" [26] has arguably changed how we think about communication effects across the social sciences [27,28]. It is therefore important for strategic communicators to spend some time trying to better understand this work as it points to the value of making choices that communicate we share someone's background and values (when that's true, which it often is).

Some of Kahan and his collaborators' work uses survey data to show that people's values are better predictors of their position on science issues than such variables as scientific knowledge or simple measures of ideology [29]. More importantly, evidence suggests that nonscientists with the most scientific knowledge seem to put their energy into learning what people within their cultural group think about scientific issues rather than what people in the scientific community think. Kahan argues this makes sense for humans because our individual ability to affect public decisions on scientific issues is likely quite small, but the consequences of taking a position against our own group could be both consequential and immediate in the form of ostracism. This means, for example, that people with high science knowledge who score relatively high on hierarchy and individualism values typically reject the science showing the threat of climate change more than people who hold those values but have less science background. For such people (e.g., conservatives), believing in climate change could lead to painful rejection from their own group, thus our tendency to engage in motivated reasoning seems to cause such people to develop beliefs that go against the scientific consensus and fit with their perceived in-group consensus. Conversely, when it comes to nuclear waste, for example, people who are relatively low on hierarchy and individualism (i.e., high on egalitarianism and communitarianism) tend to develop beliefs that lead them to reject the scientific consensus that such wastes can be stored safely. Put differently, those with strong cultural values and relatively high scientific knowledge— as well as numeracy [24]—seem to be the people who tend to become the most polarized from each other and from the scientific community if scientific findings seem incommensurate with their values. The idea is not that such people purposefully shape their views. Instead, it is simply that a host of forces cause all of us to seek out and pay more attention to information that affirms our values.

What Might Cause a Person to Perceive Shared Values with the Scientific Community?

While the survey results are interesting, Kahan has also used experiments embedded within his surveys to explain why people's values affect what they learn, how they feel, and what they do about scientific issues. An initial study focused on the perceived risk of a vaccine for human papillomavirus (HPV) is illustrative. The HPV vaccine was selected for a 2007 study because all credible public health officials agreed that preteen girls should receive it to prevent cervical cancer, which could occur as a result of HPV infection. A problem arose, argues Kahan, because the main way people contract HPV is through sex, and the marketing effort to make the vaccine mandatory for young girls seemed to threaten religious groups, which tend to be high on hierarchical and individualistic values [23].

Kahan and his collaborators designed an experiment that revealed the danger of allowing values to "pollute" public discourse related to science [30,31]. In the experiment, 1,500 Americans who were part of a large survey panel were randomly assigned to one of several different conditions. About a sixth of the survey respondents (i.e., about 250) were simply given a survey about their cultural values and the risks and benefits of the HPV vaccines. Another sixth of the respondents were shown either a short pro-vaccine or anti-vaccine message before answering the same survey questions. The remaining respondents (i.e., about 1,000 people) saw either the pro- or anti-vaccine message coupled with a description and photo of one of four different people who were described as the source of the information. The research team designed the ostensible authors through a series of pretests so that people would recognize them as being a hierarchical individualist, an egalitarian individualist, a hierarchical communitarian, or an egalitarian communitarian. They did this through both photos and book titles associated with the photos. For example, the egalitarian communitarian author had a bushy beard, a smile, and an informal button-up shirt, whereas the hierarchical individualist looked like a banker in a white shirt and tie. For book titles, the individualist egalitarian was described as writing books with such titles as *A Free Market Defense of Workplace Equality*, whereas the hierarchical communitarian was described as having written books like *How "Women's Liberation" Hurts Women and Men and Children Too!* All were white men of a similar age to keep that part consistent.

Kahan and his colleagues generally found that those with hierarchical and individualist values were the most likely to see the HPV vaccine as risky. Further, these risk perceptions were strengthened when they received the message that the HPV vaccine poses risks, which is the message designed to support their values. Risk perceptions were even higher in cases where a participant in the experiment also received the message from a scientist who seemed to share their values based on the scientist's supposed photograph and book titles. The opposite pattern occurred for those with relatively stronger egalitarian and communitarian values [23].

Kahan and his colleagues used a similar experimental design for a study conducted in 2009 but focused on the expertise of scientists studying global warming, concealed weapons permits, and nuclear waste storage. In this case, the experimental component of the study again used a combination of photos and book titles alongside statements about whether a policy involved high or low risk. They again found that people who saw an argument that matched their values from a researcher who looked like they probably shared their values responded more positively. For example, 88% of egalitarian respondents who read a message by an expert who said that global warming represents a high risk agreed that the researcher was a "trustworthy and knowledgeable expert" whereas only 23% of hierarchical individualists gave this response. In contrast, 86% of hierarchical individualists assigned to read an excerpt from a researcher who said that global warming was a low risk agreed that the researcher was likely a "trustworthy and knowledgeable expert." The same pattern—in reverse—occurred for the concealed weapons issue, and a similar (but less pronounced) pattern occurred on the issue of nuclear waste (with hierarchical individualists somewhat tending to be the ones favoring experts who saw low risk). To us, this points to the fact that people will tend to use whatever cues they have (e.g., photos, biographies) to try to figure out what values someone holds.

Kahan and his colleagues' results suggest to us that science communicators should pay attention to what aspect of themselves they are making most available through their communication choices (or nonchoices). In other words, science communicators might sometimes want to highlight that people share a social identity with others involved in scientific issues. For example, communication researchers Sol Hart and Erik Nisbet did a study where they showed residents of upstate New York a newspaper article that described the victims of climate change as being local farmers, farmers in Georgia, or farmers in France [32]. The idea behind this variation was that people would identify more with local farmers than farmers who were more "socially distant." And, indeed, the results found that people did identify more strongly with people close to them (who they might expect to be more likely to share their values), and such identification had a small effect on climate change mitigation policies support. The effect of local vs. nonlocal farmers was especially important for the more conservative respondents who became even less likely to support climate change mitigation policies when they had read the story about distant farmers. In terms of tactics, however, the point remains that communication choices involving identity can matter.

The fact that people rely so heavily on their existing cultural values when evaluating scientific issues and members of the scientific community can also be discouraging. Nevertheless, the positive version of this situation is that science communicators can make choices so they are communicating in ways that affirm, rather than challenge, people's values. Kahan makes this point quite strongly in a commentary he wrote for *Science* in 2013 in which he criticizes the HPV vaccine's manufacturer and public health advocates for rushing the vaccine's approval. He notes that the vaccine might not have been opposed "had it not been introduced as a mandatory, girls-only shot for sexually transmitted disease in a nationwide legislative campaign" and if "parents' first exposure to information on HPV vaccine would not have been from partisan news outlines" [5, p. 54].

Kahan returned to this theme for a 2016 study about the Zika virus, a mosquito-borne disease that emerged in late 2015 as a potential threat of microcephaly (i.e., an abnormally small head with accompanying cognitive issues) to babies born from infected mothers. According to Kahan and his colleagues, the Zika virus provided an opportunity to show the danger of imbuing scientific issues with cultural meaning due to the virus's potential association with both climate change and immigration. The study itself was especially simple and involved assigning participants to read one of three articles about the true risks of the Zika virus that were similar but had slightly different content aimed at describing the issue as being a general public health issue, an immigration issue, or a global-warming issue. In addition to reading the article, respondents also answered questions about their values, how much they worried about Zika, basic knowledge about Zika, general scientific understanding, and support for potential policies aimed at controlling the virus.

The study's results once again showed the importance of values. In general, the pattern was what the study's authors expected. A single news article about Zika in terms of global warming made those who tended toward being hierarchical and individualistic slightly less concerned about Zika (although not less supportive of Zika policies). In contrast, a story that puts Zika in the context of immigration generally had the opposite effect. The public health context was relatively less polarizing. Of special interest was the finding that people in the immigration and global-warming conditions tended to end up with less Zika knowledge and, even, baseless concerns about the virus. The authors note that this means people in the polarizing conditions may have processed the article content less carefully—or incorrectly—because they were likely using their values to make sense of the content on the page. The failure to find policy effects was explained in terms of the fact that participants in the study read a single story but warned that cumulative exposure to this type of content might prove more problematic. Again, Kahan's key warning about science communication is that people with strong values will try to figure out what people in their cultural group are supposed to believe.

One other thing to note in Kahan's work is it highlights that science communicators might inadvertently signal values through choices such as book titles or sartorial choice. To our knowledge, Kahan has not tested what might happen if science communicators made a point of talking about themselves and the issues they care about in a way that seeks to affirm their audiences' values. Similarly, we have not seen research that focuses on what would happen if science communicators prioritized communicating in ways that highlight similarities or respect for others' values so that people do not feel attacked.

Note that we are suggesting two different types of related communication objectives: signaling shared values and signaling respect for others' values (even if you do not specifically or completely share them). Climate scientist Katharine Hayhoe—an evangelical Christian Canadian living in Texas with her pastor husband—is a model for this type of communication tactic in her many efforts to let her fellow

Christians know about the values that drive her desire to study the threat of climate change [33]. Through public talks and writing, media interviews, and a web series, Hayhoe has consistently tried to connect with potential climate skeptics through a combination of both openness about her values and respect for others' values in the form of politeness and good humor. Where other climate communicators have sought to shame those who reject climate change, Hayhoe has distinguished herself as a positive voice for the value of science in solving real challenges [34].

Although we do not know of any specific research on communicating shared values or respect for values in the realm of science communication, a line of research from work on procedural justice (see chapter 5) provides some limited evidence that we think might be helpful. For example, the group engagement model suggests that one way to get people to feel like they are part of your group is to treat them fairly, including showing respect and listening to their points of view [35]. This builds on the seminal work around social identity by Henry Tajfel and John Turner that highlights the central role of people's perceptions of who they are as members of society driving their social behaviors [36,37]. The group engagement model builds on this idea to show that how people are treated is a key driver of their identification with a group, and this identification can lead to positive behavior on behalf of the group.

A primary test of the group engagement model appeared in a 2009 journal article by professors Steven Blader and Tom Tyler. For the project, an initial study saw the researchers collect surveys from 112 employees of an American company as well as surveys from these employees' bosses [38]. The surveys asked employees how much they identified with their work group, how much pride they felt in that group, and how much respect they felt from their group and these measures were combined to capture strength of social identity. These employees also answered questions about the fairness of workplace decisions and processes, as well as how fair and satisfied they felt about their rewards. The bosses answered questions about the degree to which they felt employees performed the type of "extra role" behavior that makes for a good employee, including things such as helping others and putting in extra effort beyond the minimum required.

The results were consistent with what the research team predicted they would find: employees who felt they worked in a fair workplace identified with their workgroup and this identification seemed to be an important driver—about equal to perceived economic incentives—of whether a boss saw an employee doing more than they expected. A follow-up study in which Blader and Tyler gave surveys to a national sample of 831 employed Americans and their bosses found some similar positive effects of perceived fair treatment and perceived fair economic outcomes on whether people identified with their coworkers, although these social identity judgments were not quite as closely connected to employee behaviors.

While the context is clearly different, the message of this study to those of us in science communication is that perceptions of fair treatment—which could include things such as perceptions of openness (chapter 5), integrity (chapter 4), and decision-maker motivation (chapter 3)—can help people identify with others. Further, identifying with others can lead to positive outcomes, such as support. Susan Fiske's model of warmth and competence [39] similarly highlights the promising impact of having positive perceptions of others on cooperation and support (chapter 3), although without the focus on identity.

It is also worth considering the reason researchers put focus on the role fairness can play in fostering shared identity. Specifically, Tyler's earlier research seemed to suggest that the effectiveness of fair process—including fair or trustworthy treatment—may decrease when people believe the decision-maker is from some other group [40–42]. In other words, people seem to rely less on how decisions get made—and more on what they get out of the decision—when they do not identify with those in charge. But again, this highlights the reality that science communicators who treat people fairly can likely help contribute to a sense of shared social identification. Classic research on social identity shows that people automatically self-categorize into different groups, depending on context (including treatment) [43], but people involved in public dialogue can "transcend their cultural biases" and come to some agreement when involved in a carefully designed discussion process [44, p. 981].

It also needs to be noted that the informal science-education community has a deep interest in identity that we simply do not have time to fully explore, but it may be relevant to science communicators interested in this topic. The National Research Council (co-chaired by Bruce Lewenstein along with education researcher Philip Bell), in their 2009 report *Learning Science in Informal Environments*, categorized "identity" as one of six "learning strands" that informal science educators often prioritize [45]. Specifically, the council argued that helping people "think about themselves as science learners and develop an identity as someone who knows about, uses, and sometimes contributes to science" was a desirable objective for the scientific community. The report highlights the many potential pathways through which a person could come to see oneself as having a science-related identity in a way that is (not by accident) similar to the focus of the STEM Ambassador Program developed at the University of Utah by Nalini Nadkarni. These identities might lead to career choices for a subset of people, but there is recognition that even people who do not pursue a career in science can benefit from believing that they are connected to science.

The report also highlights the challenge of helping people to see themselves as being connected to science when those whom they might typically see involved in scientific positions do not look or sound like them or others they care about. Similarly, the types of issues that someone sees the scientific community trying to solve may not resonate with the cultural context within which they find themselves. For example, someone without a steady paycheck may find it hard to understand why the government spends millions of dollars on research trying to understand fruit-fly genetics. In 2019, for reasons like these, the American Association for the Advancement of Science launched an IF/THEN Ambassador Program that, in its first iteration, selected women based on their scientific acumen and diversity across a range of metrics, including race or ethnic background but also age, field, career pathway, geography, and other factors [46]. The women receive various types of communication training—including training for a variety of traditional and online channels—and support, including networking within the group, and the hope was they would find ways to get involved in "empowering current innovators and inspiring the next generation of pioneers."

The IF/THEN Ambassador Program is part of an IF/THEN coalition that includes a range of philanthropies, companies, and nongovernmental organizations all focused on getting more women to choose science careers, both through ensuring positive role models and also by changing the communicative behavior of the scientific community. For example, a coalition partner group called 500 Women Scientists has focused on changing behavior within the scientific community to ensure that it is a group within which women and people from other marginalized communities want to identify [47,48]. This means addressing sexual harassment in science [49] and taking stances on scientific issues they believe matter to Americans, such as the separation of children from their parents [50] and environmental protection [51]. Efforts to identify and recognize that we share values with people who don't look or sound like us cannot be a substitute for ensuring actual diversity, equity, and inclusion.

Again, a key takeaway for science communicators is that our tactical choices—including our communicative behaviors—can affect whether someone identifies with science or believes we share or respect their values. As with other potential objectives, these tactics include the content of what we say and do, the style or tone of our communication, and choices about who communicates and the channels through which we communicate. And, as with the other trustworthiness-related objectives discussed in previous chapters, the consequences of doing an effective job is having the type of diverse scientific community and positive relationships that make it possible for science to flourish.

Scientists' Willingness to Prioritize Showing Their Values

Our 2015–16 scientist survey also had a block of questions focused on values. The results again point to the fact that science communicators have positive views about communicating values but have not spent much time thinking about communicating shared values as a potential objective. Specifically, we asked scientists about their views about the objective of "demonstrating that scientists share community values" (table 6.1). Scientists from across disciplines appeared quite willing to prioritize this objective, giving it an average score of about 5 on our 7-point "very low importance" to "very high importance" scale. They gave it slightly higher absolute scores on our measures for ethicality and whether it was possible to achieve for a good communicator. On the other hand, the agreement scores for the normative belief questions asking respondents if a scientist prioritizing this objective would be well regarded averaged a little below 5 on the 7-point scale, suggesting a little bit of ambivalence about colleagues' views. Similarly, scientists were about evenly divided on whether they think their colleagues would prioritize this objective. On average, scientists generally seemed to think they had the skill to pursue this objective—giving themselves agreement scores in the mid-4 range—but many had clearly not given this objective much thought prior to the survey. The agreement score for prior consideration of the objective was below the mid-point of the 7-point scale. Indeed, this objective tended to have middle-range to low-range scores on most measures when compared to the other objectives that we asked about in 2015-16 (see appendix B tables), but it performed particularly poorly in terms of prior consideration, sitting in last place alongside the objective of framing (chapter 11). The objective also faired especially poorly relative to other measures on whether respondents thought achieving this objective was possible for a skilled communicator and whether they had the skills needed to achieve this objective.

Our initial research on why scientists might choose different objectives found similar results about "demonstrating values" as an objective to what we have reported in previous chapters [52,53]. The perceived ethicality of this objective along with previous consideration were again among the best statistical predictors of being willing to prioritize the objective of demonstrating shared values, though all of the variables were sometimes significant for some of the societies

Table 6.1.

Scientists' average assessment of the perceived importance of "demonstrating that scientists share community values" and associated beliefs about this objective in the context of different communication channels and different scientific societies (on a scale of 1 to 7)

	Priority[1]	Ethicality[2]	Peer norms[3]	Peer priority[4]	Achievability[5]	My skills[6]	Prior thought[7]	Sample size range
General								
Face-to-face	5.31	5.45	4.72	4.19	5.51	4.61	3.77	371–379
Media	5.17	5.39	4.71	4.22	5.51	4.28	3.63	323–331
Online	4.94	5.25	4.50	4.00	5.35	4.13	3.38	376–383
Biological								
Face-to-face	5.39	5.36	4.86	4.31	5.60	4.77	3.85	345–352
Online	5.28	5.47	4.87	4.19	5.48	4.34	3.54	323–333
Geophysical								
Face-to-face	5.01	5.24	4.54	4.06	5.40	4.69	3.78	313–316
Media	4.94	5.16	4.58	4.09	5.46	4.43	3.64	315–321
Online	4.89	5.22	4.43	3.93	5.37	4.41	3.60	268–277
Geological								
Face-to-face	5.15	5.25	4.59	4.07	5.40	4.72	3.66	244–255
Media	5.23	5.34	4.66	4.31	5.40	4.58	3.60	233–247
Online	5.15	5.29	4.65	4.26	5.44	4.58	3.80	229–240
Ecological								
Face-to-face	5.08	5.34	4.43	4.08	5.57	4.55	3.78	342–347
Chemical								
Face-to-face	5.33	5.27	4.86	4.37	5.44	4.51	3.87	179–184
Media	5.00	5.16	4.61	4.11	5.27	4.18	3.47	157–159
Online	5.03	5.15	4.55	3.99	5.34	4.26	3.27	151–156
Biochemical								
Face-to-face	5.27	5.34	4.62	4.18	5.57	4.50	3.61	368–371
Social								
Media	4.25	4.84	4.12	3.80	5.01	4.50	3.42	862–921

Notes: For the "priority" statement, respondents were given a list of objectives (including the objective noted in the table title) and asked to rate each objective between "very low importance" (1) and "very high importance" (7). For all other statements, respondents selected between "strongly disagree" (1) and "strongly agree" (7). Respondents were all faculty with PhDs at US-based universities. Standard deviations in appendix B tables.

[1] "In general, what are the most important or unimportant communication objectives that scientists such as yourself should have when taking part in [mode*]? Please remember that not every objective can be the most important objective." *Respondents were assigned to see all questions in the context of only one of three potential modes: face-to-face engagement, media engagement, or online engagement.

[2] "This objective is ethical."

[3] "Scientists who pursue this objective would be well regarded by their peers."

[4] "My colleagues would put a high priority on this objective."

[5] "Achieving this objective is possible for a good communicator."

[6] "I have the skills needed to achieve this objective."

[7] "Prior to this survey, I had thought a lot about this potential objective."

from which we drew our sample. These results suggest that a trainer wanting to get a science communicator to consider this objective might need to first make sure the communicator knows the objective exists and then ensure they perceive it as ethical (which most do anyway). The trainer might then turn to speaking about the efficacy of the objective in achieving relevant goals.

In terms of views about tactics relevant to this objective, our research has not specifically mentioned value-focused tactics, but we have asked about the tactic of telling stories to help connect with audiences. Our sense is that this tactic might be useful in communicating values. Our expectation—though we have not seen any studies on this yet—is that scientists' stories about their work might tell others a lot about scientists' values. The Canadian scientists we studied for our initial work on willingness to prioritize various communication tactics were quite willing to tell stories, averaging about 5.5 on a 7-point scale agree–disagree scale. They also agreed that telling stories to connect is ethical (5.5 out of 7), normatively acceptable to colleagues (5.0 out of 7), likely to be effective (5.3 out of 7), and something they have the skill to do (5.7 out 7) [54]. They were about equally likely to agree and disagree that they had thought previously about the storytelling as a way to connect (4.1 out of 7). Our simple modeling to understand what factors statistically predict willingness suggested that all of the variables were associated with willingness but efficacy-related beliefs—that is, that the tactic was likely to be effective and something the scientist had the skill to enact—were relatively highly correlated with willingness to prioritize the tactic. We interpret this to mean that getting science communicators to share stories that help people understand scientists' values may require convincing communicators that they have the ability to tell such stories and that such stories have potential impact.

Looking Forward

Communicating shared values or group identity has not been a topic either of us has spent a substantial time studying despite its likely

Preparing to Prioritize Communicating Shared Values and Identity as a Communication Objective

The following are eight questions that science communicators should consider when deciding whether to prioritize communicating to ensure that others believe the scientific community shares their values or some aspect of their identity as a communication objective. In many cases, communicating shared identity and values might involve directly communicating what values underlie your research choices, but it could also involve communicating about your background or context, if relevant.

THE GOAL QUESTION

1. Given the behavior you want from your specific audience (i.e., your goal), why do you think it would be helpful if your chosen audience believed you shared some aspect of their values?

THE PREPARATION QUESTIONS

2. What does your chosen audience believe about your values and is there meaningful opportunity to change these views?
3. What do you believe about your chosen audience's values?

THE TACTICS QUESTIONS

4. What could you do to potentially increase the likelihood that those with whom you are communicating see you as sharing some aspect of their values, including choices about messages, behaviors, tone/style, communication channel, and communication source?
5. What could you do to learn about your chosen audience's values and identities?

THE EVALUATION QUESTIONS

6. Did your chosen audience perceive you as sharing some aspect of their values?
7. What did you learn about your audience's values?

THE ETHICS QUESTION

8. Are you being honest about your values?

connection to other trustworthiness-related beliefs. Going forward, we hope to be able to give additional focus to this topic. We also hope to see others asking practical but theory-driven questions about how to ensure that science communicators can best communicate about values and identity. This could include trying to ensure others recognize situations when the scientific community shares something with their audiences, but it could also involve scientists purposefully trying to better understand stakeholders' values and identities and where they intersect with their own. Perhaps most importantly, it must also include active efforts to expand the scientific community to include people that we have previously and currently marginalized. Doing so is both the right thing and the thing that will likely expand the scientific consensus on key issues while better allowing us to ensure that science has a positive impact on society.

REFERENCES

1. Nadkarni, Nalini M., Caitlin Q. Weber, Shelley V. Goldman, Dennis L. Schatz, Sue Allen, and Rebecca Menlove. "Beyond the Deficit Model: The Ambassador Approach to Public Engagement." *BioScience* 69, no. 4 (2019): 305–13. https://doi.org/10.1093/biosci/biz018.

2. Sofia, Madeline K., Maia Stern, and Becky Harlan. "Tree Scientist Inspires Next Generation . . . Through Barbie." Videos: Maddie About Science. *National Public Radio*, October 18, 2019. https://www.npr.org/2019/09/22/762385293/video-tree-scientist-inspires-next-generation-through-barbie.

3. Kahan, Dan M. "The Gun Control Debate: A Culture-Theory Manifesto." *Washington and Lee Law Review* 60, no. 1 (2003).

4. Douglas, Mary, and Aaron Wildavsky. *Risk and Culture: An Essay on the Selection of Technologocial and Environmental Dangers.* Berkeley: University of California Press, 1982.

5. Kahan, Dan M. "A Risky Science Communication Environment for Vaccines." *Science* 342, no. 6154 (2013): 53–54. https://doi.org/10.1126/science.1245724.

6. Schwartz, Shalom H., and Klaus Boehnke. "Evaluating the Structure of Human Values with Confirmatory Factor Analysis." *Journal of Research in Personality* 38, no. 3 (June 2004): 230–55.

7. Besley, John C. "Media Exposure and Core Values." *Journalism and Mass Communication Quarterly* 85, no. 2 (2008): 311–30. https://doi.org/10.1177/107769900808500206.

8. Rokeach, Milton. *The Nature of Human Values.* New York: Free Press, 1973.

9. Inglehart, Ronald, and Daphna Oyserman. "Individualism, Autonomy, Self-Expression." In *Comparing Cultures: Dimensions of Culture in a Comparative*

Perspective, edited by Henk Vinken, Joseph Soeters, and Peter Ester, 74–96. Leiden: Brill, 2004.

10. Inglehart, Ronald, and Paul R. Abramson. "Measuring Postmaterialism." *American Political Science Review* 93, no. 3 (September 1999): 665–77.

11. Inglehart, Ronald. "Public Support for Environmental-Protection: Objective Problems and Subjective Values in 43 Societies." *PS: Political Science & Politics* 28, no. 1 (March 1995): 57–72.

12. Besley, John C., and Anthony Dudo. *Landscaping Overview of the North American Science Communication Training Community: Topline Takeaways from Trainer Interviews*. N.p.: Kavli Foundation, Rita Allen Foundation, David and Lucile Packard Foundation, and Gordon and Betty Moore Foundation, 2017. http://www.informalscience.org/sites/default/files/Communication Training Landscape Overview Final.pdf.

13. Wildavsky, Aaron, and Karl Dake. "Theories of Risk Perception: Who Fears What and Why?" *Daedalus* 119, no. 4 (Fall 1990): 41–60.

14. Schwartz, Shalom. "A Theory of Cultural Value Orientations: Explication and Applications." *Comparative Sociology* 5, no. 2–3 (2006): 137–82. https://doi.org /10.1163/156913306778667357.

15. Slovic, Paul. "Perception of Risk." *Science* 236, no. 4799 (1987): 280–85. https://doi.org/10.1126/science.3563507.

16. Jamieson, Kathleen Hall, Dan Kahan, and Dietram A. Scheufele, eds. *The Oxford Handbook on the Science of Science Communication*. Oxford Library of Psychology. New York: Oxford University Press, 2017.

17. Dake, Karl. "Orienting Dispositions in the Perception of Risk: An Analysis of Contemporary Worldviews and Cultural Biases." *Journal of Cross-Cultural Psychology* 22, no. 1 (1991): 61–82. https://doi.org/10.1177 /0022022191221006.

18. Gastil, John, Donald Braman, Dan M. Kahan, and Paul Slovic. "The 'Wildavsky Heuristic': The Cultural Orientation of Mass Political Opinion." Public Law Working Paper No. 107, Yale Law School, New Haven, CT, October 2005. http://dx.doi.org/10.2139/ssrn.834264.

19. Kahan, Dan M., Kathleen Hall Jamieson, Asheley Landrum, and Kenneth Winneg. "Culturally Antagonistic Memes and the Zika Virus: An Experimental Test." *Journal of Risk Research* 20, no. 1 (2017): 1–40.

20. Kahan, Dan M. "Nanotechnology and Society: The Evolution of Risk Perceptions." *Nature Nanotechnology* 4, no. 11 (2009): 705–06. https://doi.org/10 .1038/nnano.2009.329.

21. Kahan, Dan M., Donald Braman, and Gregory N. Mandel. "Risk and Culture: Is Synthetic Biology Different?" Harvard Law School Program on Risk Regulation Research Paper No. 09-2, Yale Law School, Public Law Working Paper No. 190, February 20, 2009. http://dx.doi.org/10.2139/ssrn.1347165.

22. Kahan, Dan M., Hank Jenkins-Smith, Tor Tarantola, Carol L. Silva, and Donald Braman. "Geoengineering and Climate Change Polarization: Testing a Two-Channel Model of Science Communication." *Annals of the American Academy*

of Political and Social Science 658, no. 1 (2015): 192–222. https://doi.org/10.1177
/0002716214559002.

23. Kahan, Dan M., D. Braman, G. L. Cohen, John Gastil, and Paul Slovic. "Who
Fears the HPV Vaccine, Who Doesn't, and Why? An Experimental Study of the
Mechanisms of Cultural Cognition." *Law and Human Behavior* 34, no. 6 (December 2010): 501–16. https://doi.org/10.1007/s10979-009-9201-0.

24. Kahan, Dan M., Ellen Peters, Maggie Wittlin, Paul Slovic, Lisa Larrimore
Ouellette, Donald Braman, and Gregory Mandel. "The Polarizing Impact of
Science Literacy and Numeracy on Perceived Climate Change Risks." *Nature
Climate Change* 2, no. 10 (2012): 732–35. https://doi.org/10.1038/nclimate1547.

25. Kahan, Dan M., and Donald Braman. "Cultural Cognition and Public
Policy." *Yale Law & Policy Review* 24 (2006): 149–72.

26. Kunda, Ziva. "The Case for Motivated Reasoning." *Psychological Bulletin*
108, no. 3 (1990): 480–98. https://doi.org/10.1037/0033-2909.108.3.480.

27. Kahan, Dan M. "The Politically Motivated Reasoning Paradigm, Part 2:
Unanswered Questions." In *Emerging Trends in the Social and Behavioral Sciences*,
edited by Robert A. Scott, Stephen M. Kosslyn, and Marlis Buchmann, Wiley
Online Library. Hoboken, NJ: John Wiley & Sons, 2015–. https://onlinelibrary
.wiley.com/doi/10.1002/9781118900772.etrds0418.

28. Kahan, Dan M. "The Politically Motivated Reasoning Paradigm, Part 1:
What Politically Motivated Reasoning Is and How to Measure It." In *Emerging
Trends in the Social and Behavioral Sciences*, edited by Robert A. Scott, Stephen M.
Kosslyn, and Marlis Buchmann, Wiley Online Library. Hoboken, NJ: John Wiley &
Sons, 2015–. https://onlinelibrary.wiley.com/doi/10.1002/9781118900772.etrds0417.

29. Kahan, Dan M., Hank Jenkins-Smith, and Donald Braman. "Cultural
Cognition of Scientific Consensus." *Journal of Risk Research* 14, no. 2 (2011): 147–74.
https://doi.org/10.1080/13669877.2010.511246.

30. Ahern, Lee, Colleen Connolly-Ahern, and Jennifer Hoewe. "Worldviews,
Issue Knowledge, and the Pollution of a Local Science Information Environment."
Science Communication 38, no. 2 (2016): 228–50. https://doi.org/10.1177/107554701
6636388.

31. Kahan, Dan M. "Misconceptions, Misinformation, and the Logic of
Identity-Protective Cognition." Cultural Cognition Project Working Paper Series
No. 164, Yale Law School, Public Law Research Paper No. 605, Yale Law &
Economics Research Paper No. 575, May 24, 2017. https://ssrn.com/abstract
=2973067.

32. Hart, P. Sol, and Erik C. Nisbet. "Boomerang Effects in Science Communication: How Motivated Reasoning and Identity Cues Amplify Opinion Polarization About Climate Mitigation Policies." *Communication Research* 39, no. 6 (2012):
701–23. https://doi.org/10.1177/0093650211416646.

33. Hayhoe, Katharine. "When Facts Are Not Enough." *Science* 360, no. 6392
(2018): 943–43. https://doi.org/10.1126/science.aau2565.

34. Schwartz, John. "Katharine Hayhoe, a Climate Explainer Who Stays above
the Storm." *New York Times*, October 11, 2016, D1.

35. Tyler, Tom R., and Steven L. Blader. "The Group Engagement Model: Procedural Justice, Social Identity, and Cooperative Behavior." *Personality and Social Psychology Review* 7, no. 4 (2003): 349–61.

36. Tajfel, Henri. "Social Psychology of Intergroup Relations." *Annual Review of Psychology* 33, no. 1 (1982): 1–39.

37. Tajfel, Henri, and John C. Turner. "An Integrative Theory of Intergroup Conflict. In *The Social Psychology of Intergroup Relations*, edited by W. Austin and S. Worchel, 33–47. Monterrey, CA: Brooks, 1979.

38. Blader, Steven L., and Tom R. Tyler. "Testing and Extending the Group Engagement Model: Linkages between Social Identity, Procedural Justice, Economic Outcomes, and Extrarole Behavior." *Journal of Applied Psychology* 94, no. 2 (March 2009): 445–64. https://doi.org/10.1037/a0013935.

39. Cuddy, Amy J. C., Susan T. Fiske, and Peter Glick. "Warmth and Competence as Universal Dimensions of Social Perception: The Stereotype Content Model and the BIAS Map." In *Advances in Experimental Social Psychology*, vol. 40, edited by Mark P. Zanna, 61–149. Cambridge, MA: Academic Press, 2008.

40. Huo, Yuen J., Heather J. Smith, Tom R. Tyler, and E. Allan Lind. "Superordinate Identification, Subgroup Identification, and Justice Concerns: Is Separatism the Problem; Is Assimilation the Answer?" *Psychological Science* 7, no. 1 (1996): 40–45. https://doi.org/10.1111/j.1467-9280.1996.tb00664.x.

41. Smith, Heather J., Tom R. Tyler, Yuen J. Huo, Daniel J. Ortiz, and E. Allan Lind. "The Self-Relevant Implications of the Group-Value Model: Group Membership, Self-Worth, and Treatment Quality." *Journal of Experimental Social Psychology* 34, no. 5 (September 1998): 470–93.

42. Tyler, Tom R., Robert J. Boeckmann, Heather J. Smith, and Yuen J. Huo. *Social Justice in a Diverse Society.* Boulder, CO: Westview, 1997.

43. Hornsey, Matthew J. "Social Identity Theory and Self-Categorization Theory: A Historical Review." *Social and Personality Psychology Compass* 2, no. 1 (2008): 204–22. https://doi.org/10.1111/j.1751-9004.2007.00066.x.

44. Gastil, John, Katherine R. Knobloch, Dan M. Kahan, and Don Braman. "Participatory Policymaking across Cultural Cognitive Divides: Two Tests of Cultural Biasing in Public Forum Design and Deliberation." *Public Administration* 94, no. 4 (2016): 970–87. https://doi.org/10.1111/padm.12255.

45. National Research Council. *Learning Science in Informal Environments: People, Places, and Pursuits.* Edited by Philip Bell, Bruce Lewenstein, Andrew W. Shouse, and Michael A. Feder. Washington, DC: National Academies Press, 2009.

46. Lohwater, Tiffany. "125 Women in STEM Selected as AAAS IF/THEN Ambassadors." *American Association for the Advancement of Science News*, September 9, 2019. https://www.aaas.org/news/125-women-stem-selected-aaas-ifthen-ambassadors.

47. 500 Women Scientists. "Who We Are." Accessed October 9, 2021. https://500womenscientists.org/who-we-are.

48. Peréz-Porro, Alicia, of 500 Women Scientists NYC. "Why Women Drop Out of Science Careers." *Voices* (blog), *Scientific American*, October 10, 2017.

https://blogs.scientificamerican.com/voices/why-women-drop-out-of-science
-careers.

49. 500 Women Scientists Leadership. "When It Comes to Sexual Harassment, Academia Is Fundamentally Broken." *Voices* (blog), *Scientific American*, August 8, 2018. https://blogs.scientificamerican.com/voices/when-it-comes-to-sexual
-harassment-academia-is-fundamentally-broken.

50. Seattle 500 Women Scientists. "Childhood Should Be Sacred." *Voices* (blog), *Scientific American*, July 2, 2018. https://blogs.scientificamerican.com/voices
/childhood-should-be-sacred.

51. 500 Women Scientists Leadership, Jewel Lipps, Jane Zelikova, Gretchen Goldman, Julia Bradley-Cook, Susan J. Cheng, and Charise Johnson. "Scientists Must Speak Up for the Green New Deal." *Observations* (blog), *Scientific American*, February 25, 2019. https://blogs.scientificamerican.com/observations/scientists
-must-speak-up-for-the-green-new-deal.

52. Besley, John C., Anthony Dudo, and Shupei Yuan. "Scientists' Views About Communication Objectives." *Public Understanding of Science* 27, no. 6 (2018): 708–30. https://doi.org/10.1177/0963662517728478.

53. Dudo, Anthony, and John C. Besley. "Scientists' Prioritization of Communication Objectives for Public Engagement." *PLOS ONE* 11, no. 2 (2016). https://doi
.org/10.1371/journal.pone.0148867.

54. Besley, John C., Kathryn O'Hara, and Anthony Dudo. "Strategic Science Communication as Planned Behavior: Understanding Scientists' Willingness to Choose Specific Tactics." *PLOS ONE* 14, no. 10 (2019): e0224039. https://doi.org/10
.1371/journal.pone.0224039.

7

Show Competence

WE HAVE NOT COME ACROSS ANY SCIENCE communication trainers in our interview studies that report putting substantial, explicit emphasis on helping science communicators ensure that people see the scientific community as highly skilled problem-solvers. That being said, simple logic suggests that helping people within the scientific community interact with others in clear and compelling ways through guided and repeated practice—the focus of many science communication trainings [1,2]—might contribute to positive beliefs about scientists' competence. For example, a team at the University of Michigan have described an improv-theater-derived game in which science communicators are asked to iteratively shrink a science message from 60 seconds, to 30 seconds, to 15 seconds [3]. The hope in doing so is to help science communicators realize that most arguments can—and should—be whittled to a core nugget of goodness. In doing so, we would fully expect a communicator to improve their delivery in a way that conveys overall competence.

Further consistent with our belief in cumulative communication effects (see chapter 1), we would expect that people who repeatedly see science communicators perform well should develop beliefs that the scientific community has strong communication skills. In contrast, a history of seeing science communicators perform poorly might contribute to negative beliefs about the scientific community's overall competence. Indeed, this chapter describes some of the research that has gone into showing how message content, source selection, and delivery might affect how people perceive science communicators' skills and knowledge. And similar to the communication objectives in our earlier chapters, only a small amount of science-communication-specific research has specifically looked at competence perceptions and associated beliefs. We therefore present a broad range of research to help us make our key points. In reviewing this research, as with elsewhere in the book, we focus primarily on things that communicators can ethically choose to control. We recognize that some audiences will infer competence from irrelevant cues, such as attractiveness, gender, sexual orientation, or race, and we believe there is an enormous need to change this tendency, which extends far beyond just science.

An interesting thing about competence beliefs (initially discussed in chapter 3) is that isolated examples of incompetence should not substantially hurt beliefs about a person or group's competence [4]. No one would reasonably judge a cook incompetent if that person were to prepare hundreds of tasty dishes and a few lousy ones. The diagnostic value of the many good meals should outweigh the diagnosticity of a botched attempt at combining chocolate ganache and liver [5]. On the other hand, we might be perfectly justified in believing that a cook who steals from the cash register or spits in the soup just once lacks integrity (chapter 4) or caring intentions (chapter 3). Similarly, a challenging aspect of competence is the fact that the types of trustworthiness-related beliefs described in chapters 3–6 tend to be more powerful than competence beliefs. Few people seem likely to want to eat the food of a cook who cares nothing about his diners' welfare, lacks the integrity to throw out contaminated food, or ignores warnings from his colleagues about potential risks. Many of us may also not want to frequent a restaurant run by someone whose values conflict substantially with our own [6,7]. Most of us, however, sometimes eat food prepared by less than amazing cooks.

Indeed, when it comes to competence, it makes sense that we rarely hear science-communication trainers and professionals put much emphasis on communicating competence. The international survey discussed in chapter 4 that Gallup did for the United Kingdom's Wellcome Trust in 2018 (table 4.1) showed that people in many countries tend to see scientists as relatively competent, at least in comparison to their ratings of scientists' warmth/benevolence and honesty/integrity. The differences between trustworthiness-related beliefs seem particularly evident in the United States. While now dated, the 2010 version of *Science and Engineering Indicators* also clearly showed that people judge scientists as relatively competent in the United States compared to other groups. For example, respondents were asked to rate various groups on the degree to which they "understand the causes of global warming" using a 5-point scale from "not at all" to "very well." For scientists, 44% of respondents chose the highest "very well" category whereas only 5% selected the highest category for elected officials and only 4% selected the highest category for business leaders. The same pattern occurred for stem cell research, income taxes, and genetically modified foods [8].

As in previous chapters, we first briefly describe the evidence that competence or ability beliefs represent a distinct type of communication objective that science communicators could prioritize, and then we describe what we know about the potential communication choices that might affect competence beliefs and what competence beliefs might affect.

How Is Competence Different?

Competence beliefs exist as a distinct way in which we make sense of other people. Researchers may debate whether it is useful to distinguish between perceived benevolence/warmth (chapter 3), integrity/honesty (chapter 4), openness/willingness to listen (chapter 5), and shared values (chapter 6), but we do not see any meaningful argument—whether conceptual [9] or statistical—when it comes to competence. What is potentially confusing, however, is that different scholars use different terms, including "competence" [10], "ability" [11], "agency" [12], "credibility" [13], or "confidence" [9] to describe what we call competence in this chapter to be consistent with Susan Fiske's widely cited work [10]. We recognize that one could argue that words such as "incompetent" or "useless" have semantic meanings that suggest both an inability to do a job and a moral element that suggest that the incompetent and useless are at least partly responsible for their poor performance. Nevertheless, the core idea of competence beliefs is simply a question of whether we think someone has the skills and intellectual capacity needed to play a role well. In the case of science, this likely means the ability to understand the natural world—or one specific aspect of the natural world—using the tools of science. Competence, in this regard, might often be situation specific (e.g., perceived cooking skill probably does not translate into a deep knowledge of chemistry), but it also likely makes sense to talk about people's overall beliefs about groups. We do this in surveys when we ask respondents to assess the degree to which scientists or politicians have the ability or capacity to understand and manage scientific issues.

The Muenster Epistemic Trustworthiness Inventory provides a good example of how competence is typically measured. Researchers Friederike Hendriks, Dorothe Kienhues, and Rainer Bromme [14] created this measure based on the now-classic benevolence/integrity/ability trichotomy from organizational psychology [11]. Using this inventory to measure competence beliefs involves asking people to use a 7-point scale to consider spectrums of word pairs that include competent–incompetent, intelligent–unintelligent, well-educated–poorly educated, professional–unprofessional, experienced–inexperienced, and qualified–unqualified. In contrast, integrity is measured with word pairs such as honest–dishonest and sincere–insincere, while benevolence is measured with word pairs such as considerate–inconsiderate and responsible–irresponsible. Similarly, an article using the warmth/

competence dichotomy to measure perceptions of doctors also asked about competence-related beliefs, such as intelligence and confidence, as well as warmth-related beliefs, such as sincerity and warmth [15].

Communicating Competence

Researchers seeking to communicate competence in social-scientific experiments have used a number of methods that provide guidance on how science communicators in the real world could convey the scientific community's competence. One common tactic used to suggest competence is simply to choose a source that people already see as competent, which often comes in the form of scientific or technical expertise. For example, a classic study on source credibility by communication research pioneer Karl Hovland published in 1951 with Walter Weiss compared how people responded to "high credibility" sources versus "low credibility" sources. The high-credibility sources included the *New England Journal of Biology and Medicine* for an article on pharmaceutical safety, the physicist Robert J. Oppenheimer for an article on atomic submarines, the *Bulletin of National Resources Planning* for an article on steel shortages, and *Fortune* magazine for an article on the future of movie theaters. In contrast, the low-credibility sources included those that readers would not likely expect to have a scientific background, including a consumer magazine (that Hovland did not name to "avoid any possible embarrassment to them"), the Soviet Union's propaganda publication *Pravda*, a well-known "anti-labor, anti–New Deal, 'rightist'" newspaper columnist (also not named in the research write-up), and a well-known gossip columnist (again, not named). Students who participated in the study tended to shift their opinion toward the direction of the high-credibility source in the short term, even though people seemed to learn an equal amount from both types of sources. The value of source credibility may decrease over time, but the key lesson for us is simply that one can take advantage of existing source beliefs. Indeed, John and our colleague Shupei Yuan have used this type of tactic in their work on aggressive risk communication to see if scientists studying genetically engineered food—in comparison to a nonscientist—might get a positive impact from communicating politely or a negative impact from communicating aggressively [16].

Choosing a source that people already see as competent might sometimes be an option, but in the long term we hope that people communicating about science will also make choices that maintain and enhance competence beliefs. One type of research in this area highlights the importance of fluency in competence perceptions, with fluent speech understood as communication "free of lengthy pauses, hesitations, repetitions, sentence changes, interruptive vocalizations, and the like" [17]. Indeed, the study in which this quotation appeared (by distinguished communication scholar Judee Burgoon) asked students in a communication class to rate their peers on competence after listening to the student give a short speech. Trained coders then judged the speeches on various measures, including fluency, and found that fluency was among the better predictors of competence scores. Other researchers have found this type of result in other cases, and the general consensus seems to be that people will often make more positive judgments of messages and the people delivering them when the communication is easier to process cognitively [18]. Less fluent messages may have some benefits (e.g., increasing the effort that people put into understanding content and thus helping avoid mistakes associated with the use of inappropriate cognitive shortcuts) [19,20], but the key for us is simply that making content easier to understand can often affect the perceived expertise of experts. We also like that fluency is a skill that most people can develop, whereas we have equity concerns about simply picking sources who audiences already see as competent.

Making content more easily processed can also affect other trustworthiness-related beliefs [21], but the effect of making content more understandable seems especially important when it comes to competence judgments. The ironically titled article "Consequences of Erudite Vernacular Utilized Irrespective of Necessity: Problems with Using Long Words Needlessly," by Princeton University cognitive psychologist Daniel Oppenheimer, explored this idea in a set of experiments that anyone who has ever seen someone try too seem knowledgeable can appreciate [22]. The first study in the set took graduate student admission essays and systematically replaced easy words with equivalent complex words from a thesaurus to make versions of the essay that were moderately complex and highly complex compared to the original. Another set of students then read randomly assigned versions of the essays and indicated whether they thought Stanford University should accept the writer to graduate school. Increasing complexity lead to lower acceptance rates and this appeared to occur most because of respondents' difficulty in making sense of the relatively more complex essays.

The second study in Oppenheimer's set made abstracts from sociology PhD dissertations less complex instead of more complex. Reading a less complex version seemed to result in higher intelligence ratings. A third study in the set saw students randomly rate two different translations of a short excerpt from a writing by French philosopher René Descartes. In this case, the students also tended to rate Descartes as less intelligent when they read a more complex translation. The clear take-home from this work is that efforts by science communicators to reduce jargon (e.g., the dejargonizer) [23] and speak in understandable ways might foster competence beliefs. One recent experiment goes so far as to argue that online readers of health information in their experiments seemed to "subconsciously punish technical language" [24].

One notable deviation from this pattern is a body of research on "neuroimage bias" that suggests that adding a neuroscience explanation to an argument can sometimes strengthen the argument, including in legal contexts [25]. This might include something like a magnetic resonance image of the brain that purports to show relevant brain activity. Our view about such efforts is that they represent an ethical rather than strategic question. From our perspective, it would seem okay to use neuroscience evidence in cases where the evidence is well accepted (i.e., fully peer-reviewed), but we would never advocate using something like bogus neuroscience in an effort to hoodwink someone just because you know it may help you achieve your goal [26]. Pragmatically, even if such tactics were to work in the short term, the long-term negative consequence for science makes such practices repugnant to us.

Another aspect of content to consider is the type of evidence that a communicator provides. We have increasingly heard from trainers about the perceived value of telling stories and using narrative evidence [27] versus reporting dry statistics. A recent study by a multi-university team tackled this question by having people read vignettes about a bank that included one person making a statistical argument and another person making an argument in the form of story about a friend's experience with the bank [28]. What the research expected—and found—is that people judged a source that used a statistical argument as more competent than someone who used a narrative argument. Using a narrative argument resulted in relatively high warmth judgments coupled with lower competence judgments. To us, this type of evidence suggests that numbers can be helpful, noting again that ethics require that the numbers be meaningful.

Beyond message content, and similar to the work of Burgoon we described, Oppenheimer also showed that production issues can affect how people's competence is judged. Specifically, he showed that difficult-to-read fonts resulted in lower author intelligence ratings, and poor quality print jobs (i.e., low toner) affected willingness to accept graduate school applicants [22]. A recent study within the science communication space similarly showed that poor audio quality—whether during a radio interview on *Science Friday* or at a conference—can negatively affect listeners' perceptions of both speaker competence and research quality [29]. Interestingly, early research suggests that speed of speech might signal competence [30,31]. As might also be expected, research outside the science context similarly points to factors such as professional attire tending to result in higher competence perceptions [32], and that there is a danger that formal dress might make experts seem less likable [33,34]. Science communicators interested in securing private-sector funding should similarly understand that even investors may have a hard time seeing past a poor quality presentation [35].

Altogether, these types of findings suggest that it may often make sense to spend resources on technical experts who can ensure that our science communication looks and sounds professional while recognizing that there are other actions that we should *not* consider. For example, we are not at all concerned about catering to the types of idiots who wrongly judge women [36], non-native speakers [37], or other discriminated-against groups as less competent. There are many reasons—all more important than short-term competence perceptions—why it is important to ensure a diverse range of science communicators, including scientific panels within academia [38]. We also recognize the danger that people may present information in ways that seems true just because of the quality of the packaging, akin to the classic smooth-talking snake-oil salesmen [39]. However, our hope is that our readers have real, meaningful knowledge to share (and learn) such that it would be a shame if they missed opportunities because of poor-quality communication.

A more positive perspective is that there is a range of tactics available to communicate the scientific community's competence. This means, for example, that non-native speakers who may find it difficult to make use of one competence-focused tactic can likely find another that does work for them. Furthermore, the impact of any one specific choice is typically going to be small such that what should matter most is the cumulative effect of people's repeated experiences with members of the scientific community saying and doing things that make them look more (or less) competent. It is also important to recognize that many of the tactics needed to communicate competence do not require extra time during a talk or extra words in an article. On the other hand, ensuring that a presentation looks professional, that an event runs smoothly, and that writing is clear may take additional preparation time or access to people who have communication expertise.

What About Controversy?

We sometimes hear science communicators worry they may drive down belief in expertise when they take unpopular positions or contradict other people in the scientific community. Our view is experts will sometimes need to tell people that a scientific consensus exists, that people who are arguing against a consensus are likely wrong, and that each new study in your social media feed doesn't mean we need to reject past insight. Science communicators cannot be expected to confirm everyone else's opinions. In these cases, as with Shupei Yuan's work on aggressive communication, the one thing we can control is *how* we communicate [40]. Do we communicate politely or in a way that makes us seem clueless or uncaring? Put differently, science communicators need to learn "how to disagree without being disagreeable" [41]. And, as best we can tell, available evidence suggests that taking a controversial position may sometimes have a minor impact on the competence of science communicators, but these effects only occur for some issues and in some contexts [42,43].

One particularly interesting study showed that while those with relatively limited knowledge about the world tended to attribute disputes between experts as the result of incompetence, those with more knowledge tended to recognize the inherent complexity of the underlying issues [44]. More sophisticated respondents were also, however, more likely to highlight concerns about an expert's integrity. Another study on the effect of comments on social media similarly found that negative comments tended to diminish the degree to which people saw a source as honest, but such comments had little effect on competence beliefs [45]. What this research did not seek to address is what might happen if a science communicator involved in a disagreement recognized the challenge and actively sought to avoid unnecessarily impugning the competence (or motives) of those with whom they disagree. Our advice is that science communicators should not worry about hurting the reputation of science when they disagree with others. If they feel they need to contradict someone to help achieve their goals they should do so to the best of their abilities, recognizing the lessons learned in chapter 3 through 6 on warmth, integrity, being willing to listen, and respecting differences.

What Does Demonstrating Perceived Competence Affect?

Competence beliefs—like the other trustworthiness-related beliefs discussed in previous chapters—are best understood as providing part of the foundation of the relationship between the scientific community and the broader society within which science takes place [46]. Practically this might mean that once people form their competence beliefs, they sometimes use these beliefs alongside other trustworthiness-related beliefs as cognitive shortcuts (i.e., heuristic or peripheral cues) to make quick judgments about communication they may not be motivated or able to process. For example, the study highlighted earlier by Burgoon found that (1) fluent communicators seemed more competent and (2) this competence was especially important in increasing the degree to which the speakers seemed persuasive. Perceived persuasiveness was measured by a set of questions asking directly about how convincing the speaker seemed, an approach that works fairly well [47].

In a classic study on credibility and persuasion, Shelly Chaiken and her colleagues asked residents of New York City in an experiment to read a product booklet for "a new answering machine" called XT-100 [48]. The participants read one of twelve systematically varied versions of the pamphlet. The variations included whether the booklet contained strong, ambiguous, or weak arguments; whether it was from an expert (*Consumer Reports*) or nonexpert (the discount store sales staff); and whether the product would be available to New Yorkers or people in the Midwest. This final condition was meant to vary how motivated the New Yorkers would be to pay close attention to the arguments in favor of the new answering machine. Chaiken and her colleagues found that the New Yorkers seemed to base their judgments about the XT-100 largely on source expertise when told that the product was for Midwesterners, suggesting that they were using source expertise as a cognitive shortcut and somewhat ignoring argument quality. In contrast, New Yorkers told that the XT-100 might be available in New York only seemed to rely on source expertise if the booklet they read contained ambiguous arguments. In other words, New Yorkers who were motivated to think about the booklet recognized both strong and weak arguments and only tended to rely on source expertise when the arguments were ambiguous.

Our colleagues Craig Trumbo and Katherine McComas have extended this thinking into the science communication space in survey research on perceptions of risk related to local cancer clusters. This work suggests that, at least to some degree, seeing government and industry sources as relatively credible (measured using elements of competence as well as integrity) might lead people to rely on heuristic processing (i.e., "fast" processing that isn't especially thoughtful) rather than systematic processing (i.e., "slow" processing that involves careful weighing of evidence) [49]. Their data implies that seeing sources as relatively less credible might prompt people to think about issues more systematically. In turn, Trumbo and McComas show that systematic processing was associated with relatively higher risk perceptions from cancer clusters, and heuristic processing was associated with somewhat lower risk perceptions. Seeing government and industry decision-makers as credible was also directly associated with lower risk perceptions.

These results were from a single survey, rather than a randomized controlled experiment, and therefore do not tell us directly about causation, but they are consistent with the general argument that it is usually better to be seen as competent rather than incompetent when communicating about risk in the context of scientific research. A number of other studies have also shown that perceived competence of scientists can affect risk and benefit beliefs, or technology acceptance, in areas such genetic modification of food [50], stem-cell research [51], nuclear energy [52], and even things like satisfaction in the environmental performance of hotels [53]. One of the most straightforward demonstrations that competence beliefs likely matter comes from a 2009 study focused on support for the use of carbon dioxide capture and storage technology [54]. This study showed that, at least in a student sample, respondents tended to perceive much higher benefits and fewer risks when the technology was said to originate with highly experienced and competent proponents of the innovation than when it was described as coming from a less competent organization.

The relationship between competence beliefs and outcomes related to risks, benefits, and acceptance might be broadly understood as being consistent with classic trust theory [11,55–57]. Specifically, we see technology acceptance and a willingness to afford scientists a role in decision-making [58] as examples of making oneself vulnerable to others, the key idea of behavioral trust. This theory is also present in the intergroup affect and stereotypes work of Susan Fiske and her colleague (discussed in chapter 3) that suggests that people are willing to "passively facilitate" (i.e., not impede) those they see as having competence and "actively facilitate" (i.e., help) those they see as being warm. The ideal, of course, is a combination of high warmth and competence [10,59,60]. And while we feel relatively positive about the degree to which most people currently see scientists as competent, we also believe that the science community needs to communicate in ways that highlight its expertise where possible. We get especially frustrated when we see science communicators who fail to prepare for communication opportunities with people outside the scientific community because we worry that it conveys incompetence, as well as disrespect (chapter 3). In isolation, these failures to prepare may not matter, but they could represent a problem if that is people's primary experience with scientists.

Scientists' Willingness to Prioritize Communicating Competence

The evidence from our past work surveying scientists suggests that they do not prioritize competence as highly as other objectives but still have positive views about the objective [61]. As shown in table 7.1, the overall priority score of respondents from across the eight scientific societies we surveyed in 2015 and 2016 tended to be just below 5 out of 7. This puts "demonstrating the scientific community's expertise"

Table 7.1.
Scientists' average assessment of the perceived importance of "demonstrating the scientific community's expertise" and associated beliefs about this objective in the context of different communication channels and different scientific societies (on a scale of 1 to 7)

	Priority[1]	Ethicality[2]	Peer norms[3]	Peer priority[4]	Achievability[5]	My skills[6]	Prior thought[7]	Sample size range
General								
Face-to-face	4.83	5.44	5.27	4.91	5.78	4.98	4.04	368–380
Media	4.90	5.53	5.28	4.87	5.77	4.69	3.80	321–332
Online	4.85	5.39	5.19	4.78	5.66	4.61	3.71	374–383
Biological								
Face-to-face	4.99	5.28	5.20	4.83	5.81	4.99	3.87	345–351
Online	4.96	5.35	5.16	4.78	5.62	4.62	3.71	328–334
Geophysical								
Face-to-face	4.66	5.30	5.18	4.90	5.72	5.09	4.14	314–316
Media	4.87	5.19	5.20	4.86	5.70	4.92	4.04	315–321
Online	4.83	5.25	5.18	4.78	5.70	4.84	3.98	267–275
Geological								
Face-to-face	4.93	5.28	5.19	4.90	5.71	5.10	4.12	248–256
Media	5.07	5.46	5.31	5.00	5.74	4.81	4.07	237–246
Online	4.96	5.37	5.17	4.84	5.63	4.91	3.93	230–237
Ecological								
Face-to-face	4.51	5.26	5.26	4.99	5.78	4.97	4.17	343–349
Chemical								
Face-to-face	4.85	5.27	5.22	4.72	5.64	4.79	3.96	179–184
Media	4.69	5.01	5.18	4.70	5.52	4.46	3.69	157–158
Online	4.85	5.20	5.06	4.66	5.58	4.49	3.56	154–155
Biochemical								
Face-to-face	4.61	5.23	5.07	4.73	5.67	4.75	3.83	369–372
Social								
Media	5.30	5.53	5.41	5.03	5.65	5.11	4.40	878–922

Notes: For the "priority" statement, respondents were given a list of objectives (including the objective noted in the table title) and asked to rate each objective between "very low importance" (1) and "very high importance" (7). For all other statements, respondents selected between "strongly disagree" (1) and "strongly agree" (7). Respondents were all faculty with PhDs at US-based universities. Standard deviations in appendix B tables.

[1] "In general, what are the most important or unimportant communication objectives that scientists such as yourself should have when taking part in [mode*]? Please remember that not every objective can be the most important objective." *Respondents were assigned to see all questions in the context of only one of three potential modes: face-to-face engagement, media engagement, or online engagement.

[2] "This objective is ethical."

[3] "Scientists who pursue this objective would be well regarded by their peers."

[4] "My colleagues would put a high priority on this objective."

[5] "Achieving this objective is possible for a good communicator."

[6] "I have the skills needed to achieve this objective."

[7] "Prior to this survey, I had thought a lot about this potential objective."

Preparing to Prioritize Competence as a Communication Objective

The following are eight questions that science communicators should consider when deciding whether to prioritize communicating that the scientific community is competent. In many cases, this could mean communicating academic and professional background, hard-won skills, and past successes and awards. Choices about how you present your research (e.g., design quality, flow) and yourself (e.g., clothing, grooming) may also communicate competence.

THE GOAL QUESTION

1. Given the behavior you want from your specific audience (i.e., your goal), why do you think it would be helpful if your chosen audience believed you are competent?

THE PREPARATION QUESTIONS

2. What does your chosen audience believe about your competence and is there meaningful opportunity to change these views?
3. What do you believe about your audience's competence?

THE TACTICS QUESTIONS

4. What could you do to potentially increase the likelihood that those with whom you are communicating see you as competent, including choices about messages, behaviors, tone/style, communication channel, and communication source?
5. What could you do to learn about your chosen audience's competence?

THE EVALUATION QUESTIONS

6. Did your chosen audience perceive you as competent?
7. What did you learn about your audience's competence?

THE ETHICS QUESTION

8. Are you being honest about your competence?

in a similar position as the objective of "hearing from other people" (chapter 5; see also appendix B tables). The most highly rated objective so far was "helping to inform people," which consistently received scores well above 6 out of 7 (chapter 2). The positive side of a priority score of 5 out of 7 is that it is still well above the scale midpoint, suggesting that scientists still see communicating competence as potentially useful. Furthermore, other measures received scores that suggest scientists see the competence objective as ethical, acceptable to peers (i.e., injunctive norms), and possible for a good communicator to achieve (i.e., response efficacy), with all three receiving above 5 out of 7. Scores were also right around 5 out of 7 for agreeing that their colleagues would prioritize communicating competence (i.e., descriptive norms) and their belief in their own ability (i.e., self-efficacy) to communicate competence. And, as with most of the objectives we measured in our surveys, there was evidence that many scientists had not thought about competence as a distinct communication objective, with scores right around 4 out of 7. We have not asked scientists about tactics related to competence objectives, but our sense is that science communicators who think they need to bolster their image of competence with a specific audience should expect colleagues to accept and support such efforts.

REFERENCES

1. Besley, John C., Anthony Dudo, Shupei Yuan, and Niveen AbiGhannam. "Qualitative Interviews with Science Communication Trainers About Communication Objectives and Goals." *Science Communication* 38, no. 3 (2016): 356–81. https://doi.org/10.1177/1075547016645640.

2. Miller, Steve, Declan Fahy, and the ESConet Team. "Can Science Communication Workshops Train Scientists for Reflexive Public Engagement? The ESConet Experience." *Science Communication* 31, no. 1 (2009): 116–26. https://doi.org/10.1177/1075547009339048.

3. Aurbach, Elyse L., Katherine E. Prater, Brandon Patterson, and Brian J. Zikmund-Fisher. "Half-Life Your Message: A Quick, Flexible Tool for Message Discovery." *Science Communication* 40, no. 5 (2018): 669–77. https://doi.org/10.1177/1075547018781917.

4. Cuddy, Amy J. C., Susan T. Fiske, and Peter Glick. "Warmth and Competence as Universal Dimensions of Social Perception: The Stereotype Content Model and the BIAS Map." In *Advances in Experimental Social Psychology*, vol. 40, edited by Mark P. Zanna, 61–149. Cambridge, MA: Academic Press, 2008.

5. BravoTV. "Padma Reveals Her Worst 'Top Chef' Dishes Ever." *The Daily Dish*, November 25, 2014. https://www.bravotv.com/the-daily-dish/padma-reveals -her-worst-top-chef-dishes-ever.

6. Monk, John. "Barbeque Eatery Owner, Segregationsit Maurice Besinger Dies at 83." *The State* (Columbia, SC), February 24, 2014. https://www.thestate .com/news/business/article13839323.html.

7. Wise, Justin. "Virginia GOP Calls for Boycott of Restaurant That Refused to Serve Sanders." *The Hill* (Washington, DC), June 25, 2018. https://thehill.com /homenews/administration/393971-virginia-gop-asks-supporters-to-boycott -restaurant-that-refused-to-serve-sarah.

8. Falkenheim, Jaquelina C. "Science and Technology: Public Attitudes and Public Understanding." In *Science and Engineering Indicators 2010*, edited by the National Science Board. Arlington VA: National Science Foundation, 2010. http://www.nsf.gov/statistics/seind10.

9. Earle, Timothy C., Michael Siegrist, and Heinz Gutscher. "Trust, Risk Perception, and the TCC Model of Cooperation." In *Trust in Cooperative Risk Management: Uncertainty and Scepticism in the Public Mind*, edited by Michael Siegrist, Timothy C. Earle, and Heinz Gutscher, 1–50. London: Earthscan, 2007.

10. Fiske, Susan T., and Cydney Dupree. "Gaining Trust as Well as Respect in Communicating to Motivated Audiences About Science Topics." *Proceedings of the National Academy of Sciences* 111, Supplement 4 (2014): 13593–97. https://doi.org/10 .1073/pnas.1317505111.

11. Schoorman, F. David, Roger C. Mayer, and James H. Davis. "An Integrative Model of Organizational Trust: Past, Present, and Future." *Academy of Management Review* 32, no. 2 (2007): 344–54. https://doi.org/10.2307/20159304.

12. Wojciszke, Bogdan, and Andrea E. Abele. "The Primacy of Communion over Agency and Its Reversals in Evaluations." *European Journal of Social Psychology* 38, no. 7 (2008): 1139–47. https://doi.org/10.1002/ejsp.549.

13. McCroskey, James C., and Thomas J. Young. "Ethos and Credibility: The Construct and Its Measurement after Three Decades." *Central States Speech Journal* 32, no. 1 (1981): 24–34. https://doi.org/10.1080/10510978109368075.

14. Hendriks, Friederike, Dorothe Kienhues, and Rainer Bromme. "Measuring Laypeople's Trust in Experts in a Digital Age: The Muenster Epistemic Trustworthiness Inventory (METI)." *PLOS ONE* 10, no. 10 (2015): e0139309. https://doi.org/10.1371/journal.pone.0139309.

15. Kraft-Todd, Gordon T., Diego A. Reinero, John M. Kelley, Andrea S. Heberlein, Lee Baer, and Helen Riess. "Empathic Nonverbal Behavior Increases Ratings of Both Warmth and Competence in a Medical Context." *PLOS ONE* 12, no. 5 (2017): e0177758. https://doi.org/10.1371/journal.pone.0177758.

16. Yuan, Shupei, Wenjuan Ma, and John C. Besley. "Should Scientists Talk About GMOs Nicely? Exploring the Effects of Communication Styles, Source Expertise, and Preexisting Attitude." *Science Communication* 41, no. 3 (2019): 267–90. https://doi.org/10.1177/1075547019837623.

17. Burgoon, Judee K., Thomas Birk, and Michael Pfau. "Nonverbal Behaviors, Persuasion, and Credibility." *Human Communication Research* 17, no. 1 (1990): 140–69. https://doi.org/10.1111/j.1468-2958.1990.tb00229.x.

18. Oppenheimer, Daniel M. "The Secret Life of Fluency." *Trends in Cognitive Sciences* 12, no. 6 (2008): 237–41. https://doi.org/10.1016/j.tics.2008.02.014.

19. Alter, Adam L., Daniel M. Oppenheimer, and Nicholas Epley. "Disfluency Prompts Analytic Thinking—But Not Always Greater Accuracy: Response to Thompson et al. (2013)." *Cognition* 128, no. 2 (August 2013): 252–55. https://doi.org/10.1016/j.cognition.2013.01.006.

20. Hernandez, Ivan, and Jesse Lee Preston. "Disfluency Disrupts the Confirmation Bias." *Journal of Experimental Social Psychology* 49, no. 1 (2013): 178–82. https://doi.org/10.1016/j.jesp.2012.08.010.

21. Reber, Rolf, Piotr Winkielman, and Norbert Schwarz. "Effects of Perceptual Fluency on Affective Judgments." *Psychological Science* 9, no. 1 (1998): 45–48. https://doi.org/10.1111/1467-9280.00008.

22. Oppenheimer, Daniel M. "Consequences of Erudite Vernacular Utilized Irrespective of Necessity: Problems with Using Long Words Needlessly." *Applied Cognitive Psychology* 20, no. 2 (March 2006): 139–56. https://doi.org/10.1002/acp.1178.

23. Rakedzon, Tzipora, Elad Segev, Noam Chapnik, Roy Yosef, and Ayelet Baram-Tsabari. "Automatic Jargon Identifier for Scientists Engaging with the Public and Science Communication Educators." *PLOS ONE* 12, no. 8 (2017): e0181742. https://doi.org/10.1371/journal.pone.0181742.

24. Thon, Franziska M., and Regina Jucks. "Believing in Expertise: How Authors' Credentials and Language Use Influence the Credibility of Online Health Information." *Health Communication* 32, no. 7 (2017): 828–36. https://doi.org/10.1080/10410236.2016.1172296.

25. Baker, D. A., Jillian M. Ware, N. J. Schweitzer, and Evan F. Risko. "Making Sense of Research on the Neuroimage Bias." *Public Understanding of Science* 26, no. 2 (2017): 251–58. https://doi.org/10.1177/0963662515604975.

26. Weisberg, Deena Skolnick, Jordan C. V. Taylor, and Emily J. Hopkins. "Deconstructing the Seductive Allure of Neuroscience Explanations." *Judgment and Decision Making* 10, no. 5 (September 2015): 429–41.

27. Besley, John C., and Anthony Dudo. *Landscaping Overview of the North American Science Communication Training Community: Topline Takeaways from Trainer Interviews.* N.p.: Kavli Foundation, Rita Allen Foundation, David and Lucille Packard Foundation, and Gordon and Betty Moore Foundation, 2017. http://www.informalscience.org/sites/default/files/Communication Training Landscape Overview Final.pdf.

28. Clark, Jenna L., Melanie C. Green, and Joseph J. P. Simons. "Narrative Warmth and Quantitative Competence: Message Type Affects Impressions of a Speaker." *PLOS ONE* 14, no. 12 (2019): e0226713. https://doi.org/10.1371/journal.pone.0226713.

29. Newman, Eryn J., and Norbert Schwarz. "Good Sound, Good Research: How Audio Quality Influences Perceptions of the Research and Researcher."

Science Communication 40, no. 2 (2018): 246–57. https://doi.org/10.1177/10755470
18759345.

30. Miller, Norman, Geoffrey Maruyama, Rex J. Beaber, and Keith Valone. "Speed of Speech and Persuasion." *Journal of Personality and Social Psychology* 34, no. 4 (1976): 615. https://doi.org/10.1080/00335636409382644.

31. Smith, Stephen M., and David R. Shaffer. "Speed of Speech and Persuasion: Evidence for Multiple Effects." *Personality and Social Psychology Bulletin* 21, no. 10 (1995): 1051–60. https://doi.org/10.1177/01461672952110006.

32. Bassett, Ronald E., Ann Q. Staton-Spicer, and Jack L. Whitehead. "Effects of Source Attire on Judgments of Credibility." *Central States Speech Journal* 30, no. 3 (1979): 282–85. https://doi.org/10.1080/10510977909368022.

33. Morris, Tracy L., Joan Gorham, Stanley H. Cohen, and Drew Huffman. "Fashion in the Classroom: Effects of Attire on Student Perceptions of Instructors in College Classes." *Communication Education* 45, no. 2 (1996): 135–48. https://doi.org/10.1080/03634529609379043.

34. Sebastian, Richard J., and Dennis Bristow. "Formal or Informal? The Impact of Style of Dress and Forms of Address on Business Students' Perceptions of Professors." *Journal of Education for Business* 83, no. 4 (2008): 196–201. https://doi.org/10.3200/joeb.83.4.196-201.

35. Clark, Colin. "The Impact of Entrepreneurs' Oral 'Pitch' Presentation Skills on Business Angels' Initial Screening Investment Decisions." *Venture Capital* 10, no. 3 (2008): 257–79. https://doi.org/10.1080/13691060802151945.

36. Fiske, Susan T., Amy J. C. Cuddy, Peter Glick, and Jun Xu. "A Model of (Often Mixed) Stereotype Content: Competence and Warmth Respectively Follow from Perceived Status and Competition." *Journal of Personality and Social Psychology* 82, no. 6 (2002): 878–902. https://doi.org/10.1037/0022-3514.82.6.878.

37. Lev-Ari, Shiri, and Boaz Keysar. "Why Don't We Believe Non-Native Speakers? The Influence of Accent on Credibility." *Journal of Experimental Social Psychology* 46, no. 6 (2010): 1093–96. https://doi.org/10.1016/j.jesp.2010.05.025.

38. Oswald, Anne-Marie M., and Srdjan Ostojic. "Curating More Diverse Scientific Conferences." *Nature Reviews Neuroscience* 21, no. 11 (2020): 589–90. https://doi.org/10.1038/s41583-020-0373-4.

39. Alter, Adam L., and Daniel M. Oppenheimer. "Uniting the Tribes of Fluency to Form a Metacognitive Nation." *Personality and Social Psychology Review* 13, no. 3 (2009): 219–35. https://doi.org/10.1177/1088868309341564.

40. Yuan, Shupei, John C. Besley, and Wenjuan Ma. "Be Mean or Be Nice? Understanding the Effects of Aggressive and Polite Communication Styles in Child Vaccination Debate." *Health Communication* 34, no. 10 (2019): 1212–21. https://doi.org/10.1080/10410236.2018.1471337.

41. Elgin, Suzette Haden. *How to Disagree without Being Disagreeable: Getting Your Point Across with the Gentle Art of Verbal Self-Defense.* New York: Wiley, 1997.

42. Beall, Lindsey, Teresa A. Myers, John E. Kotcher, Emily K. Vraga, and Edward W. Maibach. "Controversy Matters: Impacts of Topic and Solution

Controversy on the Perceived Credibility of a Scientist Who Advocates." *PLOS ONE* 12, no. 11 (2017): e0187511. https://doi.org/10.1371/journal.pone.0187511.

43. Vraga, Emily, Teresa Myers, John Kotcher, Lindsey Beall, and Ed Maibach. "Scientific Risk Communication About Controversial Issues Influences Public Perceptions of Scientists' Political Orientations and Credibility." *Royal Society Open Science* 5, no. 2 (2018): 170505. https://doi.org/10.1098/rsos.170505.

44. Dieckmann, Nathan F., Branden B. Johnson, Robin Gregory, Marcus Mayorga, Paul K. J. Han, and Paul Slovic. "Public Perceptions of Expert Disagreement: Bias and Incompetence or a Complex and Random World?" *Public Understanding of Science* 26, no. 3 (2017): 325–38. https://doi.org/10.1177/0963662515603271.

45. Gierth, Lukas, and Rainer Bromme. "Attacking Science on Social Media: How User Comments Affect Perceived Trustworthiness and Credibility." *Public Understanding of Science* 29, no. 2 (2020): 230–47. https://doi.org/10.1177/0963662519889275.

46. Hon, Linda Childers, and James E. Grunig. *Guidelines for Measuring Relationships in Public Relations*. Gainesville, FL: Institute for Public Relations, 1999. http://www.instituteforpr.org/topics/measuring-relationships.

47. Dillard, James Price, Kirsten M. Weber, and Renata G. Vail. "The Relationship between the Perceived and Actual Effectiveness of Persuasive Messages: A Meta-Analysis with Implications for Formative Campaign Research." *Journal of Communication* 57, no. 4 (2007): 613–31. https://doi.org/10.1111/j.1460-2466.2007.00360.x.

48. Chaiken, Shelly, and Durairaj Maheswaran. "Heuristic Processing Can Bias Systematic Processing: Effects of Source Credibility, Argument Ambiguity, and Task Importance on Attitude Judgment." *Journal of Personality and Social Psychology* 66, no. 3 (1994): 460–73. http://dx.doi.org/10.1037/0022-3514.66.3.460.

49. Trumbo, Craig W., and Katherine A. McComas. "The Function of Credibility in Information Processing for Risk Perception." *Risk Analysis* 23, no. 2 (April 2003): 343–53.

50. Allum, Nick C. "An Empirical Test of Competing Theories of Hazard-Related Trust: The Case of GM Food." *Risk Analysis* 27, no. 4 (2007): 935–46. https://doi.org/10.1111/j.1539-6924.2007.00933.x.

51. Critchley, C. R. "Public Opinion and Trust in Scientists: The Role of the Research Context, and the Perceived Motivation of Stem Cell Researchers." *Public Understanding of Science* 17, no. 3 (July 2008): 309–27.

52. Besley, John C. "Public Engagement and the Impact of Fairness Perceptions on Decision Favorability and Acceptance." *Science Communication* 32, no. 2 (June 2010): 256–80. https://doi.org/10.1177/1075547009358624.

53. Gao, Yixing, and Anna S. Mattila. "Improving Consumer Satisfaction in Green Hotels: The Roles of Perceived Warmth, Perceived Competence, and CSR Motive." *International Journal of Hospitality Management* 42 (September 2014): 20–31. https://doi.org/10.1016/j.ijhm.2014.06.003.

54. Terwel, Bart W., Fieke Harinck, Naomi Ellemers, and Dancker D. L. Daamen. "Competence-Based and Integrity-Based Trust as Predictors of Acceptance of Carbon Dioxide Capture and Storage (CCS)." *Risk Analysis* 29, no. 8 (2009): 1129–40. https://doi.org/10.1111/j.1539-6924.2009.01256.x.

55. Colquitt, Jason A., Brent A. Scott, and Jeffery A. LePine. "Trust, Trustworthiness, and Trust Propensity: A Meta-Analytic Test of Their Unique Relationships with Risk Taking and Job Performance." *Journal of Applied Psychology* 92, no. 4 (2007): 909–27. https://doi.org/10.1037/0021-9010.92.4.909.

56. Colquitt, Jason A., and Jessica B. Rodell. "Justice, Trust, and Trustworthiness: A Longitudinal Analysis Integrating Three Theoretical Perspectives." *Academy of Management Journal* 54, no. 6 (2011): 1183–206. https://doi.org/10.5465/amj.2007.0572.

57. Peters, Richard G., Vincent T. Covello, and David B. McCallum. "The Determinants of Trust and Credibility in Environmental Risk Communication: An Empirical Study." *Risk Analysis* 17, no. 1 (February 1997): 43–54.

58. National Science Board. "Science and Technology: Public Attitudes and Public Understanding." In *Science and Engineering Indicators 2012*. Arlington, VA: National Science Foundation, 2012. http://www.nsf.gov/statistics/seind12.

59. Malone, Chris, and Susan T. Fiske. *The Human Brand: How We Relate to People, Products, and Companies*. San Francisco: Jossey-Bass, 2013.

60. Cuddy, Amy J. C., Susan T. Fiske, and Peter Glick. "The BIAS Map: Behaviors from Intergroup Affect and Stereotypes." *Journal of Personality and Social Psychology* 92, no. 4 (2007): 631–48. https://doi.org/10.1037/0022-3514.92.4.631.

61. Besley, John C., Anthony Dudo, and Shupei Yuan. "Scientists' Views About Communication Objectives." *Public Understanding of Science* 27, no. 6 (2018): 708–30. https://doi.org/10.1177/0963662517728478.

8

Share Risks and Benefits

COMPASS SCIENCE COMMUNICATION has established itself as one of the most sophisticated, experienced, and comprehensive training organizations within the science communication community. They provide traditional training for groups of scientists as well as specialized coaching and support to scientists working on specific projects that might benefit from deeper-level help. Some of their work focuses on communication with topic-specific stakeholders, as well as the media, but they also maintain staff in Washington, DC, to support science communicators who want lawmakers to consider specific pieces of evidence or paths forward on important issues. We are fortunate to be recipients of their training and have enjoyed many opportunities to discuss the science communication field with the COMPASS team over the years. Anthony also joined their advisory board in 2021.

The tool that COMPASS is likely best known for is its Message Box [1,2], which plays an important role in their training and is meant to help scientists identify a specific audience and topic around which they can hone a potential message (i.e., improve message tactics). When we look at the Message Box, we see a helpful tool that puts a primary emphasis on the objectives of communicating the risks and benefits related to an area of research. It does so by asking potential communicators to identify an issue and answer a set of four questions. These questions are meant to help the communicators see their issue through four lenses.

The first of these lenses is about identifying the specific problem (i.e., a specific risk or challenge) that a communicator's research tries to help address. COMPASS counsels that a problem is often core to a research question and might "reveal itself through a troubling trend in the data, or a situation that will have a negative effect on people or the environment" [1, p. 11]. Next, they ask potential communicators to think about an answer to the question "So what?" from the perspective of their chosen audience. In describing what might constitute a good answer to the "so what" question, COMPASS focuses largely on the benefits that someone might accrue from the solutions suggested by research. This might include telling a policymaker or an organization how a specific area of research might support their agenda or benefit the policymaker's own stakeholders, including constituents, funders, members, or readers.

The Message Box's third lens focuses even more directly on these benefits and asks potential communicators to identify specific positive outcomes that might come from the types of solutions suggested by the research. And the fourth asks communicators to articulate in more detail the solution itself that the communicator thinks their research suggests. This quadrant is meant to include the behavior that the science communicator thinks will provide expected benefits that solve the stated problem. Whereas the three other sections of the Message Box focus on risks and benefits, the solution section seems a bit like a behavioral goal. It might also include an element of self-efficacy (chapter 10) inasmuch as COMPASS suggests that the solutions section can include content that addresses issues of what an audience can personally do to help solve a problem.

We are glad that COMPASS's work on the Message Box has become a widely used tool that helps science communicators focus their attention on a specific and important objective that is not traditional scientific knowledge (chapter 2). Too few trainers offer this level of clarity. And, at the risk of being trite, focusing on communicating benefits and risks likely offers far more benefits than risks. And beyond the Message Box, we also appreciate that COMPASS focuses on additional objectives and deeper discussions about linking risk and benefits communication to behavioral goals.

Our conversations with other trainers around the country have convinced us that COMPASS isn't alone in encouraging communicators to prioritize communication about risks and benefits. After scientific knowledge beliefs (chapter 2), risks and benefit beliefs are the twin communication objectives that trainers are most likely to tell us they emphasize in their courses. A focus on communicating the benefits of research (but not the risks) can also be seen in activities such as the annual Golden Goose Award that the American Association for the Advancement of Science's Office of Government Relations gives to researchers "whose seemingly obscure, federally funded research has led to major breakthrough" [3]. Our assumption is they want to communicate, through the award, that science funding can often provide unexpected benefits and that they believe that policymakers who believe in such benefits are more likely to ensure robust science funding.

How people think about risks and benefits is a large topic and the subject of a range of theories as well as a key component of other theories. This chapter's aim, therefore, is to provide (1) a high-level sense of some different ways that researchers think about risk and benefit beliefs, and (2) what we know about the origins and consequences of such beliefs. This is also the start of three chapters built around social science theory about increasing the odds that people will choose certain behaviors (i.e., behavior change) [4]. Chapters 3 through 7 focused on trustworthiness-related beliefs because we think trustworthiness gets discussed too vaguely in discussions of science communication strategy. Science communicators who want to have a cumulative, long-term impact need to make sure that people perceive the scientific community as trustworthy before they can have much influence on benefit or risk beliefs (this chapter), normative beliefs (chapter 9), or self-efficacy beliefs (chapter 10). Those interested in theory may recognize these three types of beliefs as the core of Icek Ajzen and Martin Fishbein's theory of planned behavior [5]. In some form, they are also part of other such theories as the health belief model [6], social cognitive theory [7], transtheoretical models [8], and protection motivation theory [9], to name a few. The integrated behavioral model attempts to summarize this literature while building on the theory of planned behavior [10,11].

One challenge of writing a chapter on risk-and-benefit beliefs comes from our effort to emphasize the role of cognitive engagement in shaping peoples' beliefs (as opposed to focusing on more automatic cognitive processes related to heuristics and biases). In contrast, much of the current literature emphasizes that people often experience risk as a feeling (chapter 12) rather than as a consequence of the slower, cumulative analytic processes that lead to stable beliefs, which we emphasize in this book. It is impossible to deny that people experience risks as a feelings [12,13] and that negative feelings are often quite powerful [14], but science communicators still likely need to communicate in ways that cognitively "engage" our audiences (and ourselves) to help people (including scientists) develop—over time—evidence-based beliefs about risks and benefits. As discussed in chapter 1, it is also important to recognize that almost all of the beliefs discussed in this book might be understood as evaluative beliefs inasmuch as they include some element of "goodness" or "badness." For example, seeing someone as dishonest likely involves both a belief about honesty and a negative evaluation.

Also, while much of the research uses terms such as "risks" and "benefits," it is also common to see benefits discussed in terms of the perceived response efficacy of a potential behavior in limiting a risk. Even more common is the discussion of risks or benefits simply as positive or negative attitudes about an issue or behavior. Again, for those interested in theory, the term "response efficacy" is often used in contexts where the focus is understanding or communicating the degree to which a behavior (e.g., exercise) or technology (e.g., solar panels) is a response that is able to provide an efficacious benefit in addressing a risk [15]. The term "attitude" is often similarly used in the context of discussing, for example, peoples' overall evaluation of a behavior or technology (e.g., is it likely to be good or bad, helpful or unhelpful) [11].

How Should We Understand Risk and Benefit Beliefs?

Formal risk analysts may try to evaluate hazards by making an assessment about the probability of an event and the severity of the consequences of that event. The uncertainty of known-unknowns and unknown-unknowns makes this tough, but social scientists understand it often does not make sense to measure peoples' risk perceptions using the same approach as a technical risk analyst [16].

One good place to start any discussion of modern risk perception research is with the work of Paul Slovic, a psychology professor at the University of Oregon and the cofounder of the nonprofit research organization Decision Research. One of the things Slovic is best known for is developing the "psychometric paradigm" of risk perception research [17,18]. At the core of this approach is the argument that we can understand perceptions of any given potential risk— whether from technologies, such as nuclear power, genetic engineering of food, or microwave ovens, or from activities, such as auto racing or downhill skiing—by using two types of measures or "dimensions": (1) the degree to which people believe that the technology or activity is relatively well-known (i.e., familiar, novel, etc.), and (2) people's sense that the risk object is something that creates an involuntary threat over which they have little control (and is thus "dreaded") [17,18]. This idea of risks having two dimensions is similar to how Susan Fiske and her colleagues argue that we can understand peoples' trustworthiness perceptions by considering warmth and competence [19]. This likely matters to us because science communicators can choose the degree to which they describe something as new and unusual as well as the degree to which they can describe something as easy or hard to control. More broadly, the scientific community should also aim to make sure they do not foist solutions on people and communities without substantial discussion and opportunity for input into technology design and deployment [20].

Slovic and his colleagues initially arrived at these two dimensions by asking four different groups of people (members of the League of Women Voters, members of a professional group, experts, and students) a series of questions about 30 different topics (e.g., smoking, electric power, handguns, food coloring, vaccinations) and used statistical techniques to figure out how many underlying ideas the questions were really capturing [18]. Science and risk communicators have used the psychometric paradigm research as a touchstone to emphasize that communicating about risks does not just mean sharing information about probabilities and consequences. The scientific community asks a lot of people when we call on our communities to accept new potential risks over which they have little control (we talk more about perceived control as self-efficacy in chapter 10). Unfortunately, to our knowledge there is no substantial body of research that has specifically sought to test messages aimed at shaping or reshaping the degree to which respondents believe that a technology is, for example, novel or voluntary. On a positive note, however, people in the scientific community have put a lot of thought into trying to design "participatory" processes aimed at giving people some actual control over technologies and research that affect their lives. Substantial work remains to be done in these areas, but ideas around responsible innovation are at the core of many efforts by thoughtful researchers to engage communities early in the process of scientific research and technology development [21] and, as discussed in chapter 6, about communicating a willingness to listen.

A second way researchers study risk and benefit beliefs is to ask survey respondents to mentally weigh the risks and benefits of something. For example, since 1979 the National Science Board has asked Americans to say in a survey whether they think "on balance, the benefits of scientific research have outweighed the harmful results, or have the harmful results of scientific research been greater than its benefits" [22]. Seventy-four percent of respondents in 2018 indicated the benefits outweighed the harms. The more common version of this type of survey question asks people to rate something like a technology or desired behavior by selecting a position between "good" and "bad" or "pleasant" and "unpleasant." Such "semantic differential" scales might give respondents something like five or seven different boxes to select from. The theory of planned behavior, for example, is one of the most common behavior change theories in the social sciences and uses this type of question as a component of a measure of attitude toward outcomes associated with a behavior [23]. Someone using the theory might want to know the degree to which a respondent thinks installing solar panels would be "effective" or "ineffective" at reducing energy costs, or the degree to which they think the process of installing would be "pleasant" or "unpleasant."

While it may sometimes make sense to ask for a single judgment about whether benefits outweigh risks, asking respondents to do mental calculus can cause people to quit surveys or provide poor quality responses [24]. It also provides less information to communicators who want to make decisions about what to emphasize when they communicate [25]. The theory of planned behavior gets around this problem by suggesting the use of both direct measures of what respondents believe about a behavior (e.g., how useful overall would it be to put in solar panels?) and questions about specific aspects of the behavior (e.g., how useful would solar panels be in reducing energy costs?). The rationale for asking about specific risks and benefits in exploratory survey work is that message designers often want to find beliefs that are correlated with a desired behavior *and* where there is a potential for communicators to try to foster change. It will rarely make sense to design a message that communicates something that everyone already believes or to emphasize beliefs that audience members see as irrelevant. Empirically, some beliefs also have little causal relationship with the desired behavior.

A third approach to measuring perceptions of risks and benefits is to simply ask people directly about how much risk or benefit they see in a technology or specific aspects of a technology. This approach seems especially useful for thinking about how to go about designing communication meant to foster risk or benefit beliefs. For example, a study on nanotechnology by researchers at the University of Wisconsin, Madison, asked respondents to use 10-point agreement–disagreement scales to indicate the degree to which they felt that nanotechnology might provide specific benefits to public health (e.g., "treat and detect new diseases") and the environment (e.g., "lead to new and better ways to clean up the environment"), as well as specific risks (e.g., "nanotech may lead to new human health problems," "nanotech may lead to contamination of water") [26]. These researchers have used similar techniques to look at such topics as biofuels [27] and genetically engineered food [28] as well.

A danger of this approach, on the other hand, is that respondents will report specific perceptions about a risk or benefit without ever having thought before about the issue using those categories [29]. One solution to this problem is to do formative research while designing the survey to ensure that you are asking about risks and benefits that people are actually thinking about (i.e., that are cognitively salient) [5]. This might mean, for example, asking people what benefits or risks first come to mind when thinking about trying a new food or accepting the construction of a new power plant. This creates a new challenge, however, in that people may not know what benefits or risks are going to be most important to their ultimate decision—and that you should communicate—until they hear relevant information. In practice, this likely means trying out arguments, seeing what seems to resonate, and adjusting as needed while always recognizing that strategic communication is not a one-off activity in which we should expect anything substantive from a single encounter.

A similar way that researchers sometimes ask about specific risk and benefit beliefs is with questions focused on whether the respondent says they believe the risks or benefits are likely to apply to themselves or whether they might happen to others [30], as well as whether they believe risks and benefits are likely to occur in the past, present, or future [31]. The procedural justice literature suggests that it makes further sense to talk about the fairness of who receives the risks and benefits of an action [32]. Such questions seem especially key to addressing potential inequities in how people experience risks or benefits. Again, however, there is rarely one correct approach; the research simply speaks to the potential value of recognizing the range of choices and figuring out over time what is ethical, reasonable, and impactful for a specific situation.

Further Challenges

One interesting thing about risk and benefit perceptions that communicators may wish to keep in mind is that risks and benefit beliefs tend to move together. In the real world, the risks and benefits of a decision are often independent. There are many things that create substantial risks but few substantial benefits (e.g., taking a selfie near a sheer drop; eating blowfish) and there are also many things that provide large benefits with few risks (e.g., wearing a seatbelt, vaccines). Most things that offer substantial risk with few benefits simply do not warrant much intellectual energy—or space on a survey. It simply does not make sense, for example, to ask someone if they believe that a risk of nuclear energy is that it will cause beetles to die in the Amazon. However, it is quite common in risk perception research to find that people who see something as risky find ways to cognitively downplay the benefits and that people who see something as beneficial tend to downplay the risks [33,34].

Equally odd is that completely unrelated risks sometimes move together. For example, both Gallup and the National Science Board have asked about a range of environmental and technological risks and found that people's fears about global warming are correlated over time with fears about water pollution and animal extinction [35], as well as nuclear power, genetic modification of crops, and various types of pollution all going up and down together [22]. This probably means that survey respondents often answer questions about specific beliefs using their general feelings of malaise or optimism about the world instead of well-considered opinions. The practical consequence for communicators interested in communicating about risks and benefits is, however, a need to recognize that communication choices often affect both risk and benefit perceptions at the same time.

In sum, there are at least three different ways researchers have studied risk and benefit beliefs about new technological or behavioral choices: (1) a psychometric approach in which new choices are classified by the degree to which something is novel and controllable, (2) a comparison approach where people are asked to weigh risks and benefits directly, and (3) a direct measurement approach in which people are asked to report the degree to which they expect a choice to create benefits or risks, including specific risks and benefits to specific people at specific times. Overall, our sense is that the final approach likely tells us the most about what scientists might want to prioritize when it comes to communicating about risks or benefits. The priority aspect here is especially important because you cannot communicate everything. Unfortunately, the existing research is rarely specific enough to tell us what to communicate in any given circumstance; that is up to formative research and judgment.

What about Uncertainty?

Anyone in the scientific community thinking about communicating risks and benefit information should ask themselves how certain they are about the relevant benefit or risk. Some communicators might worry that communicating about such uncertainty might dissuade people from doing a desirable behavior or stopping an undesirable behavior. As noted in chapter 1, our view is that the choice to communicate uncertainty should be about ethics rather than strategy. We think, ethically, science communicators should articulate, at least to some degree, how certain they are about whether any given choice will provide benefits or risks. It then becomes a (potentially challenging) tactical question of how to do that in an understandable way. We do not have the space here to provide guidance on how to communicate uncertainty, but a range of researchers have compiled evidence-based summaries of good practice [36–38].

Our key point is that we would never want a science communicator to think they should hide uncertainty because of a concern about whether sharing such information will have negative effects on potential audiences. We worry far more about the potential negative consequences of people coming to believe that scientists are being dishonest, whether by hiding uncertainty when it exists or feigning uncertainty when it mostly doesn't. The scientific community, in this regard, cannot and should not risk its reputation by communicating uncertainty strategically, like the tobacco and fossil fuel companies [39]. It should be reassuring, however, that the available evidence suggests that communicating uncertainty in respectful ways only rarely has substantial negative effects on how people view scientists or science. And the negative examples tend to be situations in which experiments amplify disagreement between scientists and others [37,38].

What Affects Risk and Benefit Perceptions?

We know from the previous chapters that most people who tend to think scientists are trustworthy—measured in different ways—tend to see more benefits and fewer risks in whatever area is being studied [40,41]. Demographic factors, such as race and gender, are also associated with risk and benefit perceptions, with women and non-white respondents tending to see more risks and fewer benefits. This is often attributed to the fact that marginalized and oppressed groups typically are the ones most vulnerable to threats and least likely to benefit from new opportunities [42–44]. However, while these types of findings may be useful for figuring out who to try to reach through behavior and communication, they do not provide much guidance to message choice. We are therefore primarily interested in the degree to which it is possible to directly communicate in a way that leads people to develop new or different beliefs about risks and benefits. We may also sometimes want to make existing beliefs more salient (i.e., top of mind).

Economists, rather than communication researchers, have done some of the most interesting research on the effect of risk and benefit information on views about technologies. For example, agricultural economist Jayson Lusk at Purdue University conducted multiple experiments on consumers' views about genetically modified (GM) food in the early 2000s [45–47]. One thing especially notable about his studies is that he used an auction technique that involves having potential consumers use real money to demonstrate their preferences. When possible, studying real behavior with real money can avoid problems that come from relying on respondents' answers to survey questions. In one study, Lusk's team gave groups of people in Texas, California, Florida, and France a cookie and then asked them how much money it would take to get them to trade their cookie for a cookie made with a GM ingredient with the understanding that they would be expected to eat the cookie at the end of the experiment [45]. Participants were not told how many rounds the experiment involved, but in each round they were asked to write down a price they would accept to trade in their regular cookie for a GM cookie. By the fourth and fifth round of bidding, the average amount of money respondents said they were willing to accept to eat the GM cookie ranged from a low of 14 cents for a group in Lubbock, Texas, to a high of $3.88 for a group in Grenoble, France. In other words, the French group indicated that it was worth an average of almost $4.00 to avoid eating a single GM cookie, but the Texas group did not really care whether they ate the GM cookie or the regular cookie.

The part of the experiment that should matter most to science communicators occurred after the fifth round of the experiment when the research team provided most participants information about the specific benefits that the genetically modified ingredients used in the cookie provided. Some groups were told that the GM ingredient helped farmers reduce pesticide use and could thus help protect the environment. Other groups were told that the reduced pesticide use would protect human health. A third set of groups were told that the GM ingredient would allow the plant to "grow at a faster rate and be resistant to drought" such that it would help lower food costs and increase food abundance in developing countries. A fourth group of participants did not receive any additional information. What the experiment ultimately found was that communicating benefit information tended to make people in most locations (except France) more willing to accept a GM cookie in comparison to the group that received no information [45]. A meta-analysis (i.e., a study of all the available studies) of additional "willingness to pay" and "willingness to accept" studies on similar topics further pointed to the potential advantages of communicating benefits [48]. We see this type of study as among the best evidence for why it is worth communicating benefit information.

More traditional experiments involving sharing information about risks and/or benefits have also generally found that such communication can often work [9,49], though not always [50]. While the size of effects is typically small, most experiments involve only one-off exposures to risk and/or benefit information in the form of a news article, brochure, or stand-alone message. We would expect more substantive impacts to result from cumulative, consistent exposure of benefit or risk messages over time [51] and in cases where it is possible to personalize risk or benefit messages so they are especially relevant to the chosen target audience [52]. On the other hand, there are issues, such as climate change, gun control, and economic policy, where people's natural tendencies to ignore information that conflicts with one's identity makes it less likely they will change their beliefs in the desired way (e.g., see the discussion of motivated cognition in chapter 6) [53]. In such cases, people may focus their cognitive effort in ways that simply adds belief to their existing position [54,55].

There is also a problem with saying that science communicators should share the benefits of their own research (or the risks of not heeding the research) in the way that trainers such as COMPASS suggest. The research we have reviewed focuses on communicating risks and benefits in the way that someone might do if they were writing an informational brochure or designing a public service announcement. We have not found research that specifically examines what happens when science communicators talk about the benefits of research in their field or try to convince others about the importance of a problem they are seeking to solve (i.e., "Here's the benefit of my research . . ."). We worry that science communicators extolling the benefits of their own research or playing up risks that they study may sometimes seem self-interested. Nevertheless, we would expect there to be acceptable ways to do so, especially if the communicator appears motivated by a desire to help others (chapter 3) and was otherwise seen as trustworthy (e.g., chapters 4–7).

One topic we have not addressed here is how different ways of presenting numbers or other visuals can affect people's risk and benefit beliefs. This is a topic we return to in chapter 12 in the context of framing.

What Do Risk and Benefit Perceptions Affect?

The logic of providing people with risk and benefit information is simply the "rational choice" argument [56] that people are more likely to behave in certain ways—including pseudobehaviors such as "supporting" research policy and funding—if they believe the behavior will benefit them without creating unmanageable risks. The opposite is also true. People are less likely to do things they believe create too much risk. In general, rational choice seems to be the case [6,34], but it is not the whole story. Two interesting findings highlight the fact that people might be slightly more attuned to the severity of a threat than they are to their personal susceptibility to the threat and that benefit beliefs are often more important than risk beliefs in predicting desired outcomes. People's perceptions of their ability to manage a threat—their sense of self-efficacy—is also tied up with risk beliefs (or emotions such as fear), but this is discussed in chapter 10.

A classic theory from health communication called the health belief model [57] predicted that people's responses to risk was likely to originate in their perceptions of (1) the severity of a health threat, (2) the susceptibility of the health threat, (3) the benefits of a specific suggested action, and (4) the barriers toward taking action. For severity, a review of studies using this model found only a small relationship with behavior [6]. While the relationship between severity and behavior is typically small, there appears to be no meaningful difference between subjects' perceptions of risk susceptibility and behavior. The more impressive finding of the analysis was the fact that the perceived benefits of a behavior—along with perceived barriers (chapter 10)— were the biggest average driver of the behavior. Other studies using similar theoretical models have also highlighted the central role that beliefs about benefits (and self-efficacy) seem to play in driving behavior [58,59]. Benefits also generally seem to be somewhat more important in the acceptance of new technologies [34].

Canadian health-promotion researchers Anca Gaston and Harry Prapavessis provide an example study focused on getting pregnant women to exercise [15]. Drawing on an established approach called the protection motivation theory, the researchers randomly assigned about 100 pregnant women into three equivalent groups. One group received a brochure promoting exercise by using fact-based arguments about the risks (both threat and severity) that pregnant women face from failing to exercise, as well as the benefits of exercise and information meant to make the reader feel they have the ability to exercise (self-efficacy, chapter 10). Another group received a brochure focused on nutrition, and a third group simply answered a survey without receiving a brochure. The exercise-focused brochure had the expected impact on the women's risk perceptions of not exercising, the benefit perceptions of exercising, and self-efficacy perceptions. More importantly, benefit beliefs around exercise, but not risk beliefs, seemed to be associated with exercise one week later. The relationship was fairly weak but consistent with past research, and again, the scope of the intervention was also quite limited.

Overall, it seems increasingly clear that successful interventions need to convince people that something is beneficial (i.e., response efficacy) while also making the desired behavior easier to do (i.e., fostering perceived and actual self-efficacy). These findings do not contradict the reality that humans have a natural tendency to react strongly to negative information [60]. Of course, scientists will also want to share risk information, but (as is discussed in chapter 10) there's a danger that risk information won't get people to change behavior if it is not accompanied by communicating a clear benefit to taking action. Of course, this also means that those proposing to create risks without benefits face a tough hurdle. For example, if a real-estate developer says they want to clear a wetland, we would expect them to have a hard time getting permission unless they can also show a benefit.

Conclusion

We think it is quite likely that science communicators who want to change behavior or garner support may need to prioritize communicating in ways that have the potential to change others' beliefs about risks and benefits—but especially benefits. Even a science communicator who just wants a decision-maker to consider scientific evidence likely needs to convince the decision-maker that considering the evidence is worthwhile. As noted, we have not seen any data that specifically shows that science communication can reliably affect the risk or benefit beliefs related to their own research, but we suspect it is possible to share information in a way that leads others to believe specific research is beneficial. We would not expect substantial impacts from any single exposure to such messages, but over time small effects might accumulate, especially where the benefits are compelling and clear.

The larger point of this chapter is that we can talk about risks and benefits in a lot of different ways. There are times where it might make sense to talk about the size of a threat, whereas other times it may make sense to talk about susceptibility or likelihood of being affected by a threat. Sometimes it may make sense to speak broadly about the balance of risks and benefits, while other times it may make sense to talk about specific benefits or risks (e.g., improved water quality or limits to economic progress). And the discussion does not stop here; in chapter 10 we cover what we know about communicating risks and benefits in the context of emotions, such as fear. In chapter 11 we talk about framing risks in ways that suggest thinking about them as concrete and near versus general and distant, as well as how different ways of presenting the same risks and benefits using different types of numerical or visual devices may affect how people respond.

We do not have data on what scientists think about the objective of communicating risks and benefits, nor have we asked about tactics related to communicating such objectives. The surveys reported in the previous chapters did not ask about these topics. The positive reception that COMPASS receives for its training makes us suspect that most science communicators are willing to share information about risks and benefits and would see value in doing so. Writing this chapter, however, also reminded us how hard it can be to communicate in ways that actually affect beliefs, and the inadvisability of expecting a large, simple relationship between people's beliefs and their behaviors.

What If My Research Does Not Suggest Risks or Benefits?

One additional topic not addressed so far is the question of how science communicators should talk about research when the risks underlying it may not seem compelling or the potential benefits are unclear. Recognizing this problem is important, but many people might not like our answer to the conundrum. It may be that scientists who cannot justify the benefits of their research, even in the long term, should think hard about their research choices. There is nothing inherently wrong with doing such research, but it may be asking too much of society to actively support such work.

We often tell our graduate students to articulate how a potential research project can help solve a real problem as early in the research process as possible. For us, asking questions about whether a project is likely to prove useful—and not just interesting to us at a given time— helps us choose what projects to prioritize. Looking back at our own research, it is easy to identify intellectually interesting projects where the real-world purpose now seems unclear. Such projects are often fun to start but often end up being unsatisfying. As peer reviewers of others' research for academic journals, we also often find ourselves asking scholars to better justify a study. And the National Science Foundation appears to be increasingly serious about asking US academics to explain "broader impacts" [61,62]. Scholars elsewhere are similarly being asked to justify the societal benefits of their research as a component of grant requests [63]. Such requests can create problems, but we are supportive of the general idea of asking scholars to think more deeply about the value of their work when asking for funding.

In the United States, one visible outcome of this commitment is the emergence of the newly established Advancing Research Impact in Society network (www.researchinsociety.org) that is aimed at helping academics think strategically about how to maximize the impact of their research. This community includes people interested in science communication as well as such related areas as formal and informal education (museums, science centers, after-school programs, etc.) and community-engaged scholarship (i.e., researchers who work directly with communities). Regardless, we still sometimes hear researchers express frustration with the expectation they should justify their research in terms of its utility instead of basic exploration and discovery. Such researchers might argue that it is often impossible to know what basic research will result in new technologies or innovations. The Golden Goose Award fits into this category in that it seeks to highlight "examples of scientific studies or research that may have seemed obscure, sounded 'funny,' or for which the results were totally unforeseen at the outset, but which ultimately led, often serendipitously, to major breakthroughs that have had significant societal impact" [3].

We are sympathetic to this view but do not think such arguments are likely to have a substantial positive impact on support for science. There is simply not good evidence for how much emphasis the scientific community should put on trying to communicate that (a) the benefits of funding basic science are large while (b) the risks of failing to support basic science are even bigger. Put differently, it is not clear to us that the reason some people do not support science funding is because the scientific community has failed to adequately communicate that such funding provides benefits. In this regard, the National Science Board regularly reports that about 8 in 10 Americans (83% in 2016) already agree, "Even if it brings no immediate benefits, scientific research that advances the frontiers of knowledge is necessary and should be supported by the federal government" [22]. As such, we are not sure how much room there is to move the needle on support for scientific funding by focusing on benefits. Our sense is that there are many clear examples of scholarship that will benefit

Preparing to Prioritize Risk and Benefit Beliefs
as a Communication Objective

The following are eight questions that science communicators should consider when deciding whether to prioritize sharing information about risk and benefit beliefs as a communication objective. In many cases, risk and benefit–related communication might involve sharing information about how a behavior or issue might contribute to positive or negative health, environmental, economic, or other quality-of-life outcomes.

THE GOAL QUESTION

1. Given the behavior you want from your specific audience (i.e., your goal), why do you think it would be helpful if your desired audience believed in specific risks or benefits?

THE PREPARATION QUESTIONS

2. What does your desired audience believe about issue- or behavior-related risks and benefits and is there meaningful room to change these beliefs?
3. What do you believe your audience believes about the relevant risks and benefits?

THE TACTICS QUESTIONS

4. What could you do to potentially increase the likelihood that those with whom you are communicating develop new or different beliefs about relevant risks and benefits, including choices about messages, behaviors, tone/style, communication channel, and communication source?
5. What could you do to learn about your chosen audience's risk and benefit beliefs?

THE EVALUATION QUESTIONS

6. Did your desired audience's beliefs about risks and benefits change?
7. What did you learn about your audience's risk and benefit beliefs?

THE ETHICS QUESTION

8. Are you being honest about risks and benefits?

society, and we should prioritize providing these scholars with opportunities to share their work.

REFERENCES

1. COMPASS Science Communication. *The Message Box Workbook: Communicating Your Science Effectively.* Portland, OR: COMPASS Science Communications, 2020. https://www.compassscicomm.org/the-message-box-workbook.

2. Baron, Nancy. *Escape from the Ivory Tower: A Guide to Making Your Science Matter.* Washington, DC: Island Press, 2010.

3. The Golden Goose Award. "General Nomination Criteria and Instructions." Accessed September 17, 2020. https://www.goldengooseaward.org/general-nomination.

4. Rice, Ronald E., and Charles K. Atkin. *Public Communication Campaigns.* 3rd ed. Thousand Oaks, CA: Sage, 2001.

5. Fishbein, Martin, and Icek Ajzen. *Predicting and Changing Behavior: The Reasoned Action Approach.* New York: Psychology Press, 2010.

6. Carpenter, Christopher J. "A Meta-Analysis of the Effectiveness of Health Belief Model Variables in Predicting Behavior." *Health Communication* 25, no. 8 (2010): 661–69. https://doi.org/10.1080/10410236.2010.521906.

7. Bandura, Albert. "Social Cognitive Theory of Mass Communication." In *Media Effects: Advances in Theory and Research,* edited by Jennings Bryant and Dolf Zillman, 121–53. Mahwah, NJ: Lawrence Erlbaum Associates, 2002.

8. Prochaska, James O., and Wayne F. Velicer. "The Transtheoretical Model of Health Behavior Change." *American Journal of Health Promotion* 12, no. 1 (1997): 38–48. https://doi.org/10.4278/0890-1171-12.1.38.

9. Neuwirth, Kurt, Sharon Dunwoody, and Robert J. Griffin. "Protection Motivation and Risk Communication." *Risk Analysis* 20, no. 5 (October 2000): 721–34.

10. Fishbein, Martin. "An Integrative Model for Behavioral Prediction and Its Application to Health Promotion." In *Emerging Theories in Health Promotion Practice and Research,* edited by Ralph J. DiClemente, Richard A. Crosby, and Michelle C. Kegler. San Francisco: Jossey-Bass, 2009.

11. Montano, Daniel E., and Danuta Kasprzyk. "Theory of Reasoned Action, Theory of Planned Behavior, and the Integrated Behavioral Model." In *Health Behavior: Theory, Research, and Practice,* edited by Karen Glanz, Barbara K. Rimer, and K. Viswanath, 95–124. San Francisco: Jossey-Bass, 2015.

12. Slovic, Paul, Melissa L. Finucane, Ellen Peters, and Donald G. MacGregor. "Risk as Analysis and Risk as Feelings: Some Thoughts About Affect, Reason, Risk, and Rationality." *Risk Analysis* 24, no. 2 (2004): 311–22.

13. Finucane, Melissa L., Ali Alhakami, Paul Slovic, and Stephen M. Johnson. "The Affect Heuristic in Judgments of Risks and Benefits." *Journal of Behavioral Decision Making* 13, no. 1 (2000): 1–17.

14. Baumeister, Roy F., Ellen Bratslavsky, Catrin Finkenauer, and Kathleen D. Vohs. "Bad Is Stronger Than Good." *Review of General Psychology* 5, no. 4 (2001): 323–70. https://doi.org/10.1037/1089-2680.5.4.323.

15. Gaston, Anca, and Harry Prapavessis. "Maternal-Fetal Disease Information as a Source of Exercise Motivation During Pregnancy." *Health Psychology* 28, no. 6 (2009): 726–33. http://dx.doi.org/10.1037/a0016702.

16. Aven, Terje, Yakov Ben-Haim, Henning Boje Andersen, Tony Cox, Enrique Lopez Droguett, Michael Greenberg, Seth Guikema, et al. *Society for Risk Analysis Glossary*. Herndon, VA: Society for Risk Analysis, 2018. https://www.sra.org/wp-content/uploads/2020/04/SRA-Glossary-FINAL.pdf.

17. Slovic, Paul. "Perception of Risk." *Science* 236, no. 4799 (1987): 280–85. https://doi.org/10.1126/science.3563507.

18. Slovic, Paul, Baruch Fischhoff, and Sarah Lichtenstein. "Rating the Risks." *Environment: Science and Policy for Sustainable Development* 21, no. 3 (1979): 14–39. https://doi.org/10.1080/00139157.1979.9933091.

19. Fiske, Susan T., and Cydney Dupree. "Gaining Trust as Well as Respect in Communicating to Motivated Audiences About Science Topics." *Proceedings of the National Academy of Sciences* 111, Supplement 4 (2014): 13593–97. https://doi.org/10.1073/pnas.1317505111.

20. Pidgeon, Nick, and Tee Rogers-Hayden. "Opening Up Nanotechnology Dialogue with the Publics: Risk Communication or 'Upstream Engagement'?" *Health, Risk & Society* 9, no. 2 (2007), 191–210. https://doi.org/10.1080/13698570701306906.

21. Gerber, Alexander. "RRI: How to 'Mainstream' the 'Upstream' Engagement." *Journal of Science Communication* 17, no. 3 (2018), Article C06. https://doi.org/10.22323/2.17030306.

22. National Science Board. "Science and Technology: Public Attitudes and Public Understanding." In *Science and Engineering Indicators 2018*. Arlington, VA: National Science Foundation, 2018. https://www.nsf.gov/statistics/2018/nsb20181/report/sections/science-and-technology-public-attitudes-and-understanding/highlights.

23. Armitage, Christopher J., and Mark Conner. "Efficacy of the Theory of Planned Behaviour: A Meta-Analytic Review." *British Journal of Social Psychology* 40, no. 4 (December 2001): 471–99. https://doi.org/10.1348/014466601164939.

24. Dillman, Don A., Jolene D. Smyth, and Leah Melani Christian. *Internet, Mail, and Mixed-Mode Surveys: The Tailored Design Method*. 3rd ed. Hoboken, NJ: John Wiley & Sons, 2009.

25. Binder, Andrew R., Michael A. Cacciatore, Dietram A. Scheufele, Bret R. Shaw, and Elizabeth A. Corley. "Measuring Risk/Benefit Perceptions of Emerging Technologies and Their Potential Impact on Communication of Public Opinion toward Science." *Public Understanding of Science* 21, no. 7 (2012): 830–47. https://doi.org/10.1177/0963662510390159.

26. Kim, Jiyoun, Sara K. Yeo, Dominique Brossard, Dietram A. Scheufele, and Michael A. Xenos. "Disentangling the Influence of Value Predispositions and Risk/Benefit Perceptions on Support for Nanotechnology among the American Public." *Risk Analysis* 34, no. 5 (2014): 965–80. https://doi.org/10.1111/risa.12141.

27. Cacciatore, Michael A., Dietram A. Scheufele, and Bret R. Shaw. "Labeling Renewable Energies: How the Language Surrounding Biofuels Can Influence Its Public Acceptance." *Energy Policy* 51 (December 2012): 673–82. https://doi.org/10.1016/j.enpol.2012.09.005.

28. Rose, Kathleen M., Dominique Brossard, and Dietram A. Scheufele. "Of Society, Nature, and Health: How Perceptions of Specific Risks and Benefits of Genetically Engineered Foods Shape Public Rejection." *Environmental Communication* (2020): 1–15. https://doi.org/10.1080/17524032.2019.1710227.

29. Gaskell, George, Katrin Hohl, and Monica M. Gerber. "Do Closed Survey Questions Overestimate Public Perceptions of Food Risks?" *Journal of Risk Research* 20, no. 8 (2017): 1038–52. https://doi.org/10.1080/13669877.2016.1147492.

30. Tyler, Tom R., and Fay L. Cook. "The Mass Media and Judgments of Risk: Distinguishing Impact on Personal and Societal Level Judgments." *Journal of Personality and Social Psychology* 47, no. 4 (1984): 693–708. https://doi.org/10.1037/0022-3514.47.4.693.

31. Roh, Sungjong, Laura N. Rickard, Katherine A. McComas, and Daniel J. Decker. "Public Understanding of 'One Health' Messages: The Role of Temporal Framing." *Public Understanding of Science* 27, no. 2 (2016): 185–96. https://doi.org/10.1177/0963662516670805.

32. Besley, John C. "Public Engagement and the Impact of Fairness Perceptions on Decision Favorability and Acceptance." *Science Communication* 32, no. 2 (June 2010): 256–80. https://doi.org/10.1177/1075547009358624.

33. Alhakami, Ali Siddiq, and Paul Slovic. "A Psychological Study of the Inverse Relationship between Perceived Risk and Perceived Benefit." *Risk Analysis* 14, no. 6 (1994): 1085–96. https://doi.org/10.1111/j.1539-6924.1994.tb00080.x.

34. Bearth, Angela, and Michael Siegrist. "Are Risk or Benefit Perceptions More Important for Public Acceptance of Innovative Food Technologies: A Meta-Analysis." *Trends in Food Science & Technology* 49 (2016): 14–23. https://doi.org/10.1016/j.tifs.2016.01.003.

35. "Environment." In Depth: Topics A to Z. *Gallup News*. Accessed February 27, 2020. https://news.gallup.com/poll/1615/environment.aspx.

36. Bostrom, Ann, Luc Anselin, and Jeremy Farris. "Visualizing Seismic Risk and Uncertainty: A Review of Related Research." In *Strategies for Risk Communication: Evolution, Evidence, Experience*, edited by W. Troy Tucker, Scott Ferson, Adam M. Finkel, and David Slavin, 29–40. Boston: Blackwell; Annals of the New York Academy of Sciences, 2008.

37. van der Bles, Anne Marthe, Sander van der Linden, Alexandra L. J. Freeman, James Mitchell, Ana B. Galvao, Lisa Zaval, and David J. Spiegelhalter. "Communicating Uncertainty About Facts, Numbers and Science." *Royal Society Open Science* 6, no. 5 (2019): 181870. https://doi.org/10.1098/rsos.181870.

38. Gustafson, Abel, and Ronald E. Rice. "A Review of the Effects of Uncertainty in Public Science Communication." *Public Understanding of Science* 29, no. 6 (2020): 614–33. https://doi.org/10.1177/0963662520942122.

39. Oreskes, Naomi, and Erik M. Conway. *Merchants of Doubt: How a Handful of Scientists Obscured the Truth on Issues from Tobacco Smoke to Global Warming.* New York: Bloomsbury, 2011.

40. Siegrist, Michael. "Factors Influencing Public Acceptance of Innovative Food Technologies and Products." *Trends in Food Science & Technology* 19, no. 11 (2008): 603–08.

41. Frewer, Lynn J., Ivo A. van der Lans, Arnout R. H. Fischer, Machiel J. Reinders, Davide Menozzi, Xiaoyong Zhang, Isabelle van den Berg, and Karin L. Zimmermann. "Public Perceptions of Agri-Food Applications of Genetic Modification: A Systematic Review and Meta-Analysis." *Trends in Food Science & Technology* 30, no. 2 (2013): 142–52. http://dx.doi.org/10.1016/j.tifs.2013.01.003.

42. Bord, Richard J., and Robert E. O'Connor. "The Gender Gap in Environmental Attitudes: The Case of Perceived Vulnerability to Risk." *Social Science Quarterly* 78, no. 4 (1997): 830–40.

43. Flynn, James, Paul Slovic, and C. K. Mertz. "Gender, Race, and Perception of Environmental Health Risks." *Risk Analysis* 14, no. 6 (Dec 1994): 1101–08.

44. Finucane, Melissa L., Paul Slovic, C. K. Mertz, James Flynn, and Theresa A. Satterfield. "Gender, Race, and Perceived Risk: The 'White Male' Effect." *Health, Risk & Society* 2, no. 2 (July 2000): 159–72. https://doi.org/10.1080/713670162.

45. Lusk, Jayson L., Lisa O. House, Carlotta Valli, Sara R. Jaeger, Melissa Moore, J.L. Morrow, and W. Bruce Traill. "Effect of Information About Benefits of Biotechnology on Consumer Acceptance of Genetically Modified Food: Evidence from Experimental Auctions in the United States, England, and France." *European Review of Agricultural Economics* 31, no. 2 (June 2004): 179–204. https://doi.org/10.1093/erae/31.2.179.

46. Lusk, Jayson L., Jutta Roosen, and John A. Fox. "Demand for Beef from Cattle Administered Growth Hormones or Fed Genetically Modified Corn: A Comparison of Consumers in France, Germany, the United Kingdom, and the United States." *American Journal of Agricultural Economics* 85, no. 1 (2003): 16–29. https://doi.org/10.1111/1467-8276.00100.

47. Lusk, Jayson L. "Effects of Cheap Talk on Consumer Willingness-to-Pay for Golden Rice." *American Journal of Agricultural Economics* 85, no. 4 (2003): 840–56. https://doi.org/10.1111/1467-8276.00492.

48. Lusk, Jayson L., Jamal Mustafa, Lauren Kurlander, Maud Roucan, and Lesley Taulman. "A Meta-Analysis of Genetically Modified Food Valuation Studies." *Journal of Agricultural and Resource Economics* 30, no. 1 (2005): 28–44.

49. Gutteling, Jan M. "A Field Experiment in Communicating a New Risk: Effects of the Source and a Message Containing Explicit Conclusions." *Basic and Applied Social Psychology* 14, no. 3 (1993): 295–316. https://doi.org/10.1207/s15324834basp1403_4.

50. Scholderer, Joachim, and Lynn J. Frewer. "The Biotechnology Communication Paradox: Experimental Evidence and the Need for a New Strategy." *Journal of Consumer Policy* 26, no. 2 (2003): 125–57. https://doi.org/10.1023/a:1023695519981.

51. Brossard, Dominique, and Anthony D. Dudo. "Cultivation of Attitudes toward Science." In *Living with Television Now: Advances in Cultivation Theory & Research*, edited by Michael Morgan, James Shanahan, and Nancy Signorielli, 120–46. New York: Peter Lang, 2012.

52. Mildenberger, Matto, Mark Lubell, and Michelle Hummel. "Personalized Risk Messaging Can Reduce Climate Concerns." *Global Environmental Change* 55 (2019): 15–24. https://doi.org/10.1016/j.gloenvcha.2019.01.002.

53. Hart, P. Sol, and Erik C. Nisbet. "Boomerang Effects in Science Communication: How Motivated Reasoning and Identity Cues Amplify Opinion Polarization About Climate Mitigation Policies." *Communication Research* 39, no. 6 (2012): 701–23. https://doi.org/10.1177/0093650211416646.

54. Frewer, Lynn J., Chaya Howard, and Richard Shepherd. "Public Concerns in the United Kingdom About General and Specific Applications of Genetic Engineering: Risk, Benefit, and Ethics." *Science, Technology, & Human Values* 22, no. 1 (1997): 98–124.

55. Gastil, John, and James P. Dillard. "Increasing Political Sophistication through Public Deliberation." *Political Communication* 16, no. 1 (1999): 3–23. https://doi.org/10.1080/105846099198749.

56. Whitely, Paul F. "Rational Choice and Political Participation: Evaluating the Debate." *Political Reseach Quarterly* 48, no. 1 (March 1995): 211–33. https://doi.org/10.2307/449128.

57. Rosenstock, Irwin M. "Historical Origins of the Health Belief Model." *Health Education Monographs* 2, no. 4 (1974): 328–35. https://doi.org/10.1177/109019817400200403.

58. Floyd, Donna L., Prentice-Dunn Steven, and Ronald W. Robers. "A Meta-Analysis of Research on Protection Motivation Theory." *Journal of Applied Social Psychology* 30, no. 2 (2000): 407–29. https://doi.org/10.1111/j.1559-1816.2000.tb02323.x.

59. Milne, Sarah, Paschal Sheeran, and Sheina Orbell. "Prediction and Intervention in Health-Related Behavior: A Meta-Analytic Review of Protection Motivation Theory." *Journal of Applied Social Psychology* 30, no. 1 (2000): 106–43. https://doi.org/10.1111/j.1559-1816.2000.tb02308.x.

60. Tierney, John, and Ray F. Baumeister. *The Power of Bad: How the Negativity Effect Rules Us and How We Can Rule It*. New York: Penguin Press, 2019.

61. Gould, Rachelle K., Kimberly J. Coleman, Daniel H. Krymkowski, Iberia Zafira, Theodora Gibbs-Plessl, and Anna Doty. "Broader Impacts in Conservation Research." *Conservation Science and Practice* 1, no. 11 (2019): e108. https://doi.org/10.1111/csp2.108.

62. Watts, Sean M., Melissa D. George, and Douglas J. Levey. "Achieving Broader Impacts in the National Science Foundation, Division of Environmental Biology." *BioScience* 65, no. 4 (2015): 397–407. https://doi.org/10.1093/biosci/biv006.

63. Wilkinson, Clare. "Evidencing Impact: A Case Study of UK Academic Perspectives on Evidencing Research Impact." *Studies in Higher Education* 44, no. 1 (2019): 72–85. https://doi.org/10.1080/03075079.2017.1339028.

9

Share What Other People
Think Is Normal

MICHIGAN STATE UNIVERSITY (MSU), where coauthor John Besley works, has a long history of conducting research on how communicating social norms can affect behavior [1]. Key beliefs about social norms might include perceptions about both what others do (e.g., do other people reuse the same towel when staying at a hotel for multiple nights?) and beliefs about what others expect (e.g., do other people think you should reuse the same towel?). Researchers typically call perceptions about others' behaviors "descriptive norms" and beliefs about others' expectations "injunctive" and/or "subjective" norms [2]. Since 2006, one of the most visible components of the norms-focused research at MSU has been a series of student-produced graphics of friendly looking cartoon ducks with images and messages designed to communicate norms around drinking (figure 9.1). The students chose ducks because of their ubiquity on the Red Cedar River in the heart of campus. And in addition to the message-specific duck graphics, the images typically included a citation for the related data and a project website address. These graphics are distributed via social media but also through physical products, such as cafeteria "table toppers," clothing, bookmarks, and posters in places where students con-

Figure 9.1. MSU Duck Campaign communicating social norms.
Used with permission from Michigan State University.

gregate [1,3]. The expectation is that communicating true norms related to alcohol use will decrease student drinking and increase behaviors that protect students who drink too much. Using MSU as an example, we argue that science communicators should consider prioritizing communicating about the sometimes-hidden behaviors and expectations of people who are important to their key audiences.

The MSU Duck Campaign is just one example of a host of efforts on college campuses to decrease problem drinking by trying to correct students' beliefs about what constitutes "normal" and expected behavior [4]. The logic of such campaigns is straightforward: students often overestimate the prevalence of campus drunkenness and make better decisions when they believe *most* other students are also making good decisions. The challenge is that anyone who has ever visited the area around a university during the weekend knows that drunk students have a way of making themselves spectacularly visible. It would be easy to believe that most students in a college town party all weekend based on frequent exposure to examples of drunken dumbassery. Less visible are the many, many students who find ways to avoid making a spectacle of themselves. Such students often drink moderately or abstain entirely. Social norms campaigns about student drinking seek to make the responsible students more visible.

Beyond alcohol, researchers have explored how communicating social norms can affect a wide range of behaviors [5,6], including health and environmental behaviors [7,8]. At the core of this research are the twin facts that people often (1) use other people's behaviors and opinions to make sense of an uncertain world, especially when they want to fit in, and (2) make mistakes when they try to assess what others think and do because they rely on their own limited experiences [2]. People are especially bad at assessing other people when the relevant behaviors and opinions are hard to observe. Worse, given how rarely humans have the motivation or ability to think deeply about most things [9], most of us will tend to use easily available information to assess social norms. Information that is harder to notice—because it is hidden from sight, like sober students in the library—is less likely to receive attention.

A classic social norms study led by persuasion guru Robert Cialdini [10], for example, showed in real-world experiments that you could decrease littering by simply picking up trash where someone might be tempted to litter [11,12]. For this set of experiments, research subjects who did not know they were in a study were given a paper flyer and then watched to see whether they littered. The wrinkle was that the research team removed all the trash bins from the area so that study participants had the choice of either keeping the flyer or throwing it in on the ground. One iteration of the experiment showed that people in a litter-free environment were less likely to litter than people in a heavily littered space. Even more interesting was the fact that seeing someone litter in the already-littered space further increased littering, while seeing someone litter in the litter-free environment resulted in the least littering of all. To Cialdini and his team, this suggested that the clean space likely communicated that tossing trash on the ground was normatively unacceptable while observing someone else violating this norm cognitively primed (i.e., made salient) participants' beliefs about the social unacceptability of littering. One thing to note, however, is that the experiment communicated the norm of the situation through the environment but also relied on people's existing beliefs about the acceptability of littering. These existing beliefs likely developed over time because of other communication.

Unfortunately, although understanding social norms is an active area of social science research, the scientists and science communication trainers we have interviewed in recent years almost never talk about the potential value of changing normative beliefs around science. Similarly, research published in science communication-focused journals—unlike research in health, risk, and environmental communication journals—rarely addresses trying to shape normative beliefs in the context of public opinion and behavior. This is too bad, although one exception is discussed later in this chapter. Ahead of that, we provide an introduction to how social scientists think about norms, including different types, followed by what we know about communicating norms and the resulting impact. Our core argument is that science communicators could likely benefit by doing more to communicate what key people (1) do about an issue (e.g., are friends and family cutting energy use; is there a scientific consensus?), and (2) expect others to do about an issue (e.g., do friends and family think cutting energy use is morally good?). As in previous chapters, much of the research discussed will come from across social science scholarship, but the core ideas are relevant to any type of science communication. Cialdini, in fact, has written extensively about norms as "social proof" in his best-selling books on persuasion; books we think all communicators should read [10,13].

Why Treat Beliefs About Social Norms as a Distinct Type of Communication Objective?

Our colleague Maria Lapinski and her coauthor Rajiv Rimal have provided a useful academic overview of key ideas for anyone hoping to affect behavior by communicating about norms [2,14]. As noted already, one step is recognizing that people regularly experience different types of norms in their life. This includes norms focused both on what others normally do (i.e., descriptive norms as the prevalence of a behavior) and on what others normally expect (i.e., injunctive norms as perceived pressure to do a behavior) [12]. Other researchers sometimes use the term "subjective norms" [15], or other such terms, rather than "injunctive norms," but we prefer the latter term because it highlights the idea that these types of norms are special in that they derive from perceptions of what people expect, which is not always the same as what people do themselves (i.e., "do what I say, not what I do"). Technically, researchers focused on subjective norms focus on expectations of a specific group that is important to the person whose behavior you are trying to affect.

Researchers also argue that descriptive and injunctive norms may affect behavior through somewhat different paths. Descriptive norms seem to affect behavior by helping people decide what to do in situations where they face ambiguity about the best course of action. Someone who does not know if it is okay to water their lawn during the dry days of late summer might look around to see what others on the same street are doing to help decide what might be okay. In contrast, complying with injunctive norms seems to affect behavior because people tend to want to fit in with the people in the groups with whom they want to affiliate [11]. Complying with injunctive norms represents a way of trying to fit in and can occur even if someone is unaware of the influence of their own beliefs about others [16]. Perceptions of group members' actual behaviors (descriptive norm beliefs) can also communicate expected behaviors (injunctive norm beliefs), and vice versa [17]. In other words, we often see behaviors as more acceptable when we see more people doing them, and we often believe more people do behaviors we perceive as socially desirable.

A related issue is recognizing that people will sometimes make distinctions between behaviors they believe are normal or expected within one group compared to another group. For example, one survey conducted by a group of MSU researchers showed that students believed there were drinking differences between (1) "people who [were] important" to the respondent, (2) fellow Michigan State University students, and (3) other university students from across the United States. This distinction between the beliefs and behaviors of important people in one's life and the norms associated with other groups is especially important when the issue involves the potential for social pressure when ignoring a norm (e.g., conservatives who support action on climate change might expect to be treated poorly by other conservatives). Another study, led by researcher Kami Silk, showed that students responded better to messages about anti-suicide norms from peers than from celebrities [18]. Indeed, one criticism of the theory of planned behavior—a dominant theory in the study of behavior change (discussed in chapter 8)—is that it includes subjective norms but not descriptive norms. One potential reason for this focus is that people seem most affected by the norms of people with whom they identify more closely [19], and so subjective norms appear more influential, especially in young people and cultures where there is more emphasis on group cohesion [20]. Our sense is that science communicators should generally seek to affect both descriptive and injunctive norms but that "reference groups" may sometimes need to be people other than target audiences' immediate friends and families (e.g., they could communicate what the majority of scientists believe).

Another key element that Lapinski and Rimal note is that perceptions about social norms are different than actual "collective" norms. Collective norms can be understood as people's actual behaviors and expectations [1,14,21]. One study by Rimal and his colleagues, for example, found that people in Malawian communities where condom use was more prevalent (i.e., the actual collective norm) were more likely to use condoms in future sexual encounters, regardless of perceived norms. Indeed, what is most interesting in social norms research is where people misjudge what others are thinking or doing such that there is the opportunity for communication to change beliefs. For this chapter's purposes, however, the key is simply to recognize that normative beliefs represent a unique type of communication objective that strategic communicators should consider as part of their planning process.

Communicating Social Norms

Many things we say and do communicate what we think is normal and expected, even small things. As with other types of beliefs, a person's perceptions about what constitutes regular and acceptable behavior will accumulate over time and become a normative belief. The sources of this cumulative exposure might include things experienced directly as well as what one reads and sees through various media channels [1]. Communication and other life experience can also serve to make the beliefs more "cognitively accessible" (i.e., salient) and thus more influential in a given decision context [22–24]. And again, like other potential communication objectives, the question for strategic science communicators becomes deciding whether it is ethical and useful to purposefully communicate norms to create new normative beliefs or to remind people of their existing beliefs.

Researchers doing experiments in this area sometimes communicate norms through implicit messages while others use explicit messages. Campus alcohol campaigns involve explicitly telling students what constitutes normal behaviors (e.g., how much the average student drinks on a weekend). In contrast, Cialdini's study on littering mentioned at the start of this chapter communicated norms implicitly when it presented the unknowing research subjects with a trash-strewn or trash-free environment [12]. They further sought to cognitively prime people's existing injunctive norms about littering behavior by arranging it so that some test subjects saw another person litter in a litter-free environment (i.e., they were making norms more salient, more cognitively accessible [23]). This priming seemed to cause people who saw someone litter in a trash-free environment to litter even less than people who only experienced a trash-free environment, without the cognitive prime.

In general, it seems that implicit messages might be more effective than explicit messages. One analysis of studies on environmental behaviors argued that this might be because explicit communication causes people to do things like mentally counterargue with the norms message in a way that prevents them from forming new normative beliefs [8]. Unfortunately, counting on implicit messages might not always be feasible for science communicators. Whereas Cialdini could signal social acceptability by tightly controlling an environment, it is harder to think of easy equivalents for science communicators (beyond encouraging members of the science community to visibly behave in ways that are consistent with scientific evidence, such as by sharing on social media when they get their kids vaccinated, use green transportation, and vote for candidates who support science). Indeed, some of Cialdini's most famous research studies aimed to increase hotel towel reuse by explicitly communicating other guests' behaviors [25] and decrease energy use by explicitly communicating research participants' energy use relative to their neighbors' use [26,27]. Similarly, our MSU colleagues have used explicit messages to affect such behaviors as the use of campus counseling services [18] and getting men to wash their hands after using the bathroom [28,29].

Another difference between the littering, towel use, and hand-washing studies versus studies of other types of behaviors is the timing of the desired behavior. In these cases, the idea is to provide people with situational cues that provide information but may or may not be encoded into memory as longer-term beliefs. In contrast, the energy-use research—similar to related work on water conservation [30] and health-focused work on topics such as sun protection [31], the use of counseling services [18], and alcohol use—was designed to foster normative beliefs with the expectation that these beliefs would be recalled and/or cognitively available at a later point in time.

What Do Social Norms Affect?

The energy-use research is particularly instructive because of its emphasis on the potential value of communicating both descriptive and injunctive norm information to affect conservation behaviors [2]. In the initial study, one problem that the research team faced in telling people about the average energy use of their neighbors was they knew that, logically, about half of their target audience was going to find out that they were using less energy than their neighbors. The fear was that letting people know they were doing relatively well might cause some people to ease off their efficiency efforts [27]. To get around this problem, the research team had the simple solution of communicating social approval by putting happy faces on a portion of energy reports that were using relatively less energy and unhappy faces on a portion of the energy reports that showed a home was using a relatively more energy. What happened was that people who were using more energy than the average tended to decrease their energy when they found out they were using more energy than others (as expected). The behavior for the people who started with relatively low energy use, however, depended on whether they saw a happy face. The people who saw a happy face tended to continue to do relatively well on their energy use whereas the people who only found out that they were using relatively less energy increased their energy use. The good news from this line of research was that a company formed to help energy companies extend the work beyond academia and ended up having a meaningful impact on customers' energy use [26].

Other factors can also influence whether communicating normative information has an effect. Perhaps the most important is that descriptive norms are less likely to affect people who already have strong beliefs about a behavior. For example, someone who thinks a behavior is immoral is unlikely to be affected by normative information. Similarly, someone who believes a behavior communicates something about their identity (e.g., owning a heavy pickup truck) or provides a substantial benefit (e.g., using a powerful pickup truck to haul a boat) might not be as susceptible to normative appeals [32].

The argument is that people who have already bought into a behavior—or are deeply "involved" in the behavior—are not experiencing uncertainty about the behavior and are therefore not deciding what to do using their beliefs about other peoples' behaviors or expectations. If you have decided that you are the type of person who really values fried food or identifies as the type of person who recycles or conserves water, then your perceptions about what others think of fast food, recycling, or water use are less likely to matter [30,32]. A team led by Wesley Schultz—who also led the energy research in which Cialdini was involved—found, for example, that they could reduce residential water use by telling people how they compared to neighbors, similar to the energy project. In this case, however, they also looked at personal norms and found that providing information about normal residential water use decreased use in people who were using more water than usual and for whom conservation was not seen as an important moral obligation. As in the energy case, providing environmental benefits information (e.g., chapter 8) rather than normative information had little impact.

One challenge of adapting the norms research to broader science communication discussions is that the norms research focuses largely on getting people to do individual behaviors, such as more handwashing or less drinking. In contrast, many of the goals that science communicators have told us they value most involve civic behaviors, including getting policymakers to use scientific evidence when making decisions (see chapter 1). Nevertheless, researchers have found that social norms messages appear able to promote such civic behaviors as voting [33,34] and cognitively engaging with political issues [35] as well as such outcomes as donations [36,37] and political participation (i.e., civic engagement) [38]. There is no reason not to expect that beliefs about social norms wouldn't similarly affect science-related civic behaviors, although we would love to see more research.

Consensus Messaging

Perhaps the most active discussion related to norms in the science communication research community focuses on the potential value of communicating that scientists have come to a consensus on an issue, such as climate change. The hypothesis is that consensus perceptions serve as "gateway beliefs" that could lead people to develop a range of additional beliefs consistent with the consensus and, in turn, support action consistent with the consensus. For example, a number of studies have found that telling people there is a near consensus among climate scientists about climate change can affect the belief that climate change is real, dangerous, and caused by humans [39–43]. In turn, these beliefs seem to be associated with support for climate change action. In addition to climate change, researchers have shown the potential value of consensus messaging on issues such as genetically modified (GM) food [44], vaccination [45], and nuclear energy [46].

Studies on consensus are often straightforward, with research teams providing some portion of study participants with information about the existence of a scientific consensus while not giving the same information to other study participants. The study participants then indicate the degree to which they believe there is a scientific consensus. They are also typically asked about other beliefs (e.g., beliefs about risks and causes) as well as policy support (a pseudobehavioral goal). For example, one early study on climate change divided their broad sample of 1,100 Americans into 11 groups and began asking them questions through an online survey tool [42]. The respondents started with distractor questions about two relatively apolitical subjects (breast cancer and drunk driving) followed by questions focused on beliefs about climate change, including a question in which respondents were asked to estimate the percentage of scientists who believe in climate change (i.e., the degree to which belief in climate change is the norm for climate scientists). For this study, these climate questions were used as a pretest of respondents' consensus beliefs. The respondents were then distracted again with questions about an animated Star Wars television program. At this point, most of the respondents were told that "97% of climate scientists have concluded that human-caused climate change is happening" alongside a logo from the American Association for the Advancement of Science

(AAAS). Respondents in 10 of the groups received slightly different versions of this message (e.g., some had additional pictures, metaphors, or a pie chart) while the eleventh group received no consensus information. They were then distracted again with questions about a Star Wars television show before being reasked additional questions about climate change, including the consensus question. Ultimately, the different consensus messages all seemed to work about equally well, driving up the perceived consensus around climate change by about 13%, while the group who received no consensus message did not change their average response at all. Later studies by researchers from the same team focused on additional climate beliefs [47] and the potential benefit of video messages [48].

At this point, the evidence seems clear that it is possible to change many people's beliefs about the degree to which scientists agree on topics. The idea of gateway beliefs has generated some disagreements on two points, however. First, there is a question about the degree to which consensus messages work on highly partisan respondents. The initial hope is that consensus messages about such issues as climate change might work well on conservatives [39,40,47], while other researchers have expressed concern that such messages might further polarize the debate and hurt the broader reputation of science [49–51]. To us, this debate reminds us why it is so important to think about audience-specific goals when designing communication. It might be that the best use of our scarce communication resources would be to shift our more moderate neighbors toward supporting action on topics such as climate change while recognizing that we should not expend resources trying to reach the unreachable. At the same time, we would like to see more emphasis on whether it is possible to design messages specifically aimed at avoiding an unwarranted negative reaction from partisan groups [50].

A second concern in the research is the fact that experimental evidence about the value of consensus messaging—like so much other communication research—relies on short-term experiments where respondents might only see a message once and where there is no substantive measure of issue-related behavior. In this regard, the data showing that it is possible to change consensus beliefs seems much stronger than the evidence showing that a change in consensus beliefs lead to substantive, long-term changes in other issue-related beliefs. The fact that different climate change beliefs are correlated, for example, does not necessarily mean that changing one type of belief will change other types of beliefs (although it is plausible) [49,52].

Finally, while we have lumped consensus messages into the discussion of social norms, our colleague Maria Lapinski points out that doing so may not make sense. From this perspective, consensus beliefs are similar to normative beliefs because they both put the attention on beliefs about others' beliefs. What is different, however, is that beliefs about injunctive norms, as discussed earlier, seem to work because people want to be part of a group that they value. Deferring to scientists might make sense in some contexts [53] or groups, but in other cases it might be that people are just using their beliefs about consensus as a way to make sense of an issue they do not understand. In this regard, it is likely to be easier to try to understand what perspective is common about experts than it is to understand the underlying science. For us right now, however, the underlying cognitive mechanism seems less important than the simple idea that communicators might sometimes want to change what people believe about others' beliefs (and expectations).

Conclusion

We would like science communication researchers and practitioners to look for more opportunities to test social norm–like messages. Americans—and we suspect people in many other countries too—want scientists to provide advice on important issues. For example, a 2019 survey by the Pew Research Center found that 60% of Americans want scientists to "play an active role in public policy debates" [54, p. 5]. Similarly, a 2010 National Science Foundation survey found that 85% of Americans want environmental scientists to have "a great deal" (48%) or "fair amount" (37%) of influence on decisions about what to do about global warming. Americans also said they want scientists to influence decisions about GM foods (81%), stem cell research (80%), nuclear power (79%) [55].

We are not suggesting that science communicators fudge agreement when it does not clearly exist. One ethical and practical challenge of communicating a shared norm or consensus is that it requires us to know if a norm exists. Colgate toothpaste notoriously got in trouble for claiming that "more than 80% of dentists recommend" the brand, but this just meant that dentists thought Colgate was one of many brands they would be happy to have their clients use [56]. We do suggest, however, it is worth sharing the information when we have strong evidence that scientists (or some other relevant group) believe something that we hope others might come to believe. Even better, given the importance of shared identity in the social norms literature, we think it would be great if people knew what scientists in their own country or region believe, not just what faceless "scientists" in some far-away place believe. Sports fans and university alumni might similarly find it helpful to know what researchers at their favorite institutions believe.

In addition to public opinion surveys, the Pew Research Center also surveys scientists about the same set of topics and compares their beliefs to the average citizen's. For example, they found in 2014 that 57% of Americans think it is unsafe to eat GM foods but only 11% of members of the AAAS hold this view [57, p. 127]. It might be natural to interpret the disagreement as evidence that people need to learn more science so that they understand GM food in the way that scientists understand GM food. However, Pew Research also reported that 67% of Americans said they did not believe scientists have a "clear understanding" of the underlying science. This additional context signals the potential value of making sure that people know when scientists agree. In this regard, just as we are happy to take restaurant advice from a local foodie friend, it makes sense for most people to focus their limited time and energy on listening to what scientists in their social group think about a complicated scientific issue rather than trying to decipher the underlying science. Communicating the "normal" opinion or behavior will not always work, but

Preparing to Prioritize Normative Beliefs
as a Communication Objective

The following are eight questions that science communicators should consider when deciding whether to prioritize sharing information about normative beliefs as a communication objective. In many cases, norm-related communication might involve sharing information about the beliefs or behaviors of people about whom your audience cares. This could include information about actual behavior or beliefs (e.g., what proportion of people in a group vaccinate) as well as what others expect (e.g., what proportion of people in a group your audience thinks vaccinate).

THE GOAL QUESTION

1. Given the behavior you want from your specific audience (i.e., your goal), why do you think it would be helpful if your chosen audience considered a certain behavior or belief as more common or more expected?

THE PREPARATION QUESTIONS

2. What does your chosen audience believe about how others behave and what others expect, and is there meaningful room to change these beliefs?
3. What do you think your audience believes about others' behaviors and expectations?

THE TACTICS QUESTIONS

4. What could you do to potentially increase the likelihood that those with whom you are communicating develop new or different beliefs about others' behaviors and expectations, including choices about messages, behaviors, tone/style, communication channel, and communication source?
5. What could you do to learn about your chosen audience's beliefs about others' behaviors and expectations?

THE EVALUATION QUESTIONS

6. Did your chosen audience's beliefs about others' behaviors and expectations change?
7. What did you learn about your audience's beliefs about others' behaviors and expectations?

THE ETHICS QUESTION

8. Are you being honest about others' behaviors and expectations?

social norms research suggests that it is often worth considering these types of objectives.

REFERENCES

1. Hembroff, Larry A., Dennis Martell, Rebecca Allen, Andrew Poole, Karen Clark, and Sandi W. Smith. "The Long-Term Effectiveness of a Social Norming Campaign to Reduce High-Risk Drinking: The Michigan State University Experience, 2000–2014." *Journal of American College Health* (2019): 1–11. https://doi .org/10.1080/07448481.2019.1674856.

2. Lapinski, Maria K., and Rajiv N. Rimal. "An Explication of Social Norms." *Communication Theory* 15, no. 2 (May 2005): 127–47. https://doi.org/10.1111/j.1468 -2885.2005.tb00329.x.

3. Michigan State University. "MSU Social Norms: About." Facebook page. Accessed October 11, 2021. https://www.facebook.com/pg/MSUSocialNorms /about.

4. Wechsler, Henry, and Toben F. Nelson. "What We Have Learned from the Harvard School of Public Health College Alcohol Study: Focusing Attention on College Student Alcohol Consumption and the Environmental Conditions That Promote It." *Journal of Studies on Alcohol and Drugs* 69, no. 4 (2008): 481–90. https:// doi.org/10.15288/jsad.2008.69.481.

5. Armitage, Christopher J., and Mark Conner. "Efficacy of the Theory of Planned Behaviour: A Meta-Analytic Review." *British Journal of Social Psychology* 40, no. 4 (December 2001): 471–99. https://doi.org/10.1348/014466601164939.

6. Schepers, Jeroen, and Martin Wetzels. "A Meta-Analysis of the Technology Acceptance Model: Investigating Subjective Norm and Moderation Effects." *Information & Management* 44, no. 1 (2007): 90–103. https://doi.org/10.1016/j.im .2006.10.007.

7. McEachan, Rosemary Robin Charlotte, Mark Conner, Natalie Jayne Taylor, and Rebecca Jane Lawton. "Prospective Prediction of Health-Related Behaviours with the Theory of Planned Behaviour: A Meta-Analysis." *Health Psychology Review* 5, no. 2 (2011): 97–144. https://doi.org/10.1080/17437199.2010.521684.

8. Bergquist, Magnus, Andreas Nilsson, and Wesley P. Schultz. "A Meta-Analysis of Field-Experiments Using Social Norms to Promote Pro-Environmental Behaviors." *Global Environmental Change* 59 (2019): 101941.

9. Petty, Richard E., and John T. Cacioppo. *The Elaboration Likelihood Model of Persuasion.* New York: Springer-Verlang, 1986.

10. Cialdini, Robert B. *Influence: Science and Practice.* 5th ed. Boston: Pearson Education, 2009.

11. Cialdini, Robert B., Carl A. Kallgren, and Raymond R. Reno. "A Focus Theory of Normative Conduct: A Theoretical Refinement and Reevaluation of the Role of Norms in Human Behavior." In *Advances in Experimental Social Psychology,* vol. 24, edited by Mark P. Zanna, 201–34. Cambridge, MA: Academic Press, 1991.

12. Cialdini, Robert B., Raymond R. Reno, and Carl A. Kallgren. "A Focus Theory of Normative Conduct: Recycling the Concept of Norms to Reduce

Littering in Public Places." *Journal of Personality and Social Psychology* 58, no. 6 (June 1990): 1015–26.

13. Cialdini, Robert B. *Pre-Suasion: A Revolutionary Way to Influence and Persuade.* 1st ed. New York: Simon & Schuster, 2016.

14. Rimal, Rajiv N., and Maria K. Lapinski. "A Re-Explication of Social Norms, Ten Years Later." *Communication Theory* 25, no. 4 (November 2015): 393–409. https://doi.org/10.1111/comt.12080.

15. Fishbein, Martin, and Icek Ajzen. *Predicting and Changing Behavior: The Reasoned Action Approach.* New York: Psychology Press, 2010.

16. Nolan, Jessica M., P. Wesley Schultz, Robert B. Cialdini, Noah J. Goldstein, and Vladas Griskevicius. "Normative Social Influence Is Underdetected." *Personality and Social Psychology Bulletin* 34, no. 7 (2008): 913–23. https://doi.org/10.1177/0146167208316691.

17. Eriksson, Kimmo, Pontus Strimling, and Julie C. Coultas. "Bidirectional Associations between Descriptive and Injunctive Norms." *Organizational Behavior and Human Decision Processes* 129 (2015): 59–69. https://doi.org/10.1016/j.obhdp.2014.09.011.

18. Silk, Kami J., Evan K. Perrault, Samantha A. Nazione, Kristin Pace, and Jan Collins-Eaglin. "Evaluation of a Social Norms Approach to a Suicide Prevention Campaign." *Journal of Health Communication* 22, no. 2 (2017): 135–42. https://doi.org/10.1080/10810730.2016.1258742.

19. Park, Hee Sun, and Sandi W. Smith. "Distinctiveness and Influence of Subjective Norms, Personal Descriptive and Injunctive Norms, and Societal Descriptive and Injunctive Norms on Behavioral Intent: A Case of Two Behaviors Critical to Organ Donation." *Human Communication Research* 33, no. 2 (2007): 194–218. https://doi.org/10.1111/j.1468-2958.2007.00296.x.

20. Rhodes, Nancy, Hillary C. Shulman, and Nikki McClaran. "Changing Norms: A Meta-Analytic Integration of Research on Social Norms Appeals." *Human Communication Research* 46, no. 2–3 (April–July 2020): 161–91. https://doi.org/10.1093/hcr/hqz023.

21. Lapinski, Maria K., John M. Kerr, Jinhua Zhao, and Robert S. Shupp. "Social Norms, Behavioral Payment Programs, and Cooperative Behaviors: Toward a Theory of Financial Incentives in Normative Systems." *Human Communication Research* 43, no. 1 (2017): 148–71. https://doi.org/10.1111/hcre.12099.

22. Rhodes, Nancy, and David R. Ewoldsen. "Attitude and Norm Accessibility and Cigarette Smoking." *Journal of Applied Social Psychology* 39, no. 10 (October 2009): 2355–72. https://doi.org/10.1111/j.1559-1816.2009.00529.x.

23. Rhodes, Nancy, David R. Ewoldsen, Lijiang Shen, Jennifer L. Monahan, and Cassie Eno. "The Accessibility of Family and Peer Norms in Young Adolescent Risk Behavior." *Communication Research* 41, no. 1 (February 2014): 3–26. https://doi.org/10.1177/0093650211429118.

24. Rasmussen, Eric E., Nancy Rhodes, Rebecca R. Ortiz, and Shawna R. White. "The Relation between Norm Accessibility, Pornography Use, and

Parental Mediation among Emerging Adults." *Media Psychology* 19, no. 3 (2016): 431–54. https://doi.org/10.1080/15213269.2015.1054944.

25. Goldstein, Noah J., Robert B. Cialdini, and Vladas Griskevicius. "A Room with a Viewpoint: Using Social Norms to Motivate Environmental Conservation in Hotels." *Journal of Consumer Research* 35, no. 3 (2008): 472–82. https://doi.org/10.1086/586910.

26. Schultz, P. Wesley, Jessica M. Nolan, Robert B. Cialdini, Noah J. Goldstein, and Vladas Griskevicius. "The Constructive, Destructive, and Reconstructive Power of Social Norms: Reprise." *Perspectives on Psychological Science* 13, no. 2 (2018): 249–54. https://doi.org/10.1177/1745691617693325.

27. Schultz, P. Wesley, Jessica M. Nolan, Robert B. Cialdini, Noah J. Goldstein, and Vladas Griskevicius. "The Constructive, Destructive, and Reconstructive Power of Social Norms." *Psychological Science* 18, no. 5 (2007): 429–34. https://doi.org/10.1111/j.1467-9280.2007.01917.x.

28. Lapinski, Maria Knight, Erin K. Maloney, Mary Braz, and Hillary C. Shulman. "Testing the Effects of Social Norms and Behavioral Privacy on Hand Washing: A Field Experiment." *Human Communication Research* 39, no. 1 (2013): 21–46. https://doi.org/10.1111/j.1468-2958.2012.01441.x.

29. Lapinski, Maria Knight, Jenn Anderson, Alicia Shugart, and Ewen Todd. "Social Influence in Child Care Centers: A Test of the Theory of Normative Social Behavior." *Health Communication* 29, no. 3 (2014): 219–32. https://doi.org/10.1080/10410236.2012.738322.

30. Schultz, P. Wesley, Alyssa Messina, Giuseppe Tronu, Eleuterio F. Limas, Rupanwita Gupta, and Mica Estrada. "Personalized Normative Feedback and the Moderating Role of Personal Norms: A Field Experiment to Reduce Residential Water Consumption." *Environment and Behavior* 48, no. 5 (2016): 686–710. https://doi.org/10.1177/0013916514553835.

31. Reid, Allecia E., and Leona S. Aiken. "Correcting Injunctive Norm Misperceptions Motivates Behavior Change: A Randomized Controlled Sun Protection Intervention." *Health Psychology* 32, no. 5 (2013): 551–60. https://doi.org/10.1037/a0028140.

32. Lapinski, Maria K., Jie Zhuang, Hyeseung Koh, and Jingyuan Shi. "Descriptive Norms and Involvement in Health and Environmental Behaviors." *Communication Research* 44, no. 3 (2017): 367–87. https://doi.org/10.1177/0093650215605153.

33. Gerber, Alan S., and Todd Rogers. "Descriptive Social Norms and Motivation to Vote: Everybody's Voting and So Should You." *Journal of Politics* 71, no. 1 (2009): 178–91. https://doi.org/10.1017/s0022381608090117.

34. Gill, James D., Lawrence A. Crosby, and James R. Taylor. "Ecological Concern, Attitudes, and Social Norms in Voting Behavior." *Public Opinion Quarterly* 50, no. 4 (1986): 537–54. https://doi.org/10.1086/269002.

35. Kam, Cindy D. "When Duty Calls, Do Citizens Answer?" *Journal of Politics* 69, no. 1 (2007): 17–29. https://doi.org/10.1111/j.1468-2508.2007.00491.x.

36. Agerström, Jens, Rickard Carlsson, Linda Nicklasson, and Linda Guntell. "Using Descriptive Social Norms to Increase Charitable Giving: The Power of

Local Norms." *Journal of Economic Psychology* 52 (2016): 147-53. https://doi.org/10.1016/j.joep.2015.12.007.

37. Croson, Rachel T. A., Femida Handy, and Jen Shang. "Gendered Giving: The Influence of Social Norms on the Donation Behavior of Men and Women." *International Journal of Nonprofit and Voluntary Sector Marketing* 15, no. 2 (2010): 199-213. https://doi.org/10.1002/nvsm.385.

38. Shulman, Hillary C., and Timothy R. Levine. "Exploring Social Norms as a Group-Level Phenomenon: Do Political Participation Norms Exist and Influence Political Participation on College Campuses?" *Journal of Communication* 62, no. 3 (June 2012): 532-52. https://doi.org/10.1111/j.1460-2466.2012.01642.x.

39. van der Linden, Sander L., Anthony Leiserowitz, and Edward Maibach. "The Gateway Belief Model: A Large-Scale Replication." *Journal of Environmental Psychology* 62 (2019): 49-58. https://doi.org/10.1016/j.jenvp.2019.01.009.

40. Lewandowsky, Stephan, Gilles E. Gignac, and Samuel Vaughan. "The Pivotal Role of Perceived Scientific Consensus in Acceptance of Science." *Nature Climate Change* 3, no. 4 (2013): 399-404. https://doi.org/10.1038/nclimate1720.

41. Cook, John, and Stephan Lewandowsky. "Rational Irrationality: Modeling Climate Change Belief Polarization Using Bayesian Networks." *Topics in Cognitive Science* 8, no. 1 (2016): 160-79. https://doi.org/10.1111/tops.12186.

42. van der Linden, Sander L., Anthony A. Leiserowitz, Geoffrey D. Feinberg, and Edward W. Maibach. "How to Communicate the Scientific Consensus on Climate Change: Plain Facts, Pie Charts or Metaphors?" *Climatic Change* 126, no. 1 (2014): 255-62. https://doi.org/10.1007/s10584-014-1190-4.

43. Ding, Ding, Edward W. Maibach, Xiaoquan Zhao, Connie Roser-Renouf, and Anthony Leiserowitz. "Support for Climate Policy and Societal Action Are Linked to Perceptions About Scientific Agreement." *Nature Climate Change* 1, no. 9 (2011): 462-66. https://doi.org/10.1038/nclimate1295.

44. Dixon, Graham. "Applying the Gateway Belief Model to Genetically Modified Food Perceptions: New Insights and Additional Questions." *Journal of Communication* 66, no. 6 (2016): 888-908. https://doi.org/10.1111/jcom.12260.

45. van der Linden, Sander L., Chris E. Clarke, and Edward W. Maibach. "Highlighting Consensus among Medical Scientists Increases Public Support for Vaccines: Evidence from a Randomized Experiment." *BMC Public Health* 15 (2015): 1207. https://doi.org/10.1186/s12889-015-2541-4.

46. Kobayashi, Keiichi. "The Impact of Perceived Scientific and Social Consensus on Scientific Beliefs." *Science Communication* 40, no. 1 (2018): 63-88. https://doi.org/10.1177/1075547017748948.

47. van der Linden, Sander L., Anthony A. Leiserowitz, Geoffrey D. Feinberg, and Edward W. Maibach. "The Scientific Consensus on Climate Change as a Gateway Belief: Experimental Evidence." *PLOS ONE* 10, no. 2 (2015). https://doi.org/10.1371/journal.pone.0118489.

48. Goldberg, Matthew H., Sander L. van der Linden, Matthew T. Ballew, Seth A. Rosenthal, Abel Gustafson, and Anthony Leiserowitz. "The Experience of Consensus: Video as an Effective Medium to Communicate Scientific Agreement

on Climate Change." *Science Communication* 41, no. 5 (2019): 659–73. https://doi.org /10.1177/1075547019874361.

49. Kahan, Dan M. "The 'Gateway Belief' Illusion: Reanalyzing the Results of a Scientific-Consensus Messaging Study." *Journal of Science Communication* 16, no. 5 (2016): 1–20. https://doi.org/10.22323/2.16050203.

50. Dixon, Graham, Jay Hmielowski, and Yanni Ma. "More Evidence of Psychological Reactance to Consensus Messaging: A Response to van der Linden, Maibach, and Leiserowitz (2019)." *Environmental Communication* (2019): 1–7. https://doi.org/10.1080/17524032.2019.1671472.

51. Dixon, Graham, and Austin Hubner. "Neutralizing the Effect of Political Worldviews by Communicating Scientific Agreement: A Thought-Listing Study." *Science Communication* 40, no. 3 (2018): 393–415. https://doi.org/10.1177 /1075547018769907.

52. Kahan, Dan M. "Climate-Science Communication and the Measurement Problem." *Political Psychology* 36 (2015): 1–43. https://doi.org/10.1111/pops.12244.

53. Lee, Chul-Joo, and Dietram A. Scheufele. "The Influence of Knowledge and Deference toward Scientific Authority: A Media Effects Model for Public Attitudes toward Nanotechnology." *Journalism & Mass Communication Quarterly* 83, no. 4 (2006): 819–34. https://doi.org/10.1177/107769900608300406.

54. Funk, Cary, Meg Hefferon, Brian Kennedy, and Courtney Johnson. *Trust and Mistrust in Americans' Views of Scientific Experts*. Washington, DC: Pew Research Center, 2019. https://www.pewresearch.org/science/2019/08/02/trust -and-mistrust-in-americans-views-of-scientific-experts.

55. National Science Board. "Science and Technology: Public Attitudes and Public Understanding." In *Science and Engineering Indicators 2012*. Arlington, VA: National Science Foundation, 2012. http://www.nsf.gov/statistics/seind12.

56. "Colgate Warned over '80%' Boast." *BBC News*, January 17, 2007. http:// news.bbc.co.uk/2/hi/uk_news/6269521.stm.

57. Pew Research Center. *Americans, Politics, and Science Issues*. Washington, DC: Pew Research Center, 2015. http://www.pewinternet.org/2015/07/01 /americans-politics-and-science-issues.

10

Foster Self-Efficacy

I THINK I CAN. I think I can. I think I can.

People—and make-believe trains [1]—are usually more likely to perform behaviors they believe they have the ability and opportunity to perform. Such beliefs are often called self-efficacy beliefs. Most science communication training programs aim to improve scientists' communication abilities—and scientists' perceptions of their communication abilities—but three programs in particular go further and make it easier for them to *actually* communicate. In other words, they try to shape scientists' perceptions about the difficulty of communicating by both building skills and removing barriers. One of these programs is the graduate-run RELATE program at the University of Michigan (www.learntorelate.org) that pairs several weeks of training with the initial goal of preparing to share research at a public event in a pub, coffeehouse, or some other local venue [2]. RELATE, in fact, stands for Researchers Expanding Lay-Audience Teaching and Engagement. Another training program that pairs building self-efficacy with opportunity is the University of Utah's STEM ambassador program (https://stemap.org), which we mentioned in chapter 6 when we discussed fostering shared-identity beliefs. In their case, the whole program is built around finding a real community partner and building real relationships [3]. Similarly, one of the special things about Portal to the Public, described in chapter 2, is that their training is built around getting scientists ready to have meaningful interactions with a wide range of guests at science centers and museums with whom they partner.

The irony is that while many science communication trainers have told us they try to increase scientists' self-efficacy in regards to communication, we rarely hear about trainers encouraging science communicators to help nonscientist audiences recognize their own abilities and capacity to act. There are certainly exceptions—communicators trying to encourage young people from underrepresented groups often seek to boost self-efficacy to encourage consideration of careers in science, technology, engineering, and math (STEM), for example [4]—but we generally think self-efficacy beliefs represent another key outcome many science communicators should consider more regularly. In other words, communicators should add self-efficacy beliefs to their pantry of potential communication objectives. If we want people to drive less, they need to believe they have the ability to drive less and still get where they need to go in a reasonable amount of time. If we want people to eat less, they need to believe they *can* eat less and still enjoy food and time with friends and family. And if we want people to support science, we need them to believe they are able to support science and have opportunities to do so.

There are always going to be people who think they possess abilities that they do not possess—psychologists David Dunning and Justin Kruger famously coined the Dunning-Kruger effect to describe this phenomenon [5]—but building self-efficacy is an often-ignored communication objective that can be prioritized by any science communicator who wants to have an impact. Stanford psychologist Albert Bandura famously articulated the idea of fostering self-efficacy in the late 1970s to help explain how direct and mediated experiences can shape the long-term beliefs that affect behavior [6]. Since then, the idea of self-efficacy has emerged as a crucial driver of whether someone will try a challenging behavior, the amount of effort that will go into achieving that behavior, and whether the effort will be sustained over time.

The concept of self-efficacy has been so influential that key behavioral theories were redeveloped to include it, including Icek Ajzen and Martin Fishbein's theory of reasoned action, a popular theory that previously explained behavior largely as an outcome of attitudes about the behavior (i.e., the risks and benefits of the behavior; chapter 8), and social norms related to the behavior (chapter 9). In the mid-1980s, Ajzen added the construct of "perceived behavioral control" and redubbed the theory of reasoned action as the theory of planned behavior in recognition that people sometimes fail to do a behavior because they are simply unable to or feel unable to [7]. To use a home improvement metaphor, we might want to construct a handy backyard shed (a behavioral goal)—and believe the shed would be beneficial (attitude) and valued by our family members (social norm)—but we may not believe we have the skills and resources needed to build something acceptable. In fact, American-based retailer Home Depot emphasized self-efficacy through the slogan "You can do it, we can help" between 2003 and 2009 before switching to "More saving, more doing" [8,9]. In doing so, Home Depot simply switched from emphasizing skill-related barriers to cost-related barriers. To use a food metaphor, my behavioral goal might be to serve homemade sourdough bread at a dinner party—and I believe that sourdough both tastes great (attitude) and would be appreciated by friends (social norm)—but I may not serve sourdough because I do not believe I have the skills or ingredients needed (lack of self-efficacy) to serve a lovely loaf. This idea of self-efficacy can be applied in most any scenario, including as a science communication objective. This chapter covers what we know about how to communicate efficacy and its outcomes. We also touch on potential downsides of helping people feel efficacious.

Why Treat Self-Efficacy as a Communication Objective

It is important to delineate what we typically mean when we talk about self-efficacy and how it is different from other such concepts as outcome expectations [6], response efficacy [10], and personal efficacy [11]. This differentiation will also be important to those interested in exploring the relevant theory and research. These concepts correspond with how some people talk about things such as the "efficacy of a new drug" in treating a disease or the "efficacy of a new technology" in solving a problem. From our perspective, these seem like alternate names for the type of objectives we prefer to call risk and benefit beliefs (chapter 8) because they focus on beliefs about positive or negative effects from performing a behavior. Self-efficacy beliefs, in contrast, seem conceptually closer to competence (or ability) beliefs (chapter 7) in their focus on whether an individual believes they have both the skills and resources needed to do a behavior [12]. However, whereas the competence belief literature focuses on perceptions of someone else's competence, self-efficacy beliefs focus on self-perceptions of competence. The theory of planned behavior uses the term "perceived behavioral control" to talk about self-efficacy and call attention to the fact that both a lack of skill (i.e., capacity, or internal control) and a lack of resources (i.e., autonomy, or external control, which could come from economic, regulatory, or time-based pressures) can create potential barriers for people considering a behavior. Those with a background in political science or political communication sometimes use the term "internal efficacy" to similarly refer to a person's sense of one's own internal competence [13].

In our own work, we have often highlighted self-efficacy beliefs when studying what makes scientists more willing to take part in communication activities. We have sometimes found that scientists who believe they have engagement skills and the time to engage tend to say they are more willing to participate in engagement activities [14–16]. We have also found that scientists' skill beliefs are associated with a willingness to prioritize novel engagement objectives [17] and tactics [18]. Others have found similar things [19].

There is some disagreement, however, in how to measure self-efficacy, as described by Albert Bandura, and perceived behavioral control, as described by the theory of planned behavior. Bandura suggests using 100-point scales to ask survey respondents how confident they are in their ability to do subtasks relevant to the goal behavior or their confidence in their ability to do a behavior in various circumstances [20]. For example, studies on quitting smoking sometimes measure self-efficacy as confidence in the ability to keep from smoking in a range of situations (at a bar, when bored, when around others who are smoking, etc.) [21]. In contrast, theory of planned behavior developers Icek Ajzen and Martin Fishbein counsel focusing on a combination of beliefs about whether someone feels they will have control over specific aspects of a goal behavior alongside the degree to which the person believes that specific aspect is likely to actually affect the goal behavior. For example, they note it might be important to know if a student who says they want to regularly attend class has reliable transportation, as well as the degree to which they believe having reliable transportation is an important driver of regular class attendance [12].

While such measurement issues are important to researchers, our sense is that the key insight for practitioners is relatively simple. Communicators need to find out whether people in their target audience are failing to do a goal behavior because they do not believe they have the skills or resources (including decision-making authority). In some cases, the communicator may find out that a true barrier exists (e.g., someone is not buying an electric car because they cannot afford an electric car), in which case they would need to look beyond communication for solutions since communication alone cannot make someone's income higher or reduce the price of an electric car. In other cases, communicators might need to build audience self-efficacy beliefs either by accentuating the audience's existing abilities or by building additional actual self-efficacy through targeted training. For example, science communicators who want local politicians to change a policy may need to (1) find ways to help the politicians recognize they have the existing ability to change the policy in a way that constituents will accept, and (2) provide the politicians (and/or their staffs) with targeted briefings aimed at helping them develop the actual technical capacity to ask the right questions and answer constituents' questions.

Communicating Self-Efficacy

Albert Bandura has argued that people can develop self-efficacy beliefs in many different ways. This can include direct experiences as well as vicarious experiences [6]. This might involve watching others (especially similar others) perform a behavior in person or online. It is also possible for someone to develop efficacy beliefs from things they read or hear, including advertisements, self-help books, or fiction.

In terms of direct experience, as noted, science communication trainers often talk about building communication self-efficacy in and of itself as a primary objective of training [22,23]. To this end, John (with the support of the American Association for the Advancement of Science) has helped a group of researchers develop a measure of self-efficacy for the training community that includes a level of agreement or disagreement with statements such as "I am good at listening to participants during public engagement with science exercises," and "I have a hard time communicating about scientific results with nonscientists." A team at the University of Missouri also used science communication self-efficacy as a primary outcome of a training program they developed [24].

It also is worth noting here that the emphasis on experiential learning to foster self-efficacy is especially important in the world of informal science education as practiced by museums, science centers, and after-school and summer programs. In these cases, there is often a clear desire to help young people believe they have the ability to be a part of the STEM community as an addition to simply learning about scientific topics [25]. Activities that foster real dialogue among nonexperts should also be expected to boost self-efficacy [26]. Indeed, beyond science contexts, many political communication scholars have pointed to self-efficacy as an outcome of the types of public dialogue that occurs in a wide range of civic settings [27,28].

Fostering self-efficacy beliefs through direct experience should often be the priority in educational and civic contexts, but doing so is not always possible. In some cases, it may be enough to communicate self-efficacy through carefully designed messages [29]. For those interested in conceptual issues, recall that the widely used theory of planned behavior [12] includes self-efficacy as a key component as does the omnibus integrated behavioral model [30] and a wide range of other key theories used by those seeking to change behavior (e.g., Bandura's social cognitive theory [31], the updated health belief model [32], protection motivation theory [33], the extended parallel process model [34], and others). At the most simple level, social scientists seeking to communicate self-efficacy typically expose people to messages (including pictures [35,36]) that provide information about what someone could do to help achieve a goal. For example, communication researchers Lauren Feldman and Sol Hart used a version of a news article edited so that some people in the experiment were told how simple it was to provide comments to a government agency on a proposed climate change plan [37]. They found that such messages can affect participation in public decision-making around climate change (at least for moderates and liberals). In other words, they showed that people will tend to do behaviors when we communicate that a behavior is easy to do.

One nuance of Feldman and Hart's work, however, is that the effects of self-efficacy might occur as a result of how such information interacts with emotions, such as hope, fear, and anger. These specific emotions are partly the subject of the next chapter (chapter 11) but Feldman and Hart's exploration of the relationship between emotions and efficacy is also central to former Michigan State professor Kim Witte's widely cited research on self-efficacy and fear (i.e., her work on the extended parallel process model) [38]. This work is important because many communicators seem to think that scare tactics in advertisements, such as "This is your brain on drugs," are inherently effective, despite a lack of evidence [39]. Witte tries instead to clarify when using a fear appeal might be effective. A core insight from the work is that telling people they face a substantial risk (chapter 8) can backfire if the target does not believe a scary threat has a feasible solution (i.e., response efficacy or behavioral benefit, also chapter 8) or that they have the ability (i.e., self-efficacy) to enact the solution. The term "parallel" in the theory's name comes from the idea that people faced with a threat for which they have no solution will tend to downplay the threat (e.g., convince themselves that smoking is not that bad, or that climate change is not real) because they are unable to take steps to deal with the problem [34].

Similar to Feldman and Hart's climate study, an initial test of the extended parallel process model involved an experiment that asked sexually active students to read randomly assigned versions of AIDS-focused educational material that varied in the degree to which it attempted to evoke threat-related fear and self-efficacy. The low efficacy message, for example, emphasized the difficulty of protecting oneself because of the potential for condoms to fail. Another study that aimed to get students to eat fruits and vegetables communicated self-efficacy by asking some respondents to recall the details of a time when they demonstrated the ability to choose healthy eating [40]. Beyond fear appeals, a broader point is that we cannot expect people to consider a behavior unless they see the behavior as beneficial, no matter how self-efficacious they feel.

One impressive effort to foster self-efficacy occurred as part of a pioneering public health intervention in the 1980s that sought to decrease heart disease. The Stanford Five-City Project saw people in chosen communities receive different types and amounts of heart disease information, as well as different amounts of guidance on how to lead healthier lives. This information reached participants through newsletters, information kits, cross-media advertising campaigns, contests, and other activities. For us, the key study was conducted by Ed Maibach (now a central figure in climate change communication research [41]) and two colleagues that used multiple waves of survey data to show that people who saw more campaign content were the most likely to increase their sense of self-efficacy over the course of the campaign. Furthermore, respondents' initial self-efficacy levels and their changes in self-efficacy seemed to result in more desirable health behavior [42].

Self-efficacy has also often been a desired outcome of "entertainment-education" campaigns that use narrative content, such as soap operas.

The use of narratives allows communicators to show people solving problems while increasing the odds that audiences will both pay attention to messages and not mentally counterargue them [43]. In contrast, most news content about health and environmental risks, as well advertisements meant to promote things like health behavior, often lack substantive self-efficacy information [44,45]. The clear implication is that communicators who want people to do a behavior need to spend at least some of their time ensuring that target audiences believe they have the skills and capacity to conduct the desired behavior. We cannot assume that people will do a behavior just because they believe the behavior is objectively beneficial (chapter 8).

What Does Self-Efficacy Affect?

Researchers in areas related to science communication have shown that self-efficacy beliefs can drive a range of desirable behaviors. Many studies focus on helping people achieve individual-level behavioral goals related to health [46,47] or the environment [48,49] by increasing self-efficacy beliefs. Health behaviors include obvious ones, such as exercise, but can also include less obvious ones, such as thinking about and using newly learned health information [50]. As noted earlier, increasing students' STEM-related efficacy is also a common goal of informal youth-oriented science education, with the expectation that doing so will increase the time and effort students put into learning STEM and considering STEM careers. Many of these studies focus on youth from groups traditionally marginalized in science fields, including minority students and young women, where a systemic history of oppression can result in low levels of self-efficacy [51]. In one widely cited study, the simple presence of female role models seemed to communicate science-related self-efficacy to female students and associated career intentions [52], while another highlighted the role of mentors [4]. Beyond career choice, one 2019 study even showed that self-efficacy beliefs made it more likely that a dog owner would take steps to control their dog's aggressive behavior [53].

What is especially interesting to us, however, is research that has focused on civic behavior rather than individual behavior. For example, Feldman and Hart's study on communicating self-efficacy about climate change examined getting people to do things like provide public comments to government officials. Similarly, a study by a group at the University of Washington showed that both personal self-efficacy and collective self-efficacy (i.e., our beliefs about the degree to which we can jointly accomplish something) were each somewhat associated with climate change concern and support for policy [54]. Our own work on scientists' public engagement activities is similar to this work in its focus on trying to understand how self-efficacy beliefs are associated with such strategic communication decisions as whether to prioritize specific tactics like storytelling or telling people about personal motivations [18], as well as overall decisions about whether to take part in engagement activities [19].

Conclusion

Fostering self-efficacy beliefs is clearly an important potential objective for science communicators who want to change public behavior. The challenge, however, is the strategic communicator's common problem of figuring out what specific behaviors one would like to see more people do. This is especially challenging when behavioral goals are semiesoteric, such as getting policymakers to use scientific evidence in decision-making or having people *not* reject technologies like genetic modification of food or nuclear energy (chapter 1). In those cases, it may be that efficacy messages do not make sense, but there may also be times when there is a need to mobilize people to take actions, such as writing letters to decision-makers or participating in public meetings, where fostering efficacy may prove important. In other words, a science communicator who wants a politician to support climate action may want to increase the self-efficacy of potential letter writers to put pressure on the politician or increase the self-efficacy of a staffer so that the staffer feels better prepared to argue for a policy to their boss.

Another potentially challenging aspect of self-efficacy is when it is misplaced [5], including when people inadvertently extrapolate expertise in one area (e.g., science) into expertise in another area (e.g., science communication). Bandura emphasized that self-efficacy beliefs can vary in their generality [6] such that it might make sense for someone to believe that they are both generally good at solving problems and also likely to do well in specific science classes [55]. This is sometimes desirable, such as when we try to give our kids the experience of success in one area of life in the hopes that it will lead to more widespread confidence that will help them tackle life's many challenges.

On the other hand, we still worry about the promotion of efficacy where it might not be warranted. Bandura, in this regard, has suggested that the best practice is to aim to provide people with accurate self-efficacy information and not seek to artificially inflate perceived self-efficacy [56]. This also seems like the most ethical practice. Psychologist Jeffrey Vancouver and his colleagues have further argued through various studies that people who feel adequately efficacious may sometimes put less effort into achieving their goals such that performance on tasks can sometimes decrease as a result of self-efficacy beliefs [57–59]. This can often be a reasonable strategy—why study more for an exam when you believe you are already prepared? But it can also sometimes backfire.

Our sense is that for most science communicators the decision about whether to emphasize self-efficacy will need to be answered by trying to figure out whether a target audience lacks a legitimate sense of self-efficacy. It will also be important to recognize that people are unlikely to do any behavior if they do not see a benefit (chapter 8) from doing the behavior (including behaviors to mitigate risks) [34]. A person might believe they are perfectly capable of recycling but still not recycle if they do not believe in the benefits of recycling. At a policy level, someone could feel that they know how to communicate with policymakers about an issue like climate change, but they are not likely to do so unless they believe that contacting the policymaker is worth the effort.

Preparing to Prioritize Self-Efficacy Beliefs as a Communication Objective

The following are eight questions that science communicators should consider when deciding whether to prioritize sharing information about self-efficacy beliefs as a communication objective. In many cases, self-efficacy-focused communication might involve sharing information about the degree to which someone has the skills and abilities, as well as the time and opportunity, to enact a desired behavior. This could include information aimed at helping someone recognize their self-efficacy or helping them develop self-efficacy.

THE GOAL QUESTION

1. Given the behavior you want from your specific audience (i.e., your goal), why do you think it would be helpful if your chosen audience believed they had more self-efficacy?

THE PREPARATION QUESTIONS

2. What does your chosen audience believe about their current level of self-efficacy, and is there meaningful room to change these beliefs?
3. What do you believe about your audience's level of actual self-efficacy?

THE TACTICS QUESTIONS

4. What could you do to potentially increase the likelihood that those with whom you are communicating develop new or different beliefs about their own self-efficacy, including choices about messages, behaviors, tone/style, communication channel, and communication source?
5. What could you do to learn about your chosen audience's self-efficacy beliefs?

THE EVALUATION QUESTIONS

6. Did your chosen audience's beliefs about their own self-efficacy change?
7. What did you learn about your audience's self-efficacy?

THE ETHICS QUESTION

8. Are you being honest about people's degrees of self-efficacy?

The question of ensuring that people have accurate self-efficacy beliefs is central to our own work around science communication training. We often worry that a lack of rigorous evaluation activity means that most science communicators have few ways of truly knowing what effects they are having on their audiences. This means they do not know whether their communication choices about tactics and objectives were effective and thus could give a false sense of self-efficacy. Inaccurate high self-efficacy might, in turn, lead to a lack of willingness to change. A lack of expertise related to setting audience-specific behavioral goals (chapter 1) and communication objectives (chapters 2–11) also means that some communicators may be focusing their attention on science knowledge–related objectives (chapter 2) and not the wide range of other objectives that social science says drives the acceptance of science and behavior. Making this argument is somewhat uncomfortable because we deeply appreciate scientists who take time away from their research to communicate, but from a strategic communication perspective, we also worry about ensuring that the resources spent on communication are put to best use. In the end, our advice, however, remains the same: Communicators need to recognize self-efficacy beliefs as a potential communication objective and prioritize building and communicating self-efficacy in cases where it is ethical and feasible.

REFERENCES

1. Piper, Watty. *The Little Engine That Could Storybook Treasury: Based on the Original Story.* New York: Platt & Munk, 2003.

2. Aurbach, Elyse L., Katherine E. Prater, Brandon Patterson, and Brian J. Zikmund-Fisher. "Half-Life Your Message: A Quick, Flexible Tool for Message Discovery." *Science Communication* 40, no. 5 (2018): 669–77. https://doi.org/10.1177/1075547018781917.

3. Nadkarni, Nalini M., Caitlin Q. Weber, Shelley V. Goldman, Dennis L. Schatz, Sue Allen, and Rebecca Menlove. "Beyond the Deficit Model: The Ambassador Approach to Public Engagement." *BioScience* 69, no. 4 (2019): 305–13. https://doi.org/10.1093/biosci/biz018.

4. MacPhee, David, Samantha Farro, and Silvia Sara Canetto. "Academic Self-Efficacy and Performance of Underrepresented STEM Majors: Gender, Ethnic, and Social Class Patterns." *Analyses of Social Issues and Public Policy* 13, no. 1 (2013): 347–69. https://doi.org/10.1111/asap.12033.

5. Dunning, David. "The Dunning–Kruger Effect: On Being Ignorant of One's Own Ignorance." In *Advances in Experimental Social Psychology*, vol. 44, edited by James M. Olson and Mark P. Zanna, 247–96. Cambridge, MA: Academic Press, 2011.

6. Bandura, Albert. "Self-Efficacy: Toward a Unifying Theory of Behavioral Change." *Psychological Review* 84, no. 2 (1977): 191–215. https://doi.org/10.1037/0033-295X.84.2.191.

7. Ajzen, Icek. "The Theory of Planned Behavior." *Organizational Behavior and Human Decision Processes* 50, no. 2 (December 1991): 179–211. https://doi.org/10.1016/0749-5978(91)90020-T.

8. Elliott, Stuart. "With Shoppers Pinching Pennies, Some Big Retailers Get the Message." *New York Times*, April 12, 2009. https://www.nytimes.com/2009/04/13/business/media/13adcol.html.

9. Elliott, Stuart. "Home Depot Taps the Weepy Part of Reality TV." *New York Times*, February 12, 2007. https://www.nytimes.com/2007/02/12/business/media/12adcol.html.

10. Floyd, Donna L., Prentice-Dunn Steven, and Ronald W. Robers. "A Meta-Analysis of Research on Protection Motivation Theory." *Journal of Applied Social Psychology* 30, no. 2 (2000): 407–29. https://doi.org/10.1111/j.1559-1816.2000.tb02323.x.

11. Milfont, Taciano L. "The Interplay between Knowledge, Perceived Efficacy, and Concern About Global Warming and Climate Change: A One-Year Longitudinal Study." *Risk Analysis* 32, no. 6 (2012): 1003–20. https://doi.org/10.1111/j.1539-6924.2012.01800.x.

12. Fishbein, Martin, and Icek Ajzen. *Predicting and Changing Behavior: The Reasoned Action Approach*. New York: Psychology Press, 2010.

13. Craig, Stephen C., Richard G. Niemi, and Glenn E. Silver. "Political Efficacy and Trust: A Report on the NES Pilot Study Items." *Political Behavior* 12, no. 3 (1990): 289–314. https://doi.org/10.1007/BF00992337.

14. Besley, John C., Anthony Dudo, Shupei Yuan, and Frank Lawrence. "Understanding Scientists' Willingness to Engage." *Science Communication* 40, no. 5 (2018): 559–90. https://doi.org/10.1177/1075547018786561.

15. Besley, John C. "What Do Scientists Think About the Public and Does It Matter to Their Online Engagement?" *Science and Public Policy* 42, no. 2 (April 2015): 201–14. https://doi.org/10.1093/scipol/scu042.

16. Besley, John C., Sang Hwa Oh, and Matthew C. Nisbet. "Predicting Scientists' Participation in Public Life." *Public Understanding of Science* 22, no. 8 (2013): 971–87. https://doi.org/10.1177/0963662512459315.

17. Besley, John C., Anthony Dudo, and Shupei Yuan. "Scientists' Views About Communication Objectives." *Public Understanding of Science* 27, no. 6 (2018): 708–30. https://doi.org/10.1177/0963662517728478.

18. Besley, John C., Kathryn O'Hara, and Anthony Dudo. "Strategic Science Communication as Planned Behavior: Understanding Scientists' Willingness to Choose Specific Tactics." *PLOS ONE* 14, no. 10 (2019): e0224039. https://doi.org/10.1371/journal.pone.0224039.

19. Bennett, Nichole, Anthony Dudo, Shupei Yuan, and John C. Besley. "Scientists, Trainers, and the Strategic Communication of Science." In *Theory and Best Practices in Science Communication Training*, edited by Todd P. Newman, 9–31. New York: Routledge, 2020.

20. Bandura, Albert. "Guide for Constructing Self-Efficacy Scales." In *Self-Efficacy Beliefs of Adolescents*, edited by Tim Urdan and Frank Pajares, 307–37. Greenwich, CT: Information Age Publishing, 2006.

21. Gwaltney, Chad J., Saul Shiffman, Gregory J. Normal, Jean A. Paty, Jon D. Kassel, Maryann Gnys, Mary Hickcox, Andrew Waters, and Mark Balabanis. "Does Smoking Abstinence Self-Efficacy Vary across Situations? Identifying Context-Specificity within the *Relapse Situation Efficacy Questionnaire*." *Journal of Consulting and Clinical Psychology* 69, no. 3 (June 2001): 516–27. http://dx.doi.org/10.1037/0022-006X.69.3.516.

22. Besley, John C., and Anthony Dudo. *Landscaping Overview of the North American Science Communication Training Community: Topline Takeaways from Trainer Interviews*. N.p.: Kavli Foundation, Rita Allen Foundation, David and Lucille Packard Foundation, and Gordon and Betty Moore Foundation, 2017. http://www.informalscience.org/sites/default/files/Communication Training Landscape Overview Final.pdf.

23. Dudo, Anthony, John C. Besley, and Shupei Yuan. "Science Communication Training in North America: Preparing Whom to Do What with What Effect?" *Science Communication* 43, no. 1 (2021): 33–63. https://doi.org/10.1177/1075547020960138.

24. Rodgers, Shelly, Ze Wang, and Jack C. Schultz. "A Scale to Measure Science Communication Training Effectiveness." *Science Communication* 42, no. 1 (2020): 90–111. https://doi.org/10.1177/1075547020903057.

25. National Research Council. *Learning Science in Informal Environments: People, Places, and Pursuits.* Edited by Philip Bell, Bruce Lewenstein, Andrew W. Shouse, and Michael A. Feder. Washington, DC: National Academies Press, 2009.

26. Zorn, Theodore E., Juliet Roper, C. Kay Weaver, and Colleen Rigby. "Influence in Science Dialogue: Individual Attitude Changes as a Result of Dialogue between Laypersons and Scientists." *Public Understanding of Science* 21, no. 7 (2012): 848–64. https://doi.org/10.1177/0963662510386292.

27. Burkhalter, Stephanie, John Gastil, and Todd Kelshaw. "A Conceptual Definition and Theoretical Model of Public Deliberation in Small Face-to-Face Groups." *Communication Theory* 12, no. 4 (November 2002): 398–422.

28. Fishkin, James S., and Robert C. Luskin. "Bringing Deliberation to the Democratic Dialogue." In *The Poll with the Human Face: The National Issues Convention Experiment in Political Communication*, edited by Maxwell McCombs and Amy Reynolds, 3–38. Mahwah, NJ: Lawrence Erlbaum Associates, 1999.

29. Dahlstrom, Michael F., Anthony Dudo, and Dominique Brossard. "Precision of Information, Sensational Information, and Self-Efficacy Information as Message-Level Variables Affecting Risk Perceptions." *Risk Analysis* 32, no. 1 (2012): 155–66. https://doi.org/10.1111/j.1539-6924.2011.01641.x.

30. Montano, Daniel E., and Danuta Kasprzyk. "Theory of Reasoned Action, Theory of Planned Behavior, and the Integrated Behavioral Model." In *Health Behavior: Theory, Research, and Practice*, edited by Karen Glanz, Barbara K. Rimer, and K. Viswanath, 95–124. San Francisco: Jossey-Bass, 2015.

31. Bandura, Albert. "Social Cognitive Theory of Mass Communication." In *Media Effects: Advances in Theory and Research*, edited by Jennings Bryant and Dolf Zillman, 121–53. Mahwah, NJ: Lawrence Erlbaum Associates, 2002.

32. Rosenstock, Irwin M., Victor J. Strecher, and Marshall H. Becker. "Social Learning Theory and the Health Belief Model." *Health Education Quarterly* 15, no. 2 (1988): 175–83. https://doi.org/10.1177/109019818801500203.

33. Rogers, Ronald W. "A Protection Motivation Theory of Fear Appeals and Attitude Change." *Journal of Psychology* 91, no. 1 (1975): 93–114. https://doi.org/10.1080/00223980.1975.9915803.

34. Maloney, Erin K., Maria K. Lapinski, and Kim Witte. "Fear Appeals and Persuasion: A Review and Update of the Extended Parallel Process Model." *Social and Personality Psychology Compass* 5, no. 4 (2011): 206–19. https://doi.org/10.1111/j.1751-9004.2011.00341.x.

35. Metag, Julia, Mike S. Schäfer, Tobias Füchslin, Tjado Barsuhn, and Katharina Kleinen-von Königslöw. "Perceptions of Climate Change Imagery: Evoked Salience and Self-Efficacy in Germany, Switzerland, and Austria." *Science Communication* 38, no. 2 (2016): 197–227. https://doi.org/10.1177/1075547016635181.

36. Hart, P. Sol, and Lauren Feldman. "The Impact of Climate Change–Related Imagery and Text on Public Opinion and Behavior Change." *Science Communication* 38, no. 4 (2016): 415–41. https://doi.org/10.1177/1075547016655357.

37. Feldman, Lauren, and P. Sol Hart. "Using Political Efficacy Messages to Increase Climate Activism: The Mediating Role of Emotions." *Science Communication* 38, no. 1 (2016): 99–127. https://doi.org/10.1177/1075547015617941.

38. Witte, Kim. "Putting the Fear Back into Fear Appeals: The Extended Parallel Process Model." *Communication Monographs* 59, no. 4 (1992): 329–49. https://doi.org/10.1080/03637759209376276.

39. Buchanan, David R., and Lawrence Wallack. "This Is the Partnership for a Drug-Free America: Any Questions?" *Journal of Drug Issues* 28, no. 2 (Spring 1998): 329–56.

40. Luszczynska, Aleksandra, Maciej Tryburcy, and Ralf Schwarzer. "Improving Fruit and Vegetable Consumption: A Self-Efficacy Intervention Compared with a Combined Self-Efficacy and Planning Intervention." *Health Education Research* 22, no. 5 (2006): 630–38. https://doi.org/10.1093/her/cyl133.

41. Leiserowitz, Anthony, Edward W. Maibach, Seth Rosenthal, John Kotcher, Parrish Bergquist, Matthew Ballew, Matthew Goldberg, and Abel Gustafson. *Climate Change in the American Mind: April 2019*. Yale University and George Mason University. New Haven, CT: Yale Program on Climate Change Communication, 2019. https://doi.org/10.17605/OSF.IO/CJ2NS.

42. Maibach, Edward, June A. Flora, and Clifford Nass. "Changes in Self-Efficacy and Health Behavior in Response to a Minimal Contact Community

Health Campaign." *Health Communication* 3, no. 1 (1991): 1–15. https://doi.org/10.1207/s15327027hc0301_1.

43. Slater, Michael D., and Donna Rouner. "Entertainment-Education and Elaboration Likelihood: Understanding the Processing of Narrative Persuasion." *Communication Theory* 12, no. 2 (May 2002): 173–91. https://doi.org/10.1111/j.1468-2885.2002.tb00265.x.

44. Evensen, Darrick T., and Christopher E. Clarke. "Efficacy Information in Media Coverage of Infectious Disease Risks: An Ill Predicament?" *Science Communication* 34, no. 3 (2012): 392–418. https://doi.org/10.1177/1075547011421020.

45. Cohen, Elisia L., Michelle D. Shumate, and Abby Gold. "Anti-Smoking Media Campaign Messages: Theory and Practice." *Health Communication* 22, no. 2 (2007): 91–102. https://doi.org/10.1080/10410230701453884.

46. Schwarzer, Ralf, Benjamin Schüz, Jochen P. Ziegelmann, Sonia Lippke, Aleksandra Luszczynska, and Urte Scholz. "Adoption and Maintenance of Four Health Behaviors: Theory-Guided Longitudinal Studies on Dental Flossing, Seat Belt Use, Dietary Behavior, and Physical Activity." *Annals of Behavioral Medicine* 33, no. 2 (2007): 156–66. https://doi.org/10.1007/BF02879897.

47. Thrasher, James F., Kamala Swayampakala, Ron Borland, Gera Nagelhout, Hua-Hie Yong, David Hammond, Maansi Bansal-Travers, Mary Thompson, and James Hardin. "Influences of Self-Efficacy, Response Efficacy, and Reactance on Responses to Cigarette Health Warnings: A Longitudinal Study of Adult Smokers in Australia and Canada." *Health Communication* 31, no. 12 (2016): 1517–26. https://doi.org/10.1080/10410236.2015.1089456.

48. Trumbo, Craig W., and Garrett J. O'Keefe. "Intention to Conserve Water: Environmental Values, Planned Behavior, and Information Effects. A Comparison of Three Communities Sharing a Watershed." *Society & Natural Resources* 14, no. 10 (2001): 889–99. https://doi.org/10.1080/089419201753242797.

49. Kim, Soojung, Se-Hoon Jeong, and Yoori Hwang. "Predictors of Pro-Environmental Behaviors of American and Korean Students: The Application of the Theory of Reasoned Action and Protection Motivation Theory." *Science Communication* 35, no. 2 (2013): 168–88. https://doi.org/10.1177/1075547012441692.

50. Rimal, Rajiv N. "Perceived Risk and Self-Efficacy as Motivators: Understanding Individuals' Long-Term Use of Health Information." *Journal of Communication* 51, no. 4 (December 2001): 633–54. https://doi.org/10.1111/j.1460-2466.2001.tb02900.x.

51. Adedokun, Omolola A., Ann B. Bessenbacher, Loran C. Parker, Lisa L. Kirkham, and Wilella D. Burgess. "Research Skills and STEM Undergraduate Research Students' Aspirations for Research Careers: Mediating Effects of Research Self-Efficacy." *Journal of Research in Science Teaching* 50, no. 8 (October 2013): 940–51. https://doi.org/10.1002/tea.21102.

52. Stout, Jane G., Nilanjana Dasgupta, Matthew Hunsinger, and Melissa A. McManus. "STEMing the Tide: Using Ingroup Experts to Inoculate Women's Self-Concept in Science, Technology, Engineering, and Mathematics (STEM)."

Journal of Personality and Social Psychology 100, no. 2 (February 2011): 255–70. http://dx.doi.org/10.1037/a0021385.

53. Williams, Emma J., and Emily Blackwell. "Managing the Risk of Aggressive Dog Behavior: Investigating the Influence of Owner Threat and Efficacy Perceptions." *Risk Analysis* 39, no. 11 (2019): 2528–42. https://doi.org/10.1111/risa .13336.

54. Bostrom, Ann, Adam L. Hayes, and Katherine M. Crosman. "Efficacy, Action, and Support for Reducing Climate Change Risks." *Risk Analysis* 39, no. 4 (2019): 805–28. https://doi.org/10.1111/risa.13210.

55. Bates, Rebecca, Elaine P. Scott, Jamie Shaffer, and Sarah Marie Painter. "Differences in Self-Efficacy among Women and Minorities in STEM." *Journal of Women and Minorities in Science and Engineering* 21, no. 1 (2015): 27–45.

56. Bandura, Albert. *Self-Efficacy: The Exercise of Control*. New York: W. H. Freeman, 1997.

57. Vancouver, Jeffrey B., Charles M. Thompson, and Amy A. Williams. "The Changing Signs in the Relationships among Self-Efficacy, Personal Goals, and Performance." *Journal of Applied Psychology* 86, no. 4 (2001): 605–20. https://doi .org/10.1037/0021-9010.86.4.605.

58. Vancouver, Jeffrey B., and Laura N. Kendall. "When Self-Efficacy Negatively Relates to Motivation and Performance in a Learning Context." *Journal of Applied Psychology* 91, no. 5 (2006): 1146–53. https://doi.org/10.1037/0021-9010.91.5 .1146.

59. Vancouver, Jeffrey B., Kristen M. More, and Ryan J. Yoder. "Self-Efficacy and Resource Allocation: Support for a Nonmonotonic, Discontinuous Model." *Journal of Applied Psychology* 93, no. 1 (2008): 35–47. https://doi.org/10.1037/0021 -9010.93.1.35.

11

Share Emotions and Frames, Carefully

THIS CHAPTER IS ABOUT COMMUNICATING to influence emotions and how people frame issues. Emotions can roughly be understood as affective responses—such as fear, anger, sadness, disgust, hope, joy, and excitement—that are used to make sense of the world, whereas framing is about how a person thinks about an issue in that world. For 10 chapters we have focused on a range of different belief types that science communicators could attempt to foster in the hopes of affecting the behavior of others or their own behavior. This chapter is different.

We described at the outset that we think it is useful to see "strategic public engagement activities" as communication designed to provide all participants—including scientists and those with whom they are communicating—the ability and motivation to process information about the experience. Our expectation is that the gradual accumulation of engagement experiences is what leads to the creation of beliefs about the world around us (e.g., factual knowledge beliefs, trustworthiness-related beliefs, risk and benefit beliefs, and normative beliefs) as well as beliefs about ourselves (e.g., self-efficacy beliefs). We also noted that our experience tells us people like using the term "engagement" because it seems most ethical to communicate in ways that might change peoples' behaviors when you are communicating evidence-based information (i.e., "true as far as we know"). For example, we feel okay saying that a motive for our research is ensuring a strong place for scientific thinking in society because we think science usually makes the world a better place. We believe communicating this information is acceptable because (1) it is true, and (2) we believe that the people in the scientific community with whom we work want to know this information. The two topics of this chapter—emotions and framing—are, however, somewhat different.

Unlike beliefs, emotions and frames cannot be "correct" or "incorrect." People genuinely experience specific emotions, and some ways to frame an issue or a technology make more sense than others. Recall, in this regard, that we roughly defined scientific knowledge in chapter 2 as true, justified beliefs. We therefore think that science communicators need to be more careful when deciding whether they pursue communication objectives related to emotions and framing. Our sense is that these objectives—especially emotions—are prone to being used in manipulative ways, or at least in ways that seem manipulative.

This difference between belief-related objectives and objectives related to emotions and framing is reflected in the ways that the latter objectives seem to be cognitively processed. We noted in chapter 1 that we are primarily interested in "slow" communication in the form of what is sometimes described as systematic [1], central route [2], analytic [3] or system 2 [4] cognitive processing. In contrast, emotions and framing are often understood to work as hidden heuristic processes. It is also likely that different emotions and framing can motivate people to think about topics more (or less) carefully [5]. In this regard, there is a compelling argument that such objectives as emotions and frames help people make sense of new and changing information.

We only devote a single combined chapter to emotion- and framing-related objectives for three main reasons. One already mentioned is that we want to use this book to emphasize slow communication designed to affect long-term beliefs. The crucial fact that people are "cognitive misers" [6] with predictable biases when they rely on heuristic processing has already been discussed extensively in publications aimed at nonresearcher audiences. Second, while we appreciate the importance of both emotions and framing, we are a little uncomfortable with the idea that the scientific community—and especially individual science communicators—would regularly rely on such tools to change behavior, especially emotional appeals that are not designed to encourage deeper-level thinking. Finally, we also feel like the breadth and depth of both the emotion and framing literature make it inadvisable to suggest we are doing more than trying to highlight some key ideas in this chapter. Our hope is that colleagues might ultimately produce a strategy-focused book on the evidence around emotion and framing-related objectives. We would further hope such a book would include a substantive discussion about how science communicators can pursue such objectives in ethical ways; something we do not have the space or expertise for here. At an academic level, these are probably the objectives where we have the least expertise.

That being said, any skilled communicator needs to be aware of how their communication choices (or failure to make choices) might affect people's emotional reactions or how audiences come to frame issues. Communicators also need to be aware of their own emotions and try to make intentional choices about how they frame issues. We said before that people will develop beliefs about trust, risks and benefits, norms, and self-efficacy whether we intend them to or not. The same is true of emotions and frames. Strategic communicators need to recognize the inherent impact of emotions and frames without necessarily trying to directly affect them. There may also be times where it is reasonable to communicate to purposefully affect people's emotions and framing of issues, such as when conducting public health or environmental campaigns. We also see little danger in getting youth excited about science. Similarly, there are likely times when we need to allow ourselves to share our own emotions or context while still recognizing that communicating how we feel or think about an issue may affect others' perspectives [7].

Emotions as a Strategic Science Communication Objective

General Affect

It would be incomplete to talk about how people respond to many scientific issues without differentiating the role of general affect (i.e., a feeling that something is positive or negative to some degree) and specific emotions. For example, when risk perception and communication pioneer Paul Slovic labeled dread as one of the two key dimensions of risk perceptions (alongside novelty) it seemed inherently affect-laden, even if it was measured in terms of beliefs about voluntariness and overall impact [8]. As noted in chapter 8, Slovic was also involved in research attempting to explain why people's risk and benefit beliefs seem to be correlated such that people who see more risks tend to see fewer benefits, and vice versa [9]. A pair of experiments led by Slovic's collaborator Melissa Finucane showed that the answer seemed to be that perceiving benefits led to a positive feeling that pushed down risk beliefs, and vice versa [10]. One way the research showed that affect was playing a heuristic role in how people judged risks and benefits was by showing that the correlation between risk and benefit beliefs increased somewhat when questionnaire respondents received less time to respond to risks and benefit questions. Put differently, the correlation between risk and benefit judgments decreased (but was still fairly high) when people were given more time to respond. Researchers in this regard sometimes intentionally constrain how much time people have to answer a survey question based on the logic that quicker answers will be more automatic and less deliberative.

Another way Finucane and her colleagues showed that people were relying on their affect as a heuristic "mental shortcut" to judge risks and benefits was by showing that providing people benefit information tended to decrease risk beliefs, and providing people risk information tended to decrease benefit beliefs. Both results—the tendency to conflate risks and benefits when rushed and the tendency to use irrelevant information to judge risks and benefits—can best be explained if people partly rely on general affect rather than specific, deeply considered beliefs when making risks and benefit judgments [11]. This tendency to use affective shortcuts can also likely be seen when people respond to technologies about which they have few pre-existing beliefs. Researcher Dan Kahan and his colleagues, for example, point at individuals' views about topics they know little about—such as nanotechnology—as outcomes that likely reflect general feelings about novel technologies, not specific beliefs about the technology itself [12].

The thing about general affect, however, is that it is typically measured by asking people the degree to which something is good or bad [13], similar to how the theory of planned behavior typically measures what it calls attitudes (chapter 8). This means that we are just telling communicators who want to change general affect that they should communicate positive or negative information, just as Finucane did in her experiment [10]. In other words, while general affect is important to understand when it comes to how people respond to risk, it offers limited help in deciding what to communicate. It may be for this reason that much of the contemporary work in this area focuses on specific emotions rather than general affect. Discrete emotions, in this regard, should be understood as somewhat temporary feelings about a target that can be of varied levels of strength and motivate both cognitive and behavioral reactions. Some common discrete emotions include anger, fear, guilt/shame, sadness, disgust, happiness/joy, and pride [14].

Discrete Emotions

One often-studied specific emotion we have already discussed is fear. Chapter 10 highlighted research, for example, that suggests that scaring people may sometimes backfire. Specifically, if a risk communicator makes their message too frightening or fails to ensure that the target audience believes they can cope with a threat, those on the receiving end will tend to do things aimed at mentally discounting or ignoring the threat rather than devoting effort to figuring out how to manage the threat [15]. The ability to cope includes believing that a solution to a scary problem exists (i.e., benefit beliefs as response efficacy; chapter 8) and believing in one's own ability to enact the solution (i.e., self-efficacy beliefs; chapter 10).

Communication and emotion researcher Robin Nabi has argued that one value of providing a somewhat scary threat message alongside efficacy messages is that the efficacy messages likely communicate hope, a positive emotion. Her research suggests that starting with a fear message about climate change, for example, and following it up with a message about the health benefits of potential climate solutions resulted in more hope than when a fear message was accompanied by an efficacy message that emphasized the health losses that might occur if we do not take action. This fear-followed-by-hope message was further associated with more willingness to take action to address climate change [16]. Others have similarly pointed to the likely importance of both fear and hope, as well as emotions such as anger, worry, and sadness, in how people respond to climate change [17–19] and other issues, such as nuclear energy [20], food risks [21], and even shark attacks [22].

The challenging role that emotions can play in how people respond to an issue is especially highlighted in an experiment that two Cornell University researchers conducted with Nabi using a video clip about climate change from the late-night television show *Jimmy Kimmel Live.* They found that showing study participants a funny clip somewhat decreased fear (and risk perceptions) but still had a net-positive impact on self-reported intent to take action to respond to climate change as a result of people perceiving the video as funny [23]. Similarly, a 2020 study showed that people experience more "mirth" as a result of an Edinburgh Fringe Festival routine by Vince Ebert, a German physicist and stand-up comic, that included audience laughter in comparison to one in which the laughter was removed, and mirth, in turn, seemed to affect people's willingness to say they would click to "like" and share the video [24]. One important challenge to studies like these is that some issues can evoke such deep, morally laden emotions (such as disgust), that it can limit a person's acceptance of potentially beneficial technologies or treatments, such as seems to be the case with genetic engineering [25] or microbes [26]. More generally, the news media may often load emotional content onto science stories [27, 28] in ways that can distract people from evidence-based decision-making.

Like the aforementioned studies that included humor, however, there seems to be substantial opportunity for science communicators to evoke positive emotions that might affect future behavior. This includes fostering hope through things like efficacy and benefit messages, as already suggested, but also through such emotions as excitement [29] and enjoyment [30]. In our own work on scientists, as might be predicted, we have found that those who expect to enjoy communicating are more likely to express willingness to communicate. To us, this suggests that people who want scientists to communicate more should find ways to make the experience pleasant (or not unpleasant)—a lesson that we imagine translates to many other goals that science communicators might have. For example, if we want people to pay attention to science information, then it probably helps if the experience is enjoyable. Science organizations like museums, zoos, and aquariums are well-aware of the importance of fostering enjoyment as a way to spark curiosity [31]. Limited evidence also suggests that science communicators can learn to use tactics such as a reasonable tone and the message of shared values in ways that help audiences feel hopeful [32].

We would further expect that many of the objectives we highlighted in previous chapters might also be associated with positive emotions. In other words, while we hesitate to encourage science communicators to purposefully try to get people to feel a certain way, we would expect people to experience such positive emotions as hope, happiness, admiration, or pride when they see caring, decent, hard-working scientists communicate. As noted above, Robin Nabi's research also highlights how efficacy information could communicate hope [16], and informal science organizations such as museums and zoos would seem silly if they did not provide guests with enjoyable and interesting experiences [33]. Conversely, the literature

Preparing to Prioritize Emotions
as a Communication Objective

The following are eight questions that science communicators should consider when deciding whether to prioritize shaping emotions as a communication objective. In many cases, emotion-focused communication will involve sharing science communicators' own emotional reactions in cases where an issue has made one feel anger, fear, guilt/shame, sadness, disgust, happiness/joy, or pride.

THE GOAL QUESTION

1. Given the behavior you want from your specific audience (i.e., your goal), why do you think it would be helpful if your chosen audience felt one or more specific emotions in response to your communication choices?

THE PREPARATION QUESTIONS

2. How does your chosen audience feel about your issue and is there meaningful room to change these feelings?
3. How do you feel about the issue?

THE TACTICS QUESTIONS

4. What could you do to potentially increase the likelihood that those with whom you are communicating experience new or different feelings in the context of the issue about which you communicate, including choices about messages, behaviors, tone/style, communication channel, and communication source?
5. What could you do to learn more about how your chosen audience feels about your issue?

THE EVALUATION QUESTIONS

6. Did your chosen audience experience emotion as a function of your communication? Did their feelings about the issue change?
7. What did you learn about your audience's feelings?

THE ETHICS QUESTION

8. Are you communicating to affect emotion in careful, respectful, and open ways?

on normative beliefs highlights how negative emotions, such as fear of being rejected, is one way that norms influence behavior [34, 35]. We look forward to research that helps further clarify how emotions affect the experience of science communication and discussions about the ethics of emotion-focused communication. One recent trend we have noticed in the literature is an emphasis on how science communicators' choices about frames can affect the emotions people experience when exposed to communication messages.

(Re)framing as a Strategic Science Communication Objective

This book started with a description of how FrameWorks Institute operates. FrameWorks is a MacArthur "genius" award–winning social scientific organization that helps progressive organizations reframe social and scientific issues [36]. We began our book with them because we appreciate their evidence-based, strategic approach to identifying behavioral goals and then working with partners to find ways to reframe issues in ways that align with those goals. Reframing is their core objective, but the challenge of framing is that—more than any other objective—each issue comes with its own set of potential framing choices. For example, a classic science communication article by sociologist William Gamson and Andre Modigliani investigated news media discourse around nuclear power and identified at least seven main ways that that media discussions were framing new technologies [37].

Robert Entman provided a classic definition of framing in a 1993 article when he said that to frame is to "select some aspects of a perceived reality and make them more salient in a communicating text, in such a way as to promote a particular problem definition, causal interpretation, moral evaluation, and/or treatment recommendation" [38]. This definition, it should be noted, focuses on communication frames rather than the corresponding "frame" that an individual might hold in their head, but the concepts are directly related [39]. FrameWorks, in this context, does its work by using social scientific methods—such as interviews, content analysis, surveys, and experiments—to try and figure out how key actors are framing issues. They then identify ways of (re)framing the issue that support their goals and provide potential science communicators (i.e., their stakeholder partners) guidance on how to deploy those frames. The objective in doing so is to reshape a conversation (and the frames in people's heads) in ways that change behaviors. In the case of technology and STEM learning, for example, after testing several different options, they advised using the metaphor of "wiring" in-school and out-of-school learning environments together. Their hypothesis was that this would help people see the choice to connect schools with such places as libraries and museums as an obvious and necessary step toward improving community infrastructure. The expectation is that accepting the "wiring" frame will lead to support (a pseudobehavior) for more resources [40].

Equivalence and Emphasis Framing

The type of framing that FrameWorks uses has sometimes been called "emphasis" framing [41] because it pushes an audience toward thinking about an issue in a specific way. For example, one experiment by Teresa Myers at George Mason University's Center for Climate Change Communication showed that framing climate change as a health issue, rather than an environmental issue or a national defense issue, seemed to generate hopeful emotions associated with support for climate change in a range of audiences, not just those who were already likely to support climate change action [42]. For emphasis framing, the issue stays the same but the content of the message—including tactical choices, such as the use of different terms, tone, visuals, metaphors, analogies, characters, and narratives—can vary in order to suggest a particular way of thinking about the underlying issue and an associated solution.

Another type of framing is often termed "equivalence" framing and involves changing the emphasis without changing the core content. The classic example is the "Asian disease" problem that Amos Tversky and Daniel Kahneman—creators of the field of decision science—used to show how little changes in presentation can affect survey respondents' answers to questionnaires in predictable ways. In the experiment, they showed that about 7 in 10 people tended to choose a health program aimed at addressing the expected death of 600 Americans when it was framed in terms of a "sure thing" to save 200 people over a program designed to provide a one-third chance of saving all 600 people and a two-thirds chance of saving no one. In contrast, people tended to gamble and choose the program with a one-third probability of saving everyone and a two-thirds probability of seeing everyone die over a program that was certain to result in 400 of 600 people dying [43]. In both cases, an average of 200 people are saved and 400 people die, but the change in wording seems to dramatically change which option respondents preferred. Everyday examples of emphasis framing might include whether we describe a glass as half-full or half-empty or whether we say something is 99% fat free or 1% fat. Similarly, evidence suggests that emphasizing real numbers often seems to have more emotional impact than those with less numeracy [44]. This means, for example, that it may matter if we talk about a 1 in 20 chance of death (or other failure) rather than a 5% chance of death.

Another version of equivalence-like framing is sometimes called gain/loss framing, which involves communicating about issues or policies in terms of the potential gains that could be obtained from enacting a solution or the losses that might occur from a failure to act. Reviews of the literature in these areas suggest that gain and loss frame studies often fail to find substantial impact [45,46]. Nevertheless, this means there are examples of studies showing that the choice about whether to focus on losses or gains can make a small difference. For example, Robin Nabi's previously mentioned 2018 framing study on climate change and emotion used gain and loss frames to affect study participants' hope and fear responses as a way to foster support for environmental behaviors [16]. The key seemed to be in the degree to which gain framing could evoke specific emotions.

Studies in gain and loss frames also highlight the thin line between equivalency framing and emphasis framing. In the real world, the choice to frame an issue in terms of gains would likely mean including benefit information (e.g., material focused on environmental gains or quality-of-life gains) whereas the choice to focus on losses might involve including risk information (e.g., environmental threats or quality of life threats). One of the leading framing researchers—Northwestern University political scientist James Druckman—helped develop the equivalency and emphasis framing terminology and has also done substantial work in the area of science communication. He has argued that the two underlying concepts likely share the same psychological processes [47]. Specifically, for framing to work, people need to have a concept available in their head (e.g., the value of saving lives) that is cognitively accessible when faced with a new situation. Put differently, framing can make specific types of beliefs (i.e., the types of beliefs discussed in previous chapters) relevant to the underlying issue [47]. For example, successfully framing climate change as a health issue might mean that an audience member would be more likely to draw on their existing beliefs about disease risks when making decisions about whether it is worth taking climate action. Indeed, for a communicator to succeed in framing an issue, the audience likely needs to see the suggested frame as relevant to the issue at hand (e.g., this is an issue where it makes sense to think about saving lives).

The key in all of this is that communicating through frames is not simply about trying to make an issue (or issue-related fact) salient, but it is also about suggesting to someone that it makes sense to think about the issue in a certain way [48]. If that way does not resonate with the audience—whether because the ideas are unfamiliar or seem irrelevant to the situation at hand—then the audience is unlikely to adopt the new way of thinking. Further, if a target audience already has a preferred way of framing an issue, it is likely more difficult to get them to adopt your preferred frame [47]. The challenge we see for practitioners is thus that is difficult to make smart framing choices without turning to groups like FrameWorks for evidence-based advice.

The challenge of identifying appropriate frames is compounded by the fact that some frames make sense for multiple issues. We sometimes call these generic frames. At the most generic level, almost any issue can be framed as being about a conflict between two (or more) sides. Framing an issue as a conflict (e.g., the Democrats said X but the Republicans said Y) does not require any specific journalistic skill and is a problem for news coverage of issues like climate change where many journalists have given too much attention to contrarian voices [49]. Conflict framing is often just lazy journalism.

A less problematic—but still potentially problematic—generic framing choice is about whether to frame an issue in "episodic" or "thematic" terms [50,51]. Framing issues episodically involves suggesting that an issue should be thought about as something that affects a single individual or a specific event. Journalists also seem to love this type of framing. This might look like an anecdote about an island facing submersion from rising seas or a scientist developing a new seed. In contrast, thematic framing puts the focus on the overall issue, rather than a specific anecdote. In any given content, a mixture of these frames is also possible (and likely). The concern about episodic framing is that, while it can be emotionally compelling [52], it often suggests solving problems one at a time (e.g., the child going hungry) rather than trying to address the underlying issue (e.g., the reason the child lacks food) [53]. Our advice to practitioners, then, is to think carefully about whether to frame something episodically.

Beyond generic frames, there are also frames that make sense for some issues but not others. As noted earlier, sociologists Gamson and Modigliani identified seven core ways that the news seemed to frame nuclear power [37]. This included framing nuclear power as an issue of economic and technological progress and another focused on whether nuclear power has adequate public accountability through rules and systems. However, the predominant way the media framed nuclear power at the time was as a question about whether it had the potential to be a runaway technology that society would have a hard time managing. There were also relatively rare frames, such as one suggesting that nuclear power be thought of in terms of energy independence for the United States.

Communication researchers Matthew Nisbet and Bruce Lewenstein showed that very similar frames could be used to understand coverage of genetically modified food [54], and another study led by Lewenstein adapted the same framing categories to study news coverage of nanotechnology [55]. Tobacco control researchers have also highlighted common frames used in the coverage of smoking regulation during the mid-1980s and early 1990s [56]. Similar to technology, this research highlights the frequency of framing tobacco control as an economic issue, but they also note common framing of tobacco as an issue of free speech or free enterprise, as well as an issue of nonsmokers' rights, deception, and the targeting of children. The key argument in the tobacco case was that tobacco-control advocates failed to make progress on smoking bans until they organized themselves to collectively prioritize messaging that framed tobacco control as being about how the tobacco industry takes away kids' freedom through youth-targeted tobacco advertising. In doing so, they used "freedom framing" to try to counteract tobacco advocates' framing of smoking bans as a violation of smoker and business freedom.

The technology and tobacco cases also highlight the centrality of values to any discussion of powerful framing. Framing a technology or issue in terms of economics seems likely to resonate with many audiences who value progress. Episodic frames also tend to emphasize individualism, and talking about an issue in terms of individual freedom seems consequently likely to be powerful to American audiences. On the other hand, frames that suggest thinking about an issue in terms of the need to protect communities or vulnerable individuals, like kids, also have the potential to resonate with many audiences. The work of the strategic science communicator, then, is often to identify a way to frame whatever they want to communicate so that it helps and does not hurt. As noted earlier, for example, framing climate change as an environmental issue or a national defense issue might work for some audiences but also has the potential to backfire for people who do not identify with environmental values or who do not think a particular framing makes sense [42]. The challenge of framing effectively also points to the importance of working collaboratively on communication strategy, a topic we'll return to in our concluding chapter.

One of our favorite examples of finding a frame that seems to resonate with a wide range of audiences is the work that the lesbian, gay, bisexual, transgender, queer (LGBTQ) community did when recognizing they would have a hard time making progress on the issue of marriage equality if they were seen to be picking a fight over rights [57]. Instead, they encouraged their community to focus on framing the issue as human equality, as being about the LGBTQ community wanting what everyone wants—to live ordinary lives filled with the love of family and friends. Love is love.

On the flip side, we must mention the work that political and corporate consultant Frank Luntz [58] did for the Republican party in the early 2000s when he recommended talking about "preserving and protecting" the environment "more wisely" and with more "common sense" while questioning the degree to which regulators were being accountable and responsible to Americans [59]. Liberal-minded researcher George Lakoff [60] become so frustrated with Republicans' apparent ability to collectively frame issues in compelling ways (e.g., calling estate taxes "death taxes") that he also tried to provide framing advice to Democrats [61]. And, as frequent survey researchers, we also appreciate how survey questions with slightly different terminology—whether "climate change" or "global warming" [62], "genetic engineering" or "genetic modification" [63], to name a few—can often result in different response patterns.

Framing to Affect "Construal Level"

One advanced-level framing-like objective that some strategic science communicators may want to pursue is to try to affect what researchers call "construal level," an extension of the idea of psychological distance [64]. At a strategic level, focusing on "construal" involves making choices about how concretely or abstractly an issue is described. A communicator proposing a policy could choose to talk concretely about right now or could be more abstract by talking about some future outcome (i.e., temporal framing). Similarly, a communicator could focus on themselves to be concrete or people more distant from them to be abstract (i.e., social distance), or things nearby versus further way (i.e., actual distance). More generally, communicators can talk about something in the abstract (e.g., a dog) or concrete (e.g., a four-month-old Labrador puppy named Wesley Besley).

Environmental communication scholars seem especially interested in the potential value of trying to shape how concretely people construe issues. For example, a former student worked with a pair of our colleagues in her dissertation to show that abstract climate change images (e.g., black and white, lacking people) fostered more abstract construal than more concrete images (e.g., colors, specific people) and that this resulted in slightly lower climate change concern [65]. Other research has used short videos [66] or news stories [19] aimed at shaping construal level in order to increase such outcomes as concern and emotions. However, while increasing emotional reactions might seem helpful, some research also suggests abstract messaging can help keep people from rejecting climate change mitigation. One danger of concrete messages seems to be that they can sometimes lead people to feel a constraint on their freedom [67].

Ultimately we continue to see framing as an essential part of communication objectives but also one where it is difficult for individual communicators to make evidence-based choices. Organizations like FrameWorks, then, seem like key actors that scientists should turn to if they think they want to try to reframe issues for people. We also think (and discuss in chapter 12) that organizations like scientific societies should get into the practice of providing members with evidence-based framing guidance, just as LGBTQ groups and Frank Luntz have provided guidance to their internal audiences. Before turning to our final chapter, however, we want to briefly highlight the fact that scientists seem open to exploring both emotion- and frame-focused communication objectives while also making a final point about the need to further explore the ethics of these types of objectives.

Willingness to Prioritize Excitement and Framing

Our 2015–16 survey asked scientists how important they saw "getting people interested or excited about science" (table 11.1) and "framing research implications so members of the public think about a topic in way that resonates with their values" as well as related questions (table 11.2). We found that "getting people interested or excited" was among the top-rated objectives, about one-third to one-fifth of a point below "helping to inform people about scientific issues" (chapter 2) and still quite close to the maximum of the scale (i.e., about 6 points out of a possible 7) (see supplementary tables in appendix B). Participating scientists from across the scientific societies with whom we conducted the survey also rated this objective as relatively ethical (our measure of attitude), normatively common and acceptable to colleagues (our measures of normative beliefs), possible, and something they were able to do. It was also among the objectives participating scientists said they had previously thought about.

In contrast, framing was a lower-tier objective across all of our question categories (see supplementary tables again in appendix B). The scientists in the survey still gave it scores well above the midpoint on most measures except those asking whether their colleagues would be likely to prioritize the objective or expect it to be prioritized, as well as the question about whether they had previously thought about the objective. In those cases, the scale was closer to the midpoint across all the societies. To us, this suggests substantial ambivalence about framing as a communication objective.

This ambivalence is also reflected in our past research aimed at understanding what makes it more likely that a scientist will see an objective as important. This work suggested that the statistical predictors of "getting people interested or excited" were different from the predictors of framing [68]. Scientists were more likely to say they believed sparking positive emotions were important if they believed doing so was possible and something that they had the skill to do. In contrast, scientists seemed to use their ethicality beliefs when deciding whether or not to prioritize framing as an objective, suggesting

Table 11.1.

Scientists' average assessment of the perceived importance of "getting people interested or excited about science" and associated beliefs about this objective in the context of different communication channels and different scientific societies (on a scale of 1 to 7)

	Priority[1]	Ethicality[2]	Peer norms[3]	Peer priority[4]	Achievability[5]	My skills[6]	Prior thought[7]	Sample size range
General								
Face-to-face	5.98	5.92	5.71	5.31	6.16	5.26	5.10	375–380
Media	5.87	5.94	5.70	5.22	6.10	4.91	4.86	323–332
Online	5.72	5.82	5.46	5.05	6.01	4.86	4.74	376–385
Biological								
Face-to-face	6.01	5.70	5.61	5.20	6.16	5.33	5.05	345–353
Online	5.92	5.75	5.54	5.13	6.10	5.10	4.76	326–329
Geophysical								
Face-to-face	5.89	5.76	5.57	5.22	6.11	5.35	5.24	314–316
Media	5.77	5.79	5.70	5.26	6.21	5.17	5.25	314–315
Online	5.84	5.72	5.47	5.03	6.17	5.11	5.00	268–273
Geological								
Face-to-face	5.91	5.81	5.55	5.14	6.07	5.39	5.25	243–248
Media	5.99	5.88	5.67	5.38	6.05	5.34	5.32	235–243
Online	5.97	5.86	5.52	5.17	6.15	5.40	5.21	229–237
Ecological								
Face-to-face	5.89	5.90	5.56	5.26	6.24	5.34	5.48	340–346
Chemical								
Face-to-face	5.74	5.62	5.52	5.22	6.04	5.21	5.05	180–181
Media	5.57	5.50	5.44	5.09	5.94	4.87	4.76	157–159
Online	5.60	5.50	5.41	4.98	6.06	4.94	4.82	150–152
Biochemical								
Face-to-face	5.94	5.69	5.51	5.10	6.07	5.08	5.03	367–369
Social								
Media	4.94	5.61	4.98	4.49	5.58	4.95	4.21	872–921

Notes: For the "priority" statement, respondents were given a list of objectives (including the objective noted in the table title) and asked to rate each objective between "very low importance" (1) and "very high importance" (7). For all other statements, respondents selected between "strongly disagree" (1) and "strongly agree" (7). Respondents were all faculty with PhDs at US-based universities. Standard deviations in appendix B tables.

[1] "In general, what are the most important or unimportant communication objectives that scientists such as yourself should have when taking part in [mode*]? Please remember that not every objective can be the most important objective." *Respondents were assigned to see all questions in the context of only one of three potential modes: face-to-face engagement, media engagement, or online engagement.

[2] "This objective is ethical."

[3] "Scientists who pursue this objective would be well regarded by their peers."

[4] "My colleagues would put a high priority on this objective."

[5] "Achieving this objective is possible for a good communicator."

[6] "I have the skills needed to achieve this objective."

[7] "Prior to this survey, I had thought a lot about this potential objective."

Table 11.2.

Scientists' average assessment of the perceived importance of "framing research implications so members of the public think about a topic in way that resonates with their values" and associated beliefs about this objective in the context of different communication channels and different scientific societies (on a scale of 1 to 7)

	Priority[1]	Ethicality[2]	Peer norms[3]	Peer priority[4]	Achievability[5]	My skills[6]	Prior thought[7]	Sample size range
General								
Face-to-face	5.27	5.30	4.81	4.34	5.53	4.54	3.87	368–379
Media	5.20	5.25	4.75	4.21	5.48	4.18	3.60	318–327
Online	5.12	5.13	4.58	4.11	5.43	4.09	3.58	368–382
Biological								
Face-to-face	5.37	5.10	4.79	4.32	5.56	4.57	3.87	344–351
Online	5.39	5.22	4.84	4.29	5.48	4.25	3.64	326–334
Geophysical								
Face-to-face	5.24	5.13	4.66	4.32	5.54	4.59	4.17	312–315
Media	5.21	5.06	4.63	4.15	5.59	4.44	4.02	314–321
Online	5.03	5.12	4.66	4.20	5.53	4.44	3.88	268–276
Geological								
Face-to-face	5.18	5.22	4.67	4.21	5.57	4.59	4.02	244–256
Media	5.17	5.14	4.71	4.34	5.43	4.44	3.86	239–245
Online	5.19	5.08	4.68	4.27	5.35	4.48	3.99	229–237
Ecological								
Face-to-face	5.33	5.28	4.64	4.31	5.70	4.60	4.38	342–345
Chemical								
Face-to-face	5.08	5.06	4.69	4.25	5.43	4.39	3.88	177–183
Media	5.12	4.80	4.52	4.06	5.28	3.97	3.38	156–158
Online	4.83	4.92	4.67	4.05	5.28	4.02	3.42	151–155
Biochemical								
Face-to-face	5.30	5.24	4.72	4.27	5.51	4.32	3.75	364–369
Social								
Media	5.07	4.90	4.42	1.43	5.28	4.69	3.88	872–921

Notes: For the "priority" statement, respondents were given a list of objectives (including the objective noted in the table title) and asked to rate each objective between "very low importance" (1) and "very high importance" (7). For all other statements, respondents selected between "strongly disagree" (1) and "strongly agree" (7). Respondents were all faculty with PhDs at US-based universities. Standard deviations in appendix B tables.

[1] "In general, what are the most important or unimportant communication objectives that scientists such as yourself should have when taking part in [mode*]? Please remember that not every objective can be the most important objective." *Respondents were assigned to see all questions in the context of only one of three potential modes: face-to-face engagement, media engagement, or online engagement.

[2] "This objective is ethical."

[3] "Scientists who pursue this objective would be well regarded by their peers."

[4] "My colleagues would put a high priority on this objective."

[5] "Achieving this objective is possible for a good communicator."

[6] "I have the skills needed to achieve this objective."

[7] "Prior to this survey, I had thought a lot about this potential objective."

to us that some scientists' concerns about the ethicality of purposeful framing may limit their desire to prioritize this type of objective. Scientists who had thought more about framing, however, were more likely to prioritize this objective suggesting more sophisticated communicators might come to see the objective as a necessary element of communication strategy. Unfortunately, we have not published research on scientists' views about emotions beyond excitement and interest, nor have we asked scientists about related tactics. We might expect that scientists would have different views about trying to spark negative emotions.

As previously noted in discussing other objectives, the main takeaway from this research is also that most scientists are open to a range of objectives—when asked—but have not necessarily spent a lot of time thinking about these objectives. Further, there are few substantive differences between scientists in different fields (or of different ages or genders) on how they think about these topics [68].

The Ethics of Emotional Communication and Framing

We remain unsure about when it is ethical to purposefully try to get someone to feel an emotion about an issue we care about, and whether it is okay to frame an issue in a certain way because you know it will resonate with a target audience. That being said, science communicators need to recognize that *failing* to make emotion or framing choices still constitutes a choice, and it does not mean that our audiences will not develop new beliefs, feelings, or framings that could affect their behavior. We have seen communicators frame issues in ways that we worry may only appeal to people like themselves or seemingly try to rile up audiences with whatever emotion the communicator is feeling.

Our best guess is that it is probably ethically acceptable to try and learn how others are feeling about issues and how they frame those issues. Similarly, we think it is probably okay to share our own feelings and preferred way to frame issues. However, we would like to see science communicators who want to suggest an emotional reaction or way of framing to be transparent about why they are doing

Preparing to Prioritize Framing
as a Communication Objective

The following are eight questions that science communicators should consider when deciding whether to prioritize reframing an issue or behavior as a communication objective. In many cases, framing-focused communication might involve a science communicator sharing how they think about an issue or presenting alternative ways to think about an issue, both in psychological terms (e.g., Does this behavior create a gain or prevent a loss?) and sociological terms (e.g., Should we think of an issue as an environmental issue or health issue?).

THE GOAL QUESTION

1. Given the behavior you want from your specific audience (i.e., your goal), why do you think it would be helpful if your chosen audience framed an issue in a specific way?

THE PREPARATION QUESTIONS

2. How does your chosen audience currently frame the issue about which you want to communicate and is there meaningful room to change these feelings?
3. How do you prefer to frame the issue? Are there frames you see as more or less applicable?

THE TACTICS QUESTIONS

4. What could you do to potentially increase the likelihood that those with whom you are communicating frame the issue about which you communicate in a different way, including choices about messages, behaviors, tone/style, communication channel, and communication source?
5. What could you do to learn more about how your chosen audience frames your issue?

THE EVALUATION QUESTIONS

6. Did your chosen audience consider or adopt an alternative or new way to frame an issue as a function of your communication? Did their feelings about the issue change?
7. What did you learn about how your audience frames your issue?

THE ETHICS QUESTION

8. Are you communicating in ways that affect how people frame an issue in a careful, respectful, and open way?

so. This might look like a scientist saying something like "It gives me hope when policymakers ask experts for their advice" or "There are different ways to frame climate change, but one way that I think makes a lot of sense involves seeing it as an emerging cause of disease." We also do not think it is necessary—or advisable—for science communicators to share every emotion, just as we do not yell at our friends when they do something that annoys us. We also worry about using emotions in ways aimed at getting people to feel shame.

Finally, returning to an idea we mentioned in chapter 1, ethical communicators need to be prepared to change how they feel or think about an issue as a result of communicating with others. This will often mean designing communication activities so that both scientists and nonscientists hear from each other, whether face-to-face or online dialogue in real time or as part of an extended process. More broadly, we hope that the science communication community can continue to have open conversations about ethics to ensure that our communication choices reflect the best parts of the scientific enterprise.

REFERENCES

1. Chaiken, Shelly. "Heuristic Versus Systematic Information Processing and the Use of Source Versus Message Cues in Persuasion." *Journal of Personality and Social Psychology* 39, no. 5 (1980): 752–66. https://doi.org/10.1037/0022-3514.39.5.752.

2. Cacioppo, John T., Chuan Feng Kao, Richard E. Petty, and Regina Rodriguez. "Cenrtral and Peripheral Routes to Persusasion: An Indivudal Difference Perspective." *Journal of Personality and Social Psychology* 51, no. 5 (November 1986): 1032–43.

3. Slovic, Paul, Melissa L. Finucane, Ellen Peters, and Donald G. MacGregor. "Risk as Analysis and Risk as Feelings: Some Thoughts About Affect, Reason, Risk, and Rationality." *Risk Analysis* 24, no. 2 (2004): 311–22.

4. Kahneman, Daniel. *Thinking, Fast and Slow.* 1st ed. New York: Farrar, Straus and Giroux, 2011.

5. Nabi, Robin L. "Exploring the Framing Effects of Emotion: Do Discrete Emotions Differentially Influence Information Accessibility, Information Seeking, and Policy Preference?" *Communication Research* 30, no. 2 (2003): 224–47. https://doi.org/10.1177/0093650202250881.

6. Fiske, Susan T., and Shelley E. Taylor. *Social Cognition: From Brains to Culture.* 1st ed. Boston: McGraw-Hill Higher Education, 2008.

7. Roeser, Sabine. "Risk Communication, Public Engagement, and Climate Change: A Role for Emotions." *Risk Analysis* 32, no. 6 (2012): 1033–40. https://doi.org/10.1111/j.1539-6924.2012.01812.x.

8. Slovic, Paul. "Perception of Risk." *Science* 236, no. 4799 (1987): 280–85. https://doi.org/10.1126/science.3563507.

9. Alhakami, Ali Siddiq, and Paul Slovic. "A Psychological Study of the Inverse Relationship between Perceived Risk and Perceived Benefit." *Risk Analysis* 14, no. 6 (1994): 1085–96. https://doi.org/10.1111/j.1539-6924.1994.tb00080.x.

10. Finucane, Melissa L., Ali Alhakami, Paul Slovic, and Stephen M. Johnson. "The Affect Heuristic in Judgments of Risks and Benefits." *Journal of Behavioral Decision Making* 13, no. 1 (2000): 1–17.

11. Loewenstein, George F., Elke U. Weber, Christopher K. Hsee, and Ned Welch. "Risk as Feelings." *Psychological Bulletin* 127, no. 2 (2001): 267–86. https://doi.org/10.1037/0033-2909.127.2.267.

12. Kahan, Dan M., Paul Slovic, Donald Braman, John Gastil, and Geoffrey L. Cohen. "Affect, Values, and Nanotechnology Risk Perceptions: An Experimental Investigation." GWU Legal Studies Research Paper No. 261. Yale Law School, Public Law Working Paper No. 155. 2nd Annual Conference on Empirical Legal Studies Paper, March 7, 2007. http://dx.doi.org/10.2139/ssrn.968652.

13. Siegrist, Michael, Carmen Keller, and Marie-Eve Cousin. "Implicit Attitudes toward Nuclear Power and Mobile Phone Base Stations: Support for the Affect Heuristic." *Risk Analysis* 26, no. 4 (2006): 1021–29. https://doi.org/10.1111/j.1539-6924.2006.00797.x.

14. Nabi, Robin L. "A Cognitive-Functional Model for the Effects of Discrete Negative Emotions on Information Processing, Attitude Change, and Recall." *Communication Theory* 9, no. 3 (1999): 292–320. https://doi.org/10.1111/j.1468-2885.1999.tb00172.x.

15. Witte, Kim. "Putting the Fear Back into Fear Appeals: The Extended Parallel Process Model." *Communication Monographs* 59, no. 4 (1992): 329–49. https://doi.org/10.1080/03637759209376276.

16. Nabi, Robin L., Abel Gustafson, and Risa Jensen. "Framing Climate Change: Exploring the Role of Emotion in Generating Advocacy Behavior." *Science Communication* 40, no. 4 (2018): 442–68. https://doi.org/10.1177/1075547018776019.

17. Bilandzic, Helena, Anja Kalch, and Jens Soentgen. "Effects of Goal Framing and Emotions on Perceived Threat and Willingness to Sacrifice for Climate Change." *Science Communication* 39, no. 4 (2017): 466–91. https://doi.org/10.1177/1075547017718553.

18. Feldman, Lauren, and P. Sol Hart. "Using Political Efficacy Messages to Increase Climate Activism: The Mediating Role of Emotions." *Science Communication* 38, no. 1 (2016): 99–127. https://doi.org/10.1177/1075547015617941.

19. Chu, Haoran, and Janet Z. Yang. "Emotion and the Psychological Distance of Climate Change." *Science Communication* 41, no. 6 (2019): 761–89. https://doi.org/10.1177/1075547019889637.

20. Besley, John C. "Does Fairness Matter in the Context of Anger About Nuclear Energy Decision Making?" *Risk Analysis* 32, no. 1 (2012): 25–38. https://doi.org/10.1111/j.1539-6924.2011.01664.x.

21. Fung, Timothy K. F., Robert J. Griffin, and Sharon Dunwoody. "Testing Links among Uncertainty, Affect, and Attitude toward a Health Behavior." *Science Communication* 40, no. 1 (2018): 33–62. https://doi.org/10.1177/107554701 7748947.

22. Myrick, Jessica Gall, and Suzannah D. Evans. "Do PSAs Take a Bite out of *Shark Week*? The Effects of Juxtaposing Environmental Messages with Violent Images of Shark Attacks." *Science Communication* 36, no. 5 (2014): 544–69. https://doi.org/10.1177/1075547014547159.

23. Skurka, Chris, Jeff Niederdeppe, and Robin Nabi. "Kimmel on Climate: Disentangling the Emotional Ingredients of a Satirical Monologue." *Science Communication* 41, no. 4 (2019): 394–421. https://doi.org/10.1177/1075547019853837.

24. Cacciatore, Michael A., Amy B. Becker, Ashley A. Anderson, and Sara K. Yeo. "Laughing with Science: The Influence of Audience Approval on Engagement." *Science Communication* 42, no. 2 (2020): 195–217. https://doi.org/10.1177 /1075547020910749.

25. Scott, Sydney E., Yoel Inbar, and Paul Rozin. "Evidence for Absolute Moral Opposition to Genetically Modified Food in the United States." *Perspectives on Psychological Science* 11, no. 3 (2016): 315–24. https://doi.org/10.1177/1745691615621275.

26. Yeo, Sara K., Ye Sun, Meaghan McKasy, and Erica Shugart. "Disgusting Microbes: The Effect of Disgust on Perceptions of Risks Related to Modifying Microbiome." *Public Understanding of Science* 28, no. 4 (2019): 433–48. https://doi .org/10.1177/0963662519832200.

27. Höijer, Birgitta. "Emotional Anchoring and Objectification in the Media Reporting on Climate Change." *Public Understanding of Science* 19, no. 6 (2010): 717–31. https://doi.org/10.1177/0963662509348863.

28. Hong, Hyehyun. "Audience Responses to Television News Coverage of Medical Advances: The Mediating Role of Audience Emotions and Identification." *Public Understanding of Science* 24, no. 6 (2015): 697–711. https://doi.org/10.1177 /0963662514544919.

29. Myrick, Jessica Gall, Lee Ahern, Ruosi Shao, and Jeff Conlin. "Technology Name and Celebrity Endorsement Effects of Autonomous Vehicle Promotional Messages: Mechanisms and Moderators." *Science Communication* 41, no. 1 (2019): 38–65. https://doi.org/10.1177/1075547018819194.

30. French, David P., Stephen Sutton, Susie J. Hennings, Jo Mitchell, Nicholas J. Wareham, Simon Griffin, Wendy Hardeman, and Ann Louise Kinmonth. "The Importance of Affective Beliefs and Attitudes in the Theory of Planned Behavior: Predicting Intention to Increase Physical Activity." *Journal of Applied Social Psychology* 35, no. 9 (September 2005): 1824–48.

31. Jensen, Eric, and Nicola Buckley. "Why People Attend Science Festivals: Interests, Motivations and Self-Reported Benefits of Public Engagement with Research." *Public Understanding of Science* 23, no. 5 (July 2014): 557–73. https://doi .org/10.1177/0963662512458624.

32. Geiger, Nathaniel, Janet K. Swim, John Fraser, and Kate Flinner. "Catalyzing Public Engagement with Climate Change through Informal Science Learning

Centers." *Science Communication* 39, no. 2 (2017): 221–49. https://doi.org/10.1177
/1075547017697980.

33. Sickler, Jessica, and John Fraser. "Enjoyment in Zoos." *Leisure Studies* 28, no. 3 (2009): 313–31. https://doi.org/10.1080/02614360903046649.

34. Glynn, Carroll J., Michael E. Huge, and Carole A. Lunney. "The Influence of Perceived Social Norms on College Students' Intention to Vote." *Political Communication* 26, no. 1 (2009): 48–64. https://doi.org/10.1080/10584600802
622860.

35. Neubaum, German, and Nicole C. Krämer. "What Do We Fear? Expected Sanctions for Expressing Minority Opinions in Offline and Online Communication." *Communication Research* 45, no. 2 (2018): 139–64. https://doi.org/10.1177
/0093650215623837.

36. FrameWorks Institute. "History." Accessed April 27, 2020. http://www
.frameworksinstitute.org/about/history.

37. Gamson, William A., and Andre Modigliani. (1989). "Media Discourse and Public Opinion on Nuclear Power: A Constructionist Approach. *American Journal of Sociology* 95, no. 1 (1989), 1–37. https://www.jstor.org/stable/2780405.

38. Entman, Robert M. "Framing: Toward Clarification of a Fractured Paradigm." *Journal of Communication* 43, no. 4 (December 1993): 51–58. https://doi
.org/10.1111/j.1460-2466.1993.tb01304.x.

39. Scheufele, Dietram A. "Framing as a Theory of Media Effects." *Journal of Communication* 49, no. 1 (Winter 1999): 103–22.

40. Moyer, Jessica, Moira O'Neil, Kevin Levay, and Andrew Volmert. *Wiring across Sites So STEM Learning Can Flow: Strategies for Communicating More Effectively About Connecting STEM Learning Environments (A FrameWorks Strategic Brief)*. Washington, DC: FrameWorks Insitute, May 2019. https://www
.frameworksinstitute.org/wp-content/uploads/2020/05/FamLAB-Strategic
-Brief.pdf.

41. Druckman, James N. "The Implications of Framing Effects for Citizen Competence." *Political Behavior* 23, no. 3 (September 2001): 225–56.

42. Myers, Teresa A., Matthew C. Nisbet, Edward W. Maibach, and Anthony A. Leiserowitz. "A Public Health Frame Arouses Hopeful Emotions About Climate Change." *Climatic Change* 113, no. 3–4 (2012): 1105–12. https://doi.org/10.1007/s10584
-012-0513-6.

43. Tversky, A., and D. Kahneman. "The Framing of Decisions and the Psychology of Choice." *Science* 211, no. 4481 (1981): 453–58.

44. Peters, Ellen. *Inumeracy in the Wild: Misunderstanding and Misusing Numbers*. New York: Oxford University Press, 2020.

45. O'Keefe, Daniel J., and Jakob D. Jensen. "The Relative Persuasiveness of Gain-Framed Loss-Framed Messages for Encouraging Disease Prevention Behaviors: A Meta-Analytic Review." *Journal of Health Communication* 12, no. 7 (2007): 623–44. https://doi.org/10.1080/10810730701615198.

46. O'Keefe, Daniel J., and Jakob D. Jensen. "The Relative Persuasiveness of Gain-Framed and Loss-Framed Messages for Encouraging Disease Detection

Behaviors: A Meta-Analytic Review." *Journal of Communication* 59, no. 2 (2009): 296–316. https://doi.org/10.1111/j.1460-2466.2009.01417.x.

47. Chong, Dennis, and James N. Druckman. "Framing Theory." *Annual Review of Political Science* 10, no. 1 (2007): 103–26. https://doi.org/10.1146/annurev.polisci .10.072805.103054.

48. Scheufele, Dietram A., and David Tewksbury. "Framing, Agenda Setting, and Priming: The Evolution of Three Media Effects Models." *Journal of Communication* 57, no. 1 (March 2007): 9–20.

49. Boykoff, Maxwell T. "From Convergence to Contention: United States Mass Media Representations of Anthropogenic Climate Change Science." *Transactions of the Institute of British Geographers* 32, no. 4 (October 2007): 477–89.

50. Iyengar, Shanto. "Framing Responsibility for Political Issues." *Annals of the American Academy of Political and Social Science* 546 (July 1996): 59–70.

51. Iyengar, Shanto. *Is Anyone Responsible? How Television Frames Political Issues*. Chicago: University of Chicago Press, 1991.

52. Gross, Kimberly. "Framing Persuasive Appeals: Episodic and Thematic Framing, Emotional Response, and Policy Opinion." *Political Psychology* 29, no. 2 (2008): 169–92. https://doi.org/10.1111/j.1467-9221.2008.00622.x.

53. Hart, Philip Solomon. "One or Many? The Influence of Episodic and Thematic Climate Change Frames on Policy Preferences and Individual Behavior Change." *Science Communication* 33, no. 1 (2011): 28–51. https://doi.org/10.1177 /1075547010366400.

54. Nisbet, Matthew C., and Bruce V. Lewenstein. "Biotechnology and the American Media: The Policy Process and the Elite Press, 1970 to 1999." *Science Communication* 23, no. 4 (June 2002): 359–91. https://doi.org/10.1177/1075547002 02300401.

55. Lewenstein, Bruce V., Jason B. Gorss, and Joanna Radin. "The Salience of Small: Nanotechnology Coverage in the American Press, 1986–2004." Annual Meeting of the International Communication Association, New York, NY, May 26–30, 2005.

56. Menashe, Claudia L. "The Power of a Frame: An Analysis of Newspaper Coverage of Tobacco Issues, United States, 1985–1996." *Journal of Health Communication* 3, no. 4 (1998): 307–25. https://doi.org/10.1080/108107398127139.

57. Movement Advancement Project and GLAAD. *Talking About LGBT Equality: Overall Approaches*. MAP's *Talking About LGBT Issues* Series, September 2011. https://www.lgbtmap.org/talking-about-lgbt-issues-overall-approaches.

58. Luntz, Frank I. *Words That Work: It's Not What You Say, It's What People Hear.* 1st paperback ed. New York: Hyperion, 2007.

59. Luntz, Frank. "The Environment: A Clean Safer, Healthier America." *The Luntz Research Companies: Straight Talk* (2002): 131–46. Accessed April 28, 2020. https://www.sourcewatch.org/index.php/File:LuntzResearch.Memo.pdf.

60. Lakoff, George. *Moral Politics: How Liberals and Conservatives Think.* 2nd ed. Chicago: University of Chicago Press, 2002.

61. Lakoff, George. *Don't Think of an Elephant! Know Your Values and Frame the Debate: The Essential Guide for Progressives.* White River Junction, VT: Chelsea Green, 2004.

62. Schuldt, Jonathon P., Sara H. Konrath, and Norbert Schwarz. "'Global Warming' or 'Climate Change'? Whether the Planet Is Warming Depends on Question Wording." *Public Opinion Quarterly* 75, no. 1 (2011): 115–24. https://doi.org/10.1093/poq/nfq073.

63. Zahry, Nagwan R., and John C. Besley. "Genetic Engineering, Genetic Modification, or Agricultural Biotechnology: Does the Term Matter?" *Journal of Risk Research*, no. 22 (2019): 16–31. https://doi.org/10.1080/13669877.2017.1351470.

64. Trope, Yaacov, and Nira Liberman. "Construal-Level Theory of Psychological Distance." *Psychological Review* 117, no. 2 (2010): 440–63. https://doi.org/10.1037/a0018963.

65. Duan, Ran, Bruno Takahashi, and Adam Zwickle. "Abstract or Concrete? The Effect of Climate Change Images on People's Estimation of Egocentric Psychological Distance." *Public Understanding of Science* 28, no. 7 (2019): 828–44. https://doi.org/10.1177/0963662519865982.

66. Jones, Charlotte, Donald W. Hine, and Anthony D. G. Marks. "The Future Is Now: Reducing Psychological Distance to Increase Public Engagement with Climate Change." *Risk Analysis* 37, no. 2 (2017): 331–41. https://doi.org/10.1111/risa.12601.

67. Katz, Sherri Jean, Sahara Byrne, and Alyssa Irene Kent. "Mitigating the Perception of Threat to Freedom through Abstraction and Distance." *Communication Research* 44, no. 7 (2017): 1046–69. https://doi.org/10.1177/0093650216647534.

68. Besley, John C., Anthony Dudo, and Shupei Yuan. "Scientists' Views About Communication Objectives." *Public Understanding of Science* 27, no. 6 (2018): 708–30. https://doi.org/10.1177/0963662517728478.

12

The Need to Take Communication More Seriously

RESEARCHING THIS BOOK REMINDED US how little we know. The "we" in this sentence includes "us" as authors but also the broader science communication field. Researchers seem to have a grip on the concepts we see as the pantry of beliefs, feelings, and frames that represent primary science communication objectives (chapters 2–11). We also have a range of well-developed theories (theory of planned behavior, health belief model, protection motivation theory, etc.) that connect these objectives to behaviors. What we lack is clear and curated evidence about what tactics (i.e., choices about message content, behaviors, tone/style, channel, and sources) can reliably affect specific objectives in various contexts, over time. We also know too little about what behaviors might result from achieving those objectives and the contexts in which these outcomes might be expected (or not expected). What we mostly see in the research are one-off, short-duration experiments that show small effects and correlational studies that show patterns of relationships between concepts. We have done these types of studies ourselves and will continue to do them, but they are not enough. Such studies provide insight on potential paths forward, but we have few real-world trials focused specifically on achieving science communication objectives and goals. We especially lack studies on objectives related to long-term trust-building through efforts to communicate caring, integrity, openness, similarity, and competence.

In the corporate world, smart companies put resources into ongoing qualitative and quantitative tracking of how stakeholders think and feel and how those beliefs, feelings, and framings are shaping behavior [1]. In the science world, however, our sense is that few organizations devote resources to researching, planning, implementing, and evaluating [2] strategic communication campaigns where the goal is to advance the place of science in our communities or our society. Individual science-oriented organizations might periodically do campaigns to advance their own interests—including recruiting desirable students, reaching funders, or promoting research—but this seems different than coordinated communication campaigns aimed at ensuring that a broad range of actors see science as a key ingredient for public decisions or for advancing evidence-based decision-making in specific contexts. Similarly, there may occasionally be health and environmental campaigns aimed at promoting individual behavior that indirectly help science thrive, but these also seem different than the type of long-term, coordinated efforts that religious, political, and industry organizations use to build strategic relationships and try to shift behavior in the directions that science suggests are needed.

It might be that some people in the scientific community have little interest in trying to help shape the communities around us and would prefer to focus on simply sharing research and hoping for the best. Such people might say we are wrong to suggest that science communication should start with setting goals such as building legitimacy and changing individual behaviors. Focusing on behavior change can sound manipulative, but our view is that wanting to change the behavior of others can be ethical if it is done carefully—with great respect for those with whom we communicate and a concomitant willingness to change our own beliefs, feelings, framing, and associated behaviors. We have also surveyed and talked to scientists and science communicators about goals (chapter 1) and found that most people in the community are comfortable with the idea that we want to do more with science communication than teach people about science. When asked, most of the people in science that we interact with say they want their policymakers and their neighbors to listen to scientists' advice and change their behavior as a result (see chapter 1). That is who this book is for. As noted, most scientists we have surveyed also seem willing to consider trying to achieve a range of communication objectives [3] and to use a range of tactics [4] to achieve their communication goals. If anything, given what we have heard in studying scientists, we think it would be unethical to pretend that much of the scientific community does not want to promote evidence-based behaviors. Some science communicators may have unrealistic expectations about the ability of science to solve problems, but many also recognize that the scientific advice they provide is always going to be just one factor people use in making decisions. This is especially true in a complex world where we need to make decisions with incomplete evidence and where we respect others' values [5].

Strategic Communication Is Difficult

The challenge we see ahead is that communicating in evidence-based ways is difficult. It is difficult because it takes time and money. It is difficult because it takes coordination, and because it takes expertise. We said in the introduction that we both shifted from studying public opinion about science to studying scientists' opinions about science communication because we wanted to help scientists communicate in more evidence-based ways. We thought that our fellow communication researchers were producing evidence about practices that could benefit those trying to advance the place of science in society. At that time, we also thought part of the task was getting more scientists to commit to communicating, but we have found that there is already a large of pool of scientists who are eager and willing to communicate [6]. As such, we turned our attention away from increasing the quantity of willing science communicators. We turned instead to trying to increase science communication quality. Our expectation was that the best path forward was to support the wonderful people who train scientists by encouraging training aimed at helping scientists think more like evidence-based strategic communicators, in addition to the existing focus on tactical skills [7]. After about a decade of such research, we now believe we may have been too optimistic about the availability of useful research and the idea that we could make progress by focusing on scientists' skills.

While we still believe increasing scientists individual-level communication skills can help, we increasingly think that improving the quality of science communication requires a team-based approach where scientists and communication experts work together to set and achieve goals [8]. Researchers Sarah Davies and Maja Horst call this an integration model of science communication [9]. At present, our sense is that much of the science communication that occurs involves individual, self-selected scientists finding ways to connect with reporters or find in-person or online audiences [10]. To use yet another food analogy, the science communication system seems largely built on the equivalent of individual home cooks working in isolation with limited training and limited reach. Many of these cooks put out consistently wonderful meals. Others have good dishes and bad dishes but keep the people around them well fed and happy. Some give people food poisoning or turn their victims off certain foods for life. There will always be a need for home cooks, and some homeschooled, hard-working geniuses will become great chefs, but most people would probably prefer to invest (or eat) in a restaurant headed by a well-trained, carefully mentored culinary expert. Similarly, while some politicians may start out by arranging their own speaking opportunities and writing their own speeches, there comes a point where they start hiring help for strategy, logistics, writing, and other specialized tasks. On the negative side, while you might defend yourself in court against a parking ticket, most people with the money would hire a lawyer for bigger cases. We think the place of science in society matters, so we think scientists need to find the resources to hire (and use) more help if they are serious about communicating with impact.

A National Science Foundation–funded project of John's has brought home the value of high-quality communication support. The project is an effort by two Long Term Ecological Research (LTER) sites in New England to improve their stakeholder engagement. This work started with the traditional idea of training scientists at the Hubbard Brook Experimental Forest in New Hampshire and the Harvard Forest in rural Massachusetts to build their communication skills. However, interviews with scientists in the first year of the project suggested ambivalence about spending precious research time on generic training. The interviews also suggested deep appreciation for the work that two public engagement specialists at the sites—Sarah Garlick and Kathy Fallon-Lambert—were already leading. The interviewed scientists expressed a desire to improve communication, but their idea of improving communication was to find better ways to collaborate with their in-house experts to set goals and then build strategies to achieve those goals. This partly shifted the research toward thinking about how to support people like Sarah and Kathy and increase scientists' buy-in for allocating resources and time to work with on-site communication experts [11].

Moving forward the hope is to figure out how to build up communication expertise across the broader LTER Network, which includes more than two dozen unique sites across the United States. If this work continues, the hypothesis is that LTER scientists will increasingly devote resources to communication infrastructure if they believe they have access to communication experts whom they see as trustworthy (i.e., caring, honest, willing to listen, similar to them in values, and competent; see chapters 3–7), as well as if they believe they benefit from improved communication (chapter 8), if they perceive their colleagues value quality communication (chapter 9), and if they believe they have the ability to obtain resources for better quality communication (chapter 10). At a tactical level, doing so will involve creating situations where scientists and communication experts work together to develop and implement strategies in ways that build both trusting relationships and other types of evaluative beliefs.

Collaborating on Science Communication Requires Shared Goals

Other things we especially appreciate about LTER sites are their size and focus. The sites tend to have fewer than 100 active scholars along with core leadership teams of fewer than a dozen. This size seems helpful because it is big enough to share work but small enough for people to potentially buy into an institutional mission and coordinate their activities. Similarly, the sites seem to be focused on a set of shared organizational research goals, and there is a recognition that achieving these goals requires thinking about more than just producing high quality research. Sites that want to continue to exist need to ensure that a range of stakeholders—including funders and their constituents, research partners, research users, fellow academics, and local communities near the site—see value in the site's ongoing work. Further, we believe that thinking their work has impact gives scientists a sense of energy and purpose.

The desire to be valued for our work and feel a sense of purpose gives organizations like the LTER Network a motive around which to set communication-focused behavioral goals for stakeholders and develop communication strategies to achieve those goals. Example objectives might include building mutually trusting relationships with civic leaders in local communities to ensure civic support for the site. For sites like Hubbard Brook and Harvard Forest, it could also likely include efforts to get regional land managers to consider changes to their forestry practices based on emerging findings, or to get advice from managers on challenges or opportunities that the researchers could try to address in future research proposals. The key is that identifying shared organizational goals likely makes communication coordination between scientists possible. This coordination includes pooling the resources needed to hire expert communicators to help scientists achieve their goals. One premise of strategic communication, in this regard, is that communication-focused goals are meant to build on organizational goals [12].

John also learned the challenge of trying to discuss communication strategy in the absence of organizational goals when a colleague invited him to an international meeting to help an interdisciplinary group of researchers strategize. The researchers were individually brilliant and committed to the value of increasing communication in their field. However, it soon became apparent that they could not agree on what they hoped to collectively accomplish through communication. They agreed they wanted more people to know more about their research, but it was not clear why they wanted to increase knowledge. Individual researchers talked about how they personally used communication to ask better scientific questions and ensure impact, but this did not translate into a collective purpose around which to coordinate and pool resources.

Closer to home, academic departments in the United States provide university faculty with shared goals around teaching, but when it comes to research, most professors run their own research groups or labs and may have a hard time identifying shared communication goals with colleagues. In our own universities, communication professionals either work at the college level (i.e., across multiple academic departments) and report to the dean's office or they work for central administration and report to a university vice president. Studies are needed to better understand the landscape of university communication from the perspective of scientists (and other researchers), but our sense is that most of the available communication expertise at universities gets devoted to recruitment, fundraising, and crisis management. Only limited communication effort seems to go toward trying to ensure that our society makes use of the scientific research that university researchers produce. That job is left to individuals and the groups they work within, most of whom likely have few communication resources.

That being said, one type of organization within universities where we have some hope for strategic discussions about communication are the institutes and centers that universities often form to bring together people and resources around a single issue. The main danger we see in these types of organizations is that the communication professionals who work for them can find themselves disconnected from the broader university and the type of mentorship, training, and career progression that communication professionals need to accrue expertise. Outside of science, our sense is that young communication professionals do best when they have the opportunity to work in established communication companies (i.e., advertising agencies or PR firms) or departments where there is the opportunity to develop both technical and strategy skills, and where there is a range of clients. We would therefore love to understand how to better connect university communicators embedded within research groups to broader communities of communication experts. Similarly, the people doing the hiring for many communication positions within universities may have research or administrative expertise but little capacity to judge communication expertise. We worry that some scientists might prioritize hiring people with tactical-level skills they recognize—such as educational expertise or media writing skills related to science—rather than the strategic skills needed to plan and evaluate communication programs [13]. One solution here may be as simple as ensuring that communication experts take part in the hiring process.

Another practical challenge that on-campus institutes and research centers face is that groups with limited budgets devoted to communication cannot afford to hire multiple people and will therefore struggle to find individuals who are able and willing to be both a strategist and a multimedia content producer comfortable with writing, video production, social media curating, and more. Once hired, communicators who are dependent on the good graces of a strong-minded researcher may also sometimes balk at "speaking truth to power" in the way that trusted communication strategists need to do when a principal—often a key actor such as a politician or executive—gets distracted from their goal. Indeed, one additional reason that being strategic in science communication is hard is that it is not fun to push back on eager, well-meaning communicators when they seem unclear about what they are trying to achieve. Asking questions like "Why do you want to correct misinformation?" or

"Why are you trying to get people excited?" can be unpleasant for both the person asking the questions and the person being asked.

One service that strategic communication firms provide their clients is access to professionals who have seen a wide range of different campaigns and who are supposed to be more concerned about the long-term reputation of their firm and themselves rather than about pleasing a client who wants to do something silly. At minimum, we agree with public relations visionary Edward Bernays's position that clients should see their communication advisors as a valued "counselor" with specific expertise, similar to a lawyer or chief financial officer [14], not just as a subordinate. PR trailblazer James Grunig similarly used surveys of PR practitioners and company leaders to argue that top-performing communication programs had a head of public relations who reported directly to the chief executive and was part of the organization's top leadership team [13]. Going forward, we hope universities can find ways to make more strategic-level communication thinkers available to researchers to help guide the activities of the skilled tacticians needed to produce content and manage stakeholder relationships. We also hope that it is possible to find communication strategists and give them time to build the trusting relationships that need to exist between a principal and their advisors.

A Bigger Role for Scientific Societies

Scientific societies are another type of organization that we have begun thinking more about in the context of finding places where resources might best help improve the overall quality of science communication. Most researchers have memberships in one or more professional associations that meet regularly to share new ideas and data, as well provide other services. This might include forums for talking about jobs, teaching, and the place of the field in society. Our colleague Shupei Yuan led a foundation-funded interview project with us and found that many of these societies in the United States employ an individual or small team of professional communicators to help with both internal communication to members as well as external communication to stakeholders, especially lawmakers [15].

Many of these societies in the United States are therefore headquartered in Washington, DC, with the biggest including groups such as the American Association for the Advancement of Science (approximately 120,000 members), the American Chemical Society (approximately 150,000 members), the American Geophysical Union (approximately 60,000 members), and the American Physical Society (over 55,000 members).

While these large societies can have impressive communication teams, interviews and surveys of communication leads at a broad range of societies convinced us of an eagerness to do more to help members but a frustration with the resources available to do the job and the limited coordination between societies. We found something similar in a project that involved interviewing organizations—many of which also were scientific societies—who manage fellowship programs for scientists who want to build communication expertise [16]. Our interviewees expressed a desire to do more but lacked the resources to push forward. Ultimately, our sense is that better understanding the communication infrastructure at scientific societies, as well as universities, represents an area where we need substantial research.

Two example areas where we would also love to see potential initial movement by societies is (1) in sponsoring public opinion surveys and interview studies focused on what scientists' fellow citizens think about specific areas of science and scientists, and (2) on providing more guidance on what communication strategies scientists should consider using when they take part in communication activities. These activities are connected inasmuch as we would like to see scientific societies using surveys and other tools (e.g., interviews, focus groups, community listening/observing, discussion fora, etc.) to make sense of how the public sees their members and the issues they care about, and then prioritizing communication aimed at addressing areas of weakness. For example, if a society's research were to suggest that many people worry about scientists' integrity [17,18] then the scientific society might develop a plan with members aimed at fostering more positive integrity beliefs (chapter 4). Such plans would likely need to include both real changes to scientists' actual behaviors and their communication.

The previous chapter's focus on framing, for example, highlighted how groups such as the FrameWorks Institute and political operatives such as Frank Luntz provide evidence-based talking points to clients. Our hope is that providing this type of guidance might become something we see more scientific societies do such that research groups and individual scientists who want to communicate can easily turn to their own scientific community for insight. Even better would be if scientific societies made an increased effort to identify promising communicators—especially communicators from diverse backgrounds that have been historically marginalized within science—and sought to give them the support they need to succeed as communicators. Political parties, for example, do this when they identify promising candidates and support their professional development as civic leaders. To our knowledge, however, no American scientific society is regularly and systematically conducting tracking polls or other communication research and sharing insights with its members.

Scientists in the United States are fortunate to have a biannual survey on public attitudes toward science published by the National Science Board [19]. Few other countries have such surveys, although the number may be increasing. However, the report and its underlying survey—which John helped write between 2014 and 2020—is somewhat general in its focus and was not designed to assist the scientific community in providing a detailed picture of how Americans see science. The Pew Research Center and Gallup similarly provide regular surveys on scientific topics but, again, not in a sustained way and not with a specific focus on helping scientists communicate more effectively. One semi-exception to this rule is a biannual survey on climate change (and other topics, on occasion) led by researchers Ed Maibach at George Mason University and Anthony Leiserowitz at Yale University. These surveys, however, are done by (very good) academics at an arm's length from practitioners and not to directly help science organizations plan and track their communication. The Climate Advocacy Lab is another example of the type of communication support [20] we would like to see more of but also would like to see built into the activities of scientific societies, rather than as a stand-alone organization dependent on raising money from donors. This group provides a range of resources—including evidence-based messaging suggestions—to members of the scientific community who want to communicate about climate change. Grassroots, pop-up organizations, such as the March for Science and ScienceDebate.org, have also done important work, but it is work we would like to have seen done as part of—or at least in coordination with—a concerted strategy organized by scientific societies and their leaders.

We were excited to see that a group of scientific societies began an effort to increase collaboration in 2019 [21]. This initiative includes support from several foundations and participation from a long list of scientific societies.

There Is No Easy Answer to Resources

We recognize that we keep suggesting the need to put more resources into communication but that there is no ready wellspring of new funding. We hope the funders of science will provide more money for communication, but, of course, every dollar spent on communication is still funding that could have gone to new research. All we can say, then, is that the scientific community—including funders and individual organizations—needs to make decisions about how much to spend on communication as well as where to spend it. This might mean more in society dues from members' pockets, and/or it might mean dollars from our grants and other sources of funding. We do not know what the correct percentage is, but effective communication does not come cheap. And, as an initial step, we suspect that a great deal of time and money is currently going into isolated, small-scale, nonstrategic science communication activities. If pooled, the money from these isolated activities might be put to better use.

One interview we did in 2019 for a project about how science-focused foundations think about science communication highlighted the potential for combining efforts [16]. One interviewee noted, for example, that their foundation was pulling back from providing individual grant recipients with supplemental funds for communication. Instead, they were asking grant recipients to take part in coordinated communication activities that the funder would help organize. We also appreciate the efforts of such groups as the Center for Advancing Research Impact in Society at the University of Missouri (www .researchinsociety.org) for bringing together researchers and practitioners interested in making sure that resources spent on "broader impacts" are put to good use and to ensure that such resources are widely available.

Any discussion of finding additional resources for communication should also recognize the value of ensuring that such resources are used to advance an inclusive version of science communication. The scientific community will benefit from ensuring that efforts to become more strategic communicators empowers those that the scientific community has often marginalized. Doing so seems both ethical and useful to ensuring that scientific community consensuses are those of more than just white men [22]. What research tells us about identity (chapter 6) further highlights the strategic value of broadening the pool of potential science communicators. Science communicators cannot ethically communicate that they share an identity and associated values with someone when they don't actually possess those identities or values. This means that the scientific community can benefit from ensuring that its membership includes a diverse range of people with a diverse range of the perspectives, experiences, identities, and other drivers of values. Put differently, the scientific community can partly communicate it shares others' values by engaging in the communicative behavior of ensuring its own diversity.

Everyone Has Their Role

We have found that talking about professionalizing science communication seems to irritate some researchers we speak with, especially young scientists who see science communication as a creative outlet for the energy that helps make them persistent scholars and for their desire to make the world better. In many cases, these young scientists also seem to feel a (very understandable) sense of frustration with inequities around race and gender and the difficulty of starting a career in science. This can include worrying about years of low-paid postdoctoral appointments, steep competition for faculty jobs, and adequate funding needed to keep those faculty jobs. We also sometimes sense (also understandable) annoyance from older scientists who have been doing a science communication activity for many years when we push them on what they hope to achieve through the activity. And, in general, we worry that what we argue in this book could be interpreted to suggest that we do not see a role for amateur, creative, or unique science communicators. We believe these interpretations would be incorrect for two reasons.

First, our hope is that all science communicators—including scientists—will increasingly seek to work with communication experts in the way that political leaders, business leaders, nongovernmental organization leaders, and other types of leaders work with their communication experts. This model would see scientists as principals in the process who rely on trusted communication advisors. This might mean that some scientists do less overall communication, but our expectation is that the communication they would do would be more impactful. We also think that working with communication experts could help scientists evaluate their impact and thus improve their ability to argue for credit for communication when they desire to do so. We often hear that many science communicators worry they receive insufficient credit from their supervisors or tenure and promotion committees for communication activities. One argument we frequently make is that communicators who ask for credit should be prepared to show impact in the same way that scholars who want credit for research and teaching typically need to show evidence of effectiveness. A further benefit of having communication professionals involved in communication is that they could prioritize ensuring that resources and opportunities reach a more diverse range of scientific voices.

Second, a key reason we think communication objectives are important is that being clear about them and their associated goals can help harness creativity. In advertising, account executives work with clients and research teams to develop creative briefs that they then give to art directors, copywriters, and other creative types. These briefs let the creative teams know what kind of campaigns to suggest and include insight about what the account team knows about where there is an opportunity to make a difference. If research says that potential clients buy meatless hamburgers based on quality and social norms, then the creative team is meant to find a way to communicate that the product works and that people the consumer cares about will appreciate the new food. Creative briefs do not constrain creativity; they guide creativity. We see a need for something similar for science communication. Our hope would be that groups like a scientific society would identify goals and then provide insight on priority objectives (e.g., ensure that stakeholders see geologists as caring and competent, or learn what issues worry stakeholders) that science communicators could creatively try to achieve when they have opportunities to share their findings. Some of these creative ideas will also likely spark research and new insight into potential good practices.

For those who do not have access to substantial communication resources, we also believe that no science communicator can go wildly wrong if they prioritize ensuring that the people with whom they interact have a positive experience. The cumulative model of communication effects that we described numerous times in this book suggests that few individual instances of communication are likely to matter on their own (unless they are really, really bad). Instead, what likely matters in the long run are the information and frames that people see and pay attention to, as well as the feelings they experience. Sometimes they will learn about the natural world and develop factual beliefs, or they might come to believe in a benefit or risk about which they had not previously known. These types of objectives are among the most well-known outcomes of science communication. Our argument is that people might equally come to learn that many scientists are caring, honest, open, or competent. Well-designed communication activities might also lead people to find out that many scientists share some of their background, or find out what their friends think about some scientific topic (i.e., social norms). Ideally, our fellow citizens might also learn about themselves and their own abilities (i.e., self-efficacy) or a new way to frame an issue. At the same time, we think science communicators should try to avoid communication (including behavior) that suggests that scientists are uncaring, dishonest, closed-minded, or incompetent, as well as communication that suggests scientists are substantially different than their neighbors, or that nonscientists are somehow deficient in skills or ability. There will always be cases where it makes sense to be assertive with people who put others in danger or who do not communicate in good faith, but this type of situation is exactly where we would like to see the scientific community come together and develop collaborative, evidence-based strategies. In the short term, biting one's tongue is sometimes strategic.

The scientific community deserves substantial credit for remaining one of the most trusted, sought-after sources of advice, but we cannot take this position for granted. We do not like "war on science" framing because of its potential to foster greater division [23], but we know there are people and groups who see advantages in undermining science's position in society [24,25]. The advantage the science community has—and the approach advocated by this book—is that we see few reasons for most scientists to get caught up in personally trying to directly respond to the forces of negativity. Instead, we hope that researchers who want to communicate can focus their attention on what they want to accomplish rather than what they want to avoid. We can take positive steps as a community to ensure that our friends and neighbors have a wide range of opportunities to engage with the scientific world and come away with the types of experiences that foster new, reality-based beliefs, feelings, and frames. We also hope that scientists continue to remember that part of asking others to engage with us is being prepared to engage with others. This means people in the scientific community need to be eager to change their own behaviors, beliefs, and feelings, and open to framing issues in new ways. For our part, we look forward to continuing to hear and learn about what we can do to continue to help make science communication more effective.

REFERENCES

1. Heath, Robert L., and Michael J. Palenchar. *Strategic Issues Management: Organizations and Public Policy Challenges.* 2nd ed. Los Angeles: Sage, 2009.

2. Sha, Bey-Ling. "2010 Practice Analysis: Professional Competencies and Work Categories in Public Relations Today." *Public Relations Review* 37, no. 3 (2011): 187-96. https://doi.org/10.1016/j.pubrev.2011.04.005.

3. Besley, John C., Anthony Dudo, and Shupei Yuan. "Scientists' Views About Communication Objectives." *Public Understanding of Science* 27, no. 6 (2018): 708-30. https://doi.org/10.1177/0963662517728478.

4. Besley, John C., Kathryn O'Hara, and Anthony Dudo. "Strategic Communication as Planned Behavior: What Shapes Scientists' Willingness to Choose Specific Tactics." Annual Meeting of the Association for Education in Journalism and Mass Communication, Washington, DC, August 2018.

5. Funtowicz, Silvio, and Jerome Ravetz. "Post-Normal Science." In *Companion to Environmental Studies*, edited by Noel Castree, Mike Hulme, and James D. Proctor, 443-47. London: Routledge, 2018.

6. Besley, John C., Anthony Dudo, Shupei Yuan, and Frank Lawrence. "Understanding Scientists' Willingness to Engage." *Science Communication* 40, no. 5 (2018): 559-90. https://doi.org/10.1177/1075547018786561.

7. Besley, John C., Anthony Dudo, Shupei Yuan, and Niveen AbiGhannam. "Qualitative Interviews with Science Communication Trainers About Communication Objectives and Goals." *Science Communication* 38, no. 3 (2016): 356-81. https://doi.org/10.1177/1075547016645640.

8. Fogg-Rogers, Laura, Margarida Sardo, and Corra Boushel. "'Robots Vs Animals': Establishing a Culture of Public Engagement and Female Role Modeling in Engineering Higher Education." *Science Communication* 39, no. 2 (2017): 195-220. https://doi.org/10.1177/1075547017696169.

9. Davies, Sarah R., and Maja Horst. *Science Communication: Culture, Identity, and Citizenship.* London: Palgrave MacMillan, 2016.

10. Besley, John C., and Anthony Dudo. *Landscaping Overview of the North American Science Communication Training Community: Topline Takeaways from Trainer Interviews.* N.p.: Kavli Foundation, Rita Allen Foundation, David and Lucille Packard Foundation, and Gordon and Betty Moore Foundation, 2017. http://www.informalscience.org/sites/default/files/Communication Training Landscape Overview Final.pdf.

11. Besley, John C., Sarah Garlick, Kathy Fallon Lambert, and Leigh Anne Tiffany. "The Role of Communication Professionals in Fostering a Culture of

Public Engagement." *International Journal of Science Education, Part B* 11, no. 3 (2021), 225–41. https://doi.org/10.1080/21548455.2021.1943763

12. Hon, Linda Childers. "Demonstrating Effectiveness in Public Relations: Goals, Objectives, and Evaluation." *Journal of Public Relations Research* 10, no. 2 (1998): 103–35. https://doi.org/10.1207/s1532754xjprr1002_02.

13. Grunig, James E., Larissa A. Grunig, and David M. Dozier. "The Excellence Theory." In *Public Relations Theory II*, edited by Carl H. Botan and Vincent Hazleton, 21–62. Mahwah, NJ: Lawrence Erlbaum Assoicates, 2006.

14. Bernays, Edward. *Crystallizing Public Opinion*. Brooklyn: Ig Publishing, 2011. First published 1923 by Liveright Publishing.

15. Yuan, Shupei, Anthony Dudo, and John C. Besley. "Scientific Societies' Support for Public Engagement: An Interview Study." *International Journal of Science Education, Part B* 9, no. 2 (2019): 140–53. https://doi.org/10.1080/21548455.2019.1576240.

16. Dudo, Anthony, John C. Besley, and Nichole Bennett. *Landscape of Science Communication Fellowship Programs in North America*. N.p.: Rita Allen Foundation, 2020. https://ritaallen.org/app/uploads/2020/06/SciEng-Fellowships-Report.pdf.

17. Gallup. *Wellcome Global Monitor: First Wave Findings*. London: Wellcome Trust, 2019. https://wellcome.ac.uk/sites/default/files/wellcome-global-monitor-2018.pdf.

18. Funk, Cary, Meg Hefferon, Brian Kennedy, and Courtney Johnson. *Trust and Mistrust in Americans' Views of Scientific Experts*. Washington, DC: Pew Research Center, 2019. https://www.pewresearch.org/science/2019/08/02/trust-and-mistrust-in-americans-views-of-scientific-experts.

19. For the most recent report, see John C. Besley and Derek Hill, "Science and Technology: Public Attitudes, Knowledge, and Interest," in *Science and Engineering Indicators 2020* (Alexandria, VA: National Science Foundation, May 2020), https://ncses.nsf.gov/pubs/nsb20207. Past reports can be found in the National Science Foundation's document library (https://www.nsf.gov/publications) by selecting "Science and Engineering Indicators" in the drop-down menu.

20. Climate Advocacy Lab. "About: Welcome to the Climate Advocacy Lab" Accessed May 5, 2020. https://climateadvocacylab.org/about-public.

21. Society Civic Science Intitiative. "About: Our Work." Accessed April 25, 2021. https://www.societycivicscience.org.

22. Oreskes, Naomi. *Why Trust Science?* Princeton, NJ: Princeton University Press, 2019.

23. Hardy, Bruce W., Meghnaa Tallapragada, John C. Besley, and Shupei Yuan. "The Effects of the 'War on Science' Frame on Scientists' Credibility." *Science Communication* 41, no. 1 (2019): 90–112. https://doi.org/10.1177/1075547018822081.

24. Oreskes, Naomi, and Erik M Conway. *Merchants of Doubt: How a Handful of Scientists Obscured the Truth on Issues from Tobacco Smoke to Global Warming*. New York: Bloomsbury, 2011.

25. Otto, Shawn Lawrence. *The War on Science: Who's Waging It, Why It Matters, What We Can Do About It*. 1st ed. Minneapolis: Milkweed Editions, 2016.

APPENDIX A
Survey Methods

Implementation and Design

The 2015–16 scientist survey collected data from members of eight scientific societies during the fall of 2015 and winter/spring of 2016 (table A.1) (Michigan State University IRB # x13-854e and University of Texas at Austin IRB #2013-08-0061). Each society was surveyed at a time convenient to society collaborators. For each survey, multiple attempts were made to obtain cooperation from member scientists with slightly different appeals in each attempt [1]. The number of attempts varied by society because of different levels of organizational willingness to email members. With the exception of the social science society, the societies themselves sent the surveys from their own membership departments on behalf of the research team because societies indicated that they did not feel comfortable providing contact information outside of the organization. All responses were sent directly to the primary investigators to ensure respondent confidentiality consistent with the intuitional review board approval for the project. We do not name the societies because we assured the participating societies that our goal was not to rank or rate societies or fields.

The survey itself typically took respondents between 15 to 25 minutes to complete. It began with questions about past public engagement and future willingness to engage. These initial questions included a definition of the three different forms of engagement as well:

- "Face-to-face engagement where you discussed science with ADULTS who are not scientists (e.g., giving a public talk or doing a demonstration)."
- "Interviews or briefings with a journalist or other media professional (e.g. from a newspaper, television, online news site, documentary film, etc.)"
- "Online engagement through websites, blogs and/or social networks (e.g., Facebook, Twitter) aimed at communicating science with ADULTS who are not scientists."

Depending on the size of the society, respondents might then have been randomly assigned to questions in the context of face-to-face communication, communication with the public through news media, or online communication (i.e., differing engagement channels). For example, a single respondent assigned to the face-to-face condition would have been asked about engagement attitudes, norms, and efficacy only within the context of that specific form of engagement. Societies with smaller memberships may have received only one of two options or a single option. Partner societies indicated the type of engagement they were interested in learning about prior to the survey. Demographic information was collected at the end of the survey.

Respondents were also asked at the beginning of the survey about their past participation in direct engagement with policymakers, defined as "direct interaction with government policymakers (e.g., elected officials, government officials, lobbyists)." However, the survey did not randomly assign any respondents to get additional questions related to this form of engagement because it seemed different enough from the other forms of engagement to require a separate project.

Sample Size and Response Rate

Respondents needed to have a PhD and be based at an American university. The goal was to obtain 383 respondents for each engagement channel, which

Table A.1.
Survey timing and sample size

Society	Survey dates	Number of attempts	Total respondents	Response rate[1] (%)	Eligible respondents[2]	Face-to-face conditions	Media conditions	Online conditions
General	10/15/15–11/10/15	5	1,263	9	1,109	385	333	391
Biological	4/25/16–6/2/16	4	1,167	6	696	356	n/a	340
Geophysical	1/25/16–3/8/16	4	2,419	10	918	316	323	279
Geological	3/8/16–4/1/16	4	1,103	10	754	259	249	246
Ecological	3/25/16–4/16/16	3	860	16	350	350	n/a	n/a
Chemical	11/12/15–12/21/15 and 5/10/16–5/19/16	5 and 3	1,919	8	501	184	160	157
Biochemical	10/26/15–11/20/15	4	513	9	375	375	n/a	n/a
Social	04/11/16–04/28/16	5	975	26	933	n/a	933	n/a
Total			10,219	n/a	5,636[3]	2,225	1,998	1,413

Note: Individual analyses may differ from these numbers due to missing data.

[1] After accounting for bounced emails due to bad or blocked addresses as well as full inboxes.

[2] Number of respondents with a PhD and working at American universities. The number of eligible respondents is different from the number of total respondents because not all participating societies had the same ability to prescreen respondents based on study criteria.

[3] Respondents could be members of more than one society. The total number of individual respondents was 5,245.

Table A.2.

Sample size by age, gender, and race

Society	Average age of respondents	Sample size reporting age	Identified male (%)	Identified female (%)	"Other, or I'd rather not say"[1] (%)	Sample size reporting sex	White (%)	Asian (%)	Hispanic/ Latino (%)	African American/ Black (%)	Sample size[2]
General	63	1,087	69	30	1	1,106	91	6	4	1	1,109
Biological	54	682	59	38	3	687	84	11	4	2	696
Geophysical	51	908	64	34	2	917	90	6	3	1	918
Geological	57	729	64	32	4	723	92	3	2	1	753
Ecological	55	345	57	42	2	343	94	2	5	1	350
Chemical	51	492	68	30	2	499	89	9	5	3	485
Biochemical	54	369	59	38	3	375	85	9	6	2	375
Social	51	926	61	39	1	931	89	4	5	3	933

Notes: Respondents were all faculty with PhDs at US-based universities. Sums may not equal 100% due to rounding of frequency reports.
[1] This question would be asked differently if fielded now based on our improved understanding of how to ask about gender and sex.
[2] Respondents could identify with racial/ethnic groups or not.

would provide a sampling margin of error of at least +/– 5% for medium to large societies. Based on research literature that used online surveys to study scientists [2,3], the project team expected about a 10% response rate and set the initial sample frame accordingly where possible. In some cases (e.g., the chemistry and geological societies), it was necessary to start with somewhat larger samples because the societies could not differentiate in their initial sampling between those who fit our study criteria and those who did not. Ultimately, the final response rate in four of the societies was similar to past online survey projects for several societies [4] and somewhat lower than hoped, and there were more noneligible members than expected. The current study is therefore cautious about using the data to describe specific societies. However, based on the substantial variance that exists within the data, it still seems reasonable to use the data to speak to the relationships between variables in the context of our hypotheses. In this regard, while we might expect that respondents with negative views about communication might be less willing to complete a survey about communication (or more willing, if they felt current discussions about engagement were a threat), we do not have any reason to think that the pattern of relationships explored would be different as a function of survey response.

An analysis (not included here) was also done to see if respondents were systematically different across early versus late waves of responses with the logic that differences would suggest that harder-to-reach respondents would respond later. These analyses found that late respondents were largely similar to early respondents. The American Association for Public Opinion Research [5] also warns that response rate should probably not be used as a measure of survey quality. Higher response rates could have been obtained using additional paper mail sampling [6,7], but that method was prohibitive due to costs associated with the large scale of the project.

REFERENCES

1. Dillman, Don A., Jolene D. Smyth, and Leah Melani Christian. *Internet, Mail, and Mixed-Mode Surveys: The Tailored Design Method.* 3rd ed. Hoboken, NJ: Wiley & Sons, 2009.

2. Dudo, Anthony, and John C. Besley. "Scientists' Prioritization of Communication Objectives for Public Engagement." *PLOS ONE* 11, no. 2 (2016): e0148867.

3. Besley, John C., Anthony Dudo, and Martin Storksdieck, "Scientists' Views About Communication Training." *Journal of Research in Science Teaching* 52, no. 2 (2015): 199–220.

4. Besley, John C. "What Do Scientists Think About the Public and Does It Matter to Their Online Engagement?" *Science and Public Policy* 42, no. 2 (April 2015): 201–14.

5. American Association for Public Opinion Research. "Response Rates: An Overview." Accessed October 14, 2021. http://www.aapor.org/Education-Resources /For-Researchers/Poll-Survey-FAQ/Response-Rates-An-Overview.aspx.

6. Pew Research Center. *Public Praises Science; Scientists Fault Public, Media.* Washington, DC: Pew Research Center, 2009. https://www.pewresearch.org /politics/2009/07/09/public-praises-science-scientists-fault-public-media.

7. Dudo, Anthony. "Toward a Model of Scientists' Public Communication Activity: The Case of Biomedical Researchers." *Science Communication* 35, no. 4 (2013): 476–501.

APPENDIX B
Supplementary Tables

See pages 127–140

Table B.1.

Scientists' average assessment of the degree to which different objectives should be prioritized with standard deviation (SD) and mean sample response (M)[1]

	Helping to inform people about scientific issues (chapter 1)		Getting people interested or excited about science (chapter 11)		Showing that the scientific community cares about society's well-being (chapter 3)		Demonstrating the scientific community's openness and transparency (chapter 4)		Showing that scientists share community values (chapter 6)		Framing research implications so members of the public think about a topic in a way that resonates with their values (chapter 11)		Hearing what others think about scientific issues (chapter 5)		Showing the scientific community's expertise (chapter 7)		Sample size
	M	SD	M	SD	M	SD	M	SD	M	SD	M	SD	M	SD	M	SD	
General																	
Face-to-face	6.21	0.92	5.98	1.05	5.71	1.11	5.49	1.19	5.31	1.23	5.27	1.35	5.17	1.21	4.83	1.39	377–381
Media	6.26	0.81	5.87	1.04	5.74	1.17	5.51	1.21	5.17	1.37	5.20	1.45	4.84	1.35	4.90	1.29	327–332
Online	6.08	0.99	5.72	1.17	5.43	1.26	5.44	1.20	4.94	1.33	5.12	1.40	4.85	1.31	4.85	1.36	382–385
Biological																	
Face-to-face	6.27	0.86	6.01	1.10	5.80	1.11	5.47	1.22	5.39	1.24	5.37	1.33	5.23	1.22	4.99	1.23	351–354
Online	6.16	0.91	5.92	1.08	5.79	1.11	5.59	1.16	5.28	1.28	5.39	1.27	5.15	1.16	4.96	1.29	332–335
Geophysical																	
Face-to-face	6.22	0.94	5.89	1.20	5.44	1.25	5.37	1.26	5.01	1.38	5.24	1.38	4.89	1.35	4.66	1.39	312–316
Media	6.34	0.80	5.77	1.17	5.49	1.16	5.44	1.25	4.94	1.42	5.21	1.42	4.72	1.32	4.87	1.38	321–322
Online	6.19	0.95	5.84	1.17	5.44	1.21	5.42	1.17	4.89	1.39	5.03	1.49	4.76	1.28	4.83	1.36	275–277
Geological																	
Face-to-face	6.21	0.88	5.91	1.08	5.60	1.12	5.41	1.24	5.15	1.36	5.18	1.43	4.93	1.35	4.93	1.37	255–257
Media	6.34	0.88	5.99	1.03	5.68	1.22	5.53	1.23	5.23	1.32	5.17	1.38	4.90	1.39	5.07	1.37	245–248
Online	6.29	0.84	5.97	1.05	5.58	1.21	5.48	1.22	5.15	1.32	5.19	1.36	4.89	1.32	4.96	1.23	237–241
Ecological																	
Face-to-face	6.18	0.92	5.89	1.10	5.46	1.20	5.23	1.27	5.08	1.34	5.33	1.3	4.83	1.29	4.51	1.34	346–350

(continued)

Table B.1.
(continued)

	Helping to inform people about scientific issues (chapter 1)		Getting people interested or excited about science (chapter 1)		Showing that the scientific community cares about society's well-being (chapter 3)		Demonstrating the scientific community's openness and transparency (chapter 4)		Showing that scientists share community values (chapter 6)		Framing research implications so members of the public think about a topic in a way that resonates with their values (chapter 11)		Hearing what others think about scientific issues (chapter 5)		Showing the scientific community's expertise (chapter 7)		Sample size
	M	SD	M	SD	M	SD	M	SD	M	SD	M	SD	M	SD	M	SD	
Chemical																	
Face-to-face	6.15	0.89	5.74	1.19	5.62	1.14	5.45	1.19	5.33	1.26	5.08	1.37	4.93	1.38	4.85	1.32	182–184
Media	5.99	1.02	5.57	1.21	5.56	1.18	5.16	1.23	5.00	1.34	5.12	1.42	4.79	1.23	4.69	1.31	157–159
Online	5.85	1.13	5.60	1.25	5.38	1.23	5.31	1.36	5.03	1.30	4.83	1.43	4.98	1.29	4.85	1.37	155–156
Biochemical																	
Face-to-face	6.07	0.97	5.94	1.03	5.71	1.14	5.56	1.13	5.27	1.33	5.30	1.34	5.10	1.25	4.61	1.34	369–374
Social																	
Media	6.06	1.08	4.94	1.46	5.05	1.47	4.95	1.41	4.25	1.60	5.07	1.56	4.47	1.49	5.30	1.38	918–924

Notes: Respondents were all faculty with PhDs at US-based universities. See specific chapters for additional details.
[1] Respondents selected between "very low importance" (1) and "very high importance" (7) for all questions. See specific chapters for additional details.

Table B.2.

Scientists' average assessment of the ethicality of different objectives with standard deviation (SD) and mean response (M)[1]

	Helping to inform people about scientific issues (chapter 1)		Getting people interested or excited about science (chapter 11)		Demonstrating the scientific community's openness and transparency (chapter 4)		Showing that the scientific community cares about society's well-being (chapter 3)		Hearing what others think about scientific issues (chapter 5)		Showing that scientists share community values (chapter 6)		Showing the scientific community's expertise (chapter 7)		Framing research implications so members of the public think about a topic in a way that resonates with their values (chapter 11)		Sample size
	M	SD	M	SD	M	SD	M	SD	M	SD	M	SD	M	SD	M	SD	
General																	
Face-to-face	6.07	1.05	5.92	1.13	5.82	1.13	5.79	1.13	5.68	1.12	5.45	1.30	5.44	1.26	5.30	1.30	369–376
Media	6.16	0.94	5.94	1.08	5.88	1.09	5.79	1.09	5.64	1.23	5.39	1.30	5.53	1.22	5.25	1.40	318–326
Online	5.96	1.07	5.82	1.17	5.71	1.18	5.65	1.23	5.47	1.26	5.25	1.31	5.39	1.26	5.13	1.44	373–380
Biological																	
Face-to-face	5.92	1.13	5.70	1.24	5.64	1.14	5.62	1.12	5.56	1.19	5.36	1.23	5.28	1.29	5.10	1.30	345–351
Online	5.88	1.06	5.75	1.20	5.66	1.17	5.74	1.12	5.57	1.21	5.47	1.11	5.35	1.29	5.22	1.25	326–330
Geophysical																	
Face-to-face	6.04	1.05	5.76	1.21	5.80	1.08	5.50	1.18	5.58	1.21	5.24	1.31	5.30	1.24	5.13	1.35	313–315
Media	6.05	1.00	5.79	1.24	5.78	1.08	5.50	1.15	5.38	1.25	5.16	1.25	5.19	1.29	5.06	1.44	313–320
Online	5.86	1.12	5.72	1.30	5.74	1.18	5.55	1.21	5.35	1.34	5.22	1.28	5.25	1.28	5.12	1.39	266–271
Geological																	
Face-to-face	5.94	1.11	5.81	1.24	5.70	1.25	5.60	1.24	5.52	1.31	5.25	1.29	5.28	1.47	5.22	1.34	243–250
Media	6.08	1.03	5.88	1.10	5.75	1.18	5.70	1.13	5.46	1.24	5.34	1.28	5.46	1.27	5.14	1.41	234–241
Online	5.92	1.20	5.86	1.18	5.76	1.08	5.66	1.16	5.31	1.32	5.29	1.29	5.37	1.31	5.08	1.46	229–237
Ecological																	
Face-to-face	6.10	1.08	5.90	1.21	5.80	1.08	5.73	1.15	5.74	1.14	5.34	1.33	5.26	1.30	5.28	1.34	340–345

(continued)

Table B.2.
(continued)

	Helping to inform people about scientific issues (chapter 1)		Getting people interested or excited about science (chapter 11)		Demonstrating the scientific community's openness and transparency (chapter 4)		Showing that the scientific community cares about society's well-being (chapter 3)		Hearing what others think about scientific issues (chapter 5)		Showing that scientists share community values (chapter 6)		Showing the scientific community's expertise (chapter 7)		Framing research implications so members of the public think about a topic in a way that resonates with their values (chapter 11)		Sample size
	M	SD	M	SD	M	SD	M	SD	M	SD	M	SD	M	SD	M	SD	
Chemical																	
Face-to-face	5.83	1.13	5.62	1.27	5.56	1.10	5.54	1.18	5.49	1.15	5.27	1.39	5.27	1.34	5.06	1.48	176–181
Media	5.81	1.17	5.50	1.25	5.47	1.21	5.55	1.14	5.28	1.21	5.16	1.24	5.01	1.39	4.80	1.54	156–159
Online	5.86	1.15	5.50	1.27	5.50	1.20	5.50	1.24	5.30	1.28	5.15	1.22	5.20	1.24	4.92	1.37	151–154
Biochemical																	
Face-to-face	5.96	0.96	5.69	1.15	5.71	1.12	5.68	1.05	5.47	1.14	5.34	1.20	5.23	1.20	5.24	1.32	364–369
Social																	
Media	5.99	1.08	5.61	1.21	5.74	1.14	5.50	1.26	5.36	1.24	4.84	1.40	5.53	1.28	4.90	1.49	862–881

Notes: Respondents were all faculty with PhDs at US-based universities. See specific chapters for additional details.
[1] Respondents selected between "strongly disagree" (1) and "strongly agree" (7) to the statement "This objective is ethical."

Table B.3.
Scientists' average assessment of injunctive norms of different objectives with standard deviation (SD) and mean response (M)[1]

	Getting people interested or excited about science (chapter 11)		Helping to inform people about scientific issues (chapter 1)		Showing the scientific community's expertise (chapter 7)		Showing that the scientific community cares about society's well-being (chapter 3)		Demonstrating the scientific community's openness and transparency (chapter 4)		Framing research implications so members of the public think about a topic in a way that resonates with their values (chapter 11)		Showing that scientists share community values (chapter 6)		Hearing what others think about scientific issues (chapter 5)		Sample size
	M	SD	M	SD	M	SD	M	SD	M	SD	M	SD	M	SD	M	SD	
General																	
Face-to-face	5.71	1.08	5.70	1.16	5.27	1.16	5.25	1.13	5.15	1.17	4.81	1.16	4.72	1.16	4.65	1.19	370–377
Media	5.70	1.09	5.79	1.04	5.28	1.12	5.20	1.05	5.24	1.19	4.75	1.21	4.71	1.18	5.64	1.18	322–328
Online	5.46	1.17	5.57	1.15	5.19	1.23	4.98	1.21	4.99	1.24	4.58	1.29	4.50	1.27	4.42	1.30	375–381
Biological																	
Face-to-face	5.61	1.16	5.59	1.22	5.20	1.16	5.19	1.24	5.13	1.22	4.79	1.27	4.86	1.25	4.71	1.29	347–353
Online	5.54	1.19	5.54	1.15	5.16	1.27	5.29	1.18	5.14	1.19	4.84	1.24	4.87	1.25	4.70	1.34	328–331
Geophysical																	
Face-to-face	5.57	1.11	5.69	1.11	5.18	1.14	5.10	1.15	5.18	1.10	4.66	1.25	4.54	1.20	4.45	1.22	313–316
Media	5.70	1.07	5.81	1.07	5.20	1.16	5.17	1.17	5.36	1.11	4.63	1.35	4.58	1.16	4.57	1.26	313–320
Online	5.47	1.21	5.54	1.13	5.18	1.19	4.99	1.20	5.07	1.16	4.66	1.28	4.43	1.22	4.36	1.24	268–274
Geological																	
Face-to-face	5.55	1.20	5.58	1.18	5.19	1.26	4.92	1.31	5.13	1.21	4.67	1.35	4.59	1.38	4.55	1.31	245–251
Media	5.67	1.16	5.76	1.13	5.31	1.22	5.13	1.25	5.32	1.15	4.71	1.30	4.66	1.30	4.59	1.30	235–243
Online	5.52	1.16	5.62	1.13	5.17	1.15	5.07	1.20	5.16	1.25	4.68	1.31	4.65	1.26	4.54	1.37	230–237
Ecological																	
Face-to-face	5.56	1.04	5.78	1.03	5.26	1.16	5.04	1.20	5.06	1.15	4.64	1.23	4.43	1.18	4.48	1.22	342–348

(continued)

Table B.3.
(continued)

	Getting people interested or excited about science (chapter 11)		Helping to inform people about scientific issues (chapter 1)		Showing the scientific community's expertise (chapter 7)		Showing that the scientific community cares about society's well-being (chapter 3)		Demonstrating the scientific community's openness and transparency (chapter 4)		Framing research implications so members of the public think about a topic in a way that resonates with their values (chapter 11)		Showing that scientists share community values (chapter 6)		Hearing what others think about scientific issues (chapter 5)		Sample size
	M	SD	M	SD	M	SD	M	SD	M	SD	M	SD	M	SD	M	SD	
Chemical																	
Face-to-face	5.52	1.10	5.51	1.06	5.22	1.06	5.12	1.11	5.12	1.09	4.69	1.30	4.86	1.26	4.61	1.21	178–181
Media	5.44	1.21	5.66	1.03	5.18	1.18	5.22	1.16	4.93	1.27	4.52	1.32	4.61	1.21	4.42	1.29	157–159
Online	5.41	1.12	5.51	1.11	5.06	1.16	5.03	1.20	4.92	1.26	4.67	1.22	4.55	1.17	4.53	1.24	152–155
Biochemical																	
Face-to-face	5.51	1.06	5.55	1.06	5.07	1.19	5.17	1.11	5.17	1.17	4.72	1.25	4.68	1.20	4.55	1.27	365–371
Social																	
Media	4.98	1.24	5.55	1.18	5.41	1.19	4.87	1.25	5.05	1.21	4.42	1.34	4.12	1.28	4.37	1.27	867–884

Notes: Respondents were all faculty with PhDs at US-based universities. See specific chapters for additional details.
[1] Respondents selected between "strongly disagree" (1) and "strongly agree" (7) to the statement "Scientists who pursue this objective would be well regarded by their peers."

Table B.4.
Scientists' average assessment of the descriptive norms of different objectives with standard deviation (SD) and mean response (M)[1]

	Helping to inform people about scientific issues (chapter 1)		Getting people interested or excited about science (chapter 11)		Showing the scientific community's expertise (chapter 6)		Showing that the scientific community cares about society's well-being (chapter 3)		Demonstrating the scientific community's openness and transparency (chapter 4)		Framing research implications so members of the public think about a topic in a way that resonates with their values (chapter 11)		Showing that scientists share community values (chapter 6)		Hearing what others think about scientific issues (chapter 5)		Sample size
	M	SD	M	SD	M	SD	M	SD	M	SD	M	SD	M	SD	M	SD	
General																	
Face-to-face	5.31	1.33	5.31	1.24	4.91	1.31	4.81	1.31	4.65	1.31	4.34	1.23	4.19	1.27	4.13	1.28	370–378
Media	5.29	1.32	5.22	1.32	4.87	1.33	4.70	1.26	4.76	1.32	4.21	1.29	4.22	1.26	5.64	1.25	322–327
Online	5.11	1.36	5.05	1.36	4.78	1.34	4.52	1.35	4.52	1.41	4.11	1.41	4.00	1.34	3.99	1.33	375–381
Biological																	
Face-to-face	5.19	1.31	5.20	1.31	4.83	1.25	4.73	1.34	4.68	1.30	4.32	1.33	4.31	1.35	4.18	1.31	347–353
Online	5.01	1.39	5.13	1.42	4.78	1.30	4.69	1.38	4.69	1.34	4.29	1.36	4.19	1.38	4.18	1.42	327–331
Geophysical																	
Face-to-face	5.35	1.31	5.22	1.23	4.90	1.29	4.67	1.30	4.73	1.26	4.32	1.29	4.06	1.27	3.98	1.26	312–316
Media	5.40	1.33	5.26	1.25	4.86	1.27	4.73	1.33	4.78	1.32	4.15	1.35	4.09	1.28	3.94	1.36	313–320
Online	5.04	1.38	5.03	1.36	4.78	1.32	4.43	1.37	4.49	1.37	4.20	1.32	3.93	1.34	3.76	1.28	267–273
Geological																	
Face-to-face	5.16	1.39	5.14	1.44	4.90	1.36	4.51	1.45	4.68	1.31	4.21	1.34	4.07	1.37	4.03	1.36	244–250
Media	5.39	1.30	5.38	1.27	5.00	1.39	4.75	1.40	4.81	1.32	4.34	1.27	4.31	1.45	4.31	1.30	236–243
Online	5.24	1.41	5.17	1.37	4.84	1.33	4.59	1.38	4.70	1.42	4.27	1.47	4.26	1.38	4.19	1.45	230–237
Ecological																	
Face-to-face	5.50	1.30	5.26	1.22	4.99	1.20	4.64	1.31	4.61	1.28	4.31	1.32	4.08	1.27	3.97	1.31	340–348

(continued)

Table B.4.
(continued)

	Helping to inform people about scientific issues (chapter 1)		Getting people interested or excited about science (chapter 11)		Showing the scientific community's expertise (chapter 6)		Showing that the scientific community cares about society's well-being (chapter 3)		Demonstrating the scientific community's openness and transparency (chapter 4)		Framing research implications so members of the public think about a topic in a way that resonates with their values (chapter 11)		Showing that scientists share community values (chapter 6)		Hearing what others think about scientific issues (chapter 5)		Sample size
	M	SD	M	SD	M	SD	M	SD	M	SD	M	SD	M	SD	M	SD	
Chemical																	
Face-to-face	5.08	1.35	5.22	1.34	4.72	1.28	4.66	1.31	4.55	1.34	4.25	1.39	4.37	1.39	4.12	1.37	178–181
Media	5.18	1.31	5.09	1.31	4.70	1.30	4.74	1.28	4.53	1.24	4.06	1.30	4.11	1.30	3.93	1.23	157–159
Online	4.93	1.41	4.98	1.38	4.66	1.40	4.45	1.35	4.30	1.37	4.05	1.31	3.99	1.29	3.94	1.31	152–155
Biochemical																	
Face-to-face	5.05	1.30	5.10	1.25	4.73	1.28	4.66	1.28	4.63	1.29	4.27	1.30	4.18	1.29	4.05	1.24	365–370
Social																	
Media	5.12	1.43	4.49	1.43	5.03	1.38	4.57	1.38	3.97	1.39	4.10	1.43	3.80	1.38	4.40	1.39	866–883

Notes: Respondents were all faculty with PhDs at US-based universities. See specific chapters for additional details.
[1] Respondents selected between "strongly disagree" (1) and "strongly agree" (7) to the statement "My colleagues would put a high priority on this objective."

Table B.5.

Scientists' average assessment of the expected impact (external efficacy) of different objectives with standard deviation (SD) and mean response (M)[1]

	Getting people interested or excited about science (chapter 11)		Helping to inform people about scientific issues (chapter 2)		Showing the scientific community's expertise (chapter 6)		Showing that the scientific community cares about society's well-being (chapter 3)		Demonstrating the scientific community's openness and transparency (chapter 4)		Hearing what others think about scientific issues (chapter 5)		Framing research implications so members of the public think about a topic in a way that resonates with their values (chapter 11)		Showing that scientists share community values (chapter 6)		Sample size
	M	SD	M	SD	M	SD	M	SD	M	SD	M	SD	M	SD	M	SD	
General																	
Face-to-face	6.16	0.86	6.11	0.85	5.78	0.97	5.76	1.01	5.57	1.05	5.54	1.06	5.53	1.10	5.51	1.06	368–376
Media	6.10	0.86	6.06	0.87	5.77	0.90	5.68	0.93	5.61	1.06	5.64	1.05	5.48	1.15	5.51	1.05	320–327
Online	6.01	0.95	5.89	0.99	5.66	1.00	5.62	1.04	5.49	1.11	5.39	1.11	5.43	1.12	5.35	1.10	370–379
Biological																	
Face-to-face	6.16	0.83	6.12	0.78	5.81	0.95	5.79	0.90	5.66	0.98	5.61	0.99	5.56	1.09	5.60	0.95	344–353
Online	6.10	0.88	5.96	0.86	5.62	1.01	5.66	0.98	5.53	1.02	5.39	1.08	5.48	1.07	5.48	1.02	327–331
Geophysical																	
Face-to-face	6.11	0.86	6.09	0.85	5.72	0.95	5.71	0.99	5.54	1.05	5.57	1.08	5.54	1.05	5.40	1.11	313–316
Media	6.21	0.82	6.19	0.79	5.70	0.98	5.67	1.01	5.60	1.08	5.40	1.18	5.59	1.06	5.46	1.06	310–319
Online	6.17	0.87	5.98	0.93	5.70	0.96	5.63	1.02	5.41	1.12	5.29	1.15	5.53	1.09	5.37	1.09	266–274
Geological																	
Face-to-face	6.07	0.98	5.99	0.93	5.71	1.08	5.68	1.07	5.57	1.05	5.55	1.10	5.57	1.09	5.40	1.19	244–251
Media	6.05	0.92	6.07	0.84	5.74	0.99	5.58	1.02	5.56	1.04	5.40	1.08	5.43	1.13	5.40	1.10	236–243
Online	6.15	0.82	5.93	0.98	5.63	1.05	5.63	1.06	5.54	1.07	5.41	1.15	5.35	1.19	5.44	1.09	230–236
Ecological																	
Face-to-face	6.24	6.24	6.20	0.72	5.78	0.90	5.76	0.86	5.60	1.00	5.65	1.03	5.70	1.07	5.57	0.97	342–347

(continued)

Table B.5.
(continued)

	Getting people interested or excited about science (chapter 11)		Helping to inform people about scientific issues (chapter 2)		Showing the scientific community's expertise (chapter 6)		Showing that the scientific community cares about society's well-being (chapter 3)		Demonstrating the scientific community's openness and transparency (chapter 4)		Hearing what others think about scientific issues (chapter 5)		Framing research implications so members of the public think about a topic in a way that resonates with their values (chapter 11)		Showing that scientists share community values (chapter 6)		Sample size
	M	SD	M	SD	M	SD	M	SD	M	SD	M	SD	M	SD	M	SD	
Chemical																	
Face-to-face	6.04	0.92	5.90	0.88	5.64	1.07	5.67	1.06	5.54	1.04	5.44	1.03	5.43	1.10	5.44	1.05	177–181
Media	5.94	0.88	5.82	0.98	5.52	1.07	5.56	1.03	5.39	1.05	5.30	1.02	5.28	1.22	5.27	1.06	157–159
Online	6.06	0.92	5.82	0.92	5.58	1.00	5.61	0.99	5.40	1.02	5.38	1.08	5.28	1.11	5.34	1.07	152–154
Biochemical																	
Face-to-face	6.07	0.86	5.99	0.82	5.67	0.96	5.72	0.94	5.49	1.03	5.48	1.01	5.51	1.09	5.57	0.97	365–370
Social																	
Media	5.58	1.03	5.86	0.94	5.65	1.02	5.36	1.03	5.30	1.09	5.04	1.18	5.28	1.11	5.01	1.19	865–881

Notes: Respondents were all faculty with PhDs at US-based universities. See specific chapters for additional details.
[1] Respondents selected between "strongly disagree" (1) and "strongly agree" (7) to the statement "Achieving this objective is possible for a good communicator."

Table B.6.

Scientists' average assessment of their personal skill (internal efficacy) to carry out different objectives with standard deviation (SD) and mean response (M)[1]

	Helping to inform people about scientific issues (chapter 1)		Getting people interested or excited about science (chapter 11)		Showing the scientific community's expertise (chapter 6)		Hearing what others think about scientific issues (chapter 5)		Showing that the scientific community cares about society's well-being (chapter 3)		Demonstrating the scientific community's openness and transparency (chapter 4)		Showing that scientists share community values (chapter 6)		Framing research implications so members of the public think about a topic in a way that resonates with their values (chapter 11)		Sample size
	M	SD	M	SD	M	SD	M	SD	M	SD	M	SD	M	SD	M	SD	
General																	
Face-to-face	5.34	1.18	5.26	1.18	4.98	1.23	4.85	1.25	4.82	1.30	4.77	1.31	4.61	1.34	4.54	1.37	370–377
Media	5.12	1.39	4.91	1.37	4.69	1.40	5.64	1.35	4.54	1.39	4.53	1.45	4.28	1.40	4.18	1.44	322–327
Online	4.97	1.41	4.86	1.46	4.61	1.44	4.47	1.46	4.38	1.52	4.43	1.47	4.13	1.51	4.09	1.47	375–380
Biological																	
Face-to-face	5.33	1.03	5.33	1.14	4.99	1.15	4.96	1.12	4.89	1.18	4.81	1.17	4.77	1.15	4.57	1.23	346–352
Online	5.05	1.35	5.10	1.37	4.62	1.37	4.71	1.35	4.58	1.30	4.55	1.33	4.34	1.34	4.25	1.39	326–330
Geophysical																	
Face-to-face	5.51	1.04	5.35	1.08	5.09	1.11	5.03	1.16	4.99	1.17	4.94	1.16	4.69	1.18	4.59	1.25	245–250
Media	5.40	1.10	5.17	1.12	4.92	1.10	4.71	1.25	4.72	1.19	4.74	1.19	4.43	1.19	4.44	1.25	313–320
Online	5.23	1.20	5.11	1.27	4.84	1.22	4.56	1.32	4.57	1.36	4.63	1.25	4.41	1.25	4.44	1.34	267–274
Geological																	
Face-to-face	5.45	1.09	5.39	1.15	5.10	1.19	5.02	1.17	4.94	1.26	4.98	1.24	4.72	1.31	4.59	1.35	245–250
Media	5.25	1.20	5.34	1.19	4.81	1.35	4.83	1.26	4.69	1.32	4.73	1.32	4.58	1.32	4.44	1.40	236–243
Online	5.33	1.23	5.40	1.31	4.91	1.31	4.71	1.35	4.77	1.37	4.76	1.34	4.58	1.40	4.48	1.38	231–234
Ecological																	
Face-to-face	5.48	1.16	5.34	1.15	4.97	1.19	4.92	1.20	4.81	1.25	4.78	1.25	4.55	1.26	4.60	1.32	341–346

(continued)

Table B.6.
(continued)

	Helping to inform people about scientific issues (chapter 1)		Getting people interested or excited about science (chapter 11)		Showing the scientific community's expertise (chapter 6)		Hearing what others think about scientific issues (chapter 5)		Showing that the scientific community cares about society's well-being (chapter 3)		Demonstrating the scientific community's openness and transparency (chapter 4)		Showing that scientists share community values (chapter 6)		Framing research implications so members of the public think about a topic in a way that resonates with their values (chapter 11)		Sample size
	M	SD	M	SD	M	SD	M	SD	M	SD	M	SD	M	SD	M	SD	
Chemical																	
Face-to-face	5.23	1.17	5.21	1.28	4.79	1.33	4.78	1.30	4.72	1.36	4.63	1.32	4.51	1.43	4.39	1.50	178–181
Media	4.88	1.33	4.87	1.36	4.46	1.26	4.46	1.21	4.42	1.28	4.37	1.38	4.18	1.24	3.97	1.50	157–158
Online	4.87	1.34	4.94	1.43	4.49	1.30	4.58	1.32	4.43	1.33	4.39	1.34	4.26	1.39	4.02	1.41	151–154
Biochemical																	
Face-to-face	5.09	1.27	5.08	1.33	4.75	1.27	4.69	1.30	4.66	1.27	4.60	1.37	4.50	1.33	4.32	1.40	368–370
Social																	
Media	5.41	1.12	5.41	1.28	5.11	1.22	4.86	1.22	4.87	1.26	4.92	1.24	4.50	1.27	4.69	1.30	866–880

Notes: Respondents were all faculty with PhDs at US–based universities. See specific chapters for additional details.
[1] Respondents selected between "strongly disagree" (1) and "strongly agree" (7) to the statement "I have the skills needed to achieve this objective."

Table B.7.
Scientists' average prior consideration of objectives with standard deviation (SD) and mean response (M)[1]

	Getting people interested or excited about science (chapter 11)		Helping to inform people about scientific issues (chapter 1)		Showing that the scientific community cares about society's well-being (chapter 3)		Showing the scientific community's expertise (chapter 7)		Demonstrating the scientific community's openness and transparency (chapter 4)		Hearing what others think about scientific issues (chapter 5)		Framing research implications so members of the public think about a topic in a way that resonates with their values (chapter 11)		Showing that scientists share community values (chapter 6)		Sample size
	M	SD	M	SD	M	SD	M	SD	M	SD	M	SD	M	SD	M	SD	
General																	
Face-to-face	5.10	1.59	5.02	1.64	4.11	1.76	4.04	1.68	3.96	1.69	3.96	1.60	3.87	1.65	3.77	1.65	368–375
Media	4.86	1.59	4.89	1.63	4.01	1.65	3.80	1.58	3.86	1.64	3.76	1.60	3.60	1.70	3.63	1.59	321–326
Online	4.74	1.74	4.80	1.77	3.82	1.73	3.71	1.64	3.74	1.71	3.67	1.66	3.58	1.71	3.38	1.62	368–378
Biological																	
Face-to-face	5.05	1.50	4.86	1.51	4.18	1.53	3.87	1.51	4.06	1.48	4.02	1.50	3.87	1.60	3.85	1.58	345–348
Online	4.76	1.72	4.67	1.68	3.98	1.71	3.71	1.65	3.79	1.64	3.83	1.61	3.64	1.69	3.54	1.69	324–330
Geophysical																	
Face-to-face	5.24	1.46	5.26	1.42	4.21	1.58	4.14	1.51	4.26	1.58	4.06	1.54	4.17	1.64	3.78	1.54	313–315
Media	5.25	1.42	5.34	1.34	4.23	1.66	4.04	1.60	4.09	1.63	3.89	1.61	4.02	1.74	3.64	1.63	313–318
Online	5.00	1.69	4.92	1.63	3.94	1.71	3.98	1.64	4.03	1.66	3.58	1.66	3.88	1.78	3.60	1.74	265–272
Geological																	
Face-to-face	5.25	1.68	5.11	1.62	4.22	1.70	4.12	1.67	3.87	1.67	4.04	1.75	4.02	1.78	3.66	1.71	245–249
Media	5.32	1.50	5.14	1.48	4.09	1.68	4.07	1.71	4.03	1.58	3.87	1.70	3.86	1.78	3.60	1.64	233–241
Online	5.21	1.50	5.07	1.51	4.10	1.68	3.93	1.60	4.06	1.67	3.98	1.64	3.99	1.72	3.80	1.66	229–237
Ecological																	
Face-to-face	5.48	1.36	5.57	1.32	4.32	1.57	4.17	1.57	4.15	1.60	4.23	1.57	4.38	1.70	3.78	1.59	339–348

(continued)

Table B.7.
(continued)

	Getting people interested or excited about science (chapter 11)		Helping to inform people about scientific issues (chapter 1)		Showing that the scientific community cares about society's well-being (chapter 3)		Showing the scientific community's expertise (chapter 7)		Demonstrating the scientific community's openness and transparency (chapter 4)		Hearing what others think about scientific issues (chapter 5)		Framing research implications so members of the public think about a topic in a way that resonates with their values (chapter 11)		Showing that scientists share community values (chapter 6)		Sample size
	M	SD	M	SD	M	SD	M	SD	M	SD	M	SD	M	SD	M	SD	
Chemical																	
Face-to-face	5.05	1.65	4.77	1.60	4.11	1.67	3.96	1.64	3.88	1.67	3.91	1.78	3.88	1.77	3.87	1.76	177–181
Media	4.76	1.64	4.67	1.61	3.96	1.57	3.69	1.51	3.64	1.57	3.50	1.50	3.38	1.74	3.47	1.52	157–158
Online	4.82	1.65	4.43	1.66	3.77	1.71	3.56	1.68	3.63	1.67	3.46	1.60	3.42	1.66	3.27	1.57	151–154
Biochemical																	
Face-to-face	5.03	1.52	4.80	1.58	4.13	1.55	3.83	1.46	3.92	1.57	3.83	1.55	3.75	1.68	3.61	1.63	363–371
Social																	
Media	4.21	1.75	5.01	1.57	3.97	1.77	4.40	1.71	3.92	1.74	3.67	1.69	3.88	1.79	3.42	1.70	862–883

Notes: Respondents were all faculty with PhDs at US-based universities. See specific chapters for additional details.

[1] Respondents selected between "strongly disagree" (1) and "strongly agree" (7) to the statement "Prior to this survey, I had thought a lot about this potential objective."

APPENDIX C

Examining Goals and Objectives Worksheets

Worksheet Section 1: Questions About Your Goals

The goal identification question: What specific behavior do you want to see in what specific group of people?*	
The other goal identification question: In what ways are you willing or eager to change your own behavior because of participating in communication with your chosen audience?	

*Behaviors could include both direct behaviors and pseudo behaviors. Direct behaviors might include a specific group of people taking scientific evidence into account when making decisions as well as such individual behaviors as taking medicine or choosing to study a specific topic. Pseudo behaviors might include broader goals such as increasing the likelihood that specific groups will see science as a legitimate source of insight or culture, including a willingness to accept/trust (i.e., not reject) new discoveries or technologies. It might also include generally positive relationships between science and society and support for robust science funding.

Worksheet Section 2: Questions About Potential Communication Objectives from the Audience's Perspective

	...your motivation is to help? (chapter 3)	...you have integrity? (chapter 4)	...you are willing to listen? (chapter 5)	...you share key values? (chapter 6)	...you are competent? (chapter 7)	...in specific risks or benefits? (chapter 8)	...a behavior is common or expected? (chapter 9)	...they have the ability to do a behavior? (chapter 10)
The goal question: Given the goal behavior you want from your chosen audience, why do you think it will be helpful if they believe...								
The preparation question: To what degree does your chosen audience believe... (And is there room for change?)								
The tactics question: What could you do* to try to ethically change the degree to which your chosen audience believes...								
The evaluation question: How much did your communication choices change the degree to which your chosen audience believes...								
The ethics question: To what degree are you being honest about whether [it makes sense to believe]...								

*(including choices about messages, behaviors, tone/style, communication channel, and communication source)

Worksheet Section 3: Questions About Potential Communication Objectives from the Communicator's Perspective

	…is motivated by a desire to help society? (chapter 3)	…is high in integrity? (chapter 4)	…is willing to listen? (chapter 5)	…shares key values with you? (chapter 6)	…is competent? (chapter 7)	…believes in specific risks or benefits? (chapter 8)	…believes a behavior is common or expected? (chapter 9)	…believes they have the ability to do a behavior? (chapter 10)
The preparation question: To what degree do *you* believe that your audience…								
The tactics question: What could you do* to try to ethically learn more about the degree to which your chosen audience…								
The evaluation question: How much did your communication choices change the degree to which *you* believe your chosen audience…								

*(including choices about messages, behaviors, tone/style, communication channel, and communication source)

Worksheet Section 4: Objectives beyond Beliefs

	…knows about specific scientific results or processes? (chapter 2)	…feels about a goal behavior in a specific way? (chapter 11)	…frames a goal behavior in a specific way? (chapter 11)
The goal question: Given the goal behavior you want from your chosen audience, why do you think it will be helpful if your chosen audience…			
The preparation questions: What do you know about what/how your chosen audience…(And is there room for change?) To what degree do you believe that your audience…			
The tactics questions: What could you ethically do* to try to change the degree to which your chosen audience… What could you ethically do* to try to learn more about the degree to which your chosen audience…			
The evaluation questions: How much did your communication choices change the degree to which your audience… How much did your communication choices change your perceived understanding of what (or how) your audience…			
The ethics question: To what degree is it acceptable to try to change what (or how) your audience…			

*(including choices about messages, behaviors, tone/style, communication channel, and communication source)

INDEX

ability in benevolence/integrity/ability trichotomy, 164–65
achievability in survey: and competency objective, 174, 176; and integrity objective, 110, 111; and knowledge objective, 53; and shared values objective, 152, 153; and sharing emotions and frames objective, 260, 261, 262; and showing warmth objective, 86, 87; and willingness to listen objective, 130, 131
action, theory of reasoned, 228
activities: focus on in engagement, 27–28, 244–45; and knowledge objective, 56–58
Advancing Research Impact in Society, 199
advisory boards, 105
affect, 8–9, 25, 247–48
affective empathy, 119
aggressive communication: and competency, 165; and integrity objective, 107–8, 111, 112; and knowledge objective, 64, 65–67; and warmth, 76–77
AIDS/HIV, 21
Ajzen, Icek, 185, 228, 230
Alan Alda Center for Communicating Science, 49–50, 118, 119
Alda, Alan, 49–50, 59
Allum, Nick, 52
ambiguity and norms, 210
American Association for the Advancement of Science IF/THEN Ambassador Program, 150–51
apologies, 106, 108
Arvai, Joe, 123–24, 128
Asbrock, Frank, 84
Asch, Solomon, 74
Association of American Universities survey, 52

attitudes, 8, 185, 188
auction techniques and measuring risk perception, 193
audience: and consensus messaging, 217; and framing, 255, 257; goals of, 28–31; knowledge expectations of, 54–56; and self-efficacy objective, 236
audio quality, 168

Bandura, Albert, 227, 229–30, 231, 232, 236
Barbie, 138–39
Bauer, Martin, 122
Becker, Julia, 84
behavior: behavior changes as end goal, 15–16; behavior goals, examples, 15–16, 39; ethics of behavior goals, 29, 34; impeding behavior, 83, 84; integrated behavioral model, 232; knowledge deficits and change in, 21–22, 52–56; need for research on, 271–73; norms' effect on, 208–9, 210–12, 252; perceived behavioral control, 228, 229; role in communication strategy, 1, 7, 19; and self-efficacy, 226–28; theory of planned behavior, 185, 188, 211, 229–30, 232; and trustworthiness, 23–24, 73; and warmth, 84–85
beliefs: and audience goals, 28–29; cumulative effect of, 38–39, 285–87; descriptive beliefs, 6; and dialogue, 27–28; and ethics of communication, 34, 35; evaluative beliefs, 6, 8; and group membership, 65; health belief model, 195; and identity conflicts in risk perception, 194; and knowledge objective, 55–56; and need for objectives, 19–20, 23; trustworthiness beliefs vs. behavior, 73; and uncertainty and

beliefs (*continued*)
  misinformation, 32. *See also* competency objective; normative beliefs objective; self-efficacy objective
benefits. *See* risk and benefits; risk and benefits objective
benevolence: and aggressive communication, 107; and apologies, 106; correlation with integrity, 102; measuring, 164–65; perceived benevolence in workplace, 79; term, 74. *See also* warmth objective
Bernays, Edward, 279
biotechnology, 60–61. *See also* genetically modified foods; genetic engineering
Blader, Steven, 148–49
Braman, Donald, 141
Bromme, Rainer, 164
Brown, Brené, 127
Burgoon, Judee, 166, 171
business: and competence, 80–82; and integrity, 103, 106, 109–10; and warmth, 81–82, 83–84, 85

Canadian survey, 52, 132, 154
Center for Advancing Research Impact, 283
Cialdini, Robert, 208–9, 212, 213
Citizen Conferences, 60–63
civic engagement: and knowledge levels, 63; and norms, 215; and self-efficacy objective, 231, 235
Climate Advocacy Lab, 281–82
clothes, 168
cognitive empathy, 119
cognitive processing: and ability, 59; and comprehension, 28; and cultural cognition, 142–43; and dialogue, 27–28, 60–63; elaboration likelihood model, 59; and emotions, 245–46; and ethics, 33–34; and fluency, 166; in formal *vs.* informal settings, 59; and framing, 245–46, 255; and jargon, 58–59; and motivation, 59; of risks and benefits, 172, 185; and self-efficacy, 232–33
coldness: and breaking bad news, 80, 85; and envy, 83; and impeding behavior, 83, 84; and perception of scientists, 76, 96
Colquitt, Jason, 79, 102
common frames, 256–57

communitarianism *vs.* individualism, 140, 141–45
Compass Science Communication, 182–84
competence: and access to information, 106; and apologies, 106, 108; in communication, 162; and fluency, 166, 171; and integrity, 96, 97, 100, 101, 102, 162, 170; measuring, 164–65; and neuroimage bias, 167–68; and self-efficacy, 229; and speech, 166, 168, 171; terms for, 164; and threat of harm, 75; trustworthiness beliefs *vs.* competence beliefs, 162–63; and values, 145, 149, 162–63; and warmth, 80–82, 168, 173
competency objective, 161–76; and controversy, 169–70; and credibility, 165–66, 171–73; effects of, 171–73; ethics of sharing, 6, 174, 176; introduction as example of sharing, 6; need for, 6, 161–63; in objectives summary list, 23; questions for, 175; research background, 163–65; research on communicating, 165–70; willingness to prioritize, 173–76
comprehension, 28, 51
conflict frames, 256
conflicts of interest, 34, 103–6, 109
consensus, 37
consensus messaging, 215–18
construal level, 258–59
control: perceived behavioral control, 228, 229; and risk perception, 186–87, 191; and self-efficacy, 228, 229, 230
controversy, 169–70
corporate social responsibility: and integrity, 108, 109–10; and warmth, 81–82, 83–84, 85
creativity, 283, 285
credibility: and competency objective, 165–66, 171–73; source credibility, 165–66, 171–72
crisis communication, 108
Cuddy, Amy, 74, 75
cultural cognition, 142–43

Davies, Sara, 274
Dawson, Emily, 126–27
decision making: and fairness, 119–20, 124–25; satisfaction with, 63–64, 123–24;

and self-efficacy objective, 230; and shared values objective, 139–47; and willingness to listen objective, 119–20, 123–25, 127–28

deliberative polling, 60–63

democracy, deliberative, 60–63

denials, 108

descriptive beliefs, 6

descriptive norms, 206, 210–11, 214–15

dialogue: and cognitive processing, 27–28, 60–63; and ethics, 35; and knowledge objective, 55–56, 60–64; and legitimacy, 64; media as, 63; and satisfaction with decision-making systems, 63–64; two-way dialogue, 26–28, 35; and warmth, 82–83; and willingness to listen objective, 122–23

direct experiences, 231

disagreements: and competency objective, 169–70; and integrity objective, 111, 112, 170; risk and benefit agreement/disagreement scales, 188, 189

discrete emotions, 248–52

diversity, equity, and inclusion (DEI): and communication strategy coordination, 281, 283; and competency objective, 169; and consensus objective, 37; and ethics, 37–38; IF/THEN Ambassador Program, 150–51; and procedural fairness, 120; and professionalization of science communication, 284; and self-efficacy objective, 234. See also marginalized groups

doctors, 79–80, 85

Douglas, Mary, 140

dread, 186, 247

drinking norms campaign, 206–8, 211, 212

Druckman, James, 255

Dunning-Kruger effect, 227

egalitarianism vs. hierarchy, 140, 141–45, 147

Einsiedel, Edna, 60–63

elaboration likelihood model, 59

emotions: and affect, 8–9, 25, 247–48; and cognitive processing, 245–46; of communicators, 246, 250; and construal level, 259; and cultural cognition, 142;

discrete, 248–52; and distraction, 250; and doctor-patient relationship, 85; and knowledge objective, 55–56; and manipulation, 245; and morality, 249–50; and need for objectives, 19–20, 23; and numeracy, 254; research background, 247–52; and risk and benefits processing, 185, 247–48; and self-efficacy, 232–33

emotions and frames, sharing objective, 244–65; challenges of, 252; and construal level, 258–59; ethics of, 9, 34, 35, 245, 246, 260–64; importance of, 244–46; introduction as example of, 5; vs. knowledge objective, 51; and manipulation, 245; in objectives summary list, 24–25; questions for, 251, 264; research background, 247–58; willingness to prioritize, 260–63

empathy, 74, 118–19, 127

emphasis framing, 253, 255

engagement, public: activities focus, 27–28, 244–45; civic engagement, 63, 215, 231, 235; group engagement model, 148–50; and knowledge objective, 55–56; scientists' participation survey, 17–19, 22, 40–42, 289–90; and shared values objective, 148–50; and willingness to listen objective, 121–22, 123, 125–26, 127–29; without addressing emotions and beliefs, 55–56. See also dialogue

entertainment-education campaigns, 233–34

Entman, Robert, 252

envy, 83

equivalence framing, 253–54

ethics: and audience goals, 28–31; and behavioral change, 29, 34; and changing of scientist behaviors, 19; and communication strategy coordination, 272–73; of competency objective, 6, 174, 176; and dialogue, 35; and diversity, equity, and inclusion (DEI), 37–38; and goals, 35–36; of integrity objective, 110, 111; of knowledge objective, 52, 53; and misinformation, 32–33; and normative beliefs objective, 212; overview of, 33–36; of risk and benefits objective, 191–92, 194–95; of self-efficacy objective,

ethics (*continued*)
236; of shared values objective, 151, 152, 153; of sharing emotions and frames objective, 9, 35, 245, 246, 260–64; and uncertainty, 32–33, 191–92; of warmth objective, 86, 87, 88; of willingness to listen objective, 130, 131, 132. *See also* integrity

evaluation phase, 1, 13, 51, 73, 237, 278, 284

evaluative beliefs, 6, 8, 19–20, 23–24, 29, 32, 79, 185

excitement, 250, 260, 261

experiences and self-efficacy, 231

expertise: and aggressive communication, 107; misplacing, 236; source expertise, 165–66, 171–72. *See also* competence

extended parallel processing model, 232–33

fairness: and group identification, 148–50; and risk and benefits perception, 189–90; and warmth, 75, 78–79; and willingness to listen objective, 119–20, 124–25

Fallon-Lambert, Kathy, 275

familiarity and risk perception, 186–87, 191

fear, 232–33, 248–49, 252, 254

Feldman, Lauren, 232

Finucane, Melissa, 247–48

Fishbein, Martin, 185, 228, 230

Fishkin, James, 62

Fiske, Susan, 74, 79, 80, 84, 95–96, 149, 173

Flame Challenge, 49–50

fluency, 107, 166, 171

FrameWorks Institute, 11–12, 252–53

framing: and audience, 255, 257; and audience goals, 28–29; challenges of, 252; common frames, 256–57; conflict frames, 256; and conflicts of interest, 34; and construal level, 258–59; defined, 252; emphasis framing, 253, 255; episodic vs. thematic, 256, 257; equivalence framing, 253–54; gain/loss, 254–55; generic frames, 256; and manipulation, 245; and need for objectives, 19–20, 23; reframing examples, 5, 11–12; research background on, 252–58; of science as long-term process, 38–39; and science societies, 281; scientists' frames, 246, 250.

See also emotions and frames, sharing objective

funding, 104–6, 109, 110, 198–201, 282–83

gain/loss framing, 254–55

Gallup. *See* Wellcome Trust

Gamson, William, 252, 256

Gardner, William, 106

Garlick, Sarah, 275

Gastil, John, 128, 141

Gaston, Anca, 196

gateway beliefs, 216, 217

General Social Survey, 96–97, 99

generic frames, 256

genetically modified foods, 61, 97, 98, 192–94, 250, 257

genetic engineering, 21, 73, 166, 189, 250, 258. *See also* biotechnology

goals: of audience, 28–31; behavior changes as end goal, 15–16; and career promotion, 16–17; challenges of identifying, 15; and coordinating communication strategy, 276–82; engagement goals in survey, 17–18; and ethics, 35–36; examples of, 15–16, 39; identification questions, 43; need for, 15–19; vs. objectives, 19–20, 25; role in communication strategy, 1, 12, 13, 14; vs. tactics, 25; worksheets for, 309–12

Golden Goose Award, 193, 199

groups: beliefs and group membership, 65; and fairness, 148–50; group engagement model, 148–50; and identity, 139, 148–50; and knowledge objective, 65; and normative beliefs objective, 210–11; and self-categorization, 149–50; and self-identity, 139; and shared values objective, 139, 142–43; and trust theory, 173; and values, 142–43; and willingness to listen objective, 126–27. *See also* marginalized groups

Grunig, James, 279

handwashing, 213, 215

harm, evaluating threat of, 75

Hart, Sol, 65, 145, 232

Hayhoe, Katharine, 147–48

health belief model, 195

Hendriks, Friederike, 164
Hibbing, John, 129
hierarchy vs. egalitarianism, 140, 141–45, 147
HIV/AIDS, 21
honesty: and being open, 34; and disagreements, 170; introduction as example of showing, 6; in objectives summary list, 23; in public perception surveys, 97, 100, 101, 102, 163; and uncertainty, 192. See also integrity
hope, 250, 253, 254
Horst, Maja, 274
Hovland, Karl, 165
HPV and risk perception, 143–44, 146
humor, 249

identity: conflicts and risk perception, 194; and group engagement model, 148–50; and groups, 139, 148–50; hierarchy vs. egalitarianism in, 140, 141–45, 147; individualism vs. communitarianism in, 140, 141–45, 147; and informal science education, 150; and norms, 211, 214–15, 219; and self-categorization, 149–50. See also shared values/identity objective
IF/THEN Ambassador Program, 150–51
implementation phase, 13
individualism vs. communitarianism, 140, 141–45
informal science education, 56–57, 126–27, 150, 231, 250
Inglehart, Ronald, 140
injunctive/subjective norms, 206, 210–11
integrated behavioral model, 232
integrity: and benevolence, 102; measuring, 164–65; public perceptions of scientists' integrity, 96–100, 101; and warmth, 75, 100–103
integrity objective, 95–113; and competence, 96, 97, 100, 101, 102, 162, 170; and conflicts of interest, 34, 103–6, 109; demand for information, 109–10; and disagreements, 111, 112, 170; effects of, 108–9; ethics of, 110, 111; and funding, 104-6, 109, 110; questions for, 113; research background, 95–100; research on communicating, 103–8; vs. willing-

ness to listen objective, 121–22; willingness to prioritize, 110–12. See also ethics; honesty
internal efficacy, 229. See also self-efficacy
introspective illusion, 30

Jamieson, Kathleen Hall, 109, 141
jargon, 14, 58–59, 166–67
jerkiness, 64, 65–67, 76, 77, 82
Jucks, Regina, 107

Kahan, Dan, 54, 64, 65, 139–45, 147, 248
Kahneman, Daniel, 253–54
Kienhues, Dorothe, 164
Kim, Sora, 81, 85
knowledge objective, 49–67; and audience expectations, 54–56; and decoding, 50–52; and dialogue, 55–56, 60–64; focus on misinformation or anti-science, 64–65; vs. framing, 51; importance of, 21–22; introduction as example of, 7; and jargon, 58–59; knowledge deficits and behavior change, 21–22, 52–56; over-reliance on, 21, 50–52; questions for, 66; tactics, 56–64
Knuth, Barbara, 123, 128
König, Lars, 107

Lakoff, George, 258
language: and competency perceptions, 166–67, 168, 171; and integrity perceptions, 107; jargon, 14, 58–59, 166–67; and warmth, 83, 84
Lapinski, Maria, 210, 211–12, 218
Lauber, Bruce, 123, 128
learning: and benefits of engagement activities, 244–45; and cultural cognition, 142; and deliberative polling, 60–63; and entertainment-education campaigns, 233–34; and knowledge objective tactics, 56–58; self-efficacy and experiential learning, 231; vs. teaching, 57–58. See also cognitive processing
legitimacy, 64, 127–28
Leiserowitz, Anthony, 281
Lewenstein, Bruce, 257
likability, 75, 76–77, 107
listening. See willingness to listen objective
littering norms, 208–9, 212–13

110, 112, 129–31. *See also* integrity objective; willingness to listen objective

Oppenheimer, Daniel, 166–67, 168

Oreskes, Naomi, 37

oversight, 105

participation, 64, 123–24, 187

peer review, 109

perceived behavioral control, 228, 229

persuasion: and credibility, 171–72; and jargon, 58–59; and knowledge objective, 58–59

Pew Research Center, 97, 218–19, 281

planned behavior, theory of, 185, 188, 211, 229–30, 232

policing and fairness, 120

policymakers: and Citizen Conferences, 61; engagement with in survey, 40–41, 42, 290; and knowledge objectives, 63; and normative beliefs objective, 184, 215; and risk and benefits objective, 184; and self-efficacy objective, 235, 236; valuing of science by, 17, 18, 273

politics: framing in, 258, 259; and perceptions of scientists, 97

polling, deliberative, 60–63

Portal to the Public, 57–58, 60, 227

Prapavessis, Harry, 196

priming and norms, 209, 212–13

print quality, 168

prior thought in survey: and competency objective, 174, 176; and integrity objective, 111, 112; and knowledge objective, 53; and shared values objective, 152, 153, 154; and sharing emotions and frames objective, 260, 261, 262; and showing warmth, 86, 87; and willingness to listen objective, 130, 131, 132

procedural fairness, 119, 127

procedural justice, 120

production quality, 168

psychometric paradigm of risk perception, 186–87

PytlikZillig, Lisa, 103

rational choice, 142, 195

reading and cognitive processing, 63

references, 107

RELATE, 226

Republican party, 258

reputation and integrity, 109

resources: and communication strategy coordination, 275, 276–77, 279, 280, 282–83; and ethics, 36; and self-efficacy objective, 229, 230; and tactics selection, 31

response efficacy, 185

Rimal, Rajiv, 210, 211–12

risk and benefits: and attitudes, 185; and competency objective, 172–73; and control, 186–87, 191; demographic factors, 192; and emotions, 185, 247–48; factors effecting, 192–95; and familiarity, 186–87, 191; measuring perception of, 186–92; as moving together, 190; and norms, 214–15; in objectives summary list, 24; and participation in decision-making, 123–24; response efficacy, 185; and self-efficacy, 195, 232–33, 236; and shared values objective, 143–45, 146; and susceptibility, 189–90, 195; and uncertainty, 191–92; unrelated risks, 190

risk and benefits objective, 182–201; approaches to, 197–98; effects of, 195–97; and ethics, 191–92; importance of, 182–86; and lack of clear risks or benefits, 198–201; questions for, 200; research background, 186–92; role in communication strategy, 8; and self-efficacy, 232–33, 236

Roskos-Ewoldsen, David, 78

Scheufele, Dietram, 63

Schultz, Wesley, 215

Science and Engineering Indicators, 96–97, 98, 163

science communication strategy: challenges of connecting theory and practice, 4, 14; cumulative effect of, 38–39, 161, 169, 184, 185, 285–87; defined, 1; evaluation phase, 14; example of mismatches in, 2–3; implementation phase, 13; integration model, 274; introduction as example of, 5–7; model diagram, 13; as more than decoding, science communication strategy (*continued*) 50–52; National Academies of Sciences approach to, 20–21; need for, 15; need for support, 273–75; professionalization of, 277–79, 283–85; research on as limited, 36–37, 271–73; science communication, defined, 7; strategy phase, 13

science communication strategy coordination, 271–87; challenges in, 273–75; and funding, 282–83; lack of, 272–73; and resources, 275, 276–77, 279, 280, 282–83; by scientific societies, 279–82; and shared goals, 276–82; by universities, 277–79

science literacy, 21–22, 52–54

scientific societies, 279–82

scientists: and career promotion, 16–17, 284; and duty, 30; emotions and frames of, 246, 250; focus on knowledge objective, 51–52, 53; identity and students, 139; openness to change, 19, 34–35, 238; public engagement survey, 17–19, 22, 40–42, 289–90; resistance to professionalization of science communication, 283–85; self-efficacy of, 229. *See also* survey of scientists (2015–2016)

scientists, perceptions of: and coldness, 76, 96; and confidence in, 96–97; general competence, 163; and integrity, 96–100, 101; and jerkiness, 64, 65–67, 76, 77, 82; and sharing knowledge, 22; surveys on, 96–97, 98, 187–88, 199, 218–19, 281; and uncertainty, 33, 192. *See also* competency objective; warmth objective

self-efficacy: and behavior, 226–28; and competence, 229; and control, 228, 229, 230; defining, 228–29; and emotions, 232–33; internal efficacy, 229; and knowledge objective, 57; measuring, 229–30; and Message Box, 193; misplaced, 227, 236; and risk and benefits, 195, 232–33, 236; of scientists, 229; and students, 227, 231, 234; and training, 226–27, 230, 231; and willingness to change, 238

self-efficacy objective, 226–38; challenges in, 235–38; effect of, 234–35; importance of, 226–27; in objectives summary list,

24; questions for, 237; research background, 227–30; research on communicating, 231–34; and resources, 229, 230; role in communication strategy, 8

shared values/identity objective, 138–56; examples of, 138–39; introduction as example of, 6; in objectives summary list, 23; questions for, 155; research background, 139–42; research on communicating, 143–51; role in communication strategy, 155–56; signaling in, 147–48; willingness to prioritize, 151–54. *See also* normative beliefs objective; values

Silk, Kami, 211

skills in survey: and integrity objective, 110, 111; and knowledge objective, 52, 53; and self-efficacy of scientists, 229; and shared values objective, 152, 153, 154; and sharing emotions and frames objective, 260, 261, 262; and showing warmth, 86, 87, 88; and willingness to listen objective, 130, 131. *See also* self-efficacy

Slovic, Paul, 141, 186–87, 247

social media, 81

source credibility, 165–66, 171–72

speech: and competency, 166, 168, 171; and integrity, 107

Stanford Five-City Project, 233

STEM education, 12, 138–39, 150–51, 226–27, 231, 234

stereotypes, 75, 77, 173

storytelling, 14, 83, 84, 87–88, 154, 168

strategy phase, 13

students, 12, 138–39, 150–51, 226–27, 231, 234

subjective norms. *See* injunctive/subjective norms

survey of scientists (2015–2016): about, 9, 22; competency objective in, 173–76; goals in, 17–18; integrity objective in, 110, 111, 112; knowledge objective in, 52, 53; methodology and demographics, 289–92; public engagement in, 17–19, 22, 40–42, 289–90; shared values objective in, 151–54; sharing emotions and frames objective in, 260–63; tables, 295–308;

warmth objective in, 85–88; willingness to listen objective in, 130, 131, 132
surveys: Canadian survey, 52, 132, 154; and communication strategy coordination, 280, 281–82; perceptions of science and scientists, 96–97, 98, 187–88, 199, 218–19, 281

tactics: *vs.* goals and objectives, 25; and knowledge objective, 56–64; need for research on, 271; over-emphasis on, 20, 22; and resource allocation, 31; role in communication strategy, 1, 12, 13, 14; uncertainty or misinformation, 32–33; and warmth objective, 83, 84, 87–88; when to choose, 15, 20
Tajfel, Henry, 148
talking and cognitive processing, 63
teaching *vs.* learning, 57–58
Theiss-Morse, Elizabeth, 129
Thibaut, John, 120
3.14 Action, 39
time and timing, 213, 247–48
Tortoriello, Macro, 103
transparency, 34, 36, 105, 109–10, 112, 129–31
Trumbo, Craig, 172
trust: and behavior goals, 23–24; beliefs *vs.* behavior, 73; willingness to be vulnerable, 73, 109, 173
trustworthiness: and behavior goals, 23–24; beliefs *vs.* behavior, 73; as central to communication strategy, 72–73, 184–85; as multi-leveled, 73; objectives, summary and list, 23–24; and risk and benefits objective, 192; and shared values objective, 145, 154–56; trust theory, 173; trustworthiness beliefs *vs.* competence beliefs, 162–63; and uncertainty, 33; Wellcome Trust survey, 97–100, 101, 163. *See also* competency objective; integrity objective; shared values/identity objective; warmth objective; willingness to listen objective
truthfulness. *See* honesty
Turner, John, 148
Tversky, Amos, 253–54
two-way dialogue, 26–28, 35
Tyler, Tom, 148–49

uncertainty, 31–33, 191–92
universities and communication strategy coordination, 277–79
University of Michigan RELATE program, 226
University of Missouri Center for Advancing Research Impact, 283
University of Utah STEM ambassador program, 138–39, 150, 226–27
utility of research, 198–99

vaccines, 73, 76, 112, 143–46, 190
values: and competence, 145, 149, 162–63; and emotions, 250; and framing, 257; and groups, 142–43; as predictive of positions, 142; and risk perception, 143–45, 146; and signaling, 147–48; valuing of science, 17, 18, 273. *See also* shared values/identity objective
Vancouver, Jeffrey, 236
van den Bos, Kees, 124–25
vicarious experiences, 231
voice, 120, 123, 124, 127–28
vulnerability, 109, 173

Walker, Laurens, 120
warmth: communicating, 78–83; and competence, 80–82, 168, 173; demand for warmth-related information, 84–85; and empathy, 74, 118–19; evaluating, 75–78; integrity as element of warmth, 100–102; and pro-social motivations, 77–78, 82, 88; in public perception surveys, 97, 100, 101; and shared values objective, 149; as term, 74
warmth objective, 72–89; demand for warmth-related information, 84–85; effect on behavior, 83–84; importance of, 75–78; *vs.* integrity objective, 75, 100–103; introduction as example of, 6; in objectives summary list, 23; questions for, 89; research background, 74–78; research on communicating, 78–83; *vs.* willingness to listen objective, 121–22; willingness to prioritize, 85–88
Weiss, Walter, 165
Wellcome Trust, 97–100, 101, 163, 190
Wildavsky, Aaron, 140